European Colonialism since 1

This masterful synthesis provides a much-needed, complete survey of European colonialism from 1700 to decolonization in the twentieth century. Written by an award-winning author, this advanced undergraduate and graduate level textbook bridges, for the first time, the early modern Atlantic empires and the later Asian and African empires of 'high imperialism'. Viewing colonialism as a phenomenon of contact between Europe and the rest of the world, the author takes an 'entangled histories' approach, considering the surprising ways in which the imperial powers of Spain, Portugal, Great Britain, France and the Netherlands displayed their identities in colonial settings, as much as in their imperial capitals. The author illuminates for students the common themes of colonial government, economic development and cultural contact across empires, and reveals the ways in which these themes played out, through contrast of the differing development, structure and impact of each empire.

JAMES R. LEHNING is Professor of History at the University of Utah. His previous publications include *To Be a Citizen: The Political Culture of the Early French Third Republic* (2001), which won the Laurence Wylie Prize in French Cultural Studies in 2003 and, as co-editor, *Europeans in the World: Sources on Cultural Contact* (2 volumes, 2002).

New Approaches To European History

Series editors
William Beik *Emory University*
T. C. W. Blanning *Sidney Sussex College, Cambridge*
Brendan Simms *Peterhouse, Cambridge*

New Approaches to European History is an important textbook series which provides concise but authoritative surveys of major themes and problems in European history since the Renaissance. Written at a level and length accessible to advanced school students and undergraduates, each book in the series addresses topics or themes that students of European history encounter daily: the series embraces both some of the more 'traditional' subjects of study and those cultural and social issues to which increasing numbers of school and college courses are devoted. A particular effort is made to consider the wider international implications of the subject under scrutiny.

To aid the student reader, scholarly apparatus and annotation is light, but each work has full supplementary bibliographies and notes for further reading: where appropriate, chronologies, maps, diagrams, and other illustrative material are also provided.

For a complete list of titles published in the series, please see:

www.cambridge.org/newapproaches

European Colonialism
since 1700

James R. Lehning

CAMBRIDGE
UNIVERSITY PRESS

CAMBRIDGE
UNIVERSITY PRESS

University Printing House, Cambridge CB2 8BS, United Kingdom

Published in the United States of America by Cambridge University Press, New York

Cambridge University Press is part of the University of Cambridge.

It furthers the University's mission by disseminating knowledge in the pursuit of education, learning and research at the highest international levels of excellence.

www.cambridge.org
Information on this title: www.cambridge.org/9780521741712

© James R. Lehning 2013

First published 2013

Printed in the United Kingdom by Bell and Bain Ltd

A catalogue record for this publication is available from the British Library

Library of Congress Cataloguing in Publication data
Lehning, James R., 1947–
European colonialism since 1700 / James R. Lehning.
  pages   cm. – (New approaches to European history)
Includes bibliographical references and index.
ISBN 978-0-521-51870-3 (hardback) – ISBN 978-0-521-74171-2 (pbk.)
1. Europe–Colonies–History.   2. Europe–Colonies–Administration–
History.   3. Europe–Territorial expansion.   4. Imperialism.
5. Postcolonialism.   I. Title.
JV135.L44 2013
325′.3094–dc23
2013009567

ISBN 978-0-521-51870-3 Hardback
ISBN 978-0-521-74171-2 Paperback

For all the Lehnings, Harrises, Moores,
Mowers, Sullivans, Seppys, Zveares,
and Hulicks in my family

Contents

Illustrations

Maps

Acknowledgments

It is a cliché, but true, that one incurs many debts writing a book like this one. It inevitably draws on the work of other scholars, and I am especially grateful to those scholars. To acknowledge all of my debts in footnotes would lead to a book that is mostly footnotes, and so the notes provide acknowledgement only where I have drawn specific information, or major interpretive points. More general works that have contributed to this book, however, are listed in the "further reading" sections at the end of each chapter.

I have also learned much about colonialism by drawing on the expertise of friends and colleagues in other fields of specialization. The discussions of the Rocky Mountain Seminar on Early American History helped me to learn about Atlantic history, and I am especially grateful to Eric Hinderaker and Chris Hodson, the organizers of the Rocky Mountain Seminar. Eric urged me in 2008 to undertake this project, and he put up with my naïve questions about early American history while I was writing it. He also organized a year-long seminar on colonialism during the 2010/11 academic year that helped me focus my thinking on a wide range of issues. That seminar, and several history department lectures, brought to Salt Lake City a number of scholars of colonialism, and discussions and conversations with Eric Jennings, Durba Ghosh, Cynthia Radding, Ann Laura Stoler, and Mark Mazower challenged my thinking and helped me refine what I wanted to say. In conversations or by reading parts of the manuscript, Eric Hinderaker, Chris Hodson, Ben Cohen, Byron Cannon, Ray Gunn, Anand Yang, Rebecca Horn, Lauren Jarvis, Peter Von Sivers, and Hugh Cagle lent their expertise, and in so doing saved me from errors.

The series editors and Michael Watson at Cambridge University Press gave me the opportunity to have my say about European colonialism. They, as well as the anonymous referees on the prospectus and the manuscript, provided valuable input and made this a much better book. Dean of Humanities Robert Newman at the University of Utah allowed me to finish the manuscript by supporting my request for a sabbatical in 2011/12. Megan Southwick and the DIGIT Cartography Lab at the University of Utah drew the maps, and the John Carter Brown Library, the British Library, the Royal Netherlands Institute of Southeast Asian and Caribbean Studies, and AP Photo provided images and gave permission for their use. Thanks to you all.

1 Introduction: writing the history of European colonialism

In the summer of 1701, around 1,300 representatives of almost forty nations gathered in Montreal to sign what became known as the Great Peace of Montreal. Only one of the nations present, the French who hosted the gathering, was European. The others were Native Americans, come to Montreal hoping to resolve a generation of conflict in the North American back country. Amid furious negotiations, great pomp and ceremony, and an outbreak of disease that killed one of the principal negotiators, these representatives concluded a peace treaty that marked an end to decades of armed conflict and brought together the French and the Indian nations of the St. Lawrence and Great Lakes regions.

Sitting astride one of the few entry points into the North American continent, the St. Lawrence River, the host city was the center of a trading network that linked the French who had founded the city some sixty years earlier with Indians further west. Bartering for furs with weapons, ammunition, other manufactured goods, and brandy, *voyageurs* from Montreal linked the markets of Montreal and Europe to the Native Americans of the interior. They were joined by missionaries who tried to convert the Indians to Catholicism, and by French authorities who concluded alliances with peoples in the Great Lakes region (the *pays d'en haut*) and beyond. These alliances recognized the French as a paternal provider and mediator, called Onontio by the Algonquians. While the French would not have accorded their allies the same sovereign status they gave themselves or other European nations, those Indian nations themselves were insistent on their independence from Onontio.

France desperately needed to be recognized as Onontio to support and defend the colony of New France. France's Indian allies were much better at fighting on the terrain of North America than were French soldiers, and they provided valuable military assistance in the French wars of the late seventeenth century with the English and their Iroquois allies. The conference at Montreal came about because at the end of the seventeenth century it proved possible to negotiate an end not only

1

to a conflict in Europe known as the War of the League of Augsburg, but also a series of conflicts in North America. With this prospect, the conference in Montreal attracted a wide range of participants. The governor-general of New France, Louis Hector de Callière, was there, as were Abenakis from Acadia and Algonquians from around the Great Lakes. Iroquoians from the area around Montreal, allies of France, were there as well. In the early summer canoes arrived from up the St. Lawrence River bearing chiefs and representatives of Native Americans from further to the north and west: Crees; Huron-Petuns; Timiskamings from the source of the Ottawa River; Miamis of the St. Joseph River; Missisaguas, Nipissings, Odawas, Ojibwas, Potawatomis, Sauks, and Winnebagos; and Illinois from the Mississippi valley. Leaders of the Iroquois Confederation, representing the Onondaga, Seneca, Oneida, and Cayuga from south of the St. Lawrence, were also there. Often enemies of the French, they had been brought to the bargaining table by the exhausting effects of decades of war.[1]

The French diplomats who negotiated the Great Peace of Montreal of 1701 viewed it as a major diplomatic achievement. The terms of the treaty increased French power in North America, giving them control of the fur trade in the west. It facilitated French entry into the interior of the North American continent, and made the French the arbiters of differences among the peoples of the Great Lakes region. Those peoples, the French hoped, would become an important reserve army for France in its conflict with England. With their support, New France, extending to the new colony of Louisiana on the lower Mississippi, would be a barrier to English penetration of the interior of the continent. The Iroquois who came to Montreal in 1701 were also vital to the French plan. The proponents within the Five Nations of a francophile policy that itself waxed and waned in influence, they had risen in power in the last decade of the seventeenth century as, with French help, warriors from the *pays d'en haut* dealt the Five Nations defeat after defeat. The Great Peace of Montreal brought security for the French by guaranteeing Iroquois neutrality in a war between the French and the English, yet kept the Five Nations strong enough to act as a buffer between the Indians of the interior and the English fur entrepôt at Albany and between New France and the English colonies in New England and New York.

But Callière and his fellow French officials were deceived. At virtually the same time as they were concluding the Peace in Montreal,

---

[1] The Five Nations of the Iroquois Confederation included the Mohawk, but they were not represented at Montreal.

anglophile Iroquois, another faction of the Five Nations, were in Albany negotiating an agreement with the English. Just like the French in Montreal, the New Yorkers who left this Albany conference were convinced that the Iroquois were "intirely ... fix'd ... in their obedience to his Majesty." Yet the Iroquois in Albany neglected to mention their commitment to the French to remain neutral in European wars. Agreeing to a massive cession of land – from western Pennsylvania to Detroit, the Chicago Portage and Michilimakinac – these Iroquois "brightened" their long-standing agreements with the English, known as the Covenant Chain, to gain English diplomatic and military protection against the French. In what some historians have called the Grand Settlement of 1701, the Iroquois were able to achieve their own goals by convincing both the French and the English of their support.[2]

I begin this account of European colonization with the Great Peace of Montreal because the event brings together many aspects of the process of colonization in the modern era. Certainly some colonial officials thought they were involved in conquest, but Callière made no pretense of subjugating in any other than symbolic form the indigenous peoples of North America whose representatives were at Montreal. Rather, as the representative of the Sun King in Versailles, he created a form of partnership that brought those peoples into a diplomatic system that was concerned with, among other things, limiting the power of France's neighbor across the English Channel. He was also seeking to ensure the primacy of French trade in the region, a move that would benefit both the French state and its merchants and manufacturers. The Great Peace therefore underscores the continuing importance of European Great Power diplomatic and economic concerns in colonial expansion, something we will see not only in the Americas but also in Asia, the Pacific, and Africa. But as a consequence of the Great Peace the French themselves took on a role in the diplomatic system of North America. They committed themselves to provide the Algonquians and

---

[2] Gilles Havard, *The Great Peace of Montreal of 1701: French-Native Diplomacy in the Seventeenth Century*, trans. Phyllis Aronoff and Howard Scott (Montreal: McGill-Queen's University Press, 2001); Anthony F. C. Wallace, "Origins of Iroquois Neutrality: The Grand Settlement of 1701," *Pennsylvania History* 24 (1957), 223–35; Daniel K. Richter, *The Ordeal of the Longhouse* (Chapel Hill: University of North Carolina Press, 1992), 211–12, and *Facing East from Indian Country: A Native History of Early America* (Cambridge, MA: Harvard University Press, 2001), 156–57; Francis Jennings, *The Invasion of America: Indians, Colonialism, and the Cant of Conquest* (Chapel Hill: University of North Carolina Press, 1975), and, *The Ambiguous Iroquois Empire: The Covenant Chain Confederation of Indian Tribes with English Colonies from its Beginnings to the Lancaster Treaty of 1744* (New York: W. W. Norton, 1984); Daniel K. Richter and James H. Merrell (eds.), *Beyond the Covenant Chain: The Iroquois and Their Neighbors in Indian North America, 1600–1800* (Syracuse University Press, 1987).

other native peoples with the European goods they needed to maintain and extend their own power and with military and diplomatic support against their enemies.

It also reminds us of the power and agency of indigenous peoples in colonization. Often these peoples made their presence known not by words that were recorded, archived, and now made available to us, but through their actions. Nonetheless, the diplomatic, economic, and political interests of the peoples that Europeans met in the course of their colonial ventures were of comparable significance to those of the Europeans. Callière was implementing a policy formulated at the court of Versailles by Louis XIV and his ministers. But in the St. Lawrence River valley, he had to reach agreement with Amerindians who lived throughout the northeastern part of North America, from the western edge of the Great Lakes, into the *pays d'en haut*, east to Acadia, and south into the Ohio valley and New York. That the Hurons, Algonquians, Iroquois, and others came to Montreal at all was the result of decisions, taken far from the view of Versailles, that it was in their interests to stop the conflicts that had marked that part of North America for decades, and those who came to Montreal calculated that the Peace would increase their own political influence. The events in both Montreal and Albany in 1701 also demonstrate the significance of cultural interactions between imperial powers and indigenous peoples. The two ceremonies drew not on the European ceremonial tradition, as elaborate as it was, but on an equally elaborate and significant collection of American ceremonies. Like many colonial relationships, they were, as Gilles Havard has noted, "a spectacular expression of this spirit of adaptation and of the intensity of cultural exchange in the diplomatic sphere."[3] Over time, these cultural exchanges would be one of the most important aspects of colonialism, moving from diplomatic negotiations to include the most intimate aspects of human lives, and mobilizing resources among both colonizers and colonized to manage those exchanges.

The diplomatic settlements at Montreal and Albany in 1701 therefore vividly display the entangled histories that made up the history of colonialism. These, we will see in the course of this book, took place at different sites, and the ways in which historians have written about colonialism reflect emphases on one or another aspect of the process. How to tell this story is not a new issue: a history of European empires has existed virtually since the first European conquest, as explorers, monarchs, and commentators sought to explain and justify the expansion

[3] Havard, *Great Peace*, 181.

of their power. Until recently, European imperialism and colonialism were portrayed in military, naval, and political terms, processes in which European states projected their power into other parts of the world and Europeans settled in the newly acquired territories. The subjects and actors in this narrative were overwhelmingly Europeans who acted upon the rest of the world. If indigenous peoples appeared at all, they were faceless and nameless participants in the process of colonialism. Non-European states were, for the most part, non-existent. But colonialism was also thought of as a phenomenon that occurred away from Europe, with only an occasional intrusion on Europe itself.

It was, in many of these accounts, the courage and daring of European explorers who "discovered" the Americas, Oceania, Asia, and Africa, and planted the flags of European nations in those parts of the world. European soldiers, sailors, and missionaries consolidated those holdings and opened the way for the colonists who followed and established the settlements that brought European civilization to the rest of the world. European statesmen made the diplomatic agreements that established the framework within which European colonialism could occur and which acknowledged each successive addition to empire. European capitalists developed the resources of the colonies. In these views, the colonial narrative has often followed an arc of growing European conquest and control, with an early modern peak that ended with the revolutions of the late eighteenth century. This was followed by the apogee of the "New Imperialism" in the late nineteenth century, and then a sudden decline and end after 1945. This approach marked historians' writings about empire in the generation after World War II, even as those empires were facing – and losing – battles with nationalist movements in the colonies.[4]

Some studies have distilled the historical experience of imperialism and colonialism into typologies. These emerged even as colonization itself proceeded. In the late nineteenth century the French political economist Paul Leroy Beaulieu distinguished between commercial, agricultural, and plantation colonies. British imperialists at the same

[4] See, for example: J. H. Parry, *The Spanish Seaborne Empire* (New York: Knopf, 1966); D. K. Fieldhouse, *The Colonial Empires* (London: Macmillan, 1966), and *Economics and Empire, 1830–1914* (Ithaca, NY: Cornell University Press, 1973); Henri Brunschwig, *French Colonialism 1871–1914* (New York: Praeger, 1966); Trevor Lloyd, *Empire: The History of the British Empire* (London: Hambledon and London, 2001); Niall Ferguson, *Empire: The Rise and Demise of the British World Order and the Lessons for Global Power* (New York: Basic Books, 2003); Jean Meyer, Jean Tarrade, Annie Rey-Goldzeiguer, and Jacques Thobie, *Histoire de la France coloniale*, 2 vols. (Paris: Armand Colin, 1990, 1991); Gilbert Comte *et al.*, *L'aventure coloniale de la France*, 2 vols. (Paris: Denoël, 1988, 1990).

time spoke of Canada, New Zealand, Australia, and South Africa (even including sometimes the United States) as "settler colonies," ignoring the presence of those who inhabited those parts of the world before the British arrived. These were seen as not only distinct from other colonies, such as India or even Ireland, but also as potential parts of a "Greater Britain" that would rescue fading British power. Some more recent academic studies also see such typologies as analytically useful. Jürgen Osterhammel, for example, describes exploitation colonies, maritime enclaves, and settlement colonies, while other historians have proposed other ways of categorizing them.[5] These certainly draw attention to common features of colonies in different empires and eras, but have a tendency to downplay the specific contexts of different colonies.

If these approaches have dominated historians' writings about colonialism, a number of factors have recently underscored their limitations. Perhaps foremost has been the process of decolonization itself, which, beginning before World War I, gaining strength between the World Wars, and culminating in the two decades after World War II, forcibly reminded European states and European colonists that colonial subjects not only existed but were capable of claiming a place in the governance of those colonies. In many instances, of course, this led to political independence from the imperial power and the recognition of the sovereignty of India, Algeria, Indonesia, and other former colonies. The obvious agency of Asians and Africans in nationalist movements during the post-World War II era strongly suggested that colonial subjects had been capable of such action in the past.

Decolonization not only lessened interest in "Imperial History" – no longer a story of European triumph and good will – but also spurred the growth of the study of the histories of the new nation-states that had achieved independence. If Western versions of the world had been, in Eric Wolf's phrase, "Europe and the people without History,"[6] in the decades after 1960 the histories of India, Southeast Asia, North Africa, and Sub-Saharan Africa became recognized specialties within the discipline. These historians insisted on the need to separate the histories of

---

[5] Paul Leroy Beaulieu, *De la colonization chez les peuples modernes*, 2nd edn. (Paris: Guillaumin et Cie, 1882), esp. 575; Duncan Bell, *The Idea of Greater Britain: Empire and the Future of World Order, 1860–1900* (Princeton University Press, 2007); Jürgen Osterhammel, *Colonialism* (Princeton: Markus Wiener Publishers, 1997), 10–12; Moses Finley, "Colonies: An Attempt at a Typology," *Transactions of the Royal Historical Society*, 5th series, 26 (1976), 167–88; James Mahoney, *Colonialism and Postcolonial Development: Spanish America in Comparative Perspective* (Cambridge University Press, 2010), 20–32.

[6] Eric Wolf, *Europe and the People without History* (Berkeley and Los Angeles: University of California Press, 1982).

the former colonies from the empires that had dominated them during the now-gone colonial era.

The past forty years have also seen significant changes in the practice of historians of Europe and the United States. The growth of World History (sometimes called global history or international history) internationalized a discipline that had usually taken the nation-state as its fundamental unit of analysis. Aiming to study historical forces that "do not respect national or even cultural boundary lines, but work their effects instead on a regional, continental, or global scale," world historians from the very beginning found imperialism and colonialism to be a significant part of their subject matter.[7] At the same time, the 1960s also saw new forms of historical analysis and writing that legitimated historical subjects and processes that, in the past, had been ignored or neglected.[8] New groups became the subjects of histories: peasants, workers, slaves, non-Europeans, and women became not exceptional and marginal participants in the story of the past, but increasingly prominent parts of that story. While many historians continued to write traditional political, diplomatic, and intellectual histories, this "New Social History" seemed to be becoming hegemonic in the discipline by the late 1970s and early 1980s, with a flood of graduate students, monographs, and journals coming into the profession, especially in the United States.

But the dominance of social history would be brief. In the 1980s, some historians, influenced initially by cultural anthropology and then by developments in philosophy and literary criticism, focused attention on the study of culture. Social historians who had grown uneasy about the emphasis in social history on broad societal structures rather than individual experience took a "cultural turn," attracted by the cultural anthropology of Clifford Geertz and his emphasis on the study

---

[7] Jerry H. Bentley, "A New Forum for Global History," *Journal of World History*, 1 (1990), iv. See William H. McNeill, *A World History* (New York: Oxford University Press, 1967), and Leften S. Stavrianos, *The World since 1500: A Global History* (Englewood Cliffs, NJ: Prentice Hall, 1966) for early versions of world history.

[8] For reflections on these developments by major participants see: Geoff Eley, *A Crooked Line: From Cultural History to the History of Society* (Ann Arbor: University of Michigan Press, 2005); Lynn Hunt, "Introduction," in Hunt (ed.), *The New Cultural History* (Berkeley and Los Angeles: University of California Press, 1989), 1–22; Victoria E. Bonnell and Lynn Hunt, "Introduction," in Bonnell and Hunt (eds.), *Beyond the Cultural Turn* (Berkeley and Los Angeles: University of California Press, 1999), 1–32; Eric Hobsbawm, *Interesting Times: A Twentieth-Century Life* (New York: Pantheon Books, 2002), esp. 282–97; and William H. Sewell, Jr., "The Political Unconscious of Social and Cultural History, or, Confessions of a Former Quantitative Historian," in *Logics of History: Social Theory and Social Transformation* (University of Chicago Press, 2005), 22–80.

of culture as an interpretive practice. Others took a "linguistic turn," influenced by post-structuralist philosophy and literary criticism. One of the most important aspects of this was the insight of the French philosopher and historian Michel Foucault that what he called "technologies of power" operated not only through the state institutions that historians had always studied, but also through various forms of knowledge. In particular, Foucault outlined an approach that emphasized the importance of the interactions between power relations and the most intimate aspects of human life, arguing that "the body is ... directly involved in a political field; power relations have an immediate hold upon it; they invest it, mark it, train it, torture it, force it to carry out tasks, to perform ceremonies, to emit signs." Subjection, in this view, can be "direct, physical, pitting force against force, bearing on material elements, and yet without involving violence; it may be calculated, organized, technically thought out; it may be subtle, make use neither of weapons nor terror and yet remain of a physical order."[9]

These influences broadened the ways in which power was understood, and made the categories of nation, class, gender, and race, often taken as unchanging givens by historians, themselves the subjects of historical analysis. But neither the "New Cultural Historians" nor Foucault himself had much to say about colonialism. Race joined gender and class in the trinity of interests for cultural historians, but colonialism remained peripheral. Foucault focused his historical studies on prisons, insanity, and sexuality in nineteenth-century France rather than the French empire. Historians of imperialism and colonialism certainly incorporated concerns about previously marginalized groups into their accounts, and it would be unfair to characterize their work as ignoring these concerns. But for many in the 1980s and 1990s their interests remained focused on more traditional aspects of the empires. The *Oxford History of the British Empire*, for example, published in five volumes between 1988 and 1999 and including contributions by many prominent scholars of the empire, largely retained the traditional emphasis on European conquest, diplomacy, settlement, and economic empire. Only after the turn of the century was it followed by a supplementary companion series that more directly addressed issues of gender, migration, race, and the environment that the original five volumes had not covered in depth.[10]

---

[9] Clifford Geertz, *The Interpretation of Cultures* (New York: Basic Books, 1973); Michel Foucault, *Discipline and Punish: The Birth of the Prison*, trans. Alan Sheridan (New York: Random House, 1977), 25–26.

[10] Wm. Roger Louis (ed.), *The Oxford History of the British Empire* (Oxford University Press, 1988–99); Philippa Levine (ed.), *Gender and Empire* (Oxford University

By then it had become clear that the "linguistic turn" and the "new cultural history" would be useful in rethinking the way in which colonialism and other relationships between Europe and the rest of the world were understood. An early, and very controversial, contribution to this came from the literary scholar Edward Said, who drew on Foucault's insights about the ways in which forms of knowledge – specifically what Said called Orientalism, the study of the Middle East – both created a subject, the undifferentiated Oriental Other, and exerted European power over those peoples.[11] In this view, European colonialism became less the actions of armies and colonial proconsuls, and more the various ways in which European discourses and forms of knowledge created colonial subjects and controlled them. The racial distinctions that were part and parcel of European colonialism were easily susceptible to this kind of analysis, and beginning in the 1990s other scholars, influenced by Foucault's emphasis on the body as a focal point of discursive power in the modern era, became interested in the ways in which colonial systems of governance controlled colonial bodies through physical spaces, labor systems, medicine, and practices concerning gender and sexuality.[12]

Exploration of the cultural aspects of colonialism was accompanied by recognition of the interplay between metropolitan and colonial cultures. One form of this has been the recent revival in popular culture of a kind of "colonial blues" that has portrayed a bittersweet memory of the colonies in films, television, and fiction.[13] Historians have shown less nostalgia for the empires, but have recognized the complex interactions between the metropolitan imperial powers and their colonies. Colonialism now appears as a phenomenon that influenced not only the histories of the places that became colonies of European powers,

Press, 2004); Philip D. Morgan and Sean Hawkins (eds.), *Black Experience and the Empire* (Oxford University Press, 2006); William Beinart and Lotte Hughes (eds.), *Environment and Empire* (Oxford University Press, 2007); Marjory Harper and Stephen Constantine (eds.), *Migration and Empire* (Oxford University Press, 2010).

[11] Edward Said, *Orientalism* (New York: Random House, 1979), and *Culture and Imperialism* (New York: Random House, 1993).

[12] Ann Laura Stoler, *Race and the Education of Desire: Foucault's History of Sexuality and the Colonial Order of Things* (Durham, NC and London: Duke University Press, 1995); Philippa Levine, *The British Empire: Sunrise to Sunset* (New York: Pearson Longman, 2007); Megan Vaughan, *Curing Their Ills: Colonial Power and African Illness* (Stanford University Press, 1991); Frederick Cooper, *Decolonization and African Society: The Labor Question in French and British Africa* (Cambridge University Press, 1996); Paul Rabinow, *French Modern: Norms and Forms of the Social Environment* (Cambridge, MA: MIT Press, 1989).

[13] The phrase is from Panivong Norindr, *Phantasmatic Indochina: French Colonial Ideology in Architecture, Film, and Literature* (Durham, NC: Duke University Press, 1996), 133.

but also the histories of those European powers themselves. In what has been called the "imperial turn," historians of the imperial powers have studied the implications of colonialism for all Europeans.[14] It has become apparent, for example, that the growing importance of colonial trade for metropolitan economies connected London dockworkers, even if they rarely left the London waterfront, with British colonies in India and Africa. Often as well the ability of governments to expand and maintain the colonial empires became a measure of their legitimacy and fitness for rule, while the popularity of empire helped European governments manage the social conflicts associated with industrialization and urbanization in the increasingly democratic political systems of eighteenth- and nineteenth-century Europe.[15] We also now see how European elite and popular culture was marked by colonialism, from the colonial subjects of Orientalist paintings to the stories of empire that Victorian youths imbibed, to popular entertainment, on stages and in international expositions, that became commonplaces for Europeans.[16] The pervasiveness of colonialism makes a modern European history without it incomplete at best, deceptive at worst, giving colonial history a position of prominence that it has rarely enjoyed in the past. Colonialism had always played some role in the narrative of modern European history. But it now joins long-standing topics such as the development of representative political institutions, national identity, human rights, urbanization, and industrialization as central elements of that history.[17]

---

[14] Antoinette Burton (ed.), *After the Imperial Turn: Thinking with and through the Nation* (Durham, NC and London: Duke University Press, 2003); Durba Ghosh, "Another Set of Imperial Turns?" *American Historical Review* 117 (2012), 772–93; Gary Wilder, "From Optic to Topic: The Foreclosure Effect of Historiographic Turns," *American Historical Review* 117 (2012), 723–45. For opposing views: P. J. Marshall, "No Fatal Impact? The Elusive History of Imperial Britain," *Times Literary Supplement*, March 12, 1993, 8–10; David Cannadine, *Ornamentalism: How the British Saw Their Empire* (New York: Oxford University Press, 2001); Bernard Porter, *The Absent-Minded Imperialists: Empire, Society and Culture in Britain* (New York: Oxford University Press, 2004).

[15] Jonathan Schneer, *London 1900: The Imperial Metropolis* (New Haven, CT: Yale University Press, 1999); Kathleen Wilson, *The Sense of the People: Politics, Culture and Imperialism in England, 1715–1785* (Cambridge University Press, 1995); Robert Tombs, *Nationhood and Nationalism in France from Boulangism to the Great War, 1889–1918* (London: HarperCollins Academic, 1991).

[16] Lynne Thornton (ed.), *The Orientalists: Painters-Travellers, 1828–1908* (Paris: ACR Édition Internationale, 1983); Leonard Ashley, *George Alfred Henty and the Victorian Mind* (San Francisco, CA: International Scholars Publications, 1999); Herman Lebovics, *True France: Wars over Cultural Identity, 1900–1945* (Ithaca, NY: Cornell University Press, 1992).

[17] Michael Adas, "'High' Imperialism and the 'New' History," in Adas (ed.), *Islam and European Expansion: The Forging of a Global Order* (Philadelphia: Temple University

Influenced by these developments, the history of European colonialism that appears in the following pages is very different from many older accounts. My version of this history seeks to take into account not only the political, diplomatic, and economic structures that linked Europe and its colonies, but also the ways in which constructions of gender, race, class, and nation worked themselves out in the broad field made up of Europe and those colonies. These colonial stories are not straightforward, easily fitted into a "rise and fall" arc, and I describe colonial history not as the inevitable growth and decline of European empires but as a series of changing relationships. It is a contingent story of shifting alliances, tactical and strategic moves, extraordinary violence, and dismal disappointments and failures. Structures of control over not only territory and indigenous populations but also cultural, gender, and sexual boundaries were continually at risk, and continually being reimagined, even as they seemed permanent and natural. Colonial ventures were often not planned, and almost never worked out as intended. Political, military, diplomatic, and commercial practices certainly joined metropole and colony together, but questions about labor, gender, race, and social and political organization also accompanied Europeans out to the colonies and came back by return ship. It is a much more complicated story than simply the conquest of other parts of the world by Europeans.

As the older accounts tell us, these structures of control had military, economic, and political qualities, in which outnumbered Europeans tried to impose their will on native peoples, for colonialism never took place on vacant land. But colonialism is also about cultural practices and remarkable intrusion into the minutest details of the lives of virtually everyone who lived in a colony. Europeans almost always thought they were winning in these relationships. But some of those indigenous peoples resisted those incursions even as others collaborated with the Europeans. Colonized peoples sought – sometimes very effectively – to affect the outcome of those negotiations, and in so doing they placed limitations on the dominion and control exercised by colonial states and administrations. Some of the colonizers themselves also upset the

Press, 1993), 311–44; Ann Stoler and Frederick Cooper, "Between Metropole and Colony: Rethinking a Research Agenda," in Stoler and Cooper (eds.), *Tensions of Empire: Colonial Cultures in a Bourgeois World* (Berkeley and Los Angeles: University of California Press, 1997), 1–58; Frederick Cooper, "The Rise, Fall, and Rise of Colonial Studies, 1951–2001," in *Colonialism in Question* (Berkeley and Los Angeles: University of California Press, 2005), 33–55; Tony Ballantyne and Antoinette Burton, "Introduction," in Ballantyne and Burton (eds.), *Moving Subjects: Gender, Mobility, and Intimacy in an Age of Global Empire* (Urbana and Chicago: University of Illinois Press, 2009).

carefully laid plans of the advocates and rulers of empire. To understand European colonialism, then, our focus must be not only on the European powers or the colonies themselves but on the contact and connections between metropoles and colonies. If we take the lessons of the Great Peace of Montreal to heart, we need to see the history of European colonial empires as an unstable pattern of negotiated settlements in which European powers and other peoples and states repeatedly structured, restructured, and reproduced their relationships.

The following pages recount the history of European colonialism since 1700 by emphasizing the different kinds of interaction that existed at different points in time between the European powers and other parts of the world. By beginning this history around 1700, we can see the twists and turns of the European relationship with other parts of the world, and how that relationship has taken different forms, from the direct control in the Atlantic colonies of the eighteenth century to the indirect links that followed the "Age of Revolution" at the turn of the nineteenth century, to the formal empires of the late nineteenth and early twentieth centuries, to the continuing effects of colonialism that mark our own time.[18] We can see the ways in which, over the course of almost three centuries, European states and their subjects created, sustained, and restructured their relationships with almost the entire rest of the world, and how colonial peoples pushed back. Acquired not so much in J. R. Seeley's famous "fit of absence of mind"[19] but through the interplay of European and indigenous decisions, conditions, and actions, the European colonial empires were the product and the expression of multiple forces. Diplomatic concerns motivated European statesmen to stake out different kinds of influence around the globe. Merchants and others sought to exploit the supposed riches of the colonies. Some Europeans tried to bring their civilization – religions that promised eternal salvation, education in a culture that valued individuals, machines that increased the productivity of human labor, political institutions that remedied the perceived ills of the colonies – to their colonial subjects. Other Europeans saw the colonies as places to make their fortunes, to escape from the cultural, psychological, and

---

[18] Some historians focusing on a specific period or empire have made similar points. See J. Gallagher and R. Robinson, "The Imperialism of Free Trade," *Economic History Review* 6, 1 (1953), 1–15; Ronald Robinson, "Non-European Foundations of European Imperialism: Sketch for a Theory of Collaboration," in Robert Owen and Bob Sutcliffe (eds.), *Studies in the Theory of Imperialism* (London: Longman, 1972), 117–42; Jeremy Adelman, "An Age of Imperial Revolutions," *American Historical Review* 113, 2 (2008), 319–40.

[19] J. R. Seeley, *The Expansion of England* (Boston: Little, Brown and Company, 1914 [1883]), 8.

other strictures of Europe. At the same time, colonial peoples pursued their own diplomatic, political, military, economic, religious, and cultural projects. Indigenous political leaders tried to confirm and consolidate their authority, while challengers sought to use the colonial authorities to unseat their opponents. Trade with Europeans brought manufactured goods into indigenous communities, and some of these goods – firearms – allowed them to defeat their enemies. Shamans and other religious leaders resisted or accommodated themselves to the messages of European missionaries in order to maintain their hold on the spiritual world of their fellows. Women and young people used the opportunities brought by colonialism to challenge the authority of husbands and fathers. In this process, European and colonial identities were put in play in multiple ways. European states, growing in power at home, sought to manage the colonial enterprise by imposing control over the actions and persons of colonizers and colonized, while those in the colonies employed numerous tactics to evade that control.

The themes of contingency, conquest, resistance, and collaboration emerge in every aspect of people's lives in each period and in the many places in which modern colonialism occurred. The next chapter begins the story with a survey of the colonial empires of France, Great Britain, the Netherlands, Portugal, Spain, and Russia at the beginning of the eighteenth century. These colonial holdings participated in, and were an outgrowth of, the conflicts between those powers. But the end of the War of Spanish Succession in the middle of the second decade of that century ushered in a period of peace between the European powers that lasted, with intermittent skirmishes, until the 1740s. This ended around the middle of the century, when a lengthy period of conflict between European powers began that lasted from the War of Austrian Succession in the 1740s and the Seven Years War in the 1750s through the American Revolution and the Wars of the French Revolution and into the early nineteenth century. This period of conflict saw a significant restructuring of the colonial empires, especially those in the Atlantic basin, and Chapter 3 takes up that part of the story. Chapters 4 and 5 describe the extension of European influence into Oceania, Asia, and Africa, as during the nineteenth century the European powers created formal empires that, by the beginning of the twentieth century, placed those regions of the world under more direct European rule than had ever been the case. This era of "High Imperialism" around the globe was accompanied in Europe itself by the creation of imperial nation-states. Colonial holdings became intrinsic parts of the politics, economics, social arrangements, and culture of the imperial powers. The characteristics of these imperial nation-states, especially in the realm of popular culture, form the subject of Chapter 6. Finally, Chapter 7 recounts the end of those formal empires, as indigenous reform and nationalist movements and the weakening of the European powers combined at the middle of the twentieth century to restructure once again the relationships between the peoples of the world and those of Europe.

FURTHER READING

Adas, Michael, ed. *Islam and European Expansion: The Forging of a Global Order.* Philadelphia: Temple University Press, 1993.

Adelman, Jeremy. "An Age of Imperial Revolutions." *American Historical Review* 113, 2 (2008), 319–40.

Ballantyne, Tony, and Antoinette Burton, eds. *Moving Subjects: Gender, Mobility, and Intimacy in an Age of Global Empire.* Urbana and Chicago: University of Illinois Press, 2009.

Beinart, William, and Lotte Hughes, eds. *Environment and Empire.* Oxford University Press, 2007.

Burton, Antoinette, ed. *After the Imperial Turn: Thinking with and through the Nation.* Durham, NC: Duke University Press, 2003.

Cooper, Frederick. *Colonialism in Question.* Berkeley and Los Angeles: University of California Press, 2005.

Gallagher, J., and R. Robinson. "The Imperialism of Free Trade." *Economic History Review* 6, 1 (1953), 1–15.

Harper, Marjory, and Stephen Constantine, eds. *Migration and Empire.* Oxford University Press, 2010.

Havard, Gilles. *The Great Peace of Montreal of 1701: French-Native Diplomacy in the Seventeenth Century*, trans. Phyllis Aronoff and Howard Scott. Montreal: McGill-Queen's University Press, 2001.

Hinderaker, Eric, and Rebecca Horn. "Territorial Crossings: Histories and Historiographies of the Early Americas." *William and Mary Quarterly* 67, 3 (2010), 395–432.

Levine, Philippa. *The British Empire: Sunrise to Sunset.* New York: Pearson Longman, 2007.

Levine, Philippa, ed. *Gender and Empire.* Oxford University Press, 2004.

Morgan, Philip D., and Sean Hawkins, eds. *Black Experience and the Empire.* Oxford University Press, 2006.

Porter, Bernard. *The Absent-Minded Imperialists: What the British Really Thought about Empire.* Oxford University Press, 2004.

Robinson, Ronald. "Non-European Foundations of European Imperialism: Sketch for a Theory of Collaboration." In Robert Owen and Bob Sutcliffe, eds., *Studies in the Theory of Imperialism.* London: Longman, 1972, 117–42.

Stoler, Ann Laura. *Race and the Education of Desire: Foucault's History of Sexuality and the Colonial Order of Things.* Durham, NC and London: Duke University Press, 1995.

Stoler, Ann Laura, and Frederick Cooper. "Between Metropole and Colony: Rethinking a Research Agenda." In Stoler and Cooper, eds., *Tensions of Empire: Colonial Cultures in a Bourgeois World*. Berkeley and Los Angeles: University of California Press, 1997, 1–58.

2   The European empires in the early eighteenth century

The European empires around the end of the seventeenth century were hardly cohesive, coherent wholes. Primarily controlled by the developing European states of Portugal, Spain, France, Great Britain, Russia, and the Netherlands, they had been pieced together slowly over the course of several centuries. In describing them we need to keep in mind the difficulties faced by Europeans as they tried to expand their trade, protect their political authority, and export their religious beliefs and ways of life to other parts of the world. The interplay of European political, diplomatic, economic, and cultural concerns with similar aspects of the places being colonized made the development of Europe's colonial empires not "smooth and linear" but, rather, temporally and spatially "lumpy," occurring in intense bursts.[1]

France

The French colonies in North America affected by the Great Peace of Montreal were only part of a collection of possessions that stretched from Acadia and Canada to the Caribbean and to South Asia. French colonies in Asia and the Americas developed slowly in the sixteenth and seventeenth centuries: French merchants at that time were more interested in trade on the coast of North Africa. But by the seventeenth century France did control several islands in the Indian Ocean, the Île de France and Île de Bourbon, which produced sugar for export to Europe. In 1674, François Martin, one of the chief proponents of French expansion in India, succeeded in negotiating the concession for what would become Pondichéry on the east coast of the subcontinent for the Compagnie des Indes Orientales, a monopoly company chartered

---

[1] William H. Sewell, Jr., "Historical Events as Transformations of Structures: Inventing Revolution at the Bastille," *Theory and Society* 25, 6 (1996), 841–81, esp. 843; Frederick Cooper adapts Sewell's concept to apply to colonialism in "Introduction," in *Colonialism in Question* (Berkeley and Los Angeles: University of California Press, 2005), 3–32.

by the French king. While at times taken over by the English, this town would remain a principal French outpost in South Asia. In all, however, French attempts prior to the eighteenth century to develop an empire in Asia remained weak and virtually stillborn (Map 1).

In the second half of the sixteenth century French efforts turned to the western shores of the Atlantic. There were failed attempts to establish settlements in South America, at Guanabara Bay (1555–60) and Maranhão (1594–1615) in Brazil. A settlement in Florida (1562–67) foundered against the opposition of Spain. But in the seventeenth century the islands of the Caribbean opened for French colonial expansion. Cardinal de Richelieu, the principal minister of Louis XIII (r. 1610–43), sponsored voyages to the Lesser Antilles (or the Windward Islands), first in the 1620s to Saint-Christophe, then in 1635 to Guadeloupe. In 1638 Martinique was claimed by France, and at about the same time France laid claim to Dominica, Saint-Barthélemy, Sainte-Croix, and Saint-Martin. By 1642 this empire in the Lesser Antilles included Marie-Galante and Grenada. The islands of Tortuga and Saint-Domingue in the Greater Antilles (or the Leeward Islands) had been used by pirates from a variety of European countries as a base for attacks on Spanish shipping, but in 1641, the French took possession of the western part of Saint-Domingue. Emigrants from France, especially Brittany, followed, and by 1677 there were about 5,000 colonists living on the western part of the island.

Europeans quickly dominated the Tainos, Arawaks, Ciboney, and Caribs who inhabited the Caribbean islands, and many of those indigenous peoples died from disease or the effects of forced labor, or were removed to smaller islands. The fertile soil of the islands made them ideal for cultivation of subtropical crops such as tobacco, cotton, cocoa, and coffee that found ready markets in Europe. In the second half of the seventeenth century these colonies turned to a more lucrative product, sugar, with the transition taking place in Martinique and Guadeloupe between 1665 and 1670, and in Saint-Domingue after 1670.

These crops were increasingly cultivated on plantations. With much of the land in the French islands allocated by the end of the seventeenth century, smaller plantations became rare, and the spread of sugar cultivation in the early eighteenth century accelerated the tendency towards large landholding by either non-residents living in France or the elite of *grands blancs* who dominated island society, wealthy whites who emigrated from France or creoles who were born in the Caribbean. White *engagés* or indentured servants obliged to work for a period of years in exchange for their passage also came from France, and once their period of indenture was completed, these immigrants and other whites

Map 1 The Americas in the eighteenth century.

formed another distinct group within white society, the *petits blancs*. Distinguished by their race and their lack of property, these poor whites worked as artisans, plantation managers, clerks, shopkeepers, and seamen. The size of this white population of *grands blancs* and *petits blancs* tended to remain steady during the eighteenth century.[2]

The expansion of plantation agriculture, and especially the shift to sugar production, meant a rapid increase in the number of slaves in the islands. The slave population grew exponentially on all of the French islands from the constant influx of new slaves from Africa, and by the early eighteenth century, more than 70 percent of the populations of each of these islands were slaves.[3] Their status and condition was regulated by the French *Code noir*, promulgated in 1685 and in effect with minor changes throughout much of the eighteenth century. While providing some protection for slaves against abusive masters, the *Code* in fact reinforced the control of slaves by their owners. In spite of the *Code*, fear of slave discontent was a constant in the French as in other slave societies in the Americas. These plantation societies faced numerous forms and instances of slave resistance to white dominance, and slave rebellions were only one form of this. Slaves at times refused to work, worked slowly, or disappeared for a brief period of time. More serious was flight from their masters, called *grand marronage*, into the back country where they created communities with other runaways that defended themselves against the authorities. These could be found wherever there were slaves, plantations, and unsettled forested areas where fugitives could hide. They existed not only in the French islands but also in the North American South, Jamaica, and the Bahia, Minas Gerais, and Alagoas regions of Brazil. They literally and symbolically reflected the instability of the colonial regimes and their tenuous authority.

The rapid growth of plantation agriculture in France's Caribbean colonies made them distinct from other French colonies in the New World: populated largely by slaves, they held a relatively small number of Europeans, who hoped to return to France after making their fortune in the sugar trade. The frequent practice by white planters of taking slave women as concubines also produced mulattos who were often considered to be free. These, joined by the occasional freed slave, made up the *gens de couleur* who competed with one another and with the *pet-*

---

[2] James Pritchard, *In Search of Empire: The French in the Americas 1670–1730* (Cambridge University Press, 2004).

[3] David Geggus, "The French Slave Trade: An Overview," *William and Mary Quarterly*, 3rd series, 58, 1 (2001), 119–38.

its blancs for employment as artisans, shopkeepers, urban laborers, and plantation overseers. Their number grew slowly over time.

The other major site for French colonial ventures was in the northern part of North America. The cod fishery off the coast of Newfoundland helped train sailors for the French navy and made French mariners increasingly familiar with the route across the North Atlantic that they took in the summer months, leading to small settlements on Newfoundland, Acadia, and Île Royale (Cape Breton Island). At the turn of the seventeenth century interest in the St. Lawrence valley began to pick up. A Compagnie de la Nouvelle France and its more significant successor, the Compagnie des Cent associés de la Nouvelle France (1627), established Quebec (1608), Trois-Rivières (1634), and Montreal (1639–40) on the St. Lawrence. These settlements were intended not only to facilitate the fur trade but also to prevent English and Dutch intrusion into the St. Lawrence valley. Voyages up the river in the 1630s began to illuminate the geography of the Great Lakes region and establish French commercial contacts with the native peoples who lived in the territories surrounding the Great Lakes. This area, unoccupied by the French but open to it commercially, would become the pendant to the small settlements along the St. Lawrence.

The French incursion into the St. Lawrence was the product of commercial and diplomatic policies of France and the actions of French investors and merchants. But the increasing presence of the French in this part of North America in the course of the seventeenth century also impacted the native peoples of the interior of North America itself, and they too helped determine how the colonial venture would turn out. As they moved up the St. Lawrence, the French found themselves involved in disputes between Iroquois and Algonquians; decisions to side with the latter set a long-term course for French Indian policy that would help shape future conflicts not only among the Indians, but also among European powers. Establishing strong trade ties with the Hurons in the region north of Lake Ontario and east of Lake Huron, the French brought European weapons and ammunition into the interior of North America, changing the balance of power among the native peoples of the interior.

At any time it was difficult for the Crown to maintain any direct control of colonial ventures, especially once the ships had left France to cross the Atlantic or to head for the Indian Ocean. These ventures were themselves usually undertaken not directly by the king's government, but by companies such as those active in New France that were chartered by the king to a group of investors and granted monopoly rights to exploit commercially a particular island or region. In this, as we will see, France differed from the Spanish monarchy, which very quickly took over direct administration of its American colonies. The French monarchy preferred private investors to take the risk of colonial ventures. Royal authorization and encouragement of these companies were therefore as far as the French Crown's colonial policy would go before the mid seventeenth century. But during the reign of Louis XIV (r. 1643–1715) this began to change. Monopoly companies continued to play a financial role, but the colonies were "royalized" in ways that paralleled the larger project of development of bureaucratic absolutism in France itself. The royal minister Jean-Baptiste Colbert (in office 1665–83) is often given a major role in this process, and he certainly took more interest in the colonies than his predecessors. For some historians, he – and the royal administration – took a preeminent place in the development of France's seventeenth-century colonies.[4] But even in provincial France it proved difficult for the king's government to control events from Versailles, and the role of the colonists themselves has frequently seemed to be more important.[5]

Whoever was responsible, the growth of New France was hardly easy. The lack of success of various monopoly companies led in 1674 to direct royal administration of New France. But it was soon returned to a new chartered company, and in 1717 it was absorbed into a new Compagnie d'Occident, established in the course of the reorganization of the finances of the French Crown by the Scottish financier John Law. This new company also took over the holdings of the monopoly company established in 1712 to exploit the lower Mississippi. In 1719 the two companies were combined by Law into a new Compagnie des Indes that controlled the royal monopolies for French trade in Senegal, Saint-Domingue, China, the East Indies, Africa, Guinée, and the West Indies. It provided the capital and security for Law's Bank and its refinancing of the French national debt. Had it been successful, Law's company might have played the same role in financing the eighteenth-century French state as did the British East India Company for Great Britain, but it collapsed in 1720 after a speculative bubble that left Law lucky to escape with his life into bankrupt exile, and that brought increased royal control over the reorganized Company.

---

[4] Jean Meyer, Jean Tarrade, Annie Rey-Goldzeiguer, and Jacques Thobie, *Histoire de la France coloniale*, vol. I, *Des origines à 1914* (Paris: Armand Colin, 1991), 77.

[5] Pritchard has most pointedly made this argument about the colonies, in *In Search of Empire*, 72–122. On absolutism in the French provinces, see William Beik, *Absolutism and Society in Seventeenth-Century France: State Power and Provincial Aristocracy in Languedoc* (Cambridge University Press, 1985).

The Company remained in intermittent existence until its final liquidation in 1826. But in spite of the prominence of the various monopoly companies in the French colonies in the seventeenth and eighteenth centuries, the French state became an increasingly important part of the colonial administration. Responsibility for the colonies was placed with the Secretary of State for the Navy, although the Controller General of Finances continued to play an important role in formulating colonial policy. Royal Secretaries of State at Versailles exploited weak administrative departments and overlapping jurisdictions to extend their personal influence, to their profit and that of their political friends. As numerous governors-general and intendants discovered to their dismay, it often proved difficult to arouse any interest in the need for funds, provisions, or even defense of the colonies on the part of their superiors in Versailles.

These needs increased as disputes between the European powers made colonies subordinate to the political conflicts and policies of Western Europe. In South Asia, these worked to the disadvantage of the French. In the Americas, though, they had more success. By the turn of the eighteenth century, the danger of English expansion in North America led to a shift from a primarily commercial approach in Canada, focused on settlements such as Quebec and Montreal that dealt primarily in furs and had to be supplied from France, towards the creation of a colony that could play an effective role in the defense of French interests in North America.

Military forts, missions, and trading posts in the Great Lakes and Illinois Country were the consequence of the decision made by Louis XIV to extend New France west and south and connect it with settlements being established in the lower Mississippi valley. The French presence there dated from an expedition in 1678 by Robert Cavelier de la Salle down the Mississippi. In 1682 he claimed the entire Mississippi valley to the Gulf of Mexico for France, establishing the basis for the territory known as Louisiana. By the eighteenth century, *voyageurs* from Montreal were making the trip to the Gulf and back with remarkable frequency, supporting W. J. Eccles' remark that New France was a river empire, following the two great rivers of North America in search of trade.[6] With the small amount of emigration from France to New France, however, this vast territory remained unpopulated by the French.

---

[6] W. J. Eccles, *France in America*, 2nd edn. (East Lansing: Michigan State University Press, 1990), 156.

If the west and Louisiana had few white settlers, the core settlements of New France in the St. Lawrence valley developed differently, slowly becoming more similar to the more populated English colonies in New England and further south. There were limited numbers of migrants from France to New France in the seventeenth and eighteenth centuries, but these were drawn from those parts of France that were most commercialized, and the migrants themselves, while they came from every level of French society, were often young, male artisans.[7] The French society that was transplanted to the St. Lawrence valley by the Company of New France and its successors and the missionaries of the Catholic Church was both urban and rural, a blend of commerce and agriculture.

Even if small by European standards, the urban settlements of the colony were commercial, political, and cultural centers. Quebec and Trois-Rivières were initially settlements intended to trade with the Indians of the interior, but within a generation they became administrative centers and, especially in the case of Quebec, looked to Europe and the fleets that sailed across the Atlantic. Montreal, in contrast, remained on the edge of the wilderness and was dominated by the fur trade's merchants and *coureurs de bois*. But a part of the purpose of the colony was to convert the Indians to Christianity, and even as the Jesuits founded missions in Huron trading villages to the west, they and other religious orders began to establish in the towns the urban religious institutions found in France. In 1635 the Jesuits established a college in Quebec, and in 1639 Ursuline nuns established a school and the Hospitalières de Saint Augustin founded a hospital there. Trois-Rivières soon also had its own schools and hospital. Montreal, established in 1640, had these urban institutions from the very beginning.

Starting in the middle of the seventeenth century, the Company granted land to seigneurs who were responsible for bringing settlers to the colony. These seigneurs offered homage to the Company, and the settlers did the same to the seigneurs and paid them feudal dues such as *cens et rente* and *lods et vente*. There was not, therefore, a landlord–tenant relationship, but rather a hierarchical relationship similar to those found in rural France at the time. This process of settlement slowly created a rural society extending from Tadoussac to Quebec and beyond of farms fronting on the banks of the St. Lawrence and extending back a few kilometers. The Company refused to grant concessions upriver from Montreal for fear that settlers there would intercept Indians bringing

---

[7] Leslie Choquette, *Frenchmen into Peasants: Modernity and Tradition in the Peopling of French Canada* (Cambridge, MA: Harvard University Press, 1997).

fur pelts to sell, and so settlement stopped just beyond the city. The strong Catholic element in the colony was reflected by the presence every few leagues of a church spire.

Relations between these settlements and the Indians in the region were always unstable, and so the society of New France quickly acquired a strong military bent as all residents were forced to defend themselves and their settlements against attacks. The military establishment maintained by the Crown contributed significantly to the economic well-being of the colony, providing customers for the artisans and shopkeepers of the towns. It was also a means by which the elite maintained their status through officer commissions for their sons. By the second half of the seventeenth century, a society dominated by merchants involved in the fur trade (especially in Montreal) and seigneurs had evolved. Below them were artisans who had been encouraged to bring their skills from France to Canada by the promise of status as a master. Some farmers in the valley also had high status, since recipients of land grants who cleared four *arpents* of land and declared their intention to remain permanently became *habitants*, a civil status that distinguished them from non-permanent wage earners. The area under wheat cultivation increased slowly, and in spite of the short growing season the colony became less dependent on the ships that annually brought supplies from France. By the 1730s, it produced a sufficient agricultural surplus in most years that wheat could be sold to the new fortress at Louisbourg, established on Île Royale to defend the entrance to the St. Lawrence. At the same time, there were tentative, but not particularly successful, attempts at establishing shipbuilding and iron-working industries.

In spite of these efforts at diversification, the fur trade remained the economic basis of France's St. Lawrence colony. French *coureurs de bois* left Montreal in the spring and autumn to trade weapons, ammunition, and other European goods with the Indian nations who gathered furs from as far west as the slopes of the Rocky Mountains. The following August or September the *coureurs'* canoes returned loaded with furs. Ottawas, Huron-Petuns, Saulteurs, Nipissings, and Potawatomis also began to bring furs to Montreal from the region north of Lake Ontario. As this trade for furs developed, European goods began to flow through Native American trade routes in the interior, and Indians came to rely on the guns, ammunition, pots, and other goods they received in exchange for their furs. The security of the fur trade against Iroquois and other Indian raiders was important for both the French and their trading partners. But its prosperity was also subject to the ability of the Company to market the furs in Europe at a profit. A glut on the market, as occurred at the beginning of the eighteenth century, was devastating for the Company and for the tax revenues of the colony. At other times, when prices were high, the *coureurs*, merchants, Company, and colonial administration did well. As the seventeenth century came to an end, the fur trade pushed the French presence further inland and the Crown subsidized the trade through the maintenance of posts in the Great Lakes region for trade between French and Indians.

The fur trade in the region of the Great Lakes created a vast area of interaction and negotiation on political, economic, and cultural levels between Europeans and Native Americans. The trade of European manufactured goods for furs was not only an economic transaction but also a renewal of the French alliance with these refugees from the Iroquois. The fur trade between Montreal and the *pays d'en haut* remained, as Richard White says, "part of the glue holding the Algonquians to the [French] alliance."[8] As late as the 1750s, a St. Joseph Potawatomi could argue "Why not love the French, since you, my father, provide for all our needs and without the French we would lack knives and all the rest?" In return, he claimed, "We respect your commands and have nothing more at heart than to obey them."[9] The attempts by the English in Albany to gain a share of this trade, and the expansionary policies of their allies, the Five Iroquois Nations, led to a series of Iroquois Wars in the seventeenth century that were only resolved, at least for a generation, in the treaties at Montreal and Albany in 1701. Traders also brought European diseases that wreaked havoc in Indian communities. As the fur trade intensified relations between the peoples of the *pays d'en haut* and the French, friendship and kinship relationships between *coureurs* and Indians were increasingly significant to the way the trade functioned. Many traders placed themselves through marriage – either formal Christian marriage or in the "manner of the country" – within the kinship networks of the Indian peoples, especially those of converts to Catholicism. These marriages made the trip west easier, as their Indian wives provided the material support traders needed to survive. They also gave these traders an advantage over others less favorably positioned. In the eighteenth century, their *métis* children would become valuable interlocutors between Europeans and Indians.[10]

---

[8] Richard White, *The Middle Ground: Indians, Empires, and Republics in the Great Lakes Region, 1650–1815* (Cambridge University Press, 1991), 94–141, esp. 105, 127. See also Brett Rushforth, "Slavery, the Fox Wars, and the Limits of Alliance," *William and Mary Quarterly*, 3rd series, 63, 1 (2006), 53–80.

[9] Quoted in White, *The Middle Ground*, 112.

[10] Susan Sleeper-Smith, *Indian Women and French Men: Rethinking Cultural Encounter in the Western Great Lakes* (Amherst: University of Massachusetts Press, 2001); Jennifer

Trade, warfare, disease, marriage, and sexual intimacy were all parts of the negotiations of empire in the "middle ground" in the North American back country, and native peoples as well as Europeans played an active role in making the history of the region. In the Ohio Country and elsewhere the increased trade brought by European contact brought subtle changes in the ways Indian societies demonstrated distinction, status, and authority. Hunting was transformed from an activity that was closely linked to male identity, reciprocity with sacred animals, and connections with the spirit world into one that, because of the demand for beaver pelts and deerskins, was increasingly organized around the desire for short-term profit. Ironically, this strengthened and rewarded important aspects of male culture, but another result was overhunting and the depletion of beaver and deer populations.[11]

It also complicated the spiritual world of Indian communities. Some Indians sought to maintain a strict boundary between their beliefs and those of the Europeans who came into their villages. A Kaskaskia elder responded to missionary activities by exhorting his people to "leave their myths to the people who come from afar, and let us cling to our own traditions."[12] In spite of this, the Jesuit missionaries that proselytized in the back country beginning in the 1620s gained some conversions by their patience and, at times, their bravery: after one Jesuit stoically suffered the amputation of his fingers during torture by the Iroquois, a Huron said that "those fingers which I see cut off are the answer to all my doubts."[13] But those conversions often were not as complete as the Jesuits would have preferred: some Indians retained belief in their traditional version of the afterlife, not the heaven and hell of Catholicism but a place much like this world. Jesuit competition did end the unquestioning allegiance that traditional shamans had enjoyed, however, and often those shamans themselves adopted some aspects of belief in the existence of the Christian God. Christian mission villages provided opportunities for Indians devastated by the wars, epidemics, and economic dislocations of the seventeenth and eighteenth centuries to create new lives and communities. This was the case for women such as the Mohawk Kateri Tekakwitha, the daughter of an Algonquin prisoner who had married a Mohawk. Her move to a Jesuit *réserve* at Kahnawake near Montreal in 1677, after the deaths of both parents

Brown, *Strangers in the Blood: Fur Trade Company Families in Indian Country* (Norman: University of Oklahoma Press, 1996).

[11] Eric Hinderaker, *Elusive Empires: Constructing Colonialism in the Ohio Valley, 1673–1800* (New York: Cambridge University Press, 1997), 54–71, esp. 66.

[12] Quoted in White, *The Middle Ground*, 58.

[13] Quoted in Alan Taylor, *American Colonies* (New York: Penguin Books, 2001), 109.

from smallpox, allowed her to escape the strictures of her Mohawk lineage and find a supportive community of women. Two decades later, the
actions of another convert to Catholicism named Marie Rouensa, the
daughter of a Kaskaskia chief, also proved disruptive of traditional relationships in her village. Her conversion to Catholicism, initial refusal of
a marriage with a French fur trader named Michel Accault, and insistence on Christian beliefs and behavior even after she capitulated to her
family's wishes and married Accault led to the wholesale conversion of
Accault and the Kaskaskia community to Catholicism.[14]

European boots were made from North American deerskins, and the
broad-brimmed hats worn by Europeans in the seventeenth and early
eighteenth centuries needed furs to stay stiff enough to keep the rain
off their wearers' faces and shoulders. The trade in furs and deerskins
heavily involved Native Americans with both France and Britain, and
the access to the European goods that they received in return, especially
weapons and ammunition, became vital for dominance and even survival
in much of the interior of North America. But fashions changed, and the
decline of the beaver trade in the 1730s was disastrous for native peoples
dependent on it. The overall diversification of the North American colonies in the middle and late eighteenth century undercut their position in
the long run. These trends affected not only those in the *pays d'en haut*
who traded with the French, but also the Iroquois further south who
dealt with the English. For the Iroquois in upstate New York, Daniel K.
Richter has told a story of depopulation from disease, economic dependence on Europeans, involvement in the conflicts between the French
and the English, and finally the loss of Iroquois lands and independence.[15] This "ordeal of the longhouse," nonetheless, was different in
some respects from that of their coastal and back-country neighbors.
Placed on the major trade routes of northeastern North America, yet
inland from the Atlantic coast, the Five Nations had time to adapt to
European incursions. They were able to expand inland against other
Indian peoples even as they became dependent on trade with Europeans.
But their advantages would not last past the 1730s: the fur trade declined
in importance, and the chaos wreaked by Iroquois wars against other
peoples opened the lands of those nations – and eventually Iroquois

---

[14] On Kateri Tekakwitha, see Daniel K. Richter, *Facing East from Indian Country: A Native History of Early America* (Cambridge, MA: Harvard University Press, 2001), 79–90, and Alan Greer, *Mohawk Saint: Catherine Tekakwitha and the Jesuits* (New York: Oxford University Press, 2005); on Marie Rouensa, see Hinderaker, *Elusive Empires*, 62–63.

[15] Daniel K. Richter, *The Ordeal of the Longhouse* (Chapel Hill: University of North Carolina Press, 1992); Richter, *Facing East from Indian Country*, 178–79.

lands – to white settlement. Increased trade, population decline, and military reverses damaged village life. The Iroquois policy of neutrality between the French and the English that was reflected in the settlements in 1701 at Montreal and Albany gained strength over the next several decades. By the 1730s, the now-Six Nations (the original five joined by the Tuscarora from present-day North Carolina in the early 1720s) had been effectively colonized by the English.

Russia

If France approached North America from the east, crossing the Atlantic to the Caribbean, Acadia, and the St. Lawrence, Russia came to it from the west. Beginning in Muscovy in northeastern Europe, the Russian empire expanded its Eurasian holdings to both the west and east between the sixteenth and the nineteenth centuries. Russian expansion to the west was limited by the states that stood in the way, Poland and Sweden, and it took three Northern Wars (1558–83, 1654–67, 1700–21) for Russia to overcome their resistance. This culminated in the partitions of Poland between 1772 and 1795 and the creation of Congress Poland in 1815. Further south, Ukraine was annexed in the decades after 1654. The conquest of Estonia and Livonia in 1710 by Peter the Great (r. 1682–1725) complemented his construction of St. Petersburg as a window on Western Europe. Finland was occupied several times during Russia's eighteenth-century wars with Sweden, but was definitively annexed in 1808–9 after the Tilsit Treaty between Tsar Alexander and Emperor Napoleon of France. Finally, in 1812, the Ottoman empire ceded to Russia the territory that became known as Bessarabia and, eventually in the twentieth century, as the Moldavian Soviet Republic and then Moldova.

Muscovite expansion to the east began in 1552 with the annexation of the khanate of Kazan, followed four years later by annexation of the khanate of Astrakhan. In the early seventeenth century, with the incentive of Siberian furs, trappers and agents of the Muscovite state moved east along the Siberian rivers, avoiding the steppe and the Kazakhs and Mongols who controlled it. They reached the Pacific in 1639, and in 1648 Okhotsk was established as a port. Only later in the seventeenth century was the tsar able to extend his control onto the steppes to the southeast of Kazan and into the Urals. Still further south, the reformed Russian state of Peter the Great pushed to the Crimea and the shores of the Black Sea. The final step in this process came in 1783, when the last khan of the Crimean Tatars was deposed and his territory incorporated into the Russian empire.

By the early nineteenth century the Russian empire was expanding south along the west coast of North America, threatening the Spanish, British, and French empires that developed in the same era. There are obvious similarities between those empires. They shared the strategic desire to increase their own power and to preempt other powers from gaining control of territories that they thought of as their own. They also shared the economic policy of exploiting the colonies for the profit of the metropole. In many instances, they also followed the same methods of divide and rule, gaining territory by reaching agreements with local rulers and governing indirectly through pragmatic co-optation of indigenous elites. All empires shared the ultimate recourse to the use of repression and violence to conquer and enforce their rule. But there were also significant differences. The missionary aspects that were so significant a part of the maritime empires were less important for Russia. There were also more pronounced distances – certainly geographic, possibly cultural – between the Western European powers and their colonies in the Americas, Asia, and Africa than between Muscovy and the non-Russians on whom it imposed its rule.[16] It is certain, in any case, that as European empires jockeyed for colonies in the eighteenth and nineteenth centuries, Russia would be a looming presence in some parts of the world.

Spain

As the French moved south along the valley of the Mississippi River, and the Russians worked their way from the Alaskan coast to California, they came into contact with the oldest and most extensive European empire in the New World, that of Spain. This empire had begun in the fifteenth and early sixteenth centuries in the Antilles, with Spanish control spreading quickly from Columbus' landing on Hispaniola to the neighboring islands of Cuba and Puerto Rico, to the mainland, and to the Pacific. The Aztec empire in Mexico was conquered in 1521. In Peru, Inca resistance, and a civil war among Spaniards, continued into the 1530s. Santiago, Chile was established in 1540. Spanish forces were also slowly subduing the more dispersed Mayan settlements on the northeast coast of South America. Further south, a permanent Spanish settlement had been established in Buenos Aires, at the mouth of the River Plate, by the 1580s, and there was a Spanish settlement

---

[16] Andreas Kappeler, *The Russian Empire: A Multiethnic History*, trans. Alfred Clayton (New York: Longman, 2001); Dominic Lieven, "The Russian Empire and the Soviet Union as Imperial Polities," *Journal of Contemporary History* 30 (1995), 607–36.

across the Pacific in the Philippine islands. Linked together by Spanish sea power, by 1700 this empire stretched from New Spain and its capital Mexico City south to the Rio de la Plata in South America, down the west coast of South America from Peru to Santiago, across the Pacific, and included important ports in the Antilles – Santo Domingo on Hispaniola, Havana on Cuba – that served as administrative centers and as staging areas for the fleets that linked the New World to the Old.

Until the end of the Seven Years War in 1763, the Pacific was, in theory and often in practice, a Spanish lake, reserved for Spanish ships and closed to trade by other European powers. The farthest outpost of this empire was Manila, the link in the Philippines between the lucrative China trade and the colonies in New Spain and Peru. First touched by Europeans in 1512, the Philippines became more attractive to the Spanish in the mid sixteenth century. A fleet from Navidad in Mexico established the first Spanish settlement at Cebu in 1565, and a returning ship from this fleet discovered the prevailing westerlies in the northern Pacific that would carry the annual galleons from Manila (founded in 1571) to the California coast and then to Acapulco. For a quarter of a millennium, until 1815, Spain traded in an empire that spanned the Pacific and Atlantic oceans and extended from Asia to Europe. Chinese and other Asian merchants brought cargoes of silk, cottons, and other products to Manila, and the galleons transported them to Acapulco, where they were unloaded and then sold or shipped to the east coast of Mexico for shipment to Spain itself. The silver from these sales was carried on the return voyage to Manila, providing specie to lubricate European trade in Asia.

In the late seventeenth century, this empire was still administered through institutions created in the mid sixteenth century and modeled on the governance of Spain itself. A Council of the Indies established in 1524 at the royal court in Spain had broad oversight responsibilities for the colonies, including legislative, judicial, financial, commercial, military, and ecclesiastical affairs. While this Council ranked below the Council of Castile in the administrative structure of the monarchy, it outranked all other royal councils. The territories in the New World were administratively organized into viceroyalties of New Spain, Peru, and after 1717 New Granada. Each of these viceroyalties was divided into smaller units called *audiencias*, which were themselves subdivided into multiple units, eventually reaching the municipality, a city or town and its hinterland. But while this might suggest a strongly centralized system in which each administrative unit reported to superiors who ultimately reported to the Crown, this impression would be illusory.

The Crown appointed viceroys, usually *peninsulares* with strong connections in the court and who saw the position as a source of wealth
and a stepping-stone to higher office in Spain itself. Baltasar Zúñiga y
Guzmán, for example served as viceroy of Navarre and Sardinia before
becoming viceroy of New Spain in 1716. The wealth he acquired in
New Spain allowed him to gain influence in court when he returned to
Spain in 1722, and in 1724 he became President of the Council of the
Indies.[17] Viceroys were responsible for virtually every aspect of administration in the viceroyalty, ruling in the name of the king. The great
distance and difficult communication with Spain, as well as the necessity of applying legislation and directives from Spain to the realities of
the New World, meant that viceroys enjoyed great power and latitude in
what policies they implemented, responding "I obey but I do not fulfill"
to legislation they chose not to put into practice.

The Crown also appointed the members of *audiencias*, advisory and
judicial bodies in subdistricts of the viceroyalities. Unlike the viceroys,
these officials were often Americans, especially as the Crown began in
the late seventeenth century to sell *audiencia* appointments in order to
meet its rising debt with the sale of the position of *alcalde del crimen*, a
magistrate, of the *audiencia* of Lima to Miguel Núñez de Sanabia. For
much of the colonial period, these officials had strong local connections
and provided the local elite with influence over judicial and political
decision-making that could last for generations: both Núñez's son and
grandson also held *audiencia* positions.[18] The same was the case for the
administrators below them. Even if they were not natives of the area in
which they held office, they soon became enmeshed in the local society,
connected with it in multiple ways. These *radicados*, as they were called,
found common cause with native sons in pursuing local interests. The
Spanish empire, like the others of its time, thus struggled to maintain
control from the center over men and events that were far away, and
while administrators on the ground enjoyed some practical latitude, the
need to consult officials in Spain often delayed decisions for years.

As with the French in North America, the Spanish relationship with
the native peoples they encountered in the Antilles, Mexico, and Central
and South America profoundly affected the colonial society of the sixteenth and seventeenth centuries. The civilizations that the Spanish
found – Mayas in Guatemala, Honduras, and the Yucatan peninsula,

[17] Mark A. Burkholder, *Biographical Dictionary of Councilors of the Indies, 1717–1808*
(Westport, CT: Greenwood Press, 1986), 142.
[18] Mark A. Burkholder and D. S. Chandler, *Biographical Dictionary of Audiencia Ministers
in the Americas, 1687–1821* (Westport, CT: Greenwood Press, 1982), 235–36.

Aztecs in central Mexico, and Incas in the Andean highlands – all ultimately found resistance to the Spanish invaders impossible. The conquests brought a combination of destruction of the existing elites, many
of whom were killed or driven into exile, and Spanish co-optation of
those willing to cooperate with the invaders. The Spanish also took
over places of prestige in the indigenous cultures, such as the Aztec
capital of Tenochtitlán, rebuilt into the capital city of Mexico. Indian
craftsmen added European skills to their own, and provided significant labor and talent for the church- and city-building that marked the
new empire. Sexual liaisons between Spanish and Indians were also
frequent, occasionally leading to marriage but more often creating illegitimate *mestizo* offspring who formed an uneasy bridge between con-
queror and conquered.

For most Indians, the conquest brought enslavement, then dramatic
changes in the agrarian economy that had supported their civilizations,
and ultimately demographic catastrophe. The conquerors found existing agriculture, manufacturing and trade, but they tried to reorient
sectors such as mining, agriculture, and textile production towards
the export market, and they introduced sugar plantations and pastoral agriculture in many places. These all rested on various forms of
forced labor initially supplied by the indigenous populations. Even in
instances in which a free wage-labor market existed, landowners and
mine owners were able to limit wages through practices such as debt
peonage, in which laborers' debts to employers prevented them from
moving to a different job.

But these developments in the agrarian economy were severely
affected by a sharp decline in the indigenous populations, and colonialism brought new groups into the populations of the Americas. In the
Caribbean islands, Mexico, and Central and South America there was
a slow increase in the Spanish population, especially as more Spanish
women emigrated to the colonies. The dramatic decline of the indigenous population after the conquest also led to an increase in African
slavery, with almost 1 million African slaves entering Spanish America
between the early sixteenth century and the beginning of the nineteenth century. In the Caribbean islands, and in the lowlands along the
Pacific, African slaves replaced the indigenous populations. Elsewhere,
the combination of indigenous, Spanish, and Africans created a mixed
population that increased throughout the colonial period.

If its most productive period came in the late sixteenth and early seventeenth centuries, when it formed an important source of resources for
Spanish dominance in Europe, this empire was in decline by the mid
seventeenth century. But it nonetheless showed signs of revival by 1700.

Population increased, as did silver production. The viceroyalties were more self-sufficient, linked by the tentacles of the administrative system to a Spain that, while it had difficulty managing local affairs in the New World, nonetheless commanded some colonial loyalty. While the empire might have seemed ripe for the picking by Spain's European enemies, their own disagreements prevented a concerted expansion of Dutch, French, or English colonial power into the Spanish realm, either in the Caribbean or in the southern areas of North America. The Spanish, like all European powers, followed mercantilist policies that restricted trade with their colonies to ships and merchants from the metropole. The Peace of Utrecht in 1713, ending the War of Spanish Succession, granted only limited trading privileges to non-Spanish merchants and ships in the territories of Spanish America. It transferred the Asiento, the privilege of supplying slaves to the Spanish colonies, from a French company to the British, but allowed only a single British ship each year to put in at Porto Bello for trade with the Spanish colonies. But Spain could not itself produce the manufactured goods needed to supply its American subjects, and so goods from Britain and France were shipped to Spanish America through Seville and, after the Peace of Utrecht, Cadiz. Smuggling also was an important way in which European goods entered the Spanish colonies, draining precious silver from the Spanish economy.

From its base in Mexico City, linked to Spain and its Caribbean colonies through the port of Veracruz, Spain pursued a halting policy of expansion to the north in the course of the seventeenth and eighteenth centuries. This expansion was dominated by the missionary impulse of Franciscans who sought to convert the native peoples of North America. The area north of the Rio Grande was first entered by Spaniards at the beginning of the sixteenth century, but those journeys had vanished into misty memory by 1581, when an expedition of the Franciscan Agustín Rodríguez journeyed north into the pueblo world that the Spaniards began calling Nuevo México. Over the next century, other Franciscans moved into the area, establishing missions that were small islands of Hispanic civilization in a sea of indigenous peoples. But the Crown and its administrators in Mexico City lacked the resources to protect the missions, which found it difficult to maintain their Indian labor force. The lack of productivity of the land, and the difficulty in persuading colonists to settle there, limited the growth of the colony. With few military resources available, the Spanish could not maintain more than nominal control over the region. Indeed, at the same time as the English were establishing Jamestown in Virginia (1607) and the French Quebec in Canada (1608), the Spanish were contemplating abandoning New Mexico. The Spanish population never was higher than 3,000 before 1700, scattered in missions along the Rio Grande as far north as Taos, with the only major settlement the mission and municipality of Santa Fe (Illustration 1).

There were few other European contenders for New Mexico in the seventeenth century, and this contributed to a lack of interest in the area by royal officials in Madrid and Mexico City. The part of North America closest to the Caribbean colonies was a different story, and the growth of the English presence on the Atlantic coast of North America after 1607 spurred Spanish efforts to consolidate their hold on both the Atlantic and Gulf coasts. Franciscans pushed the Spanish presence inland there as in New Mexico, establishing missions along the Atlantic coast north of St. Augustine (itself established in 1565) as far as Santa Catalina and across the Florida panhandle as far west as the Apalachicola River. But the population of St. Augustine was only between 1,400 and 1,500 in 1700, a total that included black slaves and Hispanicized Indians.[19] Both New Mexico and Florida were small, expensive for the Crown, and unable to support themselves, let alone turn a profit.

Conquest brought missionary efforts to the Indians throughout the Spanish empire, a task enjoined upon the conquerors by papal bulls of 1493. Dominicans, Jesuits, Augustinians, Franciscans, and others accompanied the *conquistadores* to the American colonies. They led campaigns of destruction of the religions of the peoples of those areas and the temples, icons, and manuscripts that were their material artifacts. Churches and clergy followed, bringing mass conversions, missions, and schools that not only taught the fundamentals of the Catholic faith but also Spanish and European crafts. Missionaries used gifts, showy vestments, elaborate ceremonies, and claims for Christianity's power of salvation and happiness to mobilize the native peoples to construct friaries for the priests and churches for worship. Many missionaries learned native languages, facilitating conversions and their ability to control the native populations. They appealed especially to younger natives, undercutting the authority of older political and religious leaders in native communities. While often fearful of the effect of the example of other Spaniards, especially soldiers, on their young charges, the missionaries tried to teach their students Castilian and to "civilize" them by making them live according to Spanish precepts. The missionary incursion transformed indigenous lives, through the introduction of new foods, crops, and livestock, exposure to raids by

---

[19] Population figures for New Mexico and St. Augustine from David J. Weber, *The Spanish Frontier in North America* (New Haven, CT: Yale University Press, 1992), 90.

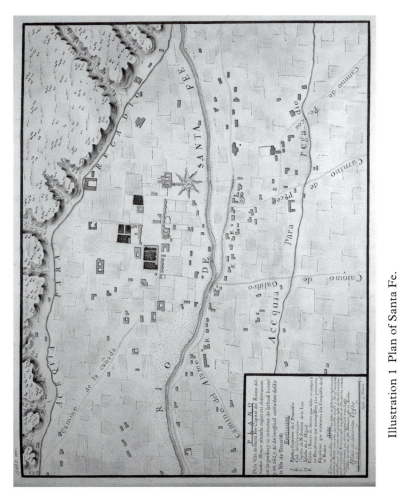

Illustration 1 Plan of Santa Fe.

other Indians not in the Spanish orbit, the disruption of family life by both missionary attention to children and the depredations of Spanish soldiers, and a new tone to factionalism in the native community. There were successes for the missionaries, with conversions of Indians who no doubt thought that it would bring them salvation, gifts, access to Spanish goods, or protection against Spanish soldiers, other Indians or the diseases that struck Indian populations but seemed to spare the Europeans, who adhered to Christianity.

But the Spanish missionaries also directly attacked native religious beliefs, and even after rejecting forced conversion as theologically unsound they relied on the force of Spanish soldiers, and on physical punishment, to prevent converts from backsliding into native beliefs or leaving the missions. The diseases that seemed to spare Europeans did not spare Indians, even if they converted to Christianity, nor were the friars protection against natural disasters such as drought and crop failure. Throughout these colonies, when it became clear to the Indians that Christianity and its proponents no longer provided them with any benefits or protection, they often returned to traditional religious practices even if the friars insisted that conversion to Christianity was irrevocable. Individuals and entire communities tried to flee the mission settlements, while others attacked individual priests and desecrated Christian shrines and the sacred objects they contained. By the seventeenth century Christianity was one of the most obvious external aspects of an Indian community in Spanish America, with the church the most important structure and the priest an important community figure. Recent studies throughout the Spanish empire have shown, however, that the Catholic faith that the missionaries brought was influenced not only by their own efforts, but also by the Guaraní, Maya, Inca, Aztec, and other peoples there. Those peoples not only demonstrated cultural resiliency in the face of the missionaries' activities, but also, through resistance, adaptation, and accommodation, helped shape popular religion in Spanish America.[20]

One aspect of this was that the missionary practice of using religious paintings and images did not always communicate what the missionaries intended. To the Maya, for example, the cross and images of the

[20] Barbara Ganson, *The Guarani under Spanish Rule in the Rio de la Plata* (Stanford University Press, 2003); Inga Clendinnen, *Ambivalent Conquests: Maya and Spaniard in Yucatan, 1517–1570*, 2nd edn. (Cambridge University Press, 2003); Sabine MacCormack, *Religion in the Andes: Vision and Imagination in Early Colonial Peru* (Princeton University Press, 1991); Erick Langer and Robert H. Jackson (eds.), *The New Latin American Mission History* (Lincoln, NE: University of Nebraska Press, 1993).

Crucifixion evoked not the sacrifice of Jesus, but their sacred "first tree," which joined the heavens, earth, and the underworld. More broadly, the translation of Christian beliefs "turned" their meanings when placed in the context of Indian beliefs. To make Christian beliefs intelligible, missionaries encouraged connections between native deities and rituals, on the one hand, with Christian practices and beliefs, on the other. But in central Mexico, this led to a weakening of the concept of evil, as the Nahua spirit with which the Christian devil was connected was a lesser deity. Further north, in the Puebla of New Mexico, this practice led to what Alan Taylor has described as a "compartmentalization" of beliefs, in which Indians retained their traditional beliefs while adding on features of Catholicism that were useful. But, he points out, this layering of Catholic beliefs over indigenous religion allowed the pueblo to conserve a strong identity that could be the basis for revolt against the Spanish, returning to their "ancient spirits" to regain their independence from the Spanish soldiers and Franciscan priests.[21]

The imperial authorities also took wealth and land from the Indian communities, as well as labor through legal and illegal forms of enslavement. By the seventeenth century this was through the *repartimiento* (in New Spain) or *mita* (in Peru). In the eighteenth century, the *mitayos agrícolas* (forced labor) and *mitayos concertados* (a form of contract labor that amounted to debt peonage) were instituted in New Granada. In these systems, the Indian community was responsible for providing a part of its male population for labor. A relatively free labor market had developed by the eighteenth century in New Spain, although the *repartimiento* never completely disappeared. In the Peruvian mines in Potosí and in New Granada, the *mita* organized a constant flow of labor to the mines.

Ultimately, the imperial powers had a predominance of force when they made a decision. But indigenous peoples also had weapons that allowed them to resist acculturation and negotiate at least some of the terms of their colonization. Migrations away from the community were a way in which Andean Indians avoided the onerous *mita* labor obligations or sought better economic opportunities in the free labor market. The indigenous community itself was an impediment to the colonizers, providing the basis for resistance to taxes, labor demands, and land seizures. On some occasions this was simply through a process by which local Spanish and Amerindian groups collaborated in maintaining local surpluses against the exactions of the colonial state, a reminder to us of

---

[21] Linda A. Curcio-Nagy, "Faith and Morals in Colonial Mexico," in Michael C. Meyer and William H. Beezley (eds.), *The Oxford History of Mexico* (Oxford University Press, 2000), 155–59; Taylor, *American Colonies*, 85.

the permeability of ethnic boundaries at the local level. Their successes were indications of the inability of colonial administrators to impose their will on a constantly shifting variety of local alliances that found common ground in opposition to the policies of the colonial state. The familiarity with the Castilian language and legal system that came to Amerindians in the Spanish colonies provided opportunities for "cultural *mestizos*" to act as mediators between Spanish and indigenous cultures and provide a voice for colonial subjects. The efforts to convert those colonial subjects to Christianity subverted indigenous religious beliefs; but they also provided a forum in which colonial subjects could combine Christian and indigenous beliefs and practices. These created occasional tensions between colonial religious authorities and Amerindians, with attempts to "extirpate" supposedly "deviant" religious beliefs at times employing the authority of the state to impose religious orthodoxy. At other times, such as by the eighteenth century in the Andes colonies of Spain, there was less tension, as missionaries overlooked indigenous beliefs and the practices of Catholic Christianity seemed to strike a chord with those converted to it.

Conflict was built into the colonial relationship, however, and Indian rebellions occurred with dismal frequency in the sixteenth and seventeenth centuries. In New Mexico the Spanish had failed to protect their Indian subjects from the raids of Apaches and other Indians in the region, who, excluded from the Spanish trading realm, took by force what they could not gain by trade from the Hopis, Zunis, and other Indians who came under Spanish control. A spectacular revolt broke out around Santa Fe in 1680, destroying the town and forcing the Spanish to retreat 300 miles south to El Paso. There they held on to a small outpost until a decade later when, in 1692, Diego de Vargas began to reassert Spanish control in New Mexico. By 1694 he had reconquered Santa Fe and gained the nominal fealty of many of the pueblos, but new missions faced determined resistance, and a rebellion in 1696 signaled continued indigenous resistance to Spanish rule.

In Florida the Spanish authorities also had difficulty controlling their English neighbors to the north. Just after the turn of the eighteenth century, English raids into Florida forced the Spanish to abandon the western province of Apalachee, and settlements in Timucua, west of St. Augustine, soon followed. The willingness of the English to trade rum, arms, and ammunition with the Indians stood in stark contrast to Spanish policies that outlawed these practices, and Spanish treatment of mission Indians was no better in Florida than in New Mexico. Only at St. Augustine, whose fort of San Marcos protected Spanish and Indians from the English, and at Pensacola Bay, founded as a port on the Gulf Coast in 1699, did the Spanish retain footholds in Florida.

Portugal

The Spanish empire was largely located in the western hemisphere, with only the Philippines as a distant appendage. But the Portuguese empire was truly global. Originating in exploration voyages that began in the early fifteenth century, it extended westwards to the Azores, Madeira, Cape Verde islands, and Brazil. There a series of settlements marked the eastern coast of the South American continent, from Belém at the mouth of the Amazon south to São Vicente. Portuguese settlements also ran along the west coast of Africa, from Tangiers and Ceuta at the Straits of Gibraltar south. Because the Portuguese had dominated the slave trade to Spanish America since the sixteenth century, they also established settlements on the Slave Coast and further south to Luanda and Benguela in Angola from which they acquired slaves. Sofala, Mozambique Island, Malindi, and Mombasa on the east coast of Africa provided way stations to India, where Goa on the west coast was the major Portuguese settlement and port. Further east, there were Portuguese settlements in Malacca, Macassar, and other Southeast Asian ports. In East Asia, Macao in China and Nagasaki in Japan were also nodes in a Portuguese world built in the fifteenth and sixteenth centuries around commerce, Catholicism, and conquest.

Sugar was the most important product of Portugal's Atlantic colonies almost from their inception in the sixteenth century until the nineteenth century. Its profitability was proved in Portugal itself and on several of the Atlantic islands, and it was introduced into Brazil soon after the Portuguese arrival there in 1500. Its cultivation focused on São Vicente in the south and in Bahia and Pernambuco, where Olinda (Illustration 2) became an important administrative center, in the northeastern part of the colony. Grown on plantations that required large investments of capital, it proved immensely profitable in the sixteenth and early seventeenth centuries for the plantation owners, not only through the sale of the sugar they produced, but also from the profits generated by the milling of sugar produced by tenants, sharecroppers, renters, or smaller landowners. As in the Caribbean islands, the Portuguese sugar plantations imported slaves from Africa to provide the labor force needed for the labor-intensive cultivation of sugarcane. Portuguese slave traders quickly moved into the trade with Brazil, and it became an important destination for those taken in West Africa by the slavers. The 850,000 slaves who entered Brazil in the seventeenth

Illustration 2 View of the town of Olinda, province of Pernambuco, Brazil, 1647.

century were more than entered all of the other European colonies in the Americas in that century combined.[22]

As in the other early modern empires, Portugal followed mercantilist policies, and tobacco, sugar, and other staples produced in Brazil were re-exported through Lisbon to other parts of Europe. By the late seventeenth century, however, sugar plantations on the Caribbean islands held by the Dutch, British, and French cut into the profits of the Brazilian plantations in Pernambuco and elsewhere, and labor costs increased as the diversification of the Brazilian economy created new uses for slave labor. The most important of these new uses came from the discovery in the 1690s and following decades of gold deposits in the area northwest of Rio de Janeiro, a region that became known as Minas Gerais. While sugar exports continued to lead the Brazilian economy well into the eighteenth century, the development of gold mining shifted population inland, attracted new immigrants from Portugal, and provided invaluable financial support for the Portuguese monarchy. The discovery of diamonds in the northern part of Minas Gerais in 1729 made the colony an even greater contributor to the prosperity of Portugal. The labor needs of the mines combined with the sugar plantations to generate strong demand for African slaves, who soon were a majority of the labor force in the mining areas. It also spurred the development of improved roads between the coast and the mining areas, and deepened commercial links between the coastal cities, the southern cattle-raising areas, and the interior. The rapid population increase, the abundance of gold, and the absence initially of almost every consumer good needed by the mining population contributed to the development of manufacturing, livestock ranching, and agriculture near the mines.

The Netherlands

The Dutch empire at the turn of the eighteenth century revolved, as it had for almost a century, around the activities of two great trading companies, the Dutch East India Company (or VOC), founded in 1602, and the Dutch West India Company (WIC), founded in 1621. Commercial companies for foreign trade had appeared in the Netherlands before the turn of the seventeenth century, but the creation of these two companies gave a new impetus and direction to Dutch efforts in the Atlantic basin and in the East Indies. The VOC was given a monopoly of Dutch trade east of the Cape of Good Hope and west of the Straits of Magellan. It

---

[22] Data from the Transatlantic Slave Trade Data Base, www.slavevoyages.org/tast/database/search.faces.

had the power to conclude treaties of peace and alliance, fight defensive wars, and build fortresses. It was also empowered to raise military and naval forces. After an initial period of low returns to its investors, the VOC became an extraordinary investment after 1634, utilizing its monopoly authority to expand its trade in Asia and distributing annual dividends in cash that ranged between 15.5 percent and 50 percent. In the period between 1715 and 1720, it distributed six annual dividends of 40 percent each.[23] The complement to the VOC was the West India Company (WIC), organized in 1621 and given a monopoly of trade with America and West Africa. It had similar powers of war and peace, maintenance of military and naval organizations, and administration. It was from the start aimed at the daunting task of challenging Spanish control of Mexico and Central and South America. It was not as successful as the VOC in gaining control of its markets or financially, and in 1674 the WIC was reorganized into a successor company whose activities largely revolved around the slave trade from West Africa to the West Indies.

The VOC sought to displace Portuguese control in South and Southeast Asia, a policy behind a successful blockade of Malacca in 1641. Similar attacks on Goa in 1603 and 1639 and against Spanish holdings in the Philippines proved less successful. The WIC, in its turn, also proved more successful against the Portuguese than against the Spanish. It established commercial links between the Netherlands and the Portuguese holdings in South America and Africa, trading for sugar in Brazil and gold, ivory, and slaves in Angola. These had, by the middle of the seventeenth century, led to the establishment of significant control by the WIC over parts of Brazil and Angola, but this was reversed by the Portuguese in the second half of the century.

With the conclusion of the Treaty of Münster in 1648, and its confirmation of the independence of the Seven Provinces from Spain, these commercial links blossomed into an impressive commercial empire with only limited territorial holdings. Indiamen left from Amsterdam, making stops at fortified posts along the route to the east. Along the Gold Coast of Africa, forts were seized in Elmina, Nassau, and Axim. After early attempts to wrest control of Mozambique away from the Portuguese failed, Cape Town was established in 1652 and became the most important provisioning and refitting port for VOC shipping to and from Asia. The Moluccas were the earliest and most important terminus of this, dating from the early sixteenth century, with the Dutch and the Portuguese competing for the trade in cloves, mace, and nutmeg.

---

[23] Charles R. Boxer, *The Dutch Seaborne Empire, 1600–1800* (New York: Alfred A. Knopf, 1965), 46.

Expansion at the expense of the Portuguese continued, and in 1641 the Dutch seized control of the port of Malacca from the Portuguese. But as the vulnerability of small posts in the Moluccas became apparent, a major fortified trading post was established at Batavia (present-day Jakarta) on the north coast of Java. This collected goods from an inter-Asian trade that linked Southeast Asia with Zeelandia in Formosa/ Taiwan and Deshima, Nagasaki, in Japan. The Dutch participated in this trade themselves, but also linked Asian traders to the Western market. Later settlements on the east and west coasts of India and Ceylon added stops to the Dutch trading network in South Asia.

While the VOC had established its presence on the waters of the south Atlantic, the Indian Ocean, and the gulfs and bays of Southeast Asia in the early seventeenth century, it remained an empire of the water for the most part, with few territorial incursions beyond the ports and factories necessary to maintain maritime shipping. Thus, while Batavia was captured in 1619, only slowly did the Dutch gain control over territories in the Indonesian archipelago, contesting local rulers for territorial control and the Portuguese and English for control of the spice trade in those islands. The company faced competition from other European powers for the trade, both in European and Asian markets, of pepper, silk, textiles, sugar, coffee, and tea. Cape Town was also originally conceived by the VOC as a port of call and little more, and it was only after the 1690s that the company began to encourage emigration – initially by French Huguenots forced out of France by the religious persecution there – and the settlement spread beyond its original footprint on the Cape peninsula. By the early eighteenth century it was producing a surplus of wheat, which was soon being shipped to Batavia.

The Dutch West India Company had begun a similar expansion in the Atlantic basin, beginning in 1630 with its conquest of Pernambuco in northeastern Brazil. This was completed by 1637, establishing a Dutch presence on the South American continent. The Dutch also settled the Caribbean islands of Curaçao, Aruba, Bonaire, Sint Eustatius, Saba, and Sint Maarten during the 1630s and 1640s. A generation later the treaties of Breda (1667) and Westminster (1674) confirmed Dutch control of Surinam. Those treaties also, however, confirmed Dutch renunciation of New Amsterdam, established on Manhattan Island in 1624, ending the Dutch presence in North America.

Great Britain

The English had colonized parts of Ireland over the course of several centuries before 1700, and in some respects, the trial-and-error process of planning and managing those ventures in Ireland proved to be a valuable experience for later efforts further away from England. This was especially the case in North America, which was very similar to Ireland in its climate and ability to produce commodities and goods that were useful and marketable in Europe. England's North American empire, with colonies from New Hampshire to Virginia that were connected by the late-seventeenth-century capture of New Amsterdam, would after the turn of the eighteenth century come to dominate a significant part of the Atlantic basin. But in many respects the key to this empire lay not in New York, as it came to be called, but further south. The English claimed Bermuda in 1609 when a fleet intended to provision the colony at Jamestown in Virginia was shipwrecked on the island, an event that may have been the basis for Shakespeare's *The Tempest*. In the Caribbean, the lack of Spanish interest in the Lesser Antilles allowed the English to establish colonies on St. Christopher (St. Kitt's) in 1624, Barbados in 1627, Nevis in 1628, and Montserrat and Antigua in 1632. These colonies became the core of the growing English presence in the New World, with more colonists coming to these West Indies colonies than to any single mainland colony. They were added to in 1655–56 with the conquest of Jamaica. Barbados led the development of an agricultural economy built around sugar export to Europe and especially to an English market that was protected after mid-century. Plantations and slavery had come to Barbados early, producing tobacco, cotton, and indigo, but while smaller planters continued to exist on the island, a small number of large sugar plantations came to dominate the island by the late seventeenth century. The sugar plantations demanded large amounts of cheap labor to grow and refine the crop, and as elsewhere this was provided by African slaves, who replaced indentured servants in growing numbers in the course of the century. In 1645, Barbados had only 5,680 slaves, but by the end of the century it had 42,000 of them.[24] The Leeward Islands, in contrast, retained more mixed economies in the seventeenth century, with indigo, tobacco, ginger, cotton, cattle, and fish in addition to sugar.

But sugar and to a lesser extent coffee spread across the islands of the British West Indies in the late seventeenth and early eighteenth

---

[24] Richard S. Dunn, *Sugar and Slaves: The Rise of the Planter Class in the English West Indies, 1624–1713* (Chapel Hill: University of North Carolina Press, 1972), 75, 87. See also Russell R. Menard, *Sweet Negotiations: Sugar, Slavery, and Plantation Agriculture in Early Barbados* (Charlottesville and London: University of Virginia Press, 2006), 25; and John J. McCusker and Russell R. Menard, *The Economy of British America, 1607–1789* (Chapel Hill: University of North Carolina Press, 1985), 153, 151 n. 10. McCusker and Menard give slightly higher estimates, but indicate that their estimates for the late seventeenth century may be too high.

centuries. Jamaica, the largest of the British West Indies but also the westernmost, developed late but came to be almost uniquely dedicated to sugar and coffee production. New plantations were established on open land on the island well into the eighteenth century. This growth depended heavily on the import of slave labor, creating a wealthy planter society that depended more on slave labor than any of the other sugar colonies in the Caribbean basin. The plantation of Worthy Park, one of the best-studied sugar plantations, shows this process.[25] Located in central Jamaica, it was established in 1670 by Francis Price. It grew slowly from the 840 acres in Price's original land patent to 1,774 acres by the time of his death in 1689. Barbados and the Windward Islands were still the major sugar producers of the West Indies at that time, and Worthy Park produced mostly livestock, provision crops, cocoa, tobacco, and indigo. Indentured white servants proved to be an undisciplined labor force, and so black slaves were acquired even before sugar became the dominant crop. But Francis Price moved slowly into sugar production, using the profits from his other crops for the capital investment to plant sugarcane, build the factory for its processing, and acquire the slaves to cultivate it. His son Charles, in all likelihood a lifelong resident of Jamaica, turned the plantation into a sugar estate by the time of his death in 1730.

The predominance of slavery in sub-tropical regions of the New World created plantation societies in which relatively small numbers of Europeans dominated large numbers of slaves of African origin or descent. Even as Francis Price was beginning the process of focusing the production of his plantation on sugar, in 1680, Worthy Park was home not only to Price and his family (his wife and four children) but also seven white indentured servants and fifty-five adult and three child slaves. By 1730, the same number of white servants – now managers and specialists in sugar production – were on a plantation overwhelmingly dedicated to sugar production. There were around 200 slaves.

---

[25] Michael Craton, *Searching for the Invisible Man: Slaves and Plantation Life in Jamaica* (Cambridge, MA: Harvard University Press, 1978), 7–15. For other plantations, see Trevor Burnard, *Mastery, Tyranny, and Desire: Thomas Thistlewood and his Slaves in the Anglo-Jamaican World* (Chapel Hill: University of North Carolina Press, 2004); Richard S. Dunn, "Sugar Production and Slave Women in Jamaica," in Ira Berlin and Philip D. Morgan (eds.), *Cultivation and Culture: Labor and the Shaping of Slave Life in the Americas* (Charlottesville: University Press of Virginia, 1993), 49–72; and "'Dreadful Idlers' in the Cane Fields: The Slave Labor Patterns on a Jamaican Sugar Estate, 1762–1831," in Barbara L. Solow and Stanley L. Engerman (eds.), *British Capitalism and Caribbean Slavery: The Legacy of Eric Williams* (Cambridge University Press, 1987), 163–90.

Jamaica was only an extreme case for the West Indies: in 1713, slaves outnumbered whites by a ratio of about 8 to 1 there. In the Leewards and Barbados, the ratio was 3 to 1.[26] The growing dependence on slave labor meant that fear of slave and maroon attacks was a constant feature of planter life in the West Indies and in the slave colonies in southern North America. Repression of slave resistance made violence in myriad forms a systemic feature of these colonial societies. Race also came to be a fundamental part of social and gender distinctions in these colonies. In Virginia, racial and gender distinctions worked together to define moral hierarchies. And while in British society in the eighteenth century property was the most important marker of social status, in plantation colonies race trumped property: as Trevor Burnard puts it with regard to Jamaica, "white skin meant freedom, dominion, and power; black skin meant slavery, submission, and powerlessness."[27]

With planters like Francis Price leading the way, by 1700 the English had made inroads into Spanish control of the Caribbean, reduced Dutch influence, and were about to challenge the French for dominance in the area. The islands formed the central node of a trading system that, increasingly after 1700, was the basis for English prosperity, bringing together sugar and rum, foodstuffs, timber, and slaves in a system that linked the West Indies to North America, western Europe, and Africa as well as Central and South America. In the eighteenth century, British ships would sail into the Pacific, challenging Spanish claims to monopoly in those waters and their shores.

The English presence on the south coast of West Africa, known as Guinea, took longer to develop and lagged behind that of the Dutch, Portuguese, and French, but by the seventeenth century English merchants were the principal rivals to the Dutch there and were moving into the slave trade east of the Gold Coast. The conflict with the Dutch became a military one in the Second Anglo-Dutch War of 1665–67, and benefitting from the decline of Dutch trade after the Third Anglo-Dutch War in 1672–74, the English gained dominance of the slave trade from the area.

England was also competing with the Portuguese and Dutch in Asia. This involved a monopoly company, the English East India Company, which received a charter from Elizabeth I in 1600. Between then and 1700, the Company slowly extended its reach into South Asia and the

---

[26] Dunn, *Sugar and Slaves*, 165; Menard, *Sweet Negotiations*.

[27] Kathleen Brown, *Good Wives, Nasty Wenches, and Anxious Patriarchs: Gender, Race, and Power in Colonial Virginia* (Chapel Hill: University of North Carolina Press, 1996); Burnard, *Mastery, Tyranny, and Desire*, 138, 270.

Indonesian archipelago. Increasingly these activities became concentrated on South Asia, and while the Company had not yet begun the emphasis on military conquest that would turn India into a British colony in the middle of the eighteenth century, it was nonetheless poised to become the dominant commercial power in South Asia. Each year it sent out Englishmen as "writers" who provided the personnel for the growing Company bureaucracy in South Asia. If the climate did not ruin the health of these young men, many of them did it themselves through drink, opium, and sex. Others, however, such as Robert Clive in the mid eighteenth century, used their entry into the Company bureaucracy as the stepping-stone to personal power and wealth, and in so doing helped expand the Company's control of India.

As with the Dutch and Portuguese, the English were attracted to the Indian Ocean and further east by the prospect of increasing their share in the spice trade. Pepper from Java, Sumatra, and the Malabar coast of India, along with cloves from the Moluccas and nutmeg and mace from the Banda Islands further east, were the commodities at the heart of this expansion. The English also found that it was advantageous as they developed the spice trade between Europe and Southeast Asia to become participants in the inter-Asian trade that extended from the Red Sea to Japan. This involved them in the trade for silk and cotton cloths, produced in Gujarat on the west coast of India and the Coromandel coast in the southeast. Tea imports from Canton grew after 1660, and by the end of the century this beverage was fashionable in England, spurring a rapid rise in imports in the first two decades of the eighteenth century. With the loss of its trading post at Bantam in western Java in 1682, the Company focused on its activities in India, and on trade in cotton calicoes that by 1700 had no competition in Europe as an item of mass consumption.

While the English went to India to trade in the seventeenth and early eighteenth centuries, they did not go there in significant numbers to colonize. In contrast, the most important focus of English colonization in the seventeenth century, and the one that involved significant attempts to transport some version of English society – and people – abroad, was on the Atlantic coast of North America. These colonies were often established by chartered companies or proprietors. In the Chesapeake region, several unsuccessful attempts to found a colony on Roanoke Island, off the coast of North Carolina, in 1585–90 were only prologues to more successful settlements in the early seventeenth century, beginning with Jamestown in Virginia in 1607. By the 1620s the colonists had maintained themselves against the powerful Indian alliance headed by the Powhatans, and population was moving up along the banks of the rivers that ran inland from Chesapeake Bay. The prosperity that followed the introduction of tobacco cultivation in the 1620s attracted large numbers of English immigrants (about 120,000 of the 500,000 who left England for the colonies in North America and the Caribbean during the seventeenth century), many of them arriving as indentured servants.[28]

By the 1670s the Chesapeake was becoming dominated by plantations cultivating tobacco, and those plantations transformed the region into a slave society with a large proportion of African slaves. This increased dramatically after 1680 in Virginia and Maryland. Slaves were never a majority of the overall population of the Chesapeake, but by 1740 in some places they made up 40 percent or more of the population.[29] The emphasis on tobacco placed a premium on the acquisition of new land, promoting farm and plantation settlement rather than towns and cities in the back country, and emphasizing the importance of water transport. For much of the seventeenth century, the expanding market for tobacco in England pulled Chesapeake society in its train. Only after the onset of falling prices after 1680 did a number of smaller farmers diversify their production away from the leaf. Even in the face of economic instability, however, the region remained dominated by tobacco plantations and the planters who owned them and controlled Chesapeake society and politics.

As in the Chesapeake, successful English settlements in New England were preceded by a disastrous attempt at Sagadahoc in Maine in 1607. But soon religious dissenters fled the growing religious and political crisis in England to found Plymouth Colony (1620) and Massachusetts Bay (1630). Connecticut (1634), Rhode Island (1644), and New Hampshire (1679) followed. By the end of the seventeenth century, the New England colonies had attracted significant emigration from England, established a web of towns throughout the region, and were under the relatively benign oversight of the newly founded Board of Trade. The colonists produced a variety of goods that made New England an important node in the developing Atlantic trading system: cod, timber, meat, corn, and the ships to carry them.

The area between New England and the Chesapeake remained relatively open until the second half of the seventeenth century. The English

---

[28] James Horn, "Tobacco Colonies: The Shaping of English Society in the Seventeenth-Century Chesapeake," in Nicholas Canny (ed.), *The Oxford History of the British Empire*, vol. I, *The Origins of Empire: British Overseas Enterprise to the Close of the Seventeenth Century* (Oxford University Press, 1988), 176–77.

[29] Ira Berlin, *Many Thousands Gone: The First Two Centuries of Slavery in North America* (Cambridge, MA: Belknap Press, 1998), 110.

seizure of the Dutch settlement of New Amsterdam in 1664 brought that town under the control of the Duke of York, the king's brother and future James II. What became New York remained a relatively international settlement and was, under both the Dutch and the English, primarily a commercial center, linking European shipping with the interior of the continent through the Hudson River and the settlement of Albany, the competitor to Montreal for the fur trade. In 1664 New Jersey was chartered in the lands south of New York, and in 1682 the first group of settlers came to Pennsylvania, west of the Delaware River from New Jersey. In both New Jersey and Pennsylvania, the climate and land were ideally suited for production of grain that could be sold to the plantation colonies in the south and the West Indies. Family farms spread through the region, producing goods that were sold through the city of Philadelphia on the Delaware River. As the English colonies in the New World became more closely linked commercially with one another and with England, the merchants of Philadelphia and New York became major participants in that trade system.

This trade with Europe depended on access to the back country of New York and Pennsylvania and the furs that, in the seventeenth century, were the principal product of that region. While the French in New France had access to the Great Lakes region through the St. Lawrence, and built trading relationships with the Hurons and other Indians in the *pays d'en haut*, the English in Albany and further south found their competition with the French blocked by the Five Nations of the Iroquois. The English and the Iroquois slowly became allies in the course of the seventeenth century. But the English were often frustrated at the independence of their Iroquois allies and their relentlessly self-interested policies, a "modern Indian politics" in which Native Americans used their geographic position, connections with trade in the interior, and military usefulness to play the English and French off against each other and maintain their own autonomy.[30] But the Iroquois alliance also opened up the trans-Appalachian west to British expansion, as they attempted to gain a share of the fur trade from that region and make Albany rather than Montreal its focal point.

The last major seventeenth-century expansion of English power in North America came in the last thirty-five years of the century, with the grant by Charles II to a number of his courtiers of a large area south of Virginia. The Carolinas were attractive to English settlers from Barbados who had been reduced to poverty by the rapid expansion

---

[30] Richter, *Looking East from Indian Country*, 164. The phrase, quoted by Richter, is from New York Indian Affairs Secretary Peter Wraxall.

of sugar plantations there in the 1640s and 1650s. With two excellent harbors – Port Royal in South Carolina and Albemarle Sound further north – the Carolinas seemed an excellent locale in which these émigrés could reconstitute to their own advantage the hierarchical planter society that existed on Barbados. A settlement was founded on the site of modern Charleston in 1670. North Carolina, in contrast, was first settled by Virginians, who came into the area in 1653, but it remained without significant colonization until after 1700.

The intention of the original settlers in the Carolinas had been to supply the Caribbean islands with food and lumber, and this trade soon became a staple part of the Carolinian economy. These activities never produced great prosperity for the region, however, and were quickly supplemented by supplying provisions for pirates, trading with the Indians, and selling Indians into slavery. More promising in the long run was the sale of buckskin, acquired from the Indians and exported to England, and supplies for the many ships that plied the routes between North America, the Caribbean islands, and England. In the early eighteenth century, some parts of South Carolina turned to rice, a crop imported into the colony around 1690 from Madagascar and the East Indies. It quickly grew in importance, as freshwater swamps were brought under cultivation and slave labor was imported from Africa. After the turn of the century, rice cultivation grew rapidly: by 1722 1.16 million acres were planted in rice, and the crop accounted for more than half of South Carolina's exports. The spread of rice cultivation made the Carolinas, Georgia, and eastern Florida a region of large rice plantations with a huge slave labor force that made up a large majority of the population.[31]

The southern part of North America was therefore a place of colonial settlement and imperial competition in the late seventeenth and early eighteenth centuries. But the colonies of Spain, France, and Great Britain in this region followed different trajectories. New Mexico and Texas grew slowly, as it proved difficult for the colonial administration in New Spain to provide security against the Apaches, Navajos, Utes, and Comanches who hemmed in the missions and other settlements and resisted attempts at conversion or subjugation. The poor agricultural prospects of the region were daunting to settlers, and there were no discoveries of precious metals to rescue these colonies as they had New Spain and Peru in earlier centuries. France's Canadian colony never attracted significant numbers of immigrants from European France – perhaps 10,250 permanent settlers in the entire French period

[31] Berlin, *Many Thousands Gone*, 143–45.

to 1760 – and one estimate is that two-thirds of those who migrated returned to France. New France did, however, show significant natural increase beginning in the last decades of the seventeenth century, and this accounts for most of the growth of the European population in the colony. While Louisiana provided the French with access to the middle of the American continent, it was badly governed, difficult to defend, and so unable to attract settlers from France that the French government was reduced to sending convicts to the colony. By 1760, about 4,000 Europeans lived in it. In contrast, while there were disparities between the different English colonies, they nonetheless grew more quickly than their Spanish or French neighbors, and by the 1760s there were significant numbers of settlers in all of them. The New England colonies had 436,900 Europeans in 1760, while the comparable figures further south were equally impressive: the Chesapeake held 312,400 Europeans, while there were 398,900 in the Middle Atlantic colonies and 119,600 in the Lower South, even though it had been colonized later.[32] The growing English population of North America east of the Appalachians, the inability of the Spanish to extend New Mexico and Texas northeastwards, and the French foothold in the Mississippi valley laid the groundwork for imperial rivalries that would dominate the second half of the century.

Colonial trade and colonial societies

In the course of the sixteenth and seventeenth centuries Europeans created much closer political links with significant parts of the Americas, East Indies, and South Asia. To some extent this was the result of rivalries between the European powers. But it was also driven by commerce, and had powerful effects on the course and strength of international trade. The Spanish need for gold and silver to finance its attempts at European dominance in the sixteenth and seventeenth centuries, and its discovery of these precious metals in Mexico and other parts of its empire, created the fleets that left from Havana and Veracruz to catch the trade winds to Seville. The discovery of gold and other valuable minerals in Minas Gerais in the late seventeenth century encouraged similar shipping between Brazil and Lisbon. Portuguese exploration

---

[32] Weber, *Spanish Frontier*, 179, 195; Pritchard, *In Search of Empire*, 16–43; Hubert Charbonneau *et al.*, *The First French Canadians: Pioneers in the Saint Lawrence Valley* (Newark, DE: University of Delaware Press, 1993), 23–41; Choquette, *Frenchmen into Peasants*, 2–22; Peter Moogk, "Reluctant Exiles: Emigrants from France in Canada before 1760," *William and Mary Quarterly*, 3rd series, 36 (1989), 463–505; McCusker and Menard, *Economy*, 103, 136, 172, 203.

along the coast of Africa and into the Indian subcontinent and the Moluccas facilitated European trade with those areas, and when the Dutch and English followed them they deepened the trade routes to Europe's Atlantic shore from Coromandel, Bengal, and Batavia, bringing the spices that had long been the spur for trade between Europe and Asia, as well as the calicoes that became the centerpiece of English trade with India in the seventeenth century. The Spanish colonies in Peru and New Spain traded with Chinese and Indian merchants through the Manila galleons. The inability of the European powers to find markets for European goods in Asia meant that gold and silver mined in the western hemisphere were needed to pay for those spices and calicoes. In turn, those European powers without access to the mines of Mexico and South America needed to sell products to the Spanish and Portuguese to acquire the precious metals they needed in Asia. The development of sugar plantations in the Atlantic islands and then in Brazil and the West Indies created another link between those colonies and the European markets for people who wished to sweeten their coffee, tea, and other foods. The naval supplies that the Carolinas produced were needed by the ships that plied the Atlantic trade routes, and further north in the English colonies the dense forests of North America provided the raw material for the New England shipbuilding industry. Fish from New England was traded to Europe and the Caribbean islands. Farms in Pennsylvania and New York produced food that was shipped south to the West Indies, where the land was too valuable as a producer of sugar and coffee to be planted in wheat. Farmers in the Hudson River valley, Long Island, northern New Jersey, and southeastern Pennsylvania were growing wheat and other grains for export, and importing slaves to help them. Through Albany and Montreal, furs from as far west as the Rockies moved from Indians who trapped them to middlemen who sold them into the European market to protect French, English, Dutch, and other North Europeans from the cold and rain and add a touch of elegance and a display of wealth to men's and women's fashions.

These trade patterns stimulated the development of colonial production in multiple ways. The desire for pepper and other Asian spices as well as Chinese tea inserted Spanish, Portuguese, Dutch, and English merchants into trade patterns that connected India, the Moluccas, China, and Japan. The European taste for sugar encouraged the clearance of land in Brazil and the West Indies and the creation of plantations that produced it. Increased shipping on the Atlantic encouraged entrepreneurs to produce the sails, ropes, and other products those ships needed. The demand for timber and furs from North America pushed Europeans into the back country, logging, establishing settlements, and bargaining with Algonquians, Iroquois, and others for furs that those nations acquired from native peoples further west.

The growth of colonial trade also affected the domestic economies of the European powers. American gold and silver gave Spain the wealth to act as a European power, and Dutch, Portuguese, and English shipping made those European nations naval powers. The demand in the colonies for European goods stimulated the production of the carriages, clothing, hats, shoes, stockings, ribbons, and other products that Europeans living in the colonies desired but were unable to produce themselves. Satisfying that demand led to standardization of goods and other innovations in commerce. The growth of the colonial market reoriented the trade of European countries away from the European market and towards those colonies. No country was more affected by this than England, which shifted its trade from dependence on continental European markets to increased involvement in the Atlantic trade with its Caribbean and North American colonies. Virtually all of the colonial powers followed mercantilist policies aimed at reserving trade with their colonies to their own subjects, ships, and ports, attempting to eliminate competitors and, in turn, stimulate the development of their own shipping, shipbuilding, and manufacturing.

The development in the sixteenth and seventeenth centuries of these empires brought Europeans to many parts of the globe. But this was not the kind of globalized economy that we know in the twenty-first century. Most trade in any part of the world remained confined to local and regional markets, and Europeans often found themselves struggling to succeed in these local market systems. At the beginning of the eighteenth century, the most important region for those Europeans was in the Atlantic basin. By this time, the various elements of trade between different parts of the Atlantic basin had coalesced into a coherent Atlantic trading complex. European goods were used to buy slaves in Africa, who were transported across the Atlantic Middle Passage to the plantations and mines of Brazil, Spanish America, the Caribbean sugar islands, and North America. Because the sugar islands devoted virtually all cultivable land to sugarcane, they imported food – especially "trash fish" for slaves and the wheat, dairy products, and meat that European colonists were accustomed to in their homelands – from the Middle Atlantic and New England colonies. Manufactured goods from Britain and France were traded for furs with the Indians in the Great Lakes region and further west, and those furs were shipped to Europe. The silver and gold mined in the Americas, the sugar produced on plantations, and other commodities grown in the Americas as well as natural resources found there were also shipped to Europe.

Nonetheless, this was not a trading system that made everyone happy, and in times of disruption, such as during the frequent wars between European powers, the interests of different groups could come to the fore. British and French merchants complained to their governments about the restrictions on their access to Spanish colonies. British merchants in particular were anxious to expand their trade throughout the Atlantic basin, and found themselves in an advantageous position when given the chance because of the quality and low price of British goods. The prosperity of Great Britain made it a strong market for colonial products such as sugar and coffee, and lumber and other products from British North America found a market in the British navy and merchant marine. French colonists in the Caribbean, on the other hand, chafed under the restrictions placed upon them by the *exclusif*, the French government's mercantilist policies that restricted trade with the French colonies to French ships and merchants. They wished to sell sugar and coffee into the ready markets of Holland and Germany. They needed slaves, which French slave traders could not supply in adequate numbers. The focus of the Caribbean islands on sugar production made them dependent on imported foodstuffs, but New France was unable to provide these in sufficient quantity, while the British colonies in North America could but were not allowed to do so. They were therefore dependent on smuggling or expensive provisioning from France itself.

The arrival of Spanish, Portuguese, Dutch, French, and English colonial regimes proved catastrophic for indigenous Americans, who died in great numbers. Europeans brought smallpox, cholera, and other European diseases with them, exacting an immediate toll after first contact. Periodic later waves of disease had serious effects on the ability of native peoples to maintain their civilizations and mount effective resistance to the encroachments of the Europeans. These demographic catastrophes were also the result of the labor regimes imposed by the colonizers. With the more or less effective power of the colonial state behind them, early colonists forced the indigenous peoples to provide labor through some version of a forced-labor system. But the indigenous populations of the New World proved to be an inadequate labor force for the mines, plantations, and other enterprises of the colonies. Migration from Europe was not strong enough to fill the need, and soon the colonists found it necessary to import labor in the form of African slaves, creating the largest forced migration in human history.

European colonialism in the New World therefore brought together peoples from vastly different places: indigenous Americans were joined by Europeans, and millions of Africans were transported across the

Atlantic to the Americas. These groups did not remain isolated from one another: Portuguese in Africa took African wives or mistresses, and the Spanish, Dutch, Portuguese, French, and English on the western shore of the Atlantic did the same with the Aztecs, Incas, and other indigenous peoples they found there, as well as with the African slaves brought to the New World. Africans also took indigenous partners. These massive population movements created an Atlantic population with a substantial *métis* component, as well as cultures made up of European, American, and African contributions. The migrations of Europeans and Africans to the New World combined with indigenous Americans to create societies that brought those different elements together in different ways. As Callière discovered at Montreal in 1701, the colonial relationship was less one of imposition of European forms and practices on colonial subjects than a complex process, operating at virtually every level of life and death, of interaction and entanglement between colonial powers and colonized peoples.

FURTHER READING

Altman, Ida, and James Horn, eds. *'To Make America': European Emigration in the Early Modern Period*. Berkeley and Los Angeles: University of California Press, 1991.

Andrien, Kenneth J. *Andean Worlds: Indigenous History, Culture, and Consciousness under Spanish Rule, 1532–1825*. Albuquerque: University of New Mexico Press, 2001.

Bailyn, Bernard, and Philip D. Morgan, eds. *Strangers within the Realm: Cultural Margins of the First British Empire*. Chapel Hill: University of North Carolina Press, 1991.

Banks, Kenneth J. *Chasing Empire across the Sea: Communications and the State in the French Atlantic, 1713–1763*. Montreal and Kingston: McGill-Queen's University Press, 2002.

Berlin, Ira. *Generations of Captivity: A History of African-American Slaves*. Cambridge, MA: Belknap Press, 2003.

Many Thousands Gone: The First Two Centuries of Slavery in North America. Cambridge, MA: Belknap Press, 1998.

Berlin, Ira, and Philip D. Morgan, eds. *Cultivation and Culture: Labor and the Shaping of Slave Life in the Americas*. Charlottesville and London: University Press of Virginia, 1993.

Bonnassieux, Pierre. *Les grandes compagnies de commerce*. New York: Burt Franklin, 1969 [reprint].

Boxer, Charles R. *The Dutch Seaborne Empire, 1600–1800*. New York: Alfred A. Knopf, 1965.

The Portuguese Seaborne Empire, 1415–1825. New York: Alfred A. Knopf, 1969.

Brown, Jennifer. *Strangers in the Blood: Fur Trade Company Families in Indian Country*. Norman: University of Oklahoma Press, 1996.

Brown, Kathleen. *Good Wives, Nasty Wenches, and Anxious Patriarchs: Gender, Race, and Power in Colonial Virginia*. Chapel Hill: University of North Carolina Press, 1996.

Burkholder, Mark A. *From Impotence to Authority: The Spanish Crown and the American Audiencias, 1687–1808*. Columbia: University of Missouri Press, 1977.

Burkholder, Mark A., and Lyman L. Johnson. *Colonial Latin America*, 6th edn. New York: Oxford University Press, 2008.

Burnard, Trevor. *Mastery, Tyranny, and Desire: Thomas Thistlewood and his Slaves in the Anglo-Jamaican World*. Chapel Hill: University of North Carolina Press, 2004.

Cahill, David. *From Rebellion to Independence in the Andes: Soundings from Southern Peru, 1750–1830*. Amsterdam: Askant Academic Publishers, 2002.

Canny, Nicholas. *Kingdom and Colony: Ireland in the Atlantic World, 1560–1800*. Baltimore, MD: Johns Hopkins University Press, 1988.

Choquette, Leslie. *Frenchmen into Peasants: Modernity and Tradition in the Peopling of French Canada*. Cambridge, MA: Harvard University Press, 1997.

Clendinnen, Inga. *Ambivalent Conquests: Maya and Spaniard in Yucatan, 1517–1570*, 2nd edn. Cambridge University Press, 2003.

Craton, Michael. *Searching for the Invisible Man: Slaves and Plantation Life in Jamaica*. Cambridge, MA: Harvard University Press, 1978.

Dechêne, Louise. *Habitants and Merchants in Seventeenth Century Montreal*, trans. Liana Viardi. Montreal and Kingston: McGill-Queen's University Press, 1992.

Drescher, Seymour. *Econocide: British Slavery in the Era of Abolition*. University of Pittsburgh Press, 1977.

Dunn, Richard S. *Sugar and Slaves: The Rise of the Planter Class in the English West Indies, 1624–1713*. Chapel Hill: University of North Carolina Press, 1972.

Eccles, W. J. *Canada under Louis XIV 1663–1701*. London and New York: Oxford University Press, 1964.

  France in America, rev. edn. East Lansing: Michigan State University Press, 1990.

Ganson, Barbara. *The Guaraní under Spanish Rule in the Río de la Plata*. Stanford University Press, 2003.

Giraud, Marcel. *Histoire de la Louisiane française*. Paris: Presses Universitaires de France, 1953.

Greer, Alan. *Mohawk Saint: Catherine Tekakwitha and the Jesuits*. New York: Oxford University Press, 2005.

Hanotaux, Gabriel, and Alfred Martineau. *Histoire des colonies françaises*, 6 vols. Paris: Plon, 1929–33.

Higman, B. W. *Plantation Jamaica 1750–1850: Capital and Control in a Colonial Economy*. Jamaica: University of the West Indies Press, 2006.

Hinderaker, Eric. *Elusive Empires: Constructing Colonialism in the Ohio Valley, 1673–1800*. New York: Cambridge University Press, 1997.

Jarvis, Michael J. *In the Eye of All Trade: Bermuda, Bermudians, and the Maritime Atlantic World, 1680–1783*. Chapel Hill: University of North Carolina Press, 2010.

Jennings, Francis. *The Ambiguous Iroquois Empire: The Covenant Chain Confederation of Indian Tribes with English Colonies from its Beginnings to the Lancaster Treaty of 1744*. New York and London: W. W. Norton, 1984.

  Empire of Fortune: Crowns, Colonies, and Tribes in the Seven Years War in America. New York and London: W. W. Norton, 1988.

  The Invasion of America: Indians, Colonialism, and the Cant of Conquest. Chapel Hill: University of North Carolina Press, 1975.

Kappeler, Andreas. *The Russian Empire: A Multiethnic History*, trans. Alfred Clayton. New York: Longman, 2001.

Langer, Erick, and Robert H. Jackson, eds. *The New Latin American Mission History*. Lincoln, NE: University of Nebraska Press, 1993.

MacCormack, Sabine. *Religion in the Andes: Vision and Imagination in Early Colonial Peru*. Princeton University Press, 1991.

McCusker, John J., and Russell R. Menard. *The Economy of British America, 1607–1789*. Chapel Hill: University of North Carolina Press, 1985.

Menard, Russell R. *Sweet Negotiations: Sugar, Slavery, and Plantation Agriculture in Early Barbados*. Charlottesville and London: University of Virginia Press, 2006.

Merrell, James H. *Into the American Woods: Negotiators on the Pennsylvania Frontier*. New York: W. W. Norton, 1999.

Paquette, Robert L., and Stanley L. Engerman, eds. *The Lesser Antilles in the Age of European Expansion*. Gainesville: University Press of Florida, 1996.

Pares, Richard. *War and Trade in the West Indies, 1739–1763*. Oxford University Press, 1936. Reprinted London: Frank Cass, 1963.

Parry, J. H. *The Spanish Seaborne Empire*. Berkeley and Los Angeles: University of California Press, 1966.

Pritchard, James. *In Search of Empire: The French in the Americas, 1670–1730*. Cambridge University Press, 2004.

Rediker, Marcus. *Villains of All Nations: Atlantic Pirates in the Golden Age*. Boston: Beacon Press, 2004.

Richter, Daniel K. *Facing East from Indian Country: A Native History of Early America*. Cambridge, MA: Harvard University Press, 2001.

  The Ordeal of the Longhouse. Chapel Hill: University of North Carolina Press, 1992.

Russell-Wood, A. J. R. *The Portuguese Empire, 1415–1808: A World on the Move*. Baltimore, MD: Johns Hopkins University Press, 1998.

Scammell, G. V. *The First Imperial Age: European Overseas Expansion, c. 1400–1715*. London: HarperCollins Academic, 1989.

Schurz, William Lytle. *The Manila Galleon*. New York: E. P. Dutton & Co., 1939.

Sheridan, Richard B. *Sugar and Slavery: An Economic History of the British West Indies, 1623–1775*. Baltimore, MD: Johns Hopkins University Press, 1973.

Sleeper-Smith, Susan. *Indian Women and French Men: Rethinking Cultural Encounter in the Western Great Lakes.* Amherst: University of Massachusetts Press, 2001.

Stein, Robert L. *The French Sugar Business in the Eighteenth Century.* Baton Rouge: Louisiana State University Press, 1988.

Subrahmanyam, Sanjay. *The Portuguese Empire in Asia, 1500–1700: A Political and Economic History.* London: Longman, 1993.

Trigger, Bruce G. *Natives and Newcomers: Canada's 'Heroic Age' Reconsidered.* Kingston and Montreal: McGill-Queen's University Press, 1985.

Trudel, Marcel. *Histoire de la Nouvelle-France.* Montreal: Fides, 1966.

Weber, David J. *The Spanish Frontier in North America.* New Haven, CT: Yale University Press, 1992.

White, Richard. *The Middle Ground: Indians, Empires, and Republics in the Great Lakes Region, 1650–1815.* Cambridge University Press, 1991.

Wilson, Kathleen. "The Performance of Freedom: Maroons and the Colonial Order in Eighteenth-Century Jamaica and the Atlantic Sound." *William and Mary Quarterly,* 3rd series, 66, 1 (2009), 45–86.

3   Restructuring the Atlantic empires

A principal minister of a European colonial power in the early 1730s, such as Robert Walpole in Great Britain or Cardinal André-Hercule de Fleury in France, might be forgiven if he looked out from Westminster or Versailles with a relatively rosy view of the world. Both men were at the height of their domestic power. They enjoyed the confidence of their royal masters, George II and Louis XV. They had created political systems, albeit of very different kinds, that effectively managed the domestic factionalism that periodically plagued European monarchies: "Cock Robin" Walpole dominated the Houses of Parliament through a combination of personal persuasiveness and what a generation later would be called "Old Corruption." Fleury was the master of backstairs deal-brokering with other ministers of state and the Royal Council. The diplomatic conflicts of the turn of the century also seemed to be over. Great Britain's colonial holdings in North America appeared to be secure, as did France's in New France, the new colony of Louisiana, and the Caribbean islands that were producers of valuable commodities like sugar and coffee.

Walpole and Fleury both left office in the early 1740s, Walpole through resignation, Fleury through death. Unfortunately for their successors, and rulers in other imperial powers of the time, neither European diplomacy, nor domestic politics, nor colonial empires remained as placid in the second half of the eighteenth century as they had seemed in 1730. This was especially the case in the Atlantic basin. Rivalries between the European powers became more intense in the 1740s, and the Atlantic colonies became a major theater for the wars that occurred in each decade of the remainder of the eighteenth century. The costs in men and money of fighting wars on a global scale made the European powers seek changes in their relationships with their Atlantic colonies. Pressures from expanding trade cracked the mercantilist economic structures of the empires, as colonial merchants pushed new policies on their imperial governments or simply evaded or ignored imperial restrictions. Between the middle of the eighteenth century and the end of the first third of the nineteenth, the control exercised by Britain, Spain, Portugal, and France over territories from Canada to the southern cone of South America changed dramatically. Often told as an "Age of Democratic Revolutions" or the creation of a "Second British Empire" characterized by a "swing to the east,"[1] this process seems more an effort by the imperial powers to restructure their relationships with their colonies and parallel efforts by colonists – by no means a single, unified group in any colony – to make that relationship more advantageous to themselves. In significant parts of the western hemisphere, this did lead to independence from the imperial power. In other parts of the Americas, the colonial relationship continued, but usually in altered form. This was a period in which colonial powers and colonial subjects contested and renegotiated their relationship. For some colonies, secession from the empire was the outcome; for others, however, the Age of Atlantic Revolution was a period of restructuring in a colonial history that would last well into the nineteenth and even the twentieth century.[2]

At least a part of the story is old-fashioned European diplomacy. This was hardly static during the eighteenth century. In Central Europe, the kingdoms of Saxony and Bavaria came increasingly under the influence of other, more successful powers such as France and Austria. Duchies in northern Italy were reduced to the status of trophies for Spanish and Austrian dukes. The United Netherlands had been an economic and diplomatic power at the beginning of the century, playing a significant role in determining British policy against Catholic France and control- ling trade in the English Channel and the Baltic. Its bankers lubricated European trade. Timber, hemp, tar, and furs from the Baltic and further east passed through its warehouses on the way to Western Europe and the Atlantic in exchange for tobacco, sugar, and spices from the East and West Indies and silks, olive oil, and wine from southern Europe. Increasingly after mid-century, though, Dutch merchants found them- selves less able to influence events, as Austria, Spain, France, and Great Britain made their own plans for the region and for trade in the Atlantic and East Indies.

At the same time, Great Britain played a bigger role in European affairs. It had become directly involved in them by the accession to

---

[1] Robert R. Palmer, *The Age of Democratic Revolutions*, 2 vols. (Princeton University Press, 1959); Vincent Harlow, *The Founding of the Second British Empire, 1763–1793*, 2 vols. (London: Longmans, Green, 1952–64).

[2] Jeremy Adelman makes this argument with respect to Spanish and Portuguese America. See Jeremy Adelman, "An Age of Imperial Revolutions," *American Historical Review* 113, 2 (2008), 319–40.

the British throne in 1688 by William of Orange and, in 1714, by the Hanoverians. Dynastic ties, common interests in trade, and Protestant religion made England and the Netherlands close friends at the beginning of the eighteenth century. But by the middle of the century, this relationship had frayed. While Dutch power declined, Britain was acting as a global power, facing off against France not only in Europe but in the Caribbean, North America, and Asia. Further east, Prussia used European wars to claw its way from the ranks of middling Central European powers to become a challenger for supremacy in that part of Europe. In the Seven Years War in the late 1750s, Prussia's king, Frederick I, not only salvaged its existence against a coalition of most European powers, but also made it one of the most significant players in continental diplomacy. Further east, the Russian empire, pushed by Tsar Peter the Great and his successors to become more European, pressed its way into continental affairs, successfully challenging Sweden for preeminence in the Baltic and becoming a contender for power in Eastern and Central Europe that all other powers had to consider in their alliances and plans.

As these different powers rose and fell, the dominance of France remained a constant in eighteenth-century diplomatic calculations. Under Louis XIV and Louis XV, France was, above all, a continental Great Power, interested in expanding its power in Europe itself. The death in 1701 of the last Habsburg king of Spain, Charles II, created a diplomatic crisis in Europe and a chance to extend French power. Charles had, in his will, left all of his holdings to Philippe, duc d'Anjou, a member of the Bourbon family that ruled France. But William III, ruler of both England and Holland, insisted on a partition of the holdings of the Spanish Habsburgs between France and Austria. Philip of Anjou took up the Spanish throne in February 1701, guaranteed by Louis XIV and French power, but opposed by England and Austria. The lengthy war that followed concluded with the Treaty of Utrecht in 1713, confirming Philip on the throne of Spain. Philip renounced his rights to the succession to the French throne, and the Treaty provided that the two thrones could never be united.

But Philip remained close to the throne of France – separated from it only by the sickly child who became Louis XV in 1715 and unlikely to adhere to his renunciation of the throne should it actually become available. French diplomats were focused more on this continental game than on the Americas. Great Britain as well tended until the 1730s to emphasize continental issues rather than Atlantic ones in its foreign policy. After the succession to the British throne by George I of Hanover in 1714, British foreign policy seemed inexorably drawn to the continent and the interests of George's German territories. These policies reflected a general sense that Britain had an important role to play on the continent and that it was vitally important to British liberties and commercial interests that the fragile balance of power on the continent be maintained. French support for the Catholic Stuart pretenders to the British throne throughout the first half of the eighteenth century did little to assuage this concern with the continent and its greatest power. While some British leaders advocated a more Atlantic policy in the first part of the eighteenth century, it was only in the years after the War of Austrian Succession in the 1740s that a "blue water" policy began to emerge as the British focus turned towards the Atlantic and the colonies on its western shores.[3] This would culminate during the Seven Years War, as William Pitt's successful policy essentially left the fighting on the continent to Britain's allies, especially the heavily subsidized Prussia of Frederick the Great. British military and naval forces instead focused on British commercial and imperial holdings in the Americas and Asia.

In Great Britain, in particular, diplomatic and imperial concerns began to merge and became closely linked to internal developments in political culture in the course of the eighteenth century. Newspapers, coffee houses, and popular theatrical productions debated public issues. Factionalism was rampant among the elite. There were anxieties about public corruption and the loyalty of some to the Hanoverian dynasty. This in particular was called into question by the Jacobite cause, with the 1745 Scottish revolt led by Bonnie Prince Charlie a reminder of its persistence. Behind these concerns loomed the French threat to British national security. As Kathleen Wilson has shown, these multiple concerns drew heavily on a language of masculinity and feminization that questioned the ability of the government to defend the nation. The victory of Admiral Vernon at Porto Bello in the War of Jenkins' Ear – virtually the only British success in that war – turned the admiral into a national hero who "supported and embodied the spectacular, if imaginary, vision of empire as an extensive, homogeneous polity bounded only by rights, liberties and duties and guided by manly and virtuous leaders."[4] Subsequent crises in British imperial fortunes, such as the Seven Years War and the American Revolution, served to solidify the links between these different discourses and, by the end

[3] Eliga H. Gould, *The Persistence of Empire: British Political Culture in the Age of the American Revolution* (Chapel Hill: University of North Carolina Press, 2000), 1–14, 35–52.

[4] Kathleen Wilson, *The Sense of the People: Politics, Culture and Imperialism in England, 1715–1785* (Cambridge University Press, 1995), 161.

of the eighteenth century, make empire – by then in South Asia rather than North America – an accepted expression of the "manly" power of a British state that was increasingly focused on disciplining its subjects both at home and in the colonies.

The British case is better studied and, because of its Atlantic emphasis, perhaps more closely related to imperial concerns. But if continental interests dominated the strategies of most of the Great Powers, the colonies of the New World could still be attractive pawns in the game of Great-Power diplomacy. There was, of course, the long-standing hope that those colonies would somehow lead to the Pacific and the lucrative trade everyone imagined could take place with China and other Asian powers. That the Spanish claimed a monopoly of trade and navigation in the Pacific, and attempted to enforce that claim by seizing the ships and cargoes of other European powers, led to the search for other routes to the Asian trade. This was one of the incentives for the continuing search for the Northwest Passage through North America, a dream that died only in the late eighteenth century.[5] The mercantilist theories that guided European economic policies also made the New World attractive. Spain profited immensely from the gold and silver brought from Mexico and Peru. Armies and allies did not come cheaply in eighteenth-century Europe, and other monarchs could only look with envy on the ability of the kings of Spain to throw their weight – accentuated by the silver in their purses – around in European affairs. There was a danger to the balance of power if one monarch controlled that silver, and access to it – or to parts of the New World, as yet unexplored, that might yield similar treasures – could be ignored only at great risk.

The expansion of Spanish America

In the course of the eighteenth century, the British in the southeast, French in the Mississippi valley, and Russians on the Pacific coast contested the Spanish for control of North America. After 1783, a new threat, the United States, joined those European powers in the struggle for the continent. In the face of this competition, the Spanish did not simply withdraw. But they did reassess the approach they had taken in the New World since the sixteenth century. Missions no longer seemed to be a realistic way of colonizing; rather, as the competition with other European powers for territory in the North American southeast and

[5] Paul W. Mapp, *The Elusive West and the Contest for Empire, 1713–1763* (Chapel Hill: University of North Carolina Press, 2011), 101–43; Glyn Williams, *Voyages of Delusion: The Quest for the Northwest Passage* (New Haven, CT: Yale University Press, 2003).

southwest unfolded in the eighteenth century, it would be the Spanish military that took the lead.

The Gulf Coast, the broad expanse from Florida to New Spain, was the site in the eighteenth century of the contest between Spain, France, and Great Britain. The trip by Robert Cavelier de La Salle from the St. Lawrence to the Gulf of Mexico in 1682 was only the beginning of French movement into the region. With the blessing of Louis XIV, who was momentarily at war with Spain, La Salle returned in 1684 to attempt to found a French colony at the mouth of the Mississippi as a base from which the French could wreak havoc on the Spanish in New Spain. Unable to find the Gulf entrance to the river, he built a fort at Matagorda Bay, very far from his intended destination but close enough to both the silver mines of New Spain and the newer colony of New Mexico that, when rumors of the settlement reached Mexico City, it elicited a strong reaction from the Spanish. They responded to the French threat by establishing a settlement at Pensacola Bay in 1698, just before a French fleet under Pierre LeMoyne d'Iberville entered the Bay.

But while the Spanish won the race, they had lost the war. The settlement they called Santa Maria de Galve was in a bay surrounded by sand barrens that could not grow food for the fledgling settlement; the Escambia River that flowed into the bay opened into Creek country, but not beyond. The bay itself proved difficult to defend. The French, on the other hand, had by a stroke of good fortune been forced to look further west, and seeking shelter from a storm d'Iberville found his way through the Mississippi delta to the great river itself. On his way back to France, he established Fort Maurepas on Biloxi Bay, giving the French two significant outposts on the coast. The French further consolidated their claim to the region with the establishment of Fort Mississippi near the mouth of the river. In the following decades, French planters attempted to create a plantation economy producing tobacco and indigo along the banks of the river, importing slaves from Africa to supplement a labor force of enslaved Indians and indentured servants. But a revolt in 1729 by the Natchez Indians, helped by African slaves, led to the end of slave importation until Louisiana was transferred to Spain in 1763. The inability of lower Mississippi tobacco to compete against Chesapeake leaf in Europe and the collapse in the 1750s of a boom in indigo cut off the development of the plantation economy, leaving Louisiana a region that produced lumber, naval stores, cattle, and other foodstuffs for the Caribbean islands. Plantation owners usually supervised the production of a broad range of products on their lands themselves, and a large proportion of the slave population lived not in the countryside, as in the

Chesapeake, the Carolinas, and even in the Middle Atlantic colonies of British North America, but in New Orleans.[6]

The advent of friendly relations between Bourbon France and Spain after 1701 prevented any Spanish efforts to dislodge the French from their foothold between New Spain and Spanish Florida. From its base in Mobile Bay (established in 1702 by the transfer of the post on Biloxi Bay) France span a trading system that ran from Pensacola in the east to the Red River in the west, and as far inland as Fort Toulouse near where the Coosa and Tallapoosa rivers joined to form the Alabama River. From New Orleans, established in 1718 and made the administrative headquarters of the colony four years later, French traders moved north up the Mississippi, past existing outposts at Natchez (1714) and Arkansas Post (1721). In the following decades furs and hides from this region moved south along the rivers to New Orleans and Mobile and then to Europe. At the same time, trading posts in what was called Upper Louisiana extended south from Detroit to Kaskaskia and Sainte-Geneviève near St. Louis (itself only established in 1764), linking Louisiana to the French colony in Canada.

The Spanish regained interest in the area north of the Rio Grande only at the end of the War of Spanish Succession, sparked by the arrival of a French expedition at the Spanish frontier post at San Juan Bautista. A Spanish expedition soon discovered a French stockade on the Red River at Natchitoches. By 1721 the French in Natchitoches looked at a new Spanish fort just 12 miles away, Nuestra Señora del Pilar de Los Adaes. While the Spanish conceded that the French colony of Louisiana extended as far as the Red River, Los Adaes became the administrative headquarters for the Spanish in East Texas.

The border between the two empires in East Texas may be seen as a microcosm of the disadvantages the Spanish faced everywhere in the New World when they came into competition with the British or the French. The distance from Mexico City made it difficult to support military operations. Spain also could not produce the cheap manufactured goods that proved the most important currency for gaining native allies in the New World. The better-developed French and British economies, in contrast, were able to do so. The French in Louisiana and Canada did not compel their trading partners to change religion, nor did the British in the Carolinas and the Ohio valley, but the Spanish did. In East Texas, the French in Natchitoches dominated the commerce with the surrounding Indians, who enjoyed French trade goods and used

[6] Ira Berlin, *Many Thousands Gone: The First Two Centuries of Slavery in North America* (Cambridge, MA: Belknap Press, 1998), 81–90, 195–200.

French arms and ammunition to threaten Los Adaes. That settlement, in contrast, was difficult for the Spanish to supply from across the Rio Grande, and they were unable to find a dependable labor supply in the indigenous population. Here, as elsewhere in North America, success meant gaining Indian allies, and while the Spanish offered religion, their competitors offered more tangible benefits.

Indeed, the Spanish and the French faced a formidable Indian power in the eighteenth and early nineteenth centuries, the Comanche empire. Beginning in the early eighteenth century, this nation extended its power across the southern plains, and by the 1760s, when France turned over Louisiana to Spain in the aftermath of the Seven Years War, the Comanches had in fact completed their own conquest of the region, making European treaties irrelevant on the ground in the southwest of North America. The expansion of Comanche power pushed Apaches south, closer to the northern provinces of New Spain. This exposed the resources of that region, especially the silver mines of Nueva Vizcaya and Coahuila, to raids by Apaches. It took some time for the Spanish to understand the tenuousness of their hold on New Spain and the regions to the north, and to formulate policies that worked with, rather than against, the native powers such as the Comanches that they faced. Only in the *Instructions* to colonial administrators promulgated in 1786 did the Spanish government recognize that gifts to Indian allies were cheaper and more effective than warfare, laying the basis for several decades of peace between the Spanish and the Comanches, Navajos, and Apaches in the southwest.

Even then, the Spanish notion that they were in control of the North American southwest was a massive exercise in self-deception and denial of the power of a Comanche empire that, well before the end of Spanish rule in 1821, had moved out of the Spanish orbit and maintained commercial ties from the Rio Grande valley to the Mississippi and Missouri rivers. In this vast territory, they traded huge quantities of furs and horses to both Indians and whites to the north and east. While Apaches had raided south of Texas in the late eighteenth century, the first few decades after Mexican independence saw the Comanche empire extend its sway even further south. In this, they took advantage of the inability of the new Mexican state to protect its northern provinces and the willingness of the newly independent Republic of Texas to allow transit across its territory by Comanche war parties heading to Mexico. In all of these relations, whether with Spaniards, Texans, other Indians, or Mexicans, the Comanches forced their diplomatic and economic partners to adopt Comanche practices and to take into account Comanche expectations. Only when the overwhelming power of the westward-expanding United States washed over the region after the mid-nineteenth-century Mexican War was the Comanche empire overcome.

While the efforts of the Spanish to move north and east from New Spain were hesitant and halting in the eighteenth century, their progress further west was different. In California Spain made its last expansive move in the New World. The Spanish authorities initially had less interest in the coast of California than they did in New Mexico and Texas. The galleon trade between Peru and Manila aroused some interest in it at the end of the sixteenth century, when the return route – north towards Japan, then following westerly winds to the California coast, then south to Acapulco – was discovered. Some officials speculated that a base on the coast of California, perhaps at Monterey Bay, would allow the galleons to refit and restore their crews after the long ocean crossing. Nothing, however, came of this for over a century.

Ministers in Madrid ignored the proposals from administrators in New Spain, but those administrators were becoming acutely aware of Russian advances southeastward from the Bering Strait. In 1741 an expedition led by Vitus Bering reached the Aleutians, opening the way for Russian trade for fur pelts with the peoples of the islands along the Pacific coast of North America. Tsar Paul I chartered a Russian–American Company in 1799 to carry on the fur trade, and a settlement established in 1801 at Novo Arkhangelski became the center of Russian efforts at colonizing North America and exploiting the sea otter fur trade with the nations who lived along the coast. Settlements further south, near Queen Charlotte Island, the Strait of Juan de Fuca, and the mouth of the Columbia River, were quickly planned by the Company, but more ambitious plans soon overcame them as Russian traders and Aleut hunters put in at Bodega Bay north of San Francisco in 1807. Temporary sojourns around Bodega Bay allowed fur hunting by the Russians and their allies. In 1812, Ivan Alexandrovich Kuskov founded "Rossiya" (Fort Ross), in a cove 30 miles north of Bodega. Never able to support itself, and facing a decline in the sea otter population as it was hunted and killed, the settlement struggled for almost thirty years until this "farthest south" of Russian colonialism in North America was abandoned in 1841.

Russian expansion, and rumors of even more competition from British and Dutch navigators, spurred the most capable of the Spanish Bourbon kings, Carlos III, to defend Spanish claims. A similarly capable administrator, José de Gálvez, strengthened the Spanish presence in the province of Sonora in northwestern New Spain and in Baja California, and pushed Spanish settlement north along the coast.

In 1769, a land expedition left San Diego to blaze a coastal path to Monterey Bay. Unable to recognize the Bay from the land – thus far, Spaniards had seen it only from the sea – the leader of this expedition, Gaspar de Portolá, decided to proceed further north in hopes of finding something that looked more like the sheltered harbor described by Sebastián Vizcaíno in 1602. Reaching Half Moon Bay, Portolá recognized landmarks described by that earlier explorer and realized he had gone past Monterey Bay. But he made the fortuitous discovery of San Francisco Bay, the best natural harbor on the west coast of North America. Monterey Bay – finally found in 1770 – became the administrative capital of the province. But Portolá's discovery of San Francisco Bay dramatically raised the stakes for the Spanish in what they called Alta California. The land route to Monterey remained open to the Spanish for only a few years, but that was long enough for settlers and livestock to make California self-sufficient. In 1775 Spanish ships not only found the Golden Gate and sailed into San Francisco Bay, but also found the Columbia River and reached the site of present-day Juneau, Alaska.

In the years following the establishment of Monterey, Franciscans under the leadership of Junípero Serra established a chain of missions between San Diego and San Francisco. In spite of the opposition of military and civil authorities, these missions remained under Franciscan control and independent of civil authorities until the end of the colonial period in 1821. With few competing civilian or military settlements, the Franciscan missions came to dominate Alta California. They produced an agricultural surplus that paid for the goods that ships brought to the province. The missions were deadly for the Indians who were brought into them as converts, and as David J. Weber noted, the irony of Alta California was that the missions expanded as the Indians died.[7] But the Hispanic population grew, and the restoration of Florida to Spain in the peace settlement of the War of American Independence in 1783 made the Spanish empire in North America a transcontinental one, extending from St. Augustine on the Atlantic to San Diego and Monterey on the Pacific.

French and British conflict in North America

European conflicts in the first half of the eighteenth century such as the War of Spanish Succession (1701–13) and the War of Austrian

---

[7] David J. Weber, *The Spanish Frontier in North America* (New Haven, CT: Yale University Press, 1992), 264.

Succession (1740–48) spilled into the Atlantic world and especially North America. Decidedly peripheral to the conflicts in Europe, these colonial wars were marked by inconclusive battles between colonial militias, Indian allies, and occasional regular troops. The French and British empires in North America remained separated by the Iroquois Confederacy in upstate New York, a flexible barrier that kept the British from moving north and the French from moving south. As Europeans moved further west, however, they faced a fluid situation in the territories west of the Alleghenies: the assumption imbedded in the logic of the Covenant Chain, that the Five Nations and their Grand Council at Onondaga could speak for the Shawnees, Delawares, and others who lived in the west, proved patently false, and those nations themselves tried to play the French and the British off against each other.

French control of the St. Lawrence River valley during the first two-thirds of the century allowed Montreal to outdistance Albany as an entrepôt for furs from the region around the Great Lakes and further west. A series of forts established a strong French presence around the Great Lakes basin, and *coureurs de bois* eventually established agricultural settlements further south in the Illinois Country between the Missouri and Kaskaskia rivers. The consolidation of Louisiana completed an arc around the British colonies on the Atlantic seaboard, which were barred from the interior not only by the Appalachian and Allegheny mountains but also by French control of the interior.

With antagonism between France and Britain focused primarily on the European continent for much of the first half of the eighteenth century, French policy intended not so much to take possession of the Ohio Country, west of the Allegheny Mountains, as to prevent the British from gaining it. This policy maintained French predominance in trade with the Indians in the area and, in time of war, would draw British resources to North America and improve French odds in a European conflict. But the situation in North America did not remain static, and as France and Britain squared off in Europe in the middle of the eighteenth century, their differences in North America became more contentious.

By the middle of the eighteenth century this conflict focused on the Forks of the Ohio River, where the Allegheny and Monongahela rivers joined. In 1744 representatives of Virginia, Maryland, and Pennsylvania negotiated the Treaty of Lancaster with the Iroquois. In this treaty, the Iroquois gave up all claims to land within the boundaries of Maryland and Virginia. While the Iroquois representative, Canasatego, may have thought he was giving up only a tenuous claim to the Shenandoah valley, the colonists took the treaty to mean that the Ohio Country, west of the Allegheny Mountains, was theirs to settle. The Virginia House of Burgesses granted a third of a million acres of land on the Ohio to a company of speculators, the Ohio Company of Virginia, who planned to resell the land at the Forks of the Ohio to settlers. The sale was delayed by the War of Austrian Succession, but that war led to incursions into the French trading monopoly in the Ohio Country. Within a year after the end of the war, a Pennsylvania trader named George Croghan had established himself in a Miami settlement called Pickawillany in the western part of the Ohio Country.

The French response to this was to place a price on Croghan's scalp and, in 1749, to send an expedition, commanded by Captain Pierre-Joseph de Céloron de Blainville, from Quebec into the Ohio Country to renew French claims. Céloron had been born in Montreal and fought against the Chickasaws in 1739, going on from there to command Fort Detroit, Fort Niagara, and Fort St.-Frédéric on Lake Champlain. He now led a flotilla from Montreal to reassert French control of the Ohio Country. His reception by the Miamis and other Indians was relatively cool, and the journey underscored the tenuousness of the French alliance with the Ohio Country Indians. This relationship was held together by trade and gifts but was now being supplanted by the better-supplied British. For the moment, the French did nothing in spite of the pessimistic report Céloron wrote upon his return to Quebec. Not so the British: beginning in 1752, the Ohio Company began to mount efforts to create a permanent settlement at the Forks of the Ohio. In that year a guide hired by the Ohio Company, Christopher Gist, concluded a vague agreement with the Delaware, Shawnee, and Mingo Indians that facilitated the establishment of a fortified trading post at the Forks. Gist was accompanied by his ally Tanaghrisson, an Iroquois half-king. His presence reflected the claim by the Onondaga Grand Council to authority over the Indians in the western back country. This claim was remarked in a report prepared a few years later, in 1763, by the British Superintendent of Indian Affairs William Johnson, who noted that the Delawares and Shawnees resided on land "allotted to them by the Six Nations," and had been the basis for the long-standing diplomatic relationship between the British and the Iroquois.[8] But both Gist and Tanaghrisson were silent about the permanent settlement implied by the trading post: the Ohio Country Indians might desire British trading goods and gifts, but did not want permanent settlers in their territory.

[8] E. B. O'Callaghan (ed.), *The Documentary History of the State of New York*, vol. I (Albany, NY: Weed, Parsons and Co., 1849), 28.

It also was not what the French wanted, since it meant the first permanent British settlement in the Ohio watershed. The counterpunch came quickly, at Pickawillany, when a company of Chippewa and Ottawa warriors accompanied by about thirty French soldiers attacked the settlement. To consolidate this victory and protect communications between New France and the French settlements in the Illinois Country, a new governor-general of New France, the marquis Duquesne, began construction of a string of forts stretching from the St. Lawrence towards the Forks of the Ohio. By the autumn of 1753, three of the forts – Presque Île on the south shore of Lake Erie, Rivière aux Boeufs on French Creek, and Fort Machault at the village of Venango – were under construction. The fourth, Fort Duquesne, was planned for the Forks of the Ohio.

The French effort to control the interior of the North American continent led Virginia to mount an expedition to the Forks. At the head of a company of 200 militiamen, the newly minted Lieutenant-Colonel George Washington set out from Alexandria in early April 1754. On May 27, he discovered a French force from the nearby Forks, and the following morning he and his Indian allies fell on the awakening French. What followed was a quick victory for Washington, followed by a massacre of most of the French. In the aftermath, Washington hastily erected a fortification nearby, Fort Necessity. By July it had become a refuge against a French force set on avenging their earlier defeat. On July 3 the French attacked, aided by Delawares, Shawnees, and Mingos who had switched their alliance from the British to the French. Washington surrendered and the next day led his men back towards Virginia. The French quickly eliminated any vestiges of British presence in the region.

The aftermath of the small engagement in 1754 between the French and British at Fort Necessity marked an important escalation of the conflict in North America. By 1756 they and their European allies were at war, a conflict known in Europe as the Seven Years War and in North America, misleadingly, as the French and Indian War. This was more than a localized war: it was, rather, a stage "on which the members of very different cultures – French, Canadian, British, Anglo-American, and Amerindian – would meet and interact in ways that were by turns violent and accommodating, shrewd and fraught with misunderstanding."[9] The events at Fort Necessity had been prologue to the early stages of the war, as the French benefitted from the support of the Indians of

---

[9] Fred Anderson, *Crucible of War: The Seven Years' War and the Fate of Empire in British North America, 1754–1766* (New York: Random House, 2000), 107.

the interior who traded more with the French than the British, and saw them as less likely to settle in the Ohio valley. But in 1759, the British captured Quebec from the French, giving them control of the St. Lawrence valley and making it difficult for the French to import the trade goods demanded by their Indian allies in the interior. With the shift of those Indians to the British side, the writing was on the wall for the French empire in Canada and the Great Lakes region. The entry of Spain into the war on the French side in 1762 only opened the way for more British victories and conquests. In 1763 a peace treaty signed in Paris ended French colonial power north of Louisiana, and severely weakened the Spanish empire, perhaps most notably in its provisions that finally ended Spanish control of the Pacific. The British gained the French colonies in Canada and on the east bank of the Mississippi. At the same time, Florida passed from Spanish control to the British, and Spain received the western part of Louisiana from the French.

The Treaty of Paris seemed to consolidate British control of North America, making London the master of a vast expanse of territory from the fur-trading areas in upper Canada to the St. Lawrence valley, and then south through New England, New York, the Middle Atlantic colonies as far south as Georgia and Florida, and into the contested Ohio Country. The weakening of French and Spanish power in the Seven Years War also had implications further south, in the Caribbean. Dominica, St. Vincent, Grenada, and Tobago were ceded to Britain in 1763, and the seventeenth-century British colonies in the Leeward Islands (Antigua, St. Kitts, Nevis, Montserrat), Barbados, and the more recently developed Jamaica contested French sugar production in Saint-Domingue, Martinique, and Guadeloupe. The region became of crucial economic importance for Great Britain in the second half of the eighteenth century.

The American Revolution

The British conflict with France and her continental allies in the Seven Years War had, for a brief period of time in 1759–61, propelled North America to the center of the concerns of the British government. But after 1761, as North America seemed secure and those interests turned elsewhere, it became a source of anxiety. The colonists, with the danger from New France past, seemed to the British commander Jeffery Amherst to be less and less cooperative in providing him with the men and materials needed to help British efforts in the West Indies. They evaded restrictions on trade with French colonies. Trade with the Indians in the North American back country expanded as well.

An even larger problem loomed through permanent emigration from the British colonies into the back country, which resumed with the end of hostilities. Settlers moved down the Shenandoah valley and into the Carolina back country as well as west from Pennsylvania and Maryland along the roads constructed by British commanders a few years earlier to connect to forts in the Ohio Country. Those forts themselves became markets for the agricultural produce of the settlers' farms. These uncontrolled, and probably uncontrollable, migrations set the stage for frequent, sometimes violent, conflicts in the 1760s between provinces over disputed boundaries, between settlers with conflicting land titles, and between Europeans and Indians.

The most immediate consequence of these attempts to assert British sovereignty over the interior came in April 1763, when the Ottawa leader Pontiac led a siege of the British garrison at Detroit, beginning a war that spread throughout the entire area west of the mountains. At its high point, the rebellion placed in question British control of virtually every stronghold they held in the interior of the continent. By the time it ended in 1765, it had significantly reinforced a British policy aimed at consolidating Westminster's control over its North American empire. It had also sharpened racial divisions between whites and Indians in the back country, laying the groundwork for decades of extraordinary violence between Native Americans and white settlers.

Even as the British army, with little help from the colonial governments, sought to re-establish control of the interior, a new ministry led by George Grenville and Lord Halifax in Westminster was energetically instituting a series of reforms in colonial administration intended to create a stable empire, restore control in the North American west, and establish a fiscal system that would use the prosperous colonies of the Atlantic seaboard to support the effort. This meant the imposition of British control on the interior to an extent that no European power had ever been able to accomplish.

The differences between Great Britain and its American colonies therefore had a significant basis in the back country, far away from the better-known story of the American Revolution on the Atlantic coast. The British empire in North America strained the resources of the metropole and, as would occur over and over again in all of the colonial powers over the next 150 years, political leaders cast about for ways to finance it. As Pontiac's Rebellion was already making clear, British policy would require a much larger army than the relatively small forces the British maintained prior to 1756, much closer to the 100,000 men in 115 regiments that comprised the British army in 1763 than the 35,000 men in 49 regiments that had existed in the early 1750s. As would happen often in the future in both the British and other empires, the cost, the imperial administrators determined, would be paid not by the metropole, but by the colonies themselves. The post-1763 British empire envisioned in London would be more tightly controlled from the center, but the costs of projecting British power would be financed at the margins. Fiscal reforms tightening collection of the tax on molasses and imposing a new tax that required revenue stamps on legal papers, newspapers, and other items, meant that those who lived in the colonies would share in the costs of the empire. But they were also to learn the responsibilities of living in the empire. The fiscal measures were to impose imperial dominion on the feckless colonists who aroused the ire of Jeffery Amherst.

It did not turn out that way. In the summer of 1765 the colonial administrations in North America found themselves faced with a series of rhetorical and violent demonstrations against the new taxes. The rhetoric declared that Parliament had no authority to tax the colonies, since the colonists were not represented in Westminster. The violence made collection of the new duties difficult if not impossible. In 1766 the Stamp Act was repealed, but replaced in June 1767 by new duties on lead, glass, paper, painter's colors, and tea. Late in 1770, Parliament repealed all of the duties except for that on tea, and relations between the colonies and Britain quieted down. This uneasy truce would last for three years, until a new Tea Act passed in May 1773 revived popular opposition to British policies. On the evening of December 16, 1773 about fifty Bostonians dressed as Indians dumped 90,000 pounds of East India Company tea into Boston harbor to prevent its importation.

The destruction of tea in Boston led to widespread condemnation of the colonists' actions by politicians in England, who were now convinced that the issue was, quite simply, the authority of the government over the colonies. The reassertion of Westminster's authority was matched by colonial preparations to defend themselves from what they saw as encroachments on their pocketbooks and liberties as Englishmen. While the debates of the decade between the Stamp Act and the imperial crisis of the mid 1770s had not been about breaking the links between London and the thirteen colonies, both sides did envisage a reformulated relationship. But events began to move beyond those concerns. In September 1774, a Continental Congress brought together delegates from many of the colonies who repeated the arguments that parliamentary authority over the colonies was limited by natural law, the British constitution, and colonial charters. As the British commander, General Thomas Gage, was urged to action by his superiors in London, the colonial militias became more active, and fighting began in earnest on April 18, 1776, when a collection of town militias in Massachusetts exchanged fire with British soldiers in Lexington, Concord, and the roads between those towns and Boston.

Over the next seven years, the American rebels slowly built up their military forces, established common governing institutions, and found European allies – France and Spain – who were willing to support them against the common enemy, Great Britain. The principal American army, commanded by George Washington, survived poor supply, physical hardship, and defeat to frustrate the better-equipped British army and navy. The French fleet finally allowed Washington to defeat the British at Yorktown in Virginia, near the Chesapeake Bay, in 1781. This defeat, and growing opposition to the war in Britain itself (notably from the former prime minister, William Pitt), forced the British to the bargaining table. Two years later, in 1783, the Peace of Paris acknowledged the independence of the thirteen British colonies east of the Alleghenies and south of the St. Lawrence as the United States of America.

The American Revolution marked the beginning of an extended period of imperial crisis for the European Atlantic empires. France and Spain took advantage of the discomfiture of Great Britain and supported the American revolt, a policy that mostly worked to the advantage of the Americans. In the Peace of Paris in 1783 Great Britain acknowledged a western boundary for the new United States that extended west as far as the Mississippi, opening up the Ohio and Illinois Country to settlement and placing the new country against Spanish-controlled Louisiana west of the Mississippi. Validated by the struggle against Great Britain and already experienced in operations against the Indians of the west, Americans moved quickly into the region in a wild scramble for western lands that accelerated American conquest of the continent and culminated in policies of the 1820s and 1830s that "removed" Native Americans from the area east of the Mississippi. The British also returned East Florida to Spain, and recognized West Florida as a Spanish possession. But Spain proved unable to defend its North American colonies against the expansionist policies of the United States and the incursions of Americans across the borders, especially in the Mississippi valley. As had been the case for over a century, Spain was unable to supply the trade goods needed to keep Indians in the southeast and southwest loyal to the Spanish authorities. Americans in Kentucky and Tennessee did so with ease. As Spain declined in power in Europe, its position in North America also declined. In 1790 it was forced to acknowledge British access to the northwest coast, in 1795 it accepted American claims to a significant part of West Florida, and in

1800 it turned over Louisiana to France. In 1803, France in turn sold the vast territory to the United States.

After 1783, the British were shorn of many of their Atlantic colonies, and they tightened control of the remaining ones in Canada and the West Indies. Within a decade, the effects of the War in North America would lead to an internal political crisis for the French monarchy with unpredicted consequences for continental politics, Atlantic diplomacy, and American colonies. The resulting generation of wars, fought both in Europe and in the Atlantic basin, not only forced imperial states to increase their exploitation of their colonies, but also created movements within those colonies that resisted that exploitation. Throughout the Atlantic, then, the end of the eighteenth and the beginning of the nineteenth century witnessed dramatic changes in the relationship between colony and metropole.

The French Caribbean islands

For France, the most immediate locus for colonial reorganization was in the Caribbean islands of Saint-Domingue, Guadeloupe, and Martinique, French possessions that were among the most important parts of what remained of the French empire after 1763. Plantation societies, these islands produced sugar and coffee for the metropole, making merchants in France and planters in the Caribbean prosperous and enslaving thousands of Africans who performed the labor of growing and processing the valuable commodities. Saint-Domingue in particular stood out as a remarkably profitable colony, with about 8,000 plantations in 1789 and numerous *sucreries*, or sugar processing plants, that produced about two-fifths of France's overseas trade (Illustration 3). Yet its planters suffered from the problems faced by many in the New World as the European powers instituted regimes – British Navigation Acts, the French *exclusif*, Spanish *Reglamentos* – that restricted trade between the colonies and Europe to benefit the colonial powers. Especially for those in the Caribbean dependent on trade, the restrictions imposed by the imperial governments created conflicts over the future organization of the empire. In the French Caribbean, relaxation of the *exclusif* during the War of American Independence increased trade between the French islands and the United States, but colonists increasingly saw their interests diverge from those of the government in Paris. The events of the last years of the eighteenth century are particularly confusing because of the shifting interests and factions of the different groups – *grands blancs*, *petits blancs*, *gens de couleur*, and slaves – who made up the islands' populations. Symptomatic of this,

Illustration 3 Caribbean sugar-processing plant, 1686.

even before news of the outbreak of revolution in France in the summer of 1789 reached the islands, a slave revolt broke out in Martinique in August 1789. This was the first of many that would follow on the three islands. The Revolutionary events in Paris that same summer weakened the ability of the colonial state to exert its authority on the other side of the Atlantic, raised the possibility of a greater voice in imperial affairs for *grands blancs*, and created the opportunity for changes in the status of people of color in the colonies. Proponents of the abolition of slavery maneuvered against the white colonists and their allies who wished to preserve the institution on which, they were convinced, the prosperity of France's most profitable colonies depended.

In the summer of 1789, assemblies were elected by whites in the islands, and a law on the colonies, passed on March 8, 1790 by the National Assembly in Paris, determined that the existing assemblies in each colony would express their opinion on the constitution, legislation, and administration to the National Assembly. Who would be allowed to vote for the members of these assemblies remained an issue, however, and in October of that year a revolt occurred in the North Province of Saint-Domingue, demanding for free colored voters the same "universal" rights proclaimed for all French citizens. This revolt was defeated by February, 1791, and its leader, Vincent Ogé, was brutally executed in Le Cap Français. But on May 15, 1791 the National Assembly granted political rights to some free people of color. The implementation of this law was resisted by whites in the colonies, creating tensions between *blancs* and *gens de couleur* that the administrators sent from France were unable to contain or resolve, and the Assembly reversed the law in September 1791. But in August 1791, two insurrections had broken out in Saint-Domingue. In the North Province, slaves on the plantations in the rural areas revolted, while in the West Province, a revolt of free people of color broke out.

The Saint-Domingue insurrections were the beginning of a decade of unrest on the island, as it became the centerpiece of French attempts to work out the implications of the rapidly changing Revolutionary movement in France on the complicated social and racial terrain of the Caribbean colonies. Events in Saint-Domingue do not seem to have been greatly inspired by the ideals of the Revolution, such as the Rights of Man proclaimed in August 1789, but the political fluctuations in Paris certainly affected the course of events by weakening central control of the empire and creating ambiguities about French policies, especially on slavery and the rights of *gens de couleur*. In a decree of April 4, 1792 the Legislative Assembly again gave extended political rights, this time to all free people of color. In April 1793 a slave insurrection

began in Guadeloupe even as the Convention sent new commissioners to Saint-Domingue to quell the ongoing revolts in the north and
west of that colony. Attempts by white colonists and some free people of color, supported by sailors from ships in the harbor, to reassert
their control over events led to a spectacular burning and destruction
of Le Cap Français, the principal port on the north coast of the colony,
on June 20, 1793. Ongoing insurrections and possible invasion by the
British and Spanish threatened the authority of the commissioner of
the Republic, Léger Félicité Sonthonax. He also faced almost certain
defeat by the rebels in Le Cap. In response to these dangers, on June 21,
1793, Sonthonax offered freedom to slaves who would fight in support
of the Republic.

Sonthonax's measure was a partial offer of emancipation, to be given
only to those male slaves who fought against the rebels in the North
Province. But it proved to be the first step towards general emancipation. With communications between Saint-Domingue and Paris difficult and time-consuming, Sonthonax and the other commissioner on
Saint-Domingue, Étienne Polverel, were unaware of the fall in May
1793 of their patron in Paris, the Girondist Jacques-Pierre Brissot.
But they undertook efforts to preserve the control of the island by the
Revolution's government and, in the late summer and fall of 1793, they
abolished slavery on the island. While they were soon recalled to Paris
to explain their conduct of affairs in Saint-Domingue, on February 4,
1794 (16 Pluviôse An II) the National Convention in Paris abolished
slavery in the entire French empire, although the decree was never
applied outside the Caribbean.

British troops invaded Saint-Domingue in September 1793 and
occupied Martinique and Guadeloupe the following spring. The
French regained control of Guadeloupe a few months later, and while
the British were never able to conquer Saint-Domingue, they did
not withdraw from that island until 1798. Their withdrawal did not
stop the fighting, for factions of free blacks and *gens de couleur* led by
Toussaint Louverture and André Rigaud began fighting one another
in the south of Saint-Domingue in July 1799. With France occupied by
European conflicts, a victorious Louverture became de facto ruler of
Saint-Domingue. In 1801, ignoring France, he wrote a new constitution that made him governor for life of the colony. In the same year soldiers mutinied in Guadeloupe against the French commander, Admiral
Jean-Baptiste Raymond de Lacrosse.

The waning of revolutionary radicalism in France, and the ascend-
ancy of Napoleon Bonaparte, led the metropolitan government to
seek to regain its profitable Caribbean colonies and reimpose slavery.

Because Martinique had been occupied by the British, the emancipation decrees of the first Republic had never been implemented there. A decree in 1802 (Floréal An X) restored the legality of slavery and the slave trade in French colonies, and when a French army regained control of Guadeloupe from the Republican military establishment in the summer of 1802, slavery was reintroduced into that colony. At the same time it was re-established in French Guiana. But on Saint-Domingue the attempt to reintroduce slavery sparked a revival of the alliance between blacks and *gens de couleur* that had dominated the island's politics in the early 1790s. In 1802 a French expedition led by General Charles-Victor-Emmanuel Leclerc arrived in Saint-Domingue to reassert French control and reimpose slavery. Louverture was captured and deported to France, where he died the following year. In Saint-Domingue, yellow fever devastated Leclerc's troops, and the rebellion forced the surrender of the French troops in November 1803. On January 1, 1804, Jean-Jacques Dessalines declared Saint-Domingue independent, giving it the original name used for the island by the indigenous peoples who had been there when the French and Spanish first came, Haiti. While it remained an outcast – slave societies in the Americas feared its influence on their own slaves, and France insisted on the payment of compensation to dispossessed plantation owners – Saint-Domingue became the first black regime outside Africa.

The impact of the French and Haitian Revolutions in the Caribbean basin is debated by historians. There is evidence from other parts of the Americas, such as Cuba, Colombia, and Louisiana, that word of the Haitian Revolution inspired discontent, unrest, and occasionally revolt by slaves. This news could pass by word of mouth in what was, after all, a seafaring world. In many slave societies there were veterans of the Haitian Revolution itself. The Revolution also created colonial refugees who, often with their slaves, moved from the French islands to Jamaica, Cuba, Venezuela, Puerto Rico, and North America and Europe. These refugees were often looked upon with distrust, but some of them helped spread sugar cultivation in Louisiana and Cuba, and coffee growing in Cuba, Jamaica, and Puerto Rico as well as word of the Revolution in Haiti.

More worrisome for colonial administrations were the black soldiers who participated in the many conflicts of the era, but then proved difficult to demobilize. The former slaves who had won victories in northern Saint-Domingue in 1791 and massacred white colonists in the course of the wars were a potential danger wherever they went. Many of them were eventually moved to Honduras, Campeche, Portobelo, and Florida, where they could continue to ply their military trade without posing a threat to existing colonial administrations. A small group who had fought for Spain and gone into exile in Honduras happened to go through Havana in 1811, hoping to return to Santo Domingo. They excited interest among the local black population, and when three months later the Aponte revolt broke out on a nearby sugar estate, the Spanish authorities were convinced there was a connection. But none was proved, and the exiles soon continued on to Santo Domingo.

The migrants certainly carried with them the stories of victorious slaves and the independence of Haiti, and there seems little doubt that slaves from the American South to Brazil and on the Caribbean islands were aware of events in Haiti. In spite of the fear the events inspired among white planters elsewhere in the Caribbean and the American south, there is no clear evidence that they incited slave revolts in those places. Nonetheless, it was hardly a period in which slaveholders could rest comfortably: the period from 1789 into the middle third of the nineteenth century was marked by numerous uprisings and conspiracies on the shores of the Caribbean. David Geggus has counted 62 in the period from 1789 to 1815, from the 1789 uprising of 300–400 slaves in the Saint-Pierre district of Martinique to multiple others in Cuba, Guadeloupe, Venezuela, Tortola, Saint Lucia, Dominica, Saint-Domingue, Louisiana, Marie-Galante, Trinidad, the Bahamas, Puerto Rico, Curaçao, Demerara, New Granada, and Tobago. Jamaicans should have seen nothing unusual in the conspiracy of 250 slaves uncovered in Saint Elizabeth in 1815: a place where slave revolts were endemic, the island had, by one calculation, a riot or revolt against slavery on average once every five years during the eighteenth century.[10] We can add as well the revolts on Barbados in 1816, in Demerara (British Guyana) in 1823, and on Jamaica in 1831–32. The links between these uprisings and the events in Haiti are uncertain, and even more problematic is the impact of the events and rhetoric in France during the Revolutionary decade. The Haitian Revolution may have been more "the stuff of nightmares in the mansions and government

---

[10] David Patrick Geggus, "Slavery, War, and Revolution in the Greater Caribbean: A Triumph or a Failure?" in David Barry Gaspar and David Patrick Geggus (eds.), *A Turbulent Time: The French Revolution and the Greater Caribbean* (Bloomington: Indiana University Press, 1997), 46–49; Yves Bénot, "The Chain of Slave Insurrections in the Caribbean, 1789–1791," in Marcel Dorigny (ed.), *The Abolitions of Slavery from L.F. Sonthonax to Victor Schoelcher, 1793, 1794, 1848* (New York: Berghahn Books, 2003), 147–54; Gad Heuman, *"The Killing Time": The Morant Bay Rebellion in Jamaica* (Knoxville: University of Tennessee Press, 1994), 34; Mary Turner, "The Jamaica Slave Rebellion of 1831," *Past and Present* 40 (1968), 108.

palaces" of the Americas than a real threat.[11] It is clear, however, that the imperial hold on the Caribbean islands was at best tenuous as the eighteenth century turned into the nineteenth. If not threatened by settlers asserting their own interests, as in the United States, it was endangered by the slaves who made up the colonial labor force.

Spanish America

As further north, the Spanish colonies in New Spain, New Granada, and Peru saw their relationship to the metropole change in the course of the eighteenth century. A stagnant Spanish economy and the demands of European warfare led to domestic reforms and efforts to increase the contribution to the Spanish budget by its colonies in the New World. Reformers such as José de Campillo y Cosió had since the middle of the eighteenth century lamented that "the Indies [were] stepmothers of the Crown when they could be the basis of its grandeur."[12] Taking a cue from these reformers, royal policies, especially during the reign of Carlos III (r. 1759–88), sought to increase trade between Spain and its colonies. These policies were intended to raise tax revenues and, by stimulating the growth in Spain of small-scale domestic manufacturing, replace the British and French goods that had been reshipped through Cadiz to the colonies (and that cost Spain precious silver) by Spanish woolen, silk, linen, and cotton goods. Wine and brandy from Andalusia and Catalonia, it was hoped, would also be shipped across the Atlantic to meet the tastes of the colonies. Sugar, tobacco, hides, cochineal, and indigo would come to Spain from the colonies to be resold in northern Europe. Reformers also hoped that these changes taken together would end the rampant smuggling of cheaper European manufactured goods that drained silver out of New Spain.

Habsburg and Bourbon mercantilist policies had limited trade to a controlled fleet sailing between Seville or Cadiz and Veracruz. But *Reglamentos* in 1765, 1778, and 1789 gradually opened more ports in Spain and the colonies to trade. These reforms were not necessarily a movement from the long-standing mercantilist policies of the Spanish empire towards free trade: rather, as Gabriel Paquette has recently argued, the reformers intended to strengthen the trading links within

---

[11] Joáo José Reis and Flávio dos Santos Gomes, "Repercussions of the Haitian Revolution in Brazil, 1791–1850," in David Patrick Geggus and Norman Fiering, eds., *The World of the Haitian Revolution* (Bloomington: Indiana University Press, 2009), 293.

[12] Quoted in Stanley J. Stein and Barbara H. Stein, *Silver, Trade, and War: Spain and America in the Making of Early Modern Europe* (Baltimore, MD: Johns Hopkins University Press, 2000), 211.

the empire while still keeping out traders from other nations and expanding the revenues of the Spanish Crown.[13] While trade increased until 1785, domestic industry never developed sufficiently to replace goods from other European countries. Silver from New Spain – mined by slaves in the area north of Mexico City from Guanajuato to Zacatecas and from Guadalajara to San Luís Potosí and then minted in Mexico City – was an increasingly crucial part of the finances of the Spanish state as it became involved in European wars, and it never completely relinquished its mercantilist control of the colonies. Rather, these fiscal policies were accompanied by tighter links between the metropole and colonies. New administrative units and officials undercut the role and influence of local oligarchies in the colonies. A major step in this process was the Ordinance of Intendants, which built on earlier reforms in Cuba and was promulgated in Peru in 1784 and in Mexico in 1786. This Ordinance abolished *repartimientos* and put new officials, the intendants, in the place of *corregidores* and *alcaldes mayores*. Administrative reformers also went after the power of the Catholic Church through the 1767 expulsion of the Jesuits, expropriation of the property of the order, and reforms that limited clerical immunity. Finally, the militia system that had developed in the colonies, creating a trained armed force primarily composed of and officered by *mestizos* and creoles, was reduced in importance and the regular army took over defense of the colonies. With army and militia officers increasingly Spaniards, the avenues of upward mobility for creoles were significantly reduced.

The administrative reforms had unintended consequences: what was enlightened rationalization in Spanish eyes threatened local interests in Spanish America, and alienated the local elite that had for centuries controlled the colonies. The increased fiscal pressures that came with the reforms generated conflict in both urban and rural communities. The attacks on the position of the Catholic Church spurred opposition from the clergy, especially the lower clergy, whose immunity was their only valuable asset. The militia reforms generated less opposition, not least because of the hardships of a military career, but they did teach the lesson that access to civilian and military office was becoming restricted to *peninsulares*, and that enlightened reform seemed to mean reducing creole influence in colonial government.

Opposition to the Bourbon attempt to tighten its rule sparked not only conflict but protest and revolt as well. Both forced labor and *repartimientos* proved difficult to abolish and continued to be a cause of unrest

[13] Gabriel Paquette, *Enlightenment, Governance, and Reform in Spain and its Empire, 1759–1808* (New York: Palgrave Macmillan, 2008), 93–126.

among Indians. The spread of hacienda agriculture, combined with population growth, created conflicts in many places between landowners and peasants over land, and the late eighteenth-century attempts by the colonial administration to extract resources more efficiently created grievances over taxes and their collection. Forced labor drafts and poor treatment of laborers did the same. Indian communities opposed the erosion of customary rights and especially the spread of hacienda lands at the expense of the holdings of those Indian communities. The *repartimiento de comercio* – the forced distribution of European goods to indigenous communities – had long been controversial in New Spain, and its spread and legalization in the Andes after 1751 generated widespread unrest among the creoles in the colonial elite and contributed to a growing climate of opposition to the colonial state. In frontier areas, such as the Rio de la Plata borderlands, royal policies in the 1770s and 1780s that encouraged settlement and the foundation of new towns and parishes undercut the local political and economic positions of absentee owners of large cattle ranches in favor of new settlers. Indigenous peoples who moved away from the missions along the Brazilian border also competed for land in the area. These conflicts created shifting alliances that the royal administration found difficult to control.[14]

The second half of the eighteenth century also was a period of popular unrest in much of Spanish America. In Mexico, local riots increased in frequency in the 1760s and continued in an almost unbroken upward curve, peaking in the period from 1806 to 1810.[15] The Andes, in contrast, experienced major revolts. In January 1780 there were a series of anti-fiscal protests, in Arequipa, Huaráz, Cerro de Pasco, La Paz, and Cochabamba, as well as other disturbances. The 1780s saw the revolt of the Comuneros in Colombia and three major rebellions in the Andes between 1780 and 1783, led by Tomás Katari, Tupac Amaru II, and Julián Apasa-Tupac Katari. These revolts were harshly repressed, but this did not end the ongoing insurgency. Everyday forms of resistance, such as refusals by Indians to provide labor service and verbal and physical abuse of officials, occurred as well throughout Spanish America. Riots against priests and Spanish officials occurred in rural Mexico. The invocation of a better past before the Spanish came, a feature of the Tupac Amaru II revolt, proved a powerful way of mobilizing Indians.

---

[14] Julio Djenderedjian, "Roots of Revolution: Frontier Settlement Policy and the Emergence of New Spaces of Power in the Río de la Plata Borderlands, 1770–1810," *Hispanic American Historical Review* 88, 4 (2008), 639–68.

[15] Eric Van Young, *The Other Rebellion: Popular Violence, Ideology, and the Mexican Struggle for Independence, 1810–1821* (Stanford University Press, 2001), 386.

Discontent by the colonial elites was therefore compounded by local conflicts that created popular discontent among poorer city-dwellers and farmers. Initially, neither those popular classes nor the creole elite envisioned independence from Spain. The Indians, free blacks, and slaves who made up the greater part of the rebels in central Mexico after 1810 were engaged, in Eric Van Young's words, in a prolonged process of cultural resistance, and "popular and elite rebel groups ... were engaged in a dialogue of the deaf in which there was considerable noise but little exchange of information." Jeremy Adelman has similarly argued that even among the creole elites, the intention until after 1815 was not independence from Spain but a restructured relationship that would protect them from popular discontent, give them a greater say in imperial affairs and protect their commercial interests. Independence movements, in that formulation, came about *"because* not *before* the Spanish empire imploded."[16]

The crisis of imperial power came, after so many opening chapters, with the French invasion of Spain in 1807. In May 1808 Napoleon forced the last Bourbons, Charles IV and Ferdinand VII, to abdicate, and placed his brother Joseph on the throne of Spain. Joseph's accession sparked a revolt organized not by the Spanish government, or what was left of it, but by provincial juntas and, in November 1808, a central junta was formed that claimed to speak for the deposed Bourbon king. The political crisis in Spain increased efforts to use the American colonies to support the Spanish government. For the creole elites of Spanish America, though, the events in the peninsula brought to a head the question of their relationship to the metropolitan center.

During the first decade of the nineteenth century the combination of popular insurgencies, creole discontent, and imperial disarray turned into major challenges to Spanish rule. This extended colonial crisis began in the viceroyalty of New Spain, where creoles and white elites were tied to Mexico by birth, property ownership, and residence. In 1810, wealthy creoles in the rich agricultural area of Querétaro launched a conspiracy against the viceregal government in Mexico City. A priest, Miguel Hidalgo y Costilla, emerged as the leader of the conspiracy. He was joined by a coalition of Indians, blacks, *mestizos*, and those of Spanish descent in an uprising that quickly spread through the intendancy of Guanajuato. But, as in the past, attacks on whites in Guanajuato convinced creoles that the revolt was an Indian revolt against whites, and it lost support from the propertied elite. By November the tide

---

[16] Van Young, *Other Rebellion*, 496, 493; Jeremy Adelman, *Sovereignty and Revolution in the Iberian Atlantic* (Princeton University Press, 2006), 219.

turned and in January 1811 the rebels were defeated at the Bridge of Calderón outside Guadalajara. Hidalgo and his chief lieutenants were captured in March, and he was shot on July 30. With the execution of Hidalgo, the leadership of the movement passed to another priest, José María Morelos, but he himself was captured and eventually executed on December 22, 1815.

The Spanish territories further south had also seen unrest since the revolts of the early 1780s. By 1810 creole juntas had been established in virtually all parts of Spanish South America, professing not only reformist aims similar to the Spanish government, but also a desire for autonomy within the empire and loyalty to the deposed king, Ferdinand VII. Those juntas rapidly collapsed in the face of internal dissension and the reassertion of authority by Spanish officials. But the restoration in 1814 of Ferdinand VII as King of Spain, and his clumsy attempts to reimpose rule from Madrid on Spanish America, proved to be the catalyst that changed discontent into movements for independence. Ferdinand instituted policies that aimed at restoring the older relationship between Spain and its American colonies, reversing Carlist trade reforms and restoring the mercantilist Spanish monopoly of trade with the New World. Coalitions of creoles, Indians, *mestizos*, and African slaves formed, collapsed, and reformed in different parts of Spanish America, forcing Ferdinand's government to use force, incur expenses, and increase the need for revenues from the American colonies.

A new revolution in Spain, in early 1820, voiced liberal demands for reform in Spain and provided the opportunity for a resurgence of dissent in Spanish America. On February 24, 1821, the commander of the royalist army in Mexico, Agustín de Iturbide, published the Plan of Iguala in conjunction with the rebel leader Vicente Guerrero. It proposed that New Spain become a separate monarchy, that a Mexican Cortes be called, and a provisional sovereign junta and then a regency be established to govern. It also gave what were called the three guarantees: continuation of the Catholic Church, independence from Spanish control, and union of Spaniards and Americans. This plan provided the basis for a broad alliance of the Mexican elite against Spanish control. In its face, the viceregal regime lasted only seven months, and on August 24, 1821, Iturbide and the new captain-general appointed by the Cortes in Spain, Juan O'Donojú, signed the Treaty of Cordoba in which O'Donojú recognized the independence of Mexico and undertook to induce the remaining royal forces in Mexico City to surrender. This occurred on September 13, and on September 27 Iturbide entered Mexico City as the head of the new government.

In other parts of Spanish America, the revolt of 1820 in Spain and the reforms of the new liberal government also reawakened hopes for reforms that brought liberals into conflict with supporters of the colonial government. Political compromises similar to those in the Plan of Iguala led Yucatán to join the new Mexican empire, and Guatemala, San Salvador, Nicaragua, Costa Rica and Honduras did so as well in late 1821. This attempt to incorporate these territories into a Mexican empire, however, itself collapsed in early 1823. In the Andes, already the site of major revolts in the 1780s, a series of revolts showed continued indigenous alienation from the colonial regime. The Pumacahua uprising occurred in 1813, and an uprising of creoles and royalists in Cuzco in 1814 was joined in 1815 by an indigenous uprising in Ocongate in the province of Quispicanchis. By 1826, these movements had ended Spanish rule. Although the crisis had initially been about reformulating the colonial relationship, by the mid 1820s a series of independent republics had replaced the provinces of the Spanish empire, and only Cuba and Puerto Rico were still controlled by Madrid.

The unrest of the early nineteenth century had a powerful effect on the society of Spanish America, and especially on the people of color who made up the majority of the population. Slaves and especially free blacks were among the most important participants in the process of winning independence for Spanish America. On the mainland by the end of the eighteenth century, most people of African descent were not slaves, but free, and most had been born free.[17] Others were former slaves who had acquired their freedom by manumission. But all of these people of color suffered from the inequities of the caste system, a collection of decrees dating from the seventeenth century that confirmed and enforced their subordinate position. The outcome of the wars of independence depended heavily on which side free black troops fought, and so one important result of the wars was the end of the caste system. The wars also affected slaves in the region, reducing owners' control over them and making it easier for slaves to flee from their owners. The need for popular support led to promises of freedom in exchange for military service, which many slaves took up. In the long run, the price of slave participation in the wars was gradual emancipation, usually in the form of "Free Womb Laws" by which the children of slave mothers were born free. Enacted in Chile in 1811, Argentina in 1813, Colombia,

---

[17] George Reid Andrews, *Afro-Latin America, 1800–2000* (Oxford University Press, 2004).

Ecuador, Peru, and Venezuela in 1821, and Uruguay in 1825, these laws set Spanish America on the course towards the abolition of slavery.

Portugal and Brazil

The late eighteenth and early nineteenth centuries also saw a restructuring of the relationship between the imperial metropole in Portugal and its colony in Brazil. Eventually, in the early nineteenth century, this led to an independent Brazil, but the process was different from those in British North America or Spanish America. As in other Atlantic empires, the growing fiscal demands of Great-Power competition led the government in Lisbon to ratchet up its efforts to control its huge South American colony as a part of the efforts by Jose I (r. 1750–77) to create a more effective state in which the colonies would provide more income as well as enhanced markets for metropolitan products. The program to increase royal power began with a campaign against the Jesuits and then other Catholic religious orders, a policy pushed by the dominant royal minister, Sebastião José de Carvalho e Melo, later the marquês de Pombal. Accusations that corrupt Jesuits in both Portugal and Brazil were undercutting royal authority and fomenting rebellion culminated in the expulsion of the order in 1759 and the confiscation of all of its properties. Royal moves against other religious orders followed, and the Catholic Church, which had been a dangerous rival for power to the monarch, was relegated to a position of social and political impotence. In the contested borderlands in the interior of South America between Brazil and the colonies of Spain, the expulsion of Jesuits from schools led to their replacement by secularizing directors who instituted new policies that prohibited the use of indigenous languages and imposed the Portuguese language on Indian children.

The following decades were marked by economic stagnation, especially in the relatively inaccessible interior of Portugal, and some recovery in the agricultural regions along its coast. Portugal had adhered to a mercantilistic approach to its South American colony, but Pombal had served earlier in his career as ambassador to Great Britain and had been impressed by the economic growth he had seen there. To achieve similar growth, he encouraged merchants in Lisbon to serve as middlemen in the trade between Brazil and European countries, especially Great Britain. He intended, he wrote in 1755, "to restore to the market places of Portugal and Brazil the commissions of which they are deprived [by foreign competition], and which are the principal substance of commerce, and the means by which there could be established the great merchant houses which had been lacking in Portugal."[18] To some extent, these policies succeeded before the 1770s because of the influx of gold from Minas Gerais into Portugal, which allowed Portugal to pay for imported goods from Britain. But one outcome of these economic trends was that Portugal ran a negative balance of trade with some regions of Brazil. British and other countries' ships openly flouted the metropolitan trade monopoly, and the purchase of commodities such as sugar, coffee, and wheat by Portugal from Brazil drained the metropole of funds. It became more difficult to pay for British imports when gold production slumped in the 1770s, and the situation worsened as Brazilian sugar producers faced competition from French and British plantations in the Caribbean.

As with British North America, these events of the late eighteenth century called into question the structure of the relationship between Portugal and its South American colony. In 1788–89 attempts by the colonial secretary, Martinho de Melo e Castro, to collect duties due the Crown precipitated an unsuccessful conspiracy in Minas to establish a Mineiro republic. In 1794 another conspiracy seemed to surface in Rio de Janeiro in the form of discussions of public issues, but while a dozen people were arrested, no conspiracy was proved and they were released after a few years in prison. In 1798, posters on the walls of Bahia called for the overthrow of metropolitan power and the establishment of a French-style republic. A strong response from the authorities led to the arrest of forty-nine persons, most of them free mulattos. Eventually, four were executed, while others were whipped and banished to other parts of the empire. Still others were imprisoned.

These conspiracies certainly reflected discontent with aspects of the relationship between Brazil and Portugal. The Bahia conspiracy must have looked at lot like the events that had occurred in the 1790s in Saint-Domingue, especially given the high proportion of mulattos and blacks in the Bahia population. Yet Portuguese colonial rule, while it was tightened in the late eighteenth century, remained less stringent than in other parts of the Atlantic world. While the colonial economy continued to be controlled by mercantilist policies that made Brazilian exports go through Portuguese ports, trade was liberalized and there were some efforts to increase exports from Brazil. The government in Lisbon also recognized the importance of slavery for significant parts of the Brazilian agricultural economy and the interests of planters in maintaining their supply of slaves. Because of these concerns, it

---

[18] Quoted in Kenneth R. Maxwell, *Pombal, Paradox of the Enlightenment* (Cambridge University Press, 1995), 60.

allowed the slave trade to Rio de Janeiro and Brazil to prosper even as other European countries were agreeing to end it, and this remained a linchpin of Portuguese colonial policy. Output of those products most dependent on slave labor – sugar, coffee, and cotton – increased most rapidly in Brazil in the years between the end of the Napoleonic Wars in 1815 and Brazilian abolition of the slave trade in 1850.[19]

The events in the Iberian peninsula sparked by the Napoleonic invasion in 1807–8 proved to be decisive in stimulating changes in the relationship between Portugal and its South American colony. The French emperor was seeking to end British resistance to his dominance of the continent by imposing a trade boycott on British goods, the Continental System. Napoleon ordered Portugal to close its ports to British ships, imprison British residents in Portugal, and confiscate their property. George Canning, the British foreign minister, pressured the regent, Dom João, to resist French demands, offering British protection if it became necessary for the royal family to leave Portugal for the safe haven of Brazil.

When Dom João failed to conform to the French demands, Napoleon sent a French army into Portugal. When that army entered the country in mid November 1807, Dom João made the decision to move his government across the Atlantic. On November 29, just a day before the French entered Lisbon, the royal family, the council of state and royal ministers, officials of the courts, treasury, army, navy, and church, thousands of aristocrats, functionaries, and assorted courtiers, along with the royal treasury, government files, a printing press, and the contents of several libraries, boarded a fleet, sailed down the Tagus, and, escorted by four British warships, headed to Bahia. What one historian called "an event unique in the history of European colonialism" – an entire imperial government moving to one of its colonies – ended on March 7, 1808, when they were greeted warmly in Rio de Janeiro by the local population.[20]

The "metropolitanization" of Brazil had profound effects on the relationship between Lisbon and Brazil, and within Brazil itself, and set the colony on a path towards greater autonomy and eventual independence. Administrative reforms tried to increase control from Rio over the different subregions of the huge colony. The protection given by Great Britain, a government committed to free trade, led to trade concessions

---

[19] David Eltis, *Economic Growth and the Ending of the Transatlantic Slave Trade* (New York: Oxford University Press, 1987), 194–95.

[20] Leslie Bethell, "The Independence of Brazil," in Bethell (ed.), *The Cambridge History of Latin America*, vol. III, *From Independence to c. 1870* (Cambridge University Press, 1985), 170.

that ended the centuries-old monopoly that Portuguese ports enjoyed on trade in and out of Brazil, thus eliminating one of the long-standing grievances of Brazilian landowners and merchants yet also spelling the end of the old colonial system. Some preferences remained for Portuguese shipping, but the increased identification of interests between the ruling government and the colony in which it was now located led to significant reforms. Dom João also revoked decrees prohibiting manufacturing, encouraged the introduction of new machinery in Brazilian shops, and gave subsidies to some industries. The close links between the Brazilian economy and the slave trade made Dom João refuse British demands for its abolition, but he did agree to forbid Portuguese slave traders to replace the British merchants that the British policy of abolition removed. The end of the Napoleonic Wars in 1815 opened the possibility of a return to Lisbon of the Portuguese government, but Dom João decided to remain in Brazil. On December 16, 1815, Brazil was raised to a status equal to Portugal, creating a dual monarchy dominated, in practice, by Brazil. Dom João finally succeeded to the throne in early 1816 upon the death of his mother, and as king he remained in the colony for the next five years.

The end of the Napoleonic Wars and the return of Portuguese freedom of movement in domestic and foreign policy led Brazilians to fear a reversion to colonial status and revival of the long-standing mercantilist favoritism of Portuguese interests. Continued British pressure to end the slave trade, viewed as vital to their interests by Brazilian plantation owners, also created tension between the king and his Brazilian subjects. But these concerns should not be seen as precursors of a movement for independence. Rather, it was the revival of the reform movement in Portugal in August 1820 and the subsequent election of a Cortes that was to write a liberal constitution for Portugal that pushed Brazil in that direction. The king faced the prospect of losing his European kingdom if he remained in Brazil, and on April 26, 1820 he, about 4,000 Portuguese, the royal jewels, the contents of the treasury, and the funds of the Banco do Brasil set sail for Lisbon. The Cortes met in January 1821, and while it was intended to include 45 representatives from Brazil as well as 100 from Portugal itself, the Brazilian deputies arrived too late to have a significant role in any decisions. As they feared, the Cortes attempted to abrogate the trade agreements that had opened up direct trade between Britain and Brazil, sought to deal directly with provincial governments in Brazil without going through Rio, and sent troop reinforcements across the Atlantic. On September 29 it ordered all royal institutions in Rio back to Lisbon. In the following weeks other changes were enacted that gave Lisbon control over

Rio, and on October 18 the Cortes ordered the prince regent in Rio, João's son Dom Pedro, to return to Lisbon.

The decrees of the Cortes were indicators that the government in Portugal intended to return the relationship between Lisbon and Rio to the pre-1808 colonial status, and when news of them arrived in Brazil in December 1821, it brought together an unlikely coalition of Portuguese-born with interests in Brazil, conservatives and moderate liberals, and extreme liberals and radicals against the reassertion of Portuguese control. Dom Pedro was persuaded to stay in Brazil, a decision he announced on January 9, 1822, and Portuguese troops who would not swear allegiance to him were forced to leave by those who did so. José Bonifácio de Andrada e Silva, a Brazilian, was appointed head of a new cabinet, and over the next year he and Dom Pedro consolidated royal power against radicals in the center and south while working to prevent dismemberment of the country. When Dom Pedro received dispatches from Lisbon emphasizing the subordination of Brazil to Lisbon, he declared Brazil separate from Portugal. On October 12, 1822 he was proclaimed Constitutional Emperor and Perpetual Defender of Brazil.

While the Brazilian story was perhaps unique in its specific details, it forms a part of the larger narrative of the end of European empires in the Americas. An account that focuses on relations between metropolitan and colonial governments, elites, and economies, and that views them fundamentally as national revolutions against the imperial center oversimplifies what happened in Brazil and elsewhere. These were not revolutions seeking an inevitable independence. Rather, in every case, there were complicated coalitions of people of indigenous, European, African, and *mestizo* origin and descent who either worked to maintain the colonial relationship or, in the process of reinventing it, created a series of newly independent nations. From the metropolitan side, there were similar efforts to change the way that relationship was structured so that the colonies would better support the ambitions of the imperial state.

The continuities of Atlantic empire

Even as many places in the Atlantic basin in the early nineteenth century saw the end of the colonial relationship with European powers, that relationship remained intact for significant parts of the Americas. It was, however, often altered by the events of the revolutionary era. In North America, while some in the newly independent United States wished to annex the vast and unexplored territories to the north of the thirteen colonies, they proved unable to do so and the colonial relationship between Great Britain and Canada continued in a reformulated way after 1783. In the Caribbean colonies, the events of the late eighteenth and early nineteenth centuries shed new light on the colonial relationship, leading in some respects to closer links between colonies and metropoles.

The collection of British territories in British North America after the conquest of 1763 brought few economic advantages and many difficult issues to the British government. Even after the loss of the thirteen American colonies British North America was not a single, unified territory, but consisted of very different places with different interests and relationships to Britain. Newfoundland, which remained largely separate from the rest of British North America, was viewed not as a colony but as a seasonal fishing station, and it took until well into the nineteenth century for the authorities in London to recognize that it had permanent residents. The Maritime territories of Nova Scotia, New Brunswick (created out of Nova Scotia), Prince Edward Island, and Cape Breton Island were most closely associated with New England, the source of many of their residents, rather than the St. Lawrence valley core of British North America.

The constitutional position in the British empire of British North America was complicated by the presence of the francophone *Canadiens* in the St. Lawrence valley. The Quebec Act of 1774 created a special set of circumstances in the province that was renamed Canada. French civil law was to be used, but English criminal law would be employed. There would be no assembly that might be dominated by potentially disloyal *Canadiens*, but they were guaranteed the free exercise of their Roman Catholic faith. Much to the relief of the British government, Canada did not join the thirteen colonies in their rebellion against the British Crown, and in a 1791 Constitutional Act Canada was divided into two territories. The francophone territory along the St. Lawrence valley, called Lower Canada, continued to exist under the terms of the Quebec Act, but was now given an assembly. Further west, north of the Great Lakes, the territory of Upper Canada was created, dominated by the growing number of anglophone immigrants who were moving towards and past the Canadian Shield.

It was in the west, around the Great Lakes, that the most important fighting took place during the War of 1812 with the United States. That war began in part over the refusal of Great Britain to recognize the possibility for British-born subjects to be naturalized as citizens of the new United States. The British position – that individuals born subjects of the king remained so for the rest of their lives – became a very practical issue during the Wars of the French Revolution and Empire, as the

British empire fought against French aims it perceived as European and global domination. The Royal Navy was the most important British weapon in this struggle, and the inability of the British Isles themselves to provide adequate numbers of sailors for the navy led to the practice of impressment by British ships of sailors on neutral ships – often American – who were, or appeared to be, British by birth. The argument of the United States and those American sailors that they had been naturalized as citizens of the United States was summarily rejected by the British. As the war was fought along the border between the United States and British North America between 1812 and 1814, it took on another dimension in the form of American militia who had emigrated to northern New York, Michigan, and Ohio from British North America but who were captured by the British and tried (and sometimes executed) as deserters from British forces.

By 1814 both the United States and the British were anxious to end the War of 1812, and the issues of national identity and impressment were passed over in the peace negotiations leading to the Treaty of Ghent. The end of the Napoleonic Wars reduced the British navy's need for sailors, ending impressment on the Atlantic, and British claims about naturalized American citizens were no longer pressed. Only as an issue in Canadian politics, through attempts by conservatives in Canada to restrict the vote for the Legislative Council to native-born British subjects, did questions about national identity continue. A decision by the Court of King's Bench in 1824 seemed to disenfranchise those residents of Upper Canada who had emigrated from the United States after 1783 (so-called Late Loyalists) by ruling that the treaty of 1783 that recognized American independence also made aliens of all Americans and their descendants. The legal controversy was resolved in 1827 by a law mandated by the British government that conceded that anyone who moved to Upper Canada after 1820, took an oath of allegiance, received a land grant, or held office in the colony was a British subject, and that allowed naturalization of later immigrants after seven years' residence.[21]

With the focus on Upper and Lower Canada, Newfoundland and the Maritime provinces were governed largely by default by the British for much of the nineteenth century. But the process of moving west away from the St. Lawrence had begun in 1811 with the grant of a large tract

[21] Alan Taylor, *The Civil War of 1812: American Citizens, British Subjects, Irish Rebels, and Indian Allies* (New York: Random House, 2010), 443–53; David Mills, *The Idea of Loyalty in Upper Canada, 1784–1850* (Kingston: McGill-Queen's University Press, 1988), 36–44.

of Hudson's Bay Company land to Thomas Douglas, the 5th Earl of Selkirk. Selkirk established the Red River Colony of Assiniboia (near the eventual site of Winnipeg). There were few mineral discoveries in the Canadian west that might have attracted permanent settlers, and for the most part this westward expansion consisted of a sparse population cultivating poor agricultural land. The new provinces did, however, produce leaders who sought greater autonomy within the framework of the British empire. Following rebellions in both Lower and Upper Canada in 1837–38, the British Parliament slowly moved towards this goal. What was called Responsible Government was granted in the 1840s, with an assembly and ministers now sharing in day-to-day governance with the governor-general appointed by London. In 1867 the Confederation was established, tying together, even if ever-so-slightly, the provinces from Newfoundland to British Columbia and making it possible to construct the trans-Canadian railway. Confederation also transferred significant powers to the Confederation government located in Ottawa, even while protecting the Catholic identity of Lower Canada (renamed Quebec).

If Canadian statesmen in 1914 could declare that the Union Jack would fly over Canada forever, there are, however, some weak points in this narrative focused on imperial relations and political institutions. The anglophone parts of the Confederation were marked by substantial immigration from Great Britain, in fact becoming more British. Native-born Canadian anglophones had difficulty making any kind of political, economic, social, or cultural mark where it really mattered to them, the imperial center in London, and so they also experienced a sense of second-class imperial citizenship. In the St. Lawrence, the most obvious and immediate problem was absorbing the 70,000 *Canadiens*, the Catholic, francophone residents of what had been New France, into the British, Protestant empire. French Canadians more accommodated themselves to anglophone rule than accepted it, and the twentieth-century revival of Québecois nationalism underscores the resilience of francophone culture. The growing number of immigrants that came into British North America in the nineteenth century made the population less and less native-born, but those immigrants brought with them their own culture, religion, and expectations. Increased female migration that balanced the sex ratio as well as the shift from the St. Lawrence settlements to the agricultural frontiers of the nineteenth century raised questions about the contributions made by women to the colonial enterprise and about constructions of masculinity and femininity. The complex roles of women both in the urban centers of the St. Lawrence valley and on the pioneer farms of the western plains have become apparent, not only in terms of their significant contributions to agricultural and industrial work but also as a focal point for the project of "civilizing" the frontier and immigrant populations. The fur trade, under a consolidated Hudson's Bay Company after 1821, continued to bring together white fur traders and Native families well into the nineteenth century. But the effects of western settlement during the nineteenth century on the native peoples of the region have also become clear: with few resources to support them, there were few Indian wars in the vast territory north of the American border, but the extinguishing of native title by legislation passed in 1871–77 proved disastrous for Canadian First Nations.

In the Caribbean colonies of France, Spain, and Great Britain, changing views about slavery and the slave trade made the first half of the nineteenth century a challenging time for colonists. Slavery had been reintroduced and confirmed by Napoleon in Guadeloupe, Martinique, and French Guiana, and in the first years after the Congress of Vienna planters were able to restock the slave labor force on their plantations. But sugar exports failed to return to Old Regime profits and the French islands stagnated. They remained French possessions, however, and in 1946 they became *Départements d'Outre-Mer*, with the same status as metropolitan *départements*.

The French sugar islands faced increased competition from Brazil and, in the nineteenth century, Cuba. That island had been a relatively unimportant part of the Spanish empire in the New World until the middle of the eighteenth century. Much of it was uninhabited, and its importance came as a collecting point for the fleets that crossed the Atlantic with the gold and silver of Mexico and other parts of Hispanic America. The island was dominated by a small number of *criollo* families who spent most of the year in Havana, Santiago, or Trinidad, but depended economically on the earnings of their plantations or ranches. The importance of urban life distinguished eighteenth-century Cuba from all other places in the Caribbean or Latin America. In contrast to Saint-Domingue or Jamaica, sugar plantations were smaller and fewer, and so there were few slaves on the island. It was also easier than in British or French colonies for slaves in Cuba to purchase their freedom, and the frequent practice among Cuban slaveholders of freeing slaves on their deathbeds meant that there were large numbers of freed slaves or mulattos, especially in the cities.

The second half of the eighteenth century, however, saw stunning changes in Cuban life. The Carlist reforms increased freedom of trade between colonies such as Cuba and other countries, and Havana became a more important port. Agricultural production, especially in the area around Havana, increased. Demand for Cuban sugar, molasses, tobacco, and coffee increased in Spain, and landholders on the island expanded plantation agriculture. Sugar exports from the island tripled between the 1770s and the early 1790s. The disruption of sugar production in Saint-Domingue during the French Revolution opened other markets to Cuban sugar, and importation of slaves from Africa increased dramatically, especially after the 1790s. In thirty years, Cuba imported over 300,000 slaves, transforming Cuba into a plantation society based on slave labor. But at the same time as the racial identities of this plantation society became the basis for inclusion of whites and exclusion of blacks, the older Cuban society that ensured the positions of free blacks remained in place.

As in other parts of Spanish America, the events of the last decades of the eighteenth century changed the relationship between Spain and Cuba. But with the example of Haiti in mind Cuban planters were fearful of the spread of revolutionary ideas to their own plantations. Having lost much of its empire in the Americas by the time of Waterloo in 1815, Spain was determined to keep the islands of Cuba and Puerto Rico, and so it maintained a strong military and police presence aimed at preventing any kind of radical political movements. Spain also resisted British attempts to impose an end to the slave trade, and it continued into the 1860s. While some planters sought more protection in the arms of the slaveholding nation to the north, the United States never fully embraced the idea, and offers by the United States to purchase the island in 1848 and 1854 were rejected by the government in Madrid.

Sugar and slavery made Cuba one of the richest colonies in the world in the first half of the nineteenth century. By the 1860s its ports were bustling with ships that took Cuban commodities to markets throughout the Atlantic basin. As early as the 1820s half of its sugar crop was sold to the United States, and by the 1860s the island was producing one quarter of the world's sugar crop. Coffee and tobacco had also become major export crops. This prosperity was, of course, unevenly shared: the wealth of the planters was the result of the labor of large numbers of slaves. With the end of slavery in the United States during the Civil War, the possibility of annexation and statehood for Cuba faded. It also convinced many of those Cubans who had favored annexation that the slave trade would soon be ended, as it indeed was in 1867. They therefore sought to gain greater control over their affairs through reforms similar to those being demanded by liberals in Spain at the time, including a constitutional assembly, reduced power for the captain-general, and greater power for municipal councils. A coup d'état in Madrid ended the prospect of liberal reforms, however, and the idea of separation from Spain began to gain ground especially among sugar planters from the east side of the island. These were isolated from Havana, had few resources with which to increase production by machinery or new slaves, and increasingly let what slaves they had be employed by other planters as wage laborers during harvests. A military rebellion in Spain that forced Queen Isabel II to flee Madrid in 1868 proved to be the catalyst: on October 10, 1868, Carlos Manuel de Céspedes, a small sugar planter, freed his slaves and issued a declaration echoing the American Declaration of Independence. This began the Ten Years' War, from 1868 to 1878, Cuba's first, but unsuccessful, attempt at independence. Only as a result of the Spanish–American War, at the turn of the century, would the island gain its independence from Spain.

Events in the British Caribbean in some respects paralleled those in Cuba. The soil on the older sugar colonies that had dominated seventeenth-century production, such as Barbados and the Leeward Islands of St. Christopher, Nevis, Antigua, and Montserrat, began to wear out around the turn of the eighteenth century. They also suffered, especially Barbados, from the effects of widespread absentee management of plantations. But Jamaica assumed a major place in sugar production in the course of the eighteenth century, and plantations there and on some of the Windward Islands, notably Grenada and Dominica, also cultivated coffee for export. But from the 1730s onwards the wealth produced for the planters by the sugar plantations in Jamaica and their fear of the unhealthy environment led many to choose to live in England and manage their Jamaican estates through attorneys or family members.

The most important issue concerning the West Indian colonies for the British government at the turn of the nineteenth century was slavery and the slave trade. A long-standing view held by planters and anti-abolitionist groups in the nineteenth century argued that the well-meaning but economically naïve abolition of the slave trade in 1807, the abolition of slavery itself in 1834, and the weakening of mercantilist protections for West Indian sugar undercut the prosperity of the West Indies plantations. In this view, the slave trade and sugar plantations were still profitable in 1807. For many abolitionists, on the other hand, the industry was already in decline by that date, and the shift to free labor brought about by abolition raised the possibility for a revival of the industry because of the supposed higher productivity of free labor. While in the 1930s Eric Williams argued that the slave trade provided the capital for the British industrial revolution and that the slave trade and slavery were no longer profitable by the beginning of the nineteenth century, those interpretations have been controversial and subsequent historians have refined their explanations of abolitionism. The contribution of slavery to the industrial revolution to some extent hinges on the relative weight given to domestic and foreign demand in the causation of British economic growth in the late eighteenth century, while the time frame selected seems to be crucial in understanding the profitability of slavery at that time. Recent historians have also emphasized non-economic factors that led the British government to abolish the trade – and eventually, in 1834, slavery itself – in the West Indies. The increased perception by many British that the empire was an empire of virtue led some to conclude that slavery conflicted with that image. As important, however, were the growth of newspapers, clubs, and coffee houses in which public opinion could be expressed, and the passage of parliamentary reform in 1832. These not only created the political culture in Great Britain in which the anti-slavery movement could bring pressure to bear on the politicians who actually made the decision to end the trade and slavery itself, but meant that politicians faced the loss of an election if they did not vote for abolition. The end of the slave trade and slavery seems, therefore, to owe a great deal to one of the first instances of an effective political lobbying campaign in the reformed Britain of the nineteenth century.[22]

The campaigns against the slave trade and then slavery itself that marked domestic British politics in the first third of the nineteenth century commanded a continued attention to the West Indies colonies, where this was not an abstraction, but a complex economic, social, cultural, and moral issue. Slave emancipation in 1834–38 forced the sugar plantations in the British West Indies to adapt to free labor, using casual labor not only during the seasons in which labor demand was highest but also throughout the year. Often working on plantations only

---

[22] The scholarship on the sugar industry and the slave trade is enormous. See Eric Williams, *Capitalism and Slavery* (Chapel Hill: University of North Carolina Press, 1944); Selwyn H. H. Carrington, *The Sugar Industry and the Abolition of the Slave Trade, 1775–1810* (Gainesville: University Press of Florida, 2002); Seymour Drescher, *Econocide: British Slavery in the Era of Abolition* (University of Pittsburgh Press, 1977), and *Abolition: A History of Slavery and Antislavery* (New York: Cambridge University Press, 2009); Eltis, *Economic Growth and the Ending of the Transatlantic Slave Trade*; Thomas Holt, "Explaining Abolitionism," *Journal of Social History* 24, 2 (1990), 371–78, and *The Problem of Freedom: Race, Labor, and Politics in Jamaica and Britain, 1832–1938* (Baltimore, MD: Johns Hopkins University Press, 1992); Christopher Leslie Brown, *Moral Capital: Foundations of British Abolitionism* (Chapel Hill: University of North Carolina Press, 2006); James Walvin, "British Abolitionism, 1787–1838," in Dorigny (ed.), *Abolitions of Slavery*, 71–78. For fuller treatment of abolitionism from the European perspective, see Chapter 6.

a few days a week, former slaves had free time to cultivate provisions on their own land.[23] As Cuba and Brazil came to dominate the production of cane sugar in the first half of the nineteenth century, and sugar beet produced in Europe took over a significant part of the world market, the economic contribution of the colony to the metropole was reduced. In Jamaica, plantations felt the full force of the shift to free labor even as they were adapting to the change in the market for their products.[24] Free labor proved to be as challenging a labor system as slavery had been, even with the plantation owners enjoying the tacit support of the colonial government. Some plantations turned to indentured laborers from South Asia. The generation after emancipation was marked by disputes between the resident whites who dominated the colonial government and its assembly, on the one hand, and former slaves who quickly moved away from the plantations to work small landholdings, on the other.

Colonial administrators and observers in London viewed many aspects of post-emancipation West Indian society with distrust. Liberal political economists everywhere in Europe during the nineteenth century believed firmly that free labor would be more productive than slave labor, and administrators in colonies everywhere therefore sought to create a free labor force out of the freed slaves or indigenous peoples who lived in the colonies. But often those peoples preferred to work on their own plots of land to grow food not for the market but for their own consumption, and they stayed away from the labor markets, on plantations and in industrial enterprises, in droves. In Jamaica, the freed slaves, who knew what labor on sugar plantations was like, worked their own land for much of the week, and only occasionally hired out their labor. Just as often, they left wage labor to return to their own farms. British administrators saw this not as enlightened self-interest on the part of the freedmen but rather as evidence of the unwillingness of Afro-Jamaicans to conform to the model of agricultural labor that had already been imposed on landed estates in rural England and Ireland. For Henry Taylor in the Colonial Office, who drafted the famous "Queen's Advice" that circulated in Jamaica in 1865, Jamaica's economic conditions would improve if only the "Labouring Classes" would work for wages "not uncertainly, or capriciously, but steadily and continuously, at the times when their labour is wanted, and for so long

---

[23] Michael Craton, *Searching for the Invisible Man: Slaves and Plantation Life in Jamaica* (Cambridge, MA: Harvard University Press, 1978), 287–88, 321–23.
[24] B. W. Higman, *Plantation Jamaica 1750–1850: Capital and Control in a Colonial Economy* (Jamaica: University of the West Indies Press, 2005), 262–67.

as it is wanted." Edward Eyre, sent to Jamaica as deputy governor in 1862 and appointed governor in 1864, was convinced that it was the laziness of blacks that was the problem.[25]

By the 1860s, when Taylor and Eyre were lecturing Jamaican blacks about their responsibilities to the economy, more intimate aspects of Afro-Jamaican life were coming under British scrutiny. The "civilizing mission" of nineteenth-century colonists was almost obsessively concerned with the sexual behavior of indigenous peoples, Africans, and peoples of African descent. In British colonies missionaries as well as civil authorities exerted great effort to control the sexual activity of blacks by enforcing monogamous, legal marriage practices and trying to reduce the number of illegitimate children. But if, as Vincent Brown has suggested, Jamaica was a demographic and social catastrophe, it was also one for Victorian morals.[26] Efforts at moralizing freed slaves were not particularly successful, and those efforts ran into the sexual exploitation of black women by white men that characterized this and other slave societies throughout the New World. As the Baptist missionaries on Jamaica noted in the middle of the nineteenth century, the white elite on the island offered not an example of the proper bourgeois family life they were trying to impose on Afro-Jamaicans, but instead "a model of disorder, licentious sexuality, illegitimacy, irregularity, with mulatto mistresses kept openly, and concubinage a completely accepted form."[27] Colonial sexuality proved to be a cultural arena in which colonial whites exercised their power, both as whites and as men, over slave and free black and mulatto women. Because of that, however, it was also a place in which the clear distinctions that administrators and clergymen tried to make between white and black, and colonizer and colonized, collapsed in interracial sexual relations and the mixed-race offspring they produced.

If the colonists had difficulty regulating the sexual behavior of slaves – and themselves – they were also unable to control the ways in which slaves faced the spiritual world. Two distinct but related spiritual practices, Obeah – shamanistic practices from Africa conducted outside formal institutions – and Myal – similar but more institutionalized ways of dealing with spiritual danger – had been present in the slave community since at least the 1760s, and missionary and administrative efforts to limit their power proved unsuccessful. Tacky's Revolt in 1760,

---

[25] Holt, *The Problem of Freedom*, 277–78.
[26] Vincent Brown, *The Reaper's Garden: Death and Power in the World of Atlantic Slavery* (Cambridge, MA: Harvard University Press, 2008), 12.
[27] Catherine Hall, *Civilising Subjects: Metropole and Colony in the English Imagination, 1830–1867* (University of Chicago Press, 2002), 72.

the most significant slave revolt of the eighteenth century in the British Caribbean, used Obeah shamans to administer oaths and provide protection for the rebels. In 1841, there was a revival of Myal among the black population, especially in the Baptist and other churches established since the beginning of the century. In October 1860, a Great Revival spread through many Moravian, Baptist, and Methodist congregations. Historians have argued that by creating a form of cultural self-expression, and by allowing black men and women the opportunity for power and authority, Revival/Myal became by the early 1860s a strong potential challenge not only to the colonists' religion but their political authority as well.[28] In 1865 these unresolved contradictions of the post-emancipation colonial project came to a head in the Morant Bay rebellion that swept over southeastern Jamaica. In its aftermath, the colony's government was changed, with the end of the Assembly in which black and mulatto Jamaicans were gaining power. Crown Colony government, in which authority was vested in a governor and an appointed council, was imposed in its place. With few dissenters, both Jamaican whites and British officials agreed that the planters knew what was best for the island.

With the constitutional change, the interests not of the peasant smallholders but rather the heirs of the sugar and coffee plantations came to dominate Jamaican society and political life. But as in the French islands, this elite would never recapture the great prosperity of the eighteenth century. For a time in the late nineteenth century the peasantry and the plantations were able to survive by producing fruits, especially bananas, for the American market. In the twentieth century, however, that industry suffered from declining prices and the black peasantry stagnated. The British effort in Jamaica to impose liberal political economy on the colony had supported the abolition of first the slave trade and then slavery itself, but it also imposed on the freedmen of the colony a model of free labor that they were unwilling to embrace. Not only the British but also other colonial powers would confront similar problems elsewhere, in South Asia and in Africa, as the expansion of European empires moved into new parts of the world in the course of the nineteenth and early twentieth centuries.

Even as the sights of European empire-builders turned to those other parts of the world, those empires continued to maintain their reach into the Americas. Great Britain continued to hold on to Canada, and it and

---

[28] Brian L. Moore and Michele A. Johnson, *Neither Led nor Driven: Contesting British Cultural Imperialism in Jamaica, 1865–1920* (Jamaica: University of the West Indies Press, 2004), 51–95.

France retained colonies in the Caribbean and on the coast of South America well into the twentieth century. Reforms such as the British attempted in Jamaica were undertaken to increase the profitability of the colonies and to fulfill a version of the imperial goal of spreading the benefits of Western civilization. The wave of decolonization there after World War II was a demonstration that these did not succeed in the long run. Nonetheless, the vestiges of eighteenth-century colonialism remain as some of those colonies today are parts of the metropole, formally integrated but reminders of the colonial past.

FURTHER READING

Anderson, Fred. *Crucible of War: The Seven Years' War and the Fate of Empire in British North America, 1754–1766*. New York: Random House, 2000.

Anderson, M. S. *The War of the Austrian Succession, 1740–1748*. London and New York: Longman, 1995.

Andrews, George Reid. *Afro-Latin America 1800–2000*. Oxford University Press, 2004.

Berlin, Ira. *Many Thousands Gone: The First Two Centuries of Slavery in North America*. Cambridge, MA: Belknap Press, 1998.

Black, Jeremy. *British Foreign Policy in the Age of Walpole*. Edinburgh: John Donald, 1985.

Blackburn, Robin. *The Overthrow of Colonial Slavery: 1776–1848*. London: Verso, 1988.

Brown, Christopher Leslie. *Moral Capital: Foundations of British Abolitionism*. Chapel Hill: University of North Carolina Press, 2006.

Brown, Gordon S. *Toussaint's Clause: The Founding Fathers and the Haitian Revolution*. Jackson: University Press of Mississippi, 2005.

Brown, Vincent. *The Reaper's Garden: Death and Power in the World of Atlantic Slavery*. Cambridge, MA: Harvard University Press, 2008.

Buckley, Roger Norman. *Slaves in Red Coats: The British West Indian Regiments, 1795–1815*. New Haven, CT: Yale University Press, 1979.

Carpentier, Alejo. *The Kingdom of this World*, trans. Harriet de Onis. New York: Farrar, Straus, and Giroux, 1957.

Childs, Matt. *The 1812 Aponte Rebellion in Cuba and the Struggle against Slavery*. Chapel Hill: University of North Carolina Press, 2006.

Cook, Warren L. *Flood Tide of Empire: Spain and the Pacific Northwest, 1543–1819*. New Haven, CT: Yale University Press, 1973.

Craton, Michael. *Empire, Enslavement, and Freedom in the Caribbean*. Princeton: Markus Wiener Publishers, 1997.

Searching for the Invisible Man: Slaves and Plantation Life in Jamaica. Cambridge, MA: Harvard University Press, 1978.

Testing the Chains: Resistance to Slavery in the British West Indies. Ithaca, NY: Cornell University Press, 1982.

Dominguez, Jorge. *Insurrection or Loyalty: The Breakdown of the Spanish American Empire*. Cambridge, MA: Harvard University Press, 1980.

Drescher, Seymour. *Abolition: A History of Slavery and Antislavery*. New York: Cambridge University Press, 2009.

Econocide: British Slavery in the Era of Abolition. University of Pittsburgh Press, 1977.

Dubois, Laurent. *Avengers of the New World: The Story of the Haitian Revolution*. Cambridge, MA: Belknap Press, 2004.

A Colony of Citizens: Revolution and Slave Emancipation in the French Caribbean, 1787–1804. Chapel Hill: University of North Carolina Press, 2004.

"An Enslaved Enlightenment: Rethinking the Intellectual History of the French Atlantic." *Social History* 31, 1 (2006), 1–14.

Duffy, Michael. *Soldiers, Sugar, and Seapower: The British Expeditions to the West Indies and the War against Revolutionary France*. Oxford: Clarendon Press, 1987.

Eltis, David. *Economic Growth and the Ending of the Transatlantic Slave Trade*. New York: Oxford University Press, 1987.

Fick, Carolyn E. *The Making of Haiti: The Saint Domingue Revolution from Below*. Knoxville: University of Tennessee Press, 1990.

Fischer, Sybille, *Modernity Disavowed: Haiti and the Cultures of Slavery in the Age of Revolution*. Durham, NC: Duke University Press, 2002.

Geggus, David. "The Enigma of Jamaica in the 1790s: New Light on the Causes of Slave Rebellions." *William and Mary Quarterly* 44, 2 (1987), 274–97.

"The French and Haitian Revolutions, and Resistance to Slavery in the Americas: An Overview." *Revue Française d'Histoire d'Outre-Mer* 76, 282–83 (1989), 107–24.

"Racial Equality, Slavery, and Colonial Secession during the Constituent Assembly." *American Historical Review* 94, 5 (1989), 1290–308.

"Slavery, War, and Revolution in Saint-Domingue: A Triumph or a Failure?" In David Barry Gaspar and Geggus, eds., *A Turbulent Time: The French Revolution and the Greater Caribbean*. Bloomington: Indiana University Press, 1997, 1–50.

Geggus, David, ed. *The Impact of the Haitian Revolution in the Atlantic World*. Columbia: University of South Carolina Press, 2001.

Geggus, David Patrick and Norman Fiering, eds. *The World of the Haitian Revolution*. Bloomington: Indiana University Press, 2009.

Gould, Eliga H. *The Persistence of Empire: British Political Culture in the Age of the American Revolution*. Chapel Hill: University of North Carolina Press, 2000.

Guardino, Peter. *The Time of Liberty: Popular Political Culture in Oaxaca, 1750–1850*. Durham, NC: Duke University Press, 2005.

Hämäläinen, Pekka. *The Comanche Empire*. New Haven, CT: Yale University Press, 2008.

Hamnett, Brian R. *Politics and Trade in Southern Mexico, 1750–1821*. Cambridge University Press, 1971.

Roots of Insurgency: Mexican Regions, 1750–1824. Cambridge University Press, 1986.

Harlow, Vincent T. *The Founding of the Second British Empire, 1763–93*, 2 vols. London: Longmans, Green, 1952–64.

Heuman, Gad. *"The Killing Time": The Morant Bay Rebellion in Jamaica*. Knoxville: University of Tennessee Press, 1994.

Higman, B. W. *Plantation Jamaica 1750–1850: Capital and Control in a Colonial Economy*. Jamaica: University of the West Indies Press, 2006.

Holt, Thomas C. *The Problem of Freedom: Race, Labor, and Politics in Jamaica and Britain, 1832–1938*. Baltimore, MD: Johns Hopkins University Press, 1992.

Hoogbergen, Wim. *The Boni Maroon Wars in Suriname*. Leiden: Brill, 1990.

Jacobsen, Nils. *Mirages of Transition: The Peruvian Altiplano, 1780–1930*. Berkeley and Los Angeles: University of California Press, 1993.

Kuethe, Allan. *Cuba, 1753–1815: Crown, Military, and Society*. Knoxville: University of Tennessee Press, 1986.

Mapp, Paul W. *The Elusive West and the Contest for Empire, 1713–1763*. Chapel Hill: University of North Carolina Press, 2011.

Maxwell, Kenneth R. *Conflicts and Conspiracies: Brazil and Portugal 1750–1808*. Cambridge University Press, 1973.

Pombal, Paradox of the Enlightenment. Cambridge University Press, 1995.

Mills, David. *The Idea of Loyalty in Upper Canada, 1784–1850*. Kingston: McGill-Queen's University Press, 1988.

Moore, Brian L., and Michele A. Johnson. *Neither Led or Driven: Contesting British Cultural Imperialism in Jamaica, 1865–1920*. Jamaica: University of the West Indies Press, 2004.

Mullin, Michael. *Africa in America: Slave Acculturation and Resistance in the American South and the British Caribbean, 1736–1831*. Urbana and Chicago: University of Illinois Press, 1992.

Murray, David J. *The West Indies and the Development of Colonial Government, 1801–1834*. Oxford: Clarendon Press, 1965.

Paquette, Gabriel. *Enlightenment, Governance, and Reform in Spain and its Empire, 1759–1808*. New York: Palgrave Macmillan, 2008.

Paquette, Robert. *Sugar is Made with Blood: The Conspiracy of La Escalera and the Conflict between Empires over Slavery in Cuba*. Middletown, CT: Wesleyan University Press, 1988.

Paquette, Robert L., and Stanley Engerman, eds. *Parts beyond the Seas: The Lesser Antilles in the Age of European Expansion*. Gainesville: University Press of Florida, 1996.

Peabody, Sue. *"There Are No Slaves in France": The Political Culture of Race and Slavery in the Ancien Régime*. New York: Oxford University Press, 1996.

Pedreira, Jorge M. "From Growth to Collapse: Portugal, Brazil, and the Breakdown of the Old Colonial System (1760–1830)." *Hispanic American Historical Review* 80, 4 (2000), 839–64.

Phelan, John Leddy. *The People and the King: The Comunero Revolution in Colombia, 1781*. Madison: University of Wisconsin Press, 1978.

Popkin, Jeremy. *You Are All Free: The Haitian Revolution and the Abolition of Slavery*. Cambridge University Press, 2010.

Rediker, Marcus. *Between the Devil and the Deep Blue Sea: Merchant Seamen, Pirates, and the Anglo-American Maritime World, 1700–1750*. Cambridge University Press, 1987.

Richardson, David, ed. *Abolition and Its Aftermath: The Historical Context 1790–1916*. London: Frank Cass, 1985.

Scott, Rebecca J. *Degrees of Freedom: Louisiana and Cuba after Slavery*. Cambridge, MA: Belknap Press, 2005.

   Slave Emancipation in Cuba: The Transition to Free Labour. Princeton University Press, 1985.

Stein, Barbara H., and Stanley J. Stein. *Edge of Crisis: War and Trade in the Spanish Atlantic, 1789–1808*. Baltimore, MD: Johns Hopkins University Press, 2008.

Stein, Stanley J., and Barbara H. Stein. *Apogee of Empire: Spain and New Spain in the Age of Charles III, 1759–1789*. Baltimore, MD: Johns Hopkins University Press, 2003.

   Silver, Trade, and War: Spain and America in the Making of Early Modern Europe. Baltimore, MD: Johns Hopkins University Press, 2000.

Taylor, Alan. *The Civil War of 1812: American Citizens, British Subjects, Irish Rebels, and Indian Allies*. New York: Random House, 2010.

Van Young, Eric. *The Other Rebellion: Popular Violence, Ideology, and the Mexican Struggle for Independence, 1810–1821*. Stanford University Press, 2001.

Walker, Charles F. *Smoldering Ashes: Cuzco and the Creation of Republican Peru, 1780–1840*. Durham, NC: Duke University Press, 1999.

Ward, J. R. *British West Indian Slavery, 1750–1834*. Oxford: Clarendon Press, 1988.

Weber, David J. *The Spanish Frontier in North America*. New Haven, CT: Yale University Press, 1992.

White, Ashli. *Encountering Revolution: Haiti and the Making of the Early Republic*. Baltimore, MD: Johns Hopkins University Press, 2010.

Wilson, Kathleen. *The Sense of the People: Politics, Culture and Imperialism in England, 1715–1785*. Cambridge University Press, 1995.

4   The new empires in Oceania and Asia

The attempts by the early modern empires of Spain, France, the Netherlands, Portugal, and Great Britain to restructure themselves in the last decades of the eighteenth century were not limited to the Atlantic basin. European ships had been in the Pacific since the sixteenth century, but now they discovered new islands and peoples. What had been largely a "Spanish lake" saw ships, and eventually settlers, from many European countries in its waters after the middle of the eighteenth century. Voyages of exploration and scientific inquiry of the late eighteenth century were followed by whalers, traders, missionaries, and convicts. The encounter with Oceania provided descriptions of plant and animal life, geological formations, and climatic conditions that helped Europeans such as Joseph Banks and Charles Darwin rethink some of the fundamental assumptions of European culture about the world. Europeans also created a fictitious island paradise in Tahiti, and attempted to recreate versions of European society in New Zealand and Australia.[1] As they did so, the interactions between Europeans and the Pacific changed.

The European relationship to Asia also changed at this time. From the shift from purely commercial to colonial links by the British East India Company in the late eighteenth century through the Revolt in 1857 and the assumption of direct control by the British government, India became the quintessential British colony. It was a subject of major importance in British politics from the 1760s on, and the financing of the British state became intimately connected to the fortunes of the British East India Company. Long-standing French religious and commercial ties to Indochina were the foundation on which missionaries and adventurous military officers built a Southeast Asian empire in the last third of the nineteenth century. Elsewhere in Asia, the Dutch East

---

[1] Greg Dening, *Islands and Beaches: Discourse on a Silent Land, Marquesas, 1774–1880* (Honolulu: University of Hawai'i Pres, 1980); Matt K. Matsuda, *Empire of Love: Histories of France and the Pacific* (Oxford University Press, 2005).

Indies became significant contributors to the revenues of the nineteenth- and twentieth-century Dutch state. All of these colonies raised issues about the relationship not only of Asians to European settlers, but also those of European descent born in Asia to the metropole in Europe.

The geographical reach of these empires was breathtaking, helped by faster ocean travel, new communications technology, and more powerful bureaucracies in the metropoles. Imperial powers that, in the sixteenth century, had been content to cross the Irish Sea and in the seventeenth and eighteenth centuries made the Atlantic a conduit for instructions and resources, now began to enclose the globe with the tentacles of their power. In all of these places, covering the globe from the Pacific shores of the Americas to the Indian Ocean, colonies proved to be sites on which Europeans worked out important concerns about social hierarchies, race, gender, and nation, defining themselves through their interactions with an "other" with whom they often had only infrequent contact. Perhaps even more remarkable was the range of human behaviors these colonial states sought to control. In seeking to define the forms of these connections, no aspect of people's lives, from justice to the environment to landholding to labor to the most intimate aspects of family, kinship, and sexuality, escaped their purview. We will see these efforts in the Pacific islands, India, Indochina, and Indonesia in this chapter. But colonialism remained a contingent phenomenon: no Leviathans, colonial states found colonists and colonized escaping from their grasp.

Pacific exploration

Prior to the eighteenth century, the Pacific Ocean had seen only passing voyages of exploration by Europeans.[2] European knowledge of the Pacific in 1700 was confined to its margins, and even then two great gaps – much of the north from southern Japan to California, all the eastern coast of New Holland (Australia) – existed. Nonetheless the Pacific was a significant contributor to the European imagination. Utopian visions in the seventeenth and eighteenth centuries began to focus on the South Seas, an area still isolated enough that it provided the opportunity to construct mythical societies. Some form of radical disjuncture, usually (as in the case of Daniel Defoe's Robinson Crusoe) shipwreck, brought observers to the islands, where they created a utopian society.

[2] Glyndwr Williams, *The Great South Sea: English Voyages and Encounters 1570–1750* (New Haven, CT: Yale University Press, 1997).

Discovery interacted with academic geography as well, and by the eighteenth century synthesizers such as the French philosopher Pierre-Louis Moreau de Maupertuis (*Lettre sur le progrès des sciences,* 1752) called for assaults on the vast blanks on the map. European rivalries and wars interfered with plans for exploration until the end of the Seven Years War in 1763, but in 1764 serious exploration of the Pacific basin began. These voyages were formally sponsored by European states, utilizing and dependent upon the resources and expertise of European navies. The principal rivals, Britain, France, and Spain, were ostensibly concerned with the advancement of knowledge, but they always kept a keen eye on commercial and geopolitical advantage. Pacific voyages by the Englishmen John Byron (1764–66), Samuel Wallis, and Philip Carteret (1767), and a Frenchman, Louis-Antoine de Bougainville (1767), prepared the ground for the work of the greatest European explorer of the Pacific, the Englishman James Cook. A series of three voyages led by Cook between 1768 and 1779 brought back to England an astonishing amount of information about virtually every aspect of the Pacific. He found New Zealand and Australia, proved that the Great Southern Continent did not exist, landed in the Hawai'ian Islands, and sailed up the coast of North America, through the Bering Strait and into the Polar Sea (Map 2).

With the outbreak of the Wars of the American Revolution and French Revolution, Europeans and their navies fought one another until after the turn of the nineteenth century, and exploration took second place. The northwest coast of North America was mapped by Spanish ships and a voyage by the Englishman George Vancouver in 1792–94, making that part of the Pacific a relatively well-known sea for Europeans. French voyages in the early nineteenth century, commanded by Louis de Freycinet (1817) and Louis-Isadore Duperrey (1822), gathered information on natural history, the situation of the native peoples, and scientific and meteorological questions in the Pacific. Missionaries, whalers, and beachcombers also increasingly joined the explorers in the Pacific islands.

Science remained a European concern, and the voyage of the *Beagle* in 1831–36 provided its naturalist, Charles Darwin, with a lifetime's worth of material to ponder. But as the nineteenth century went on, explorers, whalers, and beachcombers gave way to other Europeans who sailed Pacific waters and came into contact with islanders. These voyages increasingly had as their goals protection of trade interests and the search for locations for possible settlement. The importance of trade with Asia and the Indian Ocean basin encouraged organizations such as the British East India Company as well as the British and French

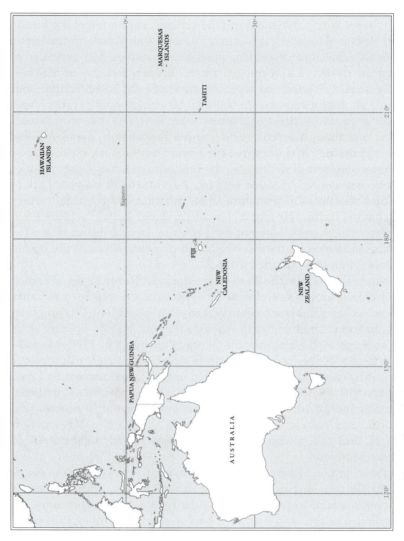

Map 2 Oceania in the nineteenth century.

governments to contemplate ways of developing that trade. While much European trade with Asia continued to go by way of the Cape of Good Hope (and after 1869 through the Suez Canal), voyages into the Pacific and Indian oceans not only improved European understanding of the region, but also mapped out the routes that would be followed by future merchant vessels. They also emphasized the need for way stations for reprovisioning on the long voyages and provided information about the best locations for those stations. European conflicts, especially the Seven Years War, the War of American Independence, and the Wars of the French Revolution and Napoleonic Empire, led England and France to consider the global reach of their conflict and to think strategically about the Pacific.

These factors came together in the last third of the eighteenth century and the first few decades of the nineteenth, as Europeans began to create permanent settlements in the Pacific and Asia. In 1789 Spain conceded to Great Britain rights to trade on the northwest coast of North America, and Americans were quick to follow. The American merchant Captain Robert Gray reached the mouth of the Columbia River in 1792, establishing the basis of an early American claim to the region. Astoria, near the mouth of that river, was established in 1811 by employees of the American fur magnate John Jacob Astor, although the settlement was unsuccessful and was abandoned in 1813 when threatened by a British ship. Other merchants sent ships to the Sandwich Islands (Hawai'i) for sandalwood, and attempted to open up the Chinese tea market to the Pacific trade.

The peoples who inhabited the Pacific islands were at times noble savages, unfathomable curiosities, and heathens awaiting salvation in the eyes of Europeans, and missionary activity was often the most important aspect of European presence into the first half of the nineteenth century. For the British, the Church Missionary Society, Wesleyans, and Roman Catholics established missions not only in Australia and New Zealand, but also on many of the Pacific islands in that period. While not necessarily intending to establish colonies, British policy there was to maintain a preponderant interest against the threat of other European powers by strengthening the power and authority of indigenous rulers. As the settlements on Australia and New Zealand grew, however, those colonies increasingly envisaged themselves as the administrators of a British suzerainty over the Pacific islands, and they pushed the British government towards annexations. Initially this was resisted in London, but by the second half of the nineteenth century, concerns about the expansionist threat of other European powers led to the declaration of British control, if not outright annexation, over many of the islands

in the western Pacific in the 1870s and 1880s. A German protectorate over New Guinea, announced in 1884, led to British annexation of
Papua, and the rise of Japan as an Asian and Pacific power furthered
these concerns even before Japan's victory in the Russo-Japanese War
in 1905. In spite of this, however, British acquisitions of Pacific islands
remained limited before 1914.

Catholic missionaries from France began competing with British
Protestant missionaries on many of the Pacific islands in the early
nineteenth century, as several religious orders sent missionaries to
the Gambier Islands, Tahiti, and the Marquesas in the 1830s to battle against Protestantism and stake out a first French claim to influence. In 1842 a French naval officer took possession for France of
the Marquesas and Tahiti, and other Pacific islands followed. These
became the Établissements français d'Océanie (EFO) in the late nineteenth century. Further west, France annexed New Caledonia in 1853.
The acquisition of land in the New Hebrides by French citizens (notably the New Caledonian nickel magnate John Higginson) drew France
into the affairs of those islands, and a loosely administered joint condo-
minium shared with the British gave way to more formal arrangements
between the two powers only in 1906.

These holdings were the subject of occasional attention by naval officers concerned about British power in the Pacific and Indian oceans, by
believers in imperialism as a source of economic prosperity, and by the
colonial lobby that developed around the turn of the twentieth century,
but they remained until well into that century isolated outposts rather
than flourishing French colonies. A small number of Catholic missionaries continued their work into the twentieth century, with priests
joined by nuns, who were useful, even in the eyes of anti-clerical republican administrators, not only because of their educational activities but
also because the moral rectitude they taught Polynesian girls seemed
protection against the debauchery and venereal disease that French
officials blamed for the decline in the indigenous population. But few
French men and women emigrated to Oceania: by one estimate, fewer
than 25,000 Frenchmen and women lived in the Pacific islands at the
turn of the twentieth century. New Caledonia was the destination of
almost all of them, and half of the French on New Caledonia were
convicts. Attempts at economic exploitation foundered on poor soil,
transportation difficulties, and lack of labor. While the islands produced fruits, sandalwood, *bêche-de-mer*, and other seafoods that could
be sold in China and Japan, these exchanges never made a significant
contribution to the metropolitan economy. Gold and nickel discoveries,
especially on New Caledonia, offered some prospects for development,

but the local population proved an unwilling labor force, and French entrepreneurs soon sought contract labor from other Pacific islands, India, Indochina, Japan, China, and Indonesia to work on plantations and in the mines. By the twentieth century, the Pacific colonies were relatively stagnant disappointments to those who had hoped for prosperity in a Pacific paradise.

The most important Pacific colonies were in Australia and New Zealand, and these were the work of British settlers. In Australia, the British established New South Wales, near Botany Bay on the east coast, as a destination for convicts condemned to transportation. The first shipload of convicts (the First Fleet) arrived in 1788 and, from then until the practice of transportation ended in 1856, a collection of Englishmen, Irish rebels, and other malcontents were sent across the two oceans to form the beginnings of the colony of Australia. But, as Alan Frost has recently argued, New South Wales was also necessary to establish a British beachhead in the South Pacific to facilitate trade in the region and to forestall Spanish and French ambitions in the region.[3] New Zealand's settlement was slower than that of Australia. Missionary activities among the Maori began soon after the turn of the nineteenth century, but a minority of white settlers were there by the 1830s. Promotion of New Zealand as a New Britain in the Pacific, as well as migration across the Tasman Sea by disappointed Australians, slowly increased its white population.

These settlements had a strong commercial emphasis almost from the very beginning. In Australia, the production of wheat and wool for the British market was soon reinforced by exploitation of gold and other metal deposits. In New Zealand, grain production developed slowly, but more important in providing an economic basis were sheep-rearing, gold that was discovered in the 1850s, 1860s, and 1870s, and what James Belich has called the "progress industry," the roads, bridges, and other infrastructure constructed by the colonial government, and the sponsorship of townships and subsequent immigration by that government.[4]

The Australian colonies each received what was called Responsible Government in the 1850s, with ministers responsible to assemblies elected by broad manhood suffrage, but it was not until 1901 that a federal government was created unifying the entire continent. This

---

[3] Alan Frost, *The Global Reach of Empire: Britain's Maritime Expansion in the Indian and Pacific Oceans, 1764–1815* (Melbourne: Miegunah Press, 2003).
[4] James Belich, *Making Peoples: A History of the New Zealanders From Polynesian Settlement to the End of the Nineteenth Century* (Honolulu: University of Hawai'i Press, 1996), 349.

government followed policies aimed at maintaining a white Australia (through Exclusion laws and restricting suffrage to whites), racial hierarchy, a primarily domestic role for women, and limited power for trade unions. These unions had become particularly strong in the depression of the 1890s, with the labor conflicts of the period between 1890 and 1894 marked especially by the participation of sheep-shearers and other rural laborers. New Zealand, in its turn, was formally annexed by Great Britain in 1840 and given Crown Colony government until Responsible Government was granted in 1852.

The most important aspect of these British possessions in the Pacific was the overwhelming importance of white settlers, and in the nineteenth and early twentieth centuries many of those settlers adhered to a combination of dedication to the British empire, which provided them with a political framework, economic ties, and cultural models, and allegiance to their Pacific home. They elaborated a triumphalist narrative of political integration of the disparate territories of these colonies, liberal democracy, economic progress under the imperial umbrella, and cultural emancipation. But these accounts marginalize important aspects of the colonization process. As in the Americas, initial contact with Europeans had severe demographic consequences for the peoples of Australia and New Zealand from disease and warfare, and the spread of European settlements appropriated lands that had supported indigenous economies and societies. But in many instances, especially in the first half-century of colonization, the "conquest" may have been more an accommodation of both British and indigenous peoples to the difficulties faced by a small number of Europeans in subduing the peoples they found in Australia and New Zealand. There was certainly violence, but Aborigines and Maoris proved capable of devising strategies of resistance, not least those that involved the use of technologies such as muskets. The Maori leader Ruatara in New Zealand at the beginning of the nineteenth century may only be a prominent example of a more common pattern: he distributed European goods and information, converted what he received into Maori terms, eased European settlement and missionary activity, and used his intermediary status to gain power with both Europeans and Maoris. In the wars of the 1810s, the 1840s, and the 1860s it proved difficult for British settlers and soldiers to achieve a definitive conquest of Maoris.[5] The stories of Ruatara and nineteenth-century New Zealand suggest that the narrative of Pacific

---

[5] Belich, *Making Peoples*, 140–78. On Ruatara, see there 141–44; on warfare, see 156–64, 204–11, 229–46.

colonization owes much to the agency and contributions of the peoples found there.

Nonetheless, the emphasis in Australia and New Zealand on Englishness had lasting implications for relations between the white settlers and the peoples they found in the Pacific, creating long-standing racial hierarchies and legal discrimination. In Australia there were few formal agreements that defined these relationships. British policies, notably the Aboriginal Protection Act passed in the 1880s, ostensibly protected Aborigines but undercut the ability of aborigine groups to survive independent of British society. But in New Zealand, the Treaty of Waitangi, concluded in 1840 between the British and many (but not all) of the Maori tribes, established at least in principle not only British sovereignty but also Maori rights and protection of their lands. Honored by whites mostly in the breach until the late twentieth century, it failed to end Maori opposition to British rule and settlement. In 1853 dissident Maoris joined together to resist further encroachments by the proclamation of a Maori king, a move that led to the Waikato Wars in the 1860s. Even after the forcible suppression of the movement for a king, Maori resistance continued through prophetic movements, the creation of a separate King Territory in the northwest part of the North Island, and to some extent accommodation of British institutions through very limited Maori representation in the New Zealand Parliament beginning in 1868.

India

Asia had been accessible to Europeans for centuries by land through the Middle East and by sea around the Cape of Good Hope. But the opening of the Pacific to European trade multiplied routes to the continent and the nearby islands. Two of the most important parts of Asia, China, and Japan, managed to avoid formal colonization by Western powers even as the European powers competed for trade and influence in East Asia. China was politically and militarily weak, but rather than this leading to colonization by a single European power, it was divided into spheres of interest by the Western powers. Within those spheres, the European powers facilitated the activities of their missionaries and merchants without taking over the emperor's government. The increasing Western influence, however, stimulated resistance from some Chinese, and this culminated in the Boxer rebellion in 1900. Its result, though, was not to lessen Western influence but to cement cooperation among the Western powers, first to crush the rebellion, and then to maintain their joint informal control of the country. Japan was better able to resist

Western colonial incursions when they arrived in the mid nineteenth century. With a stronger central government, the Japanese were able to impose restrictions on Western traders who wished to open up the Japanese market for Western goods, and the program of Westernization and armament undertaken by Japan in the late nineteenth century made it a competitor for power in the Pacific by the time of World War I. The Japanese themselves undertook colonial expansion, conquering Korea in 1900 and expanding into Manchuria and the Pacific in the 1930s, expansion that only ended with their defeat in World War II.

The Portuguese, Danish, Dutch, French, and British had contended for influence in South Asia and in the East Indies since the spice trade opened up in the early seventeenth century. The Portuguese retained control of the Molucca Islands, but in the late eighteenth and early nineteenth centuries the British East India Company consolidated its influence on the western shore of the Malay Peninsula in the settlements at Malacca, Penang, Dinding, and Singapore. These were grouped together under British East India Company control as the Straits Settlements in 1826. In the course of the nineteenth century the British slowly accumulated influence on the Malay mainland although the indigenous sultans of the various Malay states remained in power. The British also gained control of Hong Kong in 1842 as a consequence of the First Opium War with China.

But the most extensive Asian territory to come under European rule was India, and by the late nineteenth century it had become the most important colony in the British empire. While the British, in the end, became the predominant European power in South Asia, that primacy was long contested. But it was not simply a contest between Europeans. The principal antagonist that faced these European powers as they sought to extend their power in South Asia in the seventeenth century was one of the great empires of the world, the Mughal empire. The empire had always been a shifting set of alliances, marked by disputes from the imperial court down to the local level, but in the late seventeenth and eighteenth centuries it faced disruptive forces, including wars of expansion and invasions from Persia and Afghanistan, that exposed its limitations, weakened it at its center, and moved authority towards regional rulers in the course of the century (Map 3).

But while earlier versions of Mughal and colonial history described this as a collapse of the central authority that opened the way for European, and especially British, expansion in the subcontinent, recent scholarship has presented a more complex story. As Mughal power weakened, it did not create anarchy, but rather a number of successor states. Local landholders took advantage of the emperor's difficulties

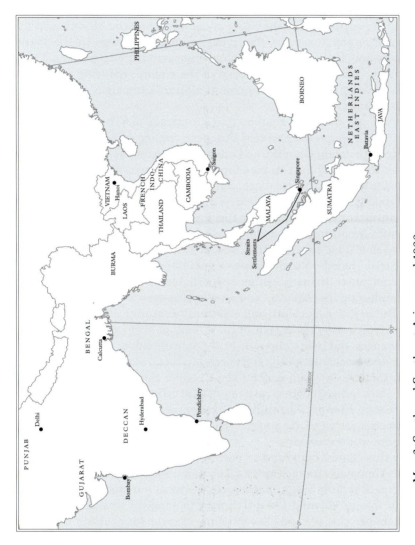

Map 3 South and Southeast Asia around 1900.

and mounted challenges to his rule. They asserted claims to rights that had previously been held by the agents of the emperor, seizing lands and prebendal rights, providing the basis for strong kinship-based groups that effectively countered the demands of the imperial state. In Bengal, Awadh, and Hyderabad autonomous hereditary kingdoms grew out of Mughal provinces, and the Sikhs in the north and the Marathas in the Deccan mounted serious challenges to imperial power. In the south, Mysore and Travancore also became important regional powers. These losses undercut the financial basis of the empire, reducing the ability of its government in Delhi to mount military campaigns to impose its authority.

It was not therefore anarchy that Europeans met, but these successor states. A series of chartered European trading companies competed with South Asian, Chinese, and other Asian merchants for a share of the trade: the British East India Company, chartered in 1600; the Dutch East India Company, established in 1602; and the French Compagnie des Indes Orientales, chartered as a joint-stock company in 1664 and the successor to a venture by the French Crown dating from 1603. There were also brief attempts by Danish and Portuguese companies to develop trade in the region, and private merchants from European countries traded on their own accounts rather than under the aegis of the companies. In many instances South Asian rulers were as successful in countering these European incursions as they were Mughal authority. But in the seventeenth and eighteenth centuries the British and the French especially made significant inroads as they competed for trade advantages and political power in the subcontinent. South Asians had little interest in purchasing European products, but Europeans brought with them silver, gold, and Japanese copper to pay for the cotton and silk cloth, indigo, pepper, cardamom, and other spices that found ready markets in Europe. The influx of these precious metals contributed to the monetization of the South Asian economy and linked it to the early modern world economy.

In this contest between the French and the British, the British East India Company emerged as the victor as it used its experience with trade and revenue farming to incorporate the local bureaucracies of Indian states into its colonial system, thereby tapping the wealth of the cities and countryside of India. But by taking over the Mughal administrative structure, the British became involved in the conflicts between central authority and the warrior lords of the countryside. The Company needed to protect its own access to the markets of India, and this meant making some sort of agreement with those warrior lords. Responding to challenges from the French, exploiting factional disputes, and using the revenues of the states they did control, the Company was able to put an ever larger, more effective army in the field against both the French and their indigenous allies, bringing the territories of those lords under the growing Company administration.

This process occurred in fits and starts from the mid eighteenth century onwards, counterpointing the conflicts between European powers elsewhere, in the Atlantic and in Europe itself. By the end of the Seven Years War in 1763 France was reduced to minor holdings in South Asia. The defeat of the Nawab of Bengal by Robert Clive at Plassey in 1757 and the installation of a new nawab by Clive effectively made Bengal a client state of the Company. The assumption in 1765 by the Company of the *diwani*, the revenues of the nawab, promised great riches and profits. Because of opposition by the British government and the British Company's Court of Directors in London to expansion and the expenditures it required, officials on the scene in India in the late eighteenth century exercised restraint in their attempts to expand Company control. Officials of the Company took up residence in princely courts, and, by monopolizing communication between the prince and the Company, and between the prince and the other Indian states, these Residents gave the Company control over the military forces of states and access as well to significant portions of the land revenues of the states.

What had been established as a trading company thus became a military and territorial power. But that position taxed the finances of the Company as well as its administrative capability. Even as the British government was dealing with unrest, revolution, and war in North America, the 1760s and 1770s saw efforts from London to reform the Company. In 1766–67 Lord Chatham attempted to reform the administration of the Company, a process that eventually led in 1773 to Lord North's Regulating Act. The India Act pushed through by William Pitt (the Younger) in 1784 established tighter control of the Company by the government even while not questioning the appropriateness of the Company as the ruler of a growing territorial presence in South Asia.

Under Lord Cornwallis (Illustration 4), who became governor-general of Bengal in 1784, the Company bureaucracy was reformed, appointments were made on merit, salaries were raised to discourage private trading by Company officials, and an emphasis was placed on professional service. But any restraint about expansion of British rule disappeared at the beginning of the nineteenth century under the governor-generalship of Richard Wellesley (1798–1805), who saw annexations in India as a part of the global conflict Britain was fighting with Revolutionary and Napoleonic France.

Illustration 4 Engraving of Charles, Marquis Cornwallis by George J. Stoddart, based on a painting by J. S. Copley.

Wellesley's legacy was a generation of Company administrators who shared his expansionist vision, and annexation became the explicit goal of the Company's officials in India. Each annexation brought the Company frontier close to new areas, and their annexation eventually took place. The assumed moral superiority of British civilization and the alleged corruption and moral bankruptcy of rule by Indian princes often served as a justification for these annexations, and supporters of annexation argued that British rule should improve the condition of Indians. The expense of the military operations connected with annexations, however, and their frequent failure to produce economic benefits for the Company or the British state served the cause of anti-annexationists. But opposition faded as the century wore on. The annexationist course of Company rule interacted with specific conditions at the local level to produce a myriad of different scenarios and frequent setbacks for the Company, but by 1857 more than a million square miles, 60 percent of the territory of India, and 75 percent of its people were under Company rule.[6]

The Company increasingly was the instrument by which the British government ruled its empire in South Asia as its trading role decreased. In 1813, a revision of the Company charter ended its monopoly on trade for all goods except tea, and that too was removed in 1833. But the Company itself was a crucial part of British political, economic, and social life in the years after Clive's victory at Plassey. Through its remittances of wealth from South Asia to England, it became an important element in the increasingly complex financing of the British state. One reason for the state intervention that culminated in Pitt's bill in 1784 was the growing perception that the prosperity of Britain depended on the Company's effective management of its Indian dominions. The financial relations between Great Britain and India have always been both controversial and difficult to unravel. British administrators insisted that the metropole was investing more in India than it drew from the colony, but some Indians insisted that the opposite was true. At the beginning of the twentieth century, Romesh Dutt claimed that the debt of British India was nothing more than a myth, calling it an "unjust tribute" that was the result of the British East India Company charging it with not only the cost of administering India but also the costs of wars in Afghanistan, China, and elsewhere outside the subcontinent, and parts of this argument have been supported by more recent historians. The economic historian H. V. Bowen concludes that while the capital returned from India may not have been significant enough to finance the industrial revolution in Britain, as some critics have claimed, it did have some impact. But whatever the actual transfers of capital between India and Great Britain, so many Britons depended on the Indian trade that the empire, in its South Asian form, acquired a central position in British identity.[7]

---

[6] Michael H. Fisher (ed.), *The Politics of the British Annexation of India, 1757–1857* (Oxford University Press, 1993), 1.

[7] P. J. Marshall, *Bengal: The British Bridgehead: Eastern India 1740–1828* (Cambridge University Press, 1987); Romesh Dutt, *The Economic History of India in the Victorian Age*

In spite of the claims that the Company's rule would remedy the supposed anarchy of South Asia, it brought the violence of military conquest and, it has recently been shown, the ordinary violence of both Company officials and non-Company Europeans to the region.[8] Company rule did not go unchallenged in India itself. In January 1779, Europeans were attacked in Calcutta and bricks thrown at the building that housed the royal supreme court and the Company's headquarters. Two years later, in August 1781, the governor, Warren Hastings, was forced to flee Benares after his troops were massacred by supporters of the raja, Chait Singh. There were also riots in parts of Awadh, brought on by attempts by British officers to enforce revenue collections, and in western Bihar. Taking place at the same time as the American Revolution, these disturbances seemed to pose a serious threat to the British position in India. They were particularly dangerous because they were concentrated in the northeast, the part of India that provided the East India Company with most of the resources it needed to maintain its operations.

C. A. Bayly has argued that such revolts were endemic in early colonial India.[9] In the countryside, attempts to increase revenues or slights to the status of local landholders led to periodic revolts. There were also conflicts between landlords and tenants, and disputes between settled peasant farmers and wandering tribes. In the cities of South Asia, there were revolts over market conditions, taxation, religion and caste, and the declining situation of artisans. The best remembered of these, the Revolt of 1857, was sparked by specific events: the annexation of Oudh and fears of pollution of Hindu and Muslim troops by an Enlistment Act that threatened to send them overseas and by the infamous Enfield rifle, which fired a cartridge smeared with animal grease. It was more widespread than was usually the case, and the soldiers were joined by a number of discontented civilians: nobles, landlords, and peasants, especially in the upper Ganges and in central India, feeling the weight of Company annexations and land assessments. Other parts of South

(London: Kegan Paul, Trench, Trubner and Co., 1916); Irfan Habib, "Colonization of the Indian Economy, 1757–1900," in Habib, *Essays in Indian History: Towards a Marxist Perception* (London: Anthem Press, 2002), 296–335, an essay originally published in 1975; H. V. Bowen, *The Business of Empire: The East India Company and Imperial Britain, 1756–1833* (Cambridge University Press, 2006); Linda Colley, *Britons: Forging the Nation, 1707–1837* (New Haven, CT: Yale University Press, 1992), 55–100; Kathleen Wilson, *The Sense of the People: Politics, Culture, and Imperialism in England, 1715–1785* (Cambridge University Press, 1995), 158–65.

[8] Elizabeth Kolsky, *Colonial Justice in British India* (Cambridge University Press, 2010).

[9] C. A. Bayly, *The New Cambridge History of India: Indian Society and the Making of the British Empire* (Cambridge University Press, 1987), 169–78.

Asia, and many of the princely states, remained loyal to the Company but, until the full weight of British military force could be brought to bear, it posed a serious threat to British control in the north. The aftermath, spurred on by rebel murders of British women, children, and wounded soldiers at Cawnpore and by newspaper reports of other atrocities, was vicious repression, including strapping rebels over the mouths of cannon that were then fired.

The revolts that marked nineteenth-century India never managed to end British rule, but they were part of a process by which the British were forced to change aspects of their rule in order to create a workable accommodation with the different parts of indigenous society. The most striking aspect of this came after the Revolt, when the government of India was reorganized, ending Company rule and creating the British Raj, which governed the subcontinent until independence in 1947. Annexations ceased and the remaining Indian princes, now viewed as the natural rulers of Indians, were cultivated as prime supports for British rule in the effort to bring government enlightened by British principles to the peoples of India. The decade after the Revolt also saw efforts to bolster the position of *taluqdars*, *zamindars*, and other local notables as a natural aristocracy who could help maintain loyalty to British rule. Ceremonial policies followed the same path: Lord Canning, the viceroy, gave titles to princes, notables. and officials who had been loyal during the Revolt, and a new British order of chivalry, the Star of India, was created in 1861 and given to Indian princes and senior officials.

There were also some efforts to expand Indian participation in the colonial state. The India Act of 1870 allowed the Government of India to appoint natives of India to any offices. But concerns about loyalty and an atmosphere of increased mistrust between the British and the peoples of South Asia hampered such efforts. On the British side, this was reinforced not only by the horrors of the Revolt and the increased isolation of the British in India, but also by the increasingly scientific racism that pervaded European social thought. On the Indian side, mistrust was fostered by the heavier weight of British rule and the assumption not only of racial superiority by the British but also the categorization of South Asians as irredeemably different and mired in traditional culture.

Especially in the second half of the nineteenth century, that traditional culture was symbolized for the British in the idea of caste as the central aspect of Hindu religion. Caste had certainly existed prior to the arrival of the British in South Asia, as an aspect of the ways in which society was organized in many parts of the subcontinent. The

Brahmins who were officials at the princely courts of the pre-colonial era emphasized their high status, and at other levels of society there were also distinctions made that in some ways drew upon Hindu beliefs. The social and economic changes that accompanied the increased British presence in places such as Bengal and Bombay in the eighteenth century encouraged the development of stronger bonds between Indian merchants to protect their livelihoods. But in the nineteenth century, the British colonial state began a process in which those distinctions became more clear-cut and rigid. Missionaries and officials had employed a language of caste in their descriptions of Indian society from the eighteenth century. They often understood caste distinctions as symptoms of the corruption and division of Indian society, contributors to the inherent tendency towards despotism that British rule would remedy. In the aftermath of the Revolt of 1857, however, and the paramount importance of maintaining public order that it underscored, caste was confirmed as the central aspect of British understandings of Indian society. The decennial census of India that was taken beginning in 1871–72, and the ethnographic survey of India, launched in 1901 and culminating in the publication of H. H. Risley's *The People of India* in 1908, made caste, Nicholas Dirks has argued, "the site for detailing a record of the customs of the people, the locus of all important information about Indian society." It became "the single most important trope for Indian society."[10] Legal codes, recruitment into the army, and criminalization of whole groups became contingent on British perceptions of caste and the characteristics it carried. By the late nineteenth century Indians themselves employed caste differences as a way, Susan Bayly argues, of "displaying markers of opposition to those of unlike and ritually inferior 'community'" and "contesting other people's advantages." Far from being a relic of pre-colonial India, caste became "an active and potent reference point" in modern India.[11]

The conquests of Clive, and the annexations by Wellesley and his successors, make up the usual account of British conquest of India. But those military and diplomatic actions were only a small part of the British effort in South Asia, for having laid claim to the subcontinent it was necessary to gain control over it. Certainly the British continued to use force in that task, as the repression that greeted indigenous opposition, from eighteenth-century riots to the Revolt in 1857 and the

[10] Nicholas Dirks, *Castes of Mind: Colonialism and the Making of Modern India* (Princeton University Press, 2001), 48–49.
[11] Susan Bayly, *The New Cambridge History of India: Caste, Society and Politics in India from the Eighteenth Century to the Modern Age* (Cambridge University Press, 1999), 189, 367.

massacre at Amritsar in 1919, indicates. But the British projected colonial power in other ways, and the decades following Plassey witnessed a political process that established colonial rule in South Asia. The extent to which the Company or Crown Raj marked a sharp break with pre-colonial India, or used pre-existing institutions and rulers has been the subject of disagreement. But what is clear is that through the use of both military and economic force, on the one hand, and diplomatic and discursive efforts, on the other, the British asserted their power over multiple areas of South Asian life. In many instances, the outcome of these processes was not conquest but limited and incomplete authority of the Company and British Raj. If these processes showed a remarkable willingness on the part of the British to intervene in the most mundane and intimate details of South Asians' lives, they also demonstrated the limits to British authority. Colonialism created sites for the interplay of British pressure and colonial resistance, accommodation, and negotiation that makes up the history not only of colonial India but also of many of the colonies that Great Britain and other European powers established in the eighteenth and nineteenth centuries.

The legal systems that the British found in Bengal (and territories annexed later) proved to be one of the most important sites on which these processes played out. While the British and other Europeans had viewed Australia and parts of New Zealand as unoccupied (*terra nullius*), they made no such claim in South Asia. But existing governments and legal codes were viewed by British observers, and many later commentators, as uncivilized and barbarian, and from soon after Plassey the Company and its officials tried to reform those codes according to Western lights. The reform has been described as a transition from Indian status-based law to British contract law, but in practice it created a situation of legal pluralism, in which litigants were able to position themselves in the legal and cultural space created by different legal codes.[12] The assumption of the *diwani* by the East India Company in 1765 made it responsible for administration of justice in Bengal, Bihar, and Orissa, and there were soon attempts to reform the indigenous legal codes and practices in those provinces. Piecemeal reforms in Warren Hastings' *Plan for the Administration of Justice* of 1772 and

---

[12] Lauren Benton, *Law and Colonial Cultures: Legal Regimes in World History 1400–1900* (New York: Cambridge University Press, 2002), esp. ch. 4. See also Benton, "Colonial Law and Cultural Difference: Jurisdictional Politics and the Formation of the Colonial State," *Comparative Studies in Society and History* 41, 3 (1999), 563–88; and Bernard Cohn, "Law and the Colonial State in India," in *Colonialism and its Forms of Knowledge: The British in India* (Princeton University Press, 1996), 57–75. For a different view, see Ranajit Guha, *Dominance without Hegemony: History and Power in Colonial India* (Cambridge, MA: Harvard University Press, 1997), esp. 60–72.

Lord Cornwallis' Legal Code for Bengal of 1793 began the process. Hastings sought to install British legal procedures and judges in Indian courts while respecting the Hindu and Muslim legal codes from the pre-colonial era by creating two courts in each district. Civil courts would use Muslim law for Muslims, and Hindu law for Hindus, in revenue and property disputes. Criminal courts would apply Muslim law universally. Cornwallis distinguished between public and private law: for the former, he drew heavily on British law and established contracts as the basis for legal relationships between individuals. Private law, in contrast, was strongly influenced by South Asian legal traditions and depended not on an individual thought of as an independent actor, as in public law, but rather on the force of religion, caste, and family in determining individual claims. Only in the nineteenth century was pre-colonial law replaced by British law. The most important step in this process was the Indian Penal Code, drafted by Thomas Macaulay in 1837 and finally instituted in 1860. A Code of Criminal Procedure was enacted in 1861. Strongly influenced by Benthamite Utilitarianism, Macaulay attempted to establish a uniform and predictable rule of law.

But legal reform was contested, British justice fragmentary, and the whole process hardly inevitable. This is evident in law concerning land use, ownership, and inheritance, an area of great concern to British administrators because of the fiscal requirements of the colonial state. Their efforts demonstrated how difficult it was to maintain the boundary between public and private law that Cornwallis envisioned. The absolute private property ownership by individuals consecrated by the public law was undercut by limitations placed on that ownership by private law that took land ownership to be a trust. The law became not so much the model of a purely capitalist system guaranteeing private property rights by contracts, but rather a system for negotiating compromises between those systems of land law that provided for community and kinship limits on private property and the demands of merchant capital. In the twentieth century, the South Asian legal system became an instrument for consolidating the positions of large landholders in order to maintain social order in the countryside and thus to allow further development of the industrial and commercial sector of the economy.[13]

These were not just abstract legal theories for Hastings, Cornwallis, and later administrators. It is now apparent that the British took over an economy that, under the Mughals, had already seen agricultural

---

[13] D. A. Washbrook, "Law, State and Agrarian Society in Colonial India," *Modern Asian Studies* 15 (1981), 649–721.

investment, expansion into new lands, experiments with new crops, and significant manufacturing and trade. This was not, however, the British perception, and legal reforms were related to fiscal reforms intended to increase productivity and revenues, and to foster the economic development of the subcontinent. They used different tenure systems in different parts of the country that, as David Ludden has shown, drew on a variety of sources for their ideas including Persian techniques adapted by the Mughals as well as Utilitarian ideas from Britain.[14] In Bengal, the role of the large landholders, the *zamindars*, was buttressed by Cornwallis' Permanent Settlement of 1793. This gave them a major role in revenue collection as well as the exercise of some judicial functions. But *zamindars* often proved unable to meet the tax payments expected of them, and in later settlements in other parts of India this attempt to create a British-style landed gentry was replaced by a system that, rather than consolidating the role of the *zamindars*, reinforced the role of the *ryots*, or larger peasant proprietors.

But the entire process underscores the contingency of imperial rule and the inability of the British to impose their will absolutely on their new subjects. The ability of the Raj to control events tapered off at the local level and these revenue systems required accommodation of local variations and the outcomes of local power conflicts between different clans. When some *zamindars* proved to be not improving landlords but exploiters of the peasantry and failed to pay their own taxes, the local district commissioner was forced to make adaptations in order to meet the revenue goals of the Company. *Ryotwari* systems also had to be altered because of local village conditions.[15] But whatever the local peculiarities of the Company's revenue schemes, they turned land into a commodity, leading to numerous local struggles for the entitlements that came from the colonial state. Especially after 1857, rural discontent appears to have been less communitarian opposition to the imposition of private property and production for the market than individuals, families, and kin groups competing with one another for benefits.[16]

The effect of these fiscal reforms on productivity was less than the British hoped. Agriculture showed immense local variation even

---

[14] David Ludden, *The New Cambridge History of India: An Agrarian History of South Asia* (Cambridge University Press, 1999), 125–28, 159–60.

[15] Robert Frykenberg, *Guntur District 1788–1848: A History of Local Influence and Central Authority in South India* (Oxford: Clarendon Press, 1965); Anand A. Yang, *The Limited Raj: Agrarian Relations in Colonial India, Saran District, 1793–1920* (Berkeley and Los Angeles: University of California Press, 1989).

[16] Ludden, *Agrarian History*, 180.

as it remained the most important sector of the Indian economy.[17] Nonetheless, agriculture was not able to lead a transformation of the South Asian economy. There were famines in the 1870s and 1890s in some districts that followed crop failures and pointed to not only the ineffectiveness of relief efforts but also the failings of transportation into the interior. But there was increased cultivation of commercial crops, and windfall price increases around mid-century may have increased some rural incomes. Notwithstanding weaknesses in times of famine, improvements in transportation after the railroad system began to be built in 1853 may have allowed peasants to produce primarily for the market and purchase foodstuffs. But the Indian agricultural sector was not the producer of capital, foreign exchange, and rising domestic spending that the agricultural revolution in eighteenth-century Great Britain seems to have been.

It is also clear that the industrial development of India, even after the middle of the nineteenth century, did not occur to an extent that one can find the "industrial revolution" hoped for by nineteenth-century British commentators. By the twentieth century only a relatively small number of Indian workers were employed in modern factory industry (1.5 million out of a population of 353 million in 1931), and these may have replaced those who previously had worked in handicraft industries rather than adding to the size of the industrial sector.[18] The industries that did develop were concentrated in specific places. Bombay was particularly favored: cotton manufacturing was overwhelmingly located in Bombay Presidency and Bombay City itself until after World War I, and there were railway repair shops and the major harbor on the Indian Ocean in the city as well. The jute industry was concentrated in Calcutta, and coal and iron mining and steel manufacturing was primarily in the western part of Bengal. In 1913, the Indian railways, mostly built through the direct intervention of the colonial state, accounted for half the railway mileage in Asia. But the development payback of this

---

[17] See Neil Charlesworth, *British Rule and the Indian Economy 1800–1914* (London: Macmillan, 1982) for a useful summary of the economic history of the Raj. For the debates about Indian economic performance, see Amiya Kumar Bagchi, *The Political Economy of Underdevelopment* (Cambridge University Press, 1982); Hamza Alavi, P. L. Burns, G. R. Knight, P. B. Mayer, and Doug McEachern, *Capitalism and Colonial Production* (London: Croom Helm, 1980); Deepak Lal, *The Hindu Equilibrium: Cultural Stability and Economic Stagnation, India 1500 BC–1980 AD*, vol. I (Oxford: Clarendon Press, 1984); Rajnarayan Chandavarkar, *Imperial Power and Popular Politics: Class, Resistance and the State in India, c. 1850–1950* (Cambridge University Press, 1998), 30–73, and *The Origins of Industrial Capitalism in India* (Cambridge University Press, 1994).

[18] Charlesworth, *British Rule*, 32.

was limited. Railway construction does not seem to have provided a strong stimulus for industrial development, as orders for rails, locomotives, and rolling stock largely went to manufacturers in Britain. Only around the turn of the twentieth century did coal imports begin to decline and an indigenous steel industry develop.

British legal reforms of commercial and property relations, and their attempts to stimulate agricultural and industrial productivity, proved less effective than hoped, and are a reminder of the limits of imperial power. The same is true of attempts to regulate other aspects of South Asians' lives such as sexual behavior, labor, and migration. Concerns about sexuality, which reappear in many other colonies in Asia and Africa, remind us that colonizers did not uniformly respect the supposed differences between Europeans and indigenous peoples, and that one task on which the colonial administrations expended much effort, and often failed, was to maintain the boundary between colonizer and colonized. Europeans also used gendered differences to assert their own difference from the societies they were in the process of colonizing. As we have seen in Australia and New Zealand, the colonial venture itself highlighted what were conceived as masculine virtues of physical daring and hard work in the explorers and settlers who created the empires. If, as Ann Laura Stoler has suggested, one aspect of the colonies was their contribution to the creation of a bourgeois self-identity for Europeans, the unwillingness of some Europeans to accomplish this was not just a personal failing, but rather redounded to the discredit of the entire colonial project in the eyes of some Europeans.[19] In settler colonies such as Australia and New Zealand this created a highly masculinized European culture, while in India the masculinity of Europeans who were making the empire was often contrasted with the effeminacy of the rulers and elites of the societies that were being conquered. Gender differences were also used by commentators to measure the contrast between European society and the societies in which it was exercising power and authority. The way in which a colonial society seemed – to European colonizers – to treat women was viewed as one of the most important indices of the relative lack of civilization of the colonized society.

The behavior of both colonizers and colonized was thus an important concern of the colonial authorities in India. British efforts along these lines, however, often demonstrated not colonial authority and power but its limits. Contention over jurisdiction introduced room for both

---

[19] Ann Laura Stoler, *Race and the Education of Desire: Foucault's "History of Sexuality" and the Colonial Order of Things* (Durham, NC: Duke University Press, 1995), esp. 95–136.

colonized and colonizer to maneuver to their advantage. Non-Company Europeans found opportunities for lawlessness, especially violence against Indians, in the colony. Often derided as "loafers" by officials, their penchant for beating, raping, and murdering Indians cast doubt on the validity of British claims to be bringing civilization to India, but also was assisted by numerous exceptions based on race in the "reform" legal codes instituted during the nineteenth century. Rather than the equal law claimed by Macaulay and other reformers, these codes "created a racialized and unequal system that provided European British subjects with special privileges and exemptions."[20]

A particular area in which British courts made judgments was that of sexual behavior. British merchants and soldiers often established households with Indian women, a practice that underscored the difficulties for the East India Company in controlling the intimate relationships of both colonizers and colonized.[21] While the Cornwallis codes of the 1790s prohibited such relationships, they nonetheless continued to occur – often not formalized in a marriage contract – and their mixed-race offspring themselves became part of the British establishment in South Asia. But the Company and criminal and civil courts usually treated these relationships as formal marriages. As they made decisions involving these relationships, they used the authority of the colonial state to define boundaries between colonizer and colonized, reinforced the paternal authority of the Company officials, and extended Company authority into the lives of native women and their children. In those same discussions, however, those women and children were able to advance their own claims.

More difficult was the justification for an extension of Company control into South Asian families in which there was no European presence. The most notable instance of this concerned the Bengali practice of sati or widow-burning, in which a widow would join her husband on his funeral pyre. Since the late eighteenth century this had horrified Company administrators.[22] Yet their efforts to deal with it demonstrated the inability to impose clear legal distinctions on the colony. The existence of sati was viewed as an indication of the barbaric character of Indian civilization, and a justification for the British presence. As British administrators and missionaries debated the relative merits, and political possibility, of using the authority of the Company to abolish

---

[20] Kolsky, *Colonial Justice*, 106.
[21] Durba Ghosh, *Sex and the Family in Colonial India: The Making of Empire* (Cambridge University Press, 2006).
[22] Lata Mani, *Contentious Traditions: The Debate on Sati in Colonial India* (Berkeley and Los Angeles: University of California Press, 1998).

the practice it became a privileged locus for the civilizing mission that informed the policies of the Company in the nineteenth century. But when it was finally abolished in 1829, it represented a significant step in interference by the Company in Bengali family practices.

While sati attracted much attention from the British because it seemed to demonstrate the great differences between British and Indian civilization and the value of British rule, British courts in India used their authority to enforce norms of behavior on both European men and Indian men and women in more mundane, everyday settings as well. In these decisions they sought to regulate relationships both between colonizer and colonized and between colonized subjects themselves. As with sati, however, these efforts brought out the contradictions and complexities of British attempts to bring British legal principles and practices to India.

This is apparent in instances of sexual violence. Sexual assaults by European men against native women often led to acquittals on the presumption that native women who were in close contact with European men were making themselves sexually available. The task was more complex in cases of sexual violence between South Asian men and women, for this involved an extension of colonial power into the native community. While imposing a legal system that purported to be more modern and humane, the British nonetheless made decisions that did little to change the difficulties in obtaining justice that pre-colonial Islamic criminal law put in the way of rape victims. Islamic law, a part of the criminal law in India until 1860, placed the heaviest burden of proof on the victim of a rape, discouraging complaints and leading to low rates of conviction in cases when a complaint was actually made. Even while condemning Islamic law as barbaric and uncivilized, British law also assumed that a woman making a rape complaint had consented to intercourse and then lied about it. In some instances judges vacated rape charges and replaced them with adultery charges against the woman who had brought the original complaint. The British law therefore tended to be similar to the pre-colonial Islamic criminal law – leading the historian of these cases to ask what was specifically colonial about the situation – and in exerting the power of the colonial state over South Asians, it made the victim the central part of the trial and brought to the foreground the character, physical appearance, and sexual behavior of the victim.[23]

---

[23] Elizabeth Kolsky, "The Rule of Colonial Indifference: Rape on Trial in Early Colonial India, 1805–1857," *Journal of Asian Studies* 69 (2010), 1093–117, and "'The Body Evidencing the Crime': Rape on Trial in Colonial India, 1860–1947," *Gender & History* 22 (2010), 109–30.

The need to manage gender relationships also informed other colonial relationships. The health dangers for Europeans of living in the tropics, and the heavy death toll that they experienced, raised fears of degeneration that played into concerns prevalent among European scientists and social theorists during the nineteenth century. There were numerous diseases that struck Europeans, but medical concerns about venereal disease, viewed as a potential threat to control over colonial subjects, were especially prominent. By associating venereal disease with "native" men controlled by their sexuality, and with "native" women who passively continued in their ignorant behavior, colonial authorities were able to build colonial hierarchies of gender, race, and nationality on the terrain of sexuality. Colonial medicine in particular, represented as modern, rational, and objective, was a specific form in which British power was projected on colonial peoples. The attempts of the British to apply a range of medical, administrative, and cultural controls of sexuality fundamentally shaped the experience of empire both in the colonies and the metropole. The empire, in this rendering, emerges as an enterprise that can be seen as "simultaneously successful and anxious, as concurrently 'home' and 'abroad,' and as always and necessarily anything but homogenous."[24]

The layering of assumptions about colonial peoples and their possible effects on the British played out in other areas as well. Increasingly in the second half of the nineteenth century Indian intellectuals who were becoming politically self-conscious, and insisting on a larger role in the governance of India, were portrayed as "effeminate babus," having an "unnatural" or "perverted" form of masculinity.[25] With concerns in Britain about the "New Woman," a militant working class, and feminist demands, discussions of British policies in India reformulated and naturalized the hierarchical relations between the British nation and its subjects. The empire – both metropole and colony – thus became the field within which versions of masculinity in both Britain and India were constructed.

The attempts by the British to control intimate details of the lives of their colonial subjects not only suggest that this was one of the most

---

[24] Philippa Levine, *Prostitution, Race and Politics: Policing Venereal Disease in the British Empire* (New York and London: Routledge, 2003), 4. For broader arguments about technology and science, see Michael Adas, *Machines as the Measure of Man: Science, Technology, and Ideologies of Western Dominance* (Ithaca, NY: Cornell University Press, 1989); and Gyan Prakash, *Another Reason: Science and the Imagination of Modern India* (Princeton University Press, 1999).

[25] Mrinalini Sinha, *Colonial Masculinity: The "Manly Englishman" and the "Effeminate Bengali" in the Late 19th Century* (Manchester University Press, 1995).

important areas of interaction between colonizer and colonized, but also shows the extraordinary effort at projecting power that colonial rule entailed. It also brings out the limits of that power, and the discursive convolutions needed to make sense of the contradictions in the colonial project. The management of gender and racial boundaries in colonial India become crucial to understanding colonialism itself. Much more complex than the conquest of princely states or the imposition of revenue systems, the history of colonial India involved multiple negotiations between a British version of how the colony should be and its ability to impose that on the people who lived in the subcontinent.

The same processes became apparent as the British attempted to manage labor practices in both agriculture and industry. Influenced by neo-classical economic theories, there was a tendency for the British to contrast a model of free labor with the restrictions placed upon labor in the India that they found. These limitations became an essential component of the British version of India as a place of underdevelopment. Their goal, therefore, became to eliminate these restrictions and create the free labor force that capitalist enterprises expected.

These concerns about free and unfree labor were first apparent in the countryside as the colonial authorities tried to create free labor systems that would, they thought, increase productivity and tax revenues. These proved only partially successful, as in many parts of India agricultural labor systems were constructed out of a combination of older labor relationships and the freer labor market that the British tried to create. One example of this was in rural Bihar, where the relationships between lords (*maliks*) and their dependent subjects (*kamias*) were transformed by the imposition of new land tenure arrangements by the British.[26] The British emphasis not on relations between people (*malik–kamia*) but on land tenure transformed *maliks* from lords into landlords, and *kamias* from dependent servants into bonded laborers. The key to this transformation was the emphasis in the Permanent Settlement of 1793 on landownership by *zamindars*, rather than the Mughal emphasis on rights to revenue collection. For many in Bihar, who did not have *zamindar* land titles, this led to pursuit of land through a variety of forms of tenure, such as subtenancy or the acquisition of peasant holdings through forced eviction or purchase. For rural laborers, the formal abolition of slavery in 1843 led to a restructuring of the *kamias* into bonded laborers, bound permanently to their landlords through debt bondage. With even low-caste but rich peasants in control of land, the

[26] Gyan Prakash, *Bonded Histories: Genealogies of Labor Servitude in Colonial India* (Cambridge University Press, 1990).

kamia labor system of debt bondage spread into new areas in spite of British attempts to end it.

Labor migration showed similar patterns of adaptation. Migration often depended on intermediary recruiters and foremen, or jobbers, whose role in both plantation and industrial enterprises seemed to limit labor freedom but facilitate its recruitment and management.[27] On the tea plantations that developed in Assam in eastern India in the 1830s, laborers were brought in as indentured labor from China and, after 1860, from Bengal and then South India. Tea plantations in the Nilgiri hills in the south of India also recruited labor in the late nineteenth century from Tamil villages in Mysore. In Assam, contractors and informal recruiters known as *sardars* were used by the plantations to recruit laborers, while in Nilgiri district owners had recourse to older practices of advance payments similar to debt bondage and to foremen, known as *maistris*, to recruit labor. By the turn of the twentieth century, these had become normal practices, as plantation owners transformed pre-colonial relationships between *sardars* or *maistris* and laborers into a labor system that met their needs.

These patterns of labor recruitment and discipline can also be found in the industrial centers of Bombay and Calcutta. The Bombay cotton industry recruited labor from distant rural areas in the southern districts of Bombay Presidency and the eastern United Provinces north of the city. The jute mills that developed in Calcutta in the 1850s and 1860s also drew labor from the countryside, in many instances from older handicraft weaving villages but also from peasant communities that cultivated rice and other crops. As the industry grew, its recruitment area expanded into the United Provinces in the northwest. The mining operations in Bengal were in rural areas, in Bihar and Orissa, and the rural population, recruited as in Bombay and Calcutta by contractors, provided the labor force for those enterprises. In these industries, workers were often hired by jobbers rather than the companies. These men wielded great power until the late 1920s, and in some respects were crucial not only for recruiting workers but also in presenting worker grievances to the textile companies. Nonetheless, their power was diffused, and was limited by their need to manage the competing demands of both employers and workers. The iron foundries, railway workshops, and engineering works in Bengal recruited labor on a more local basis, but still drew from rural communities around Calcutta.

---

[27] Barbara Evans, "Constructing a Plantation Labor Force: The Plantation–Village Nexus in South India," *Indian Social and Economic History Review* 32 (1995), 155–76.

Thus, the labor systems found on plantations and in industrial enterprises continued to include informal aspects that limited the function-
ing of a completely free labor market as described by neo-classical
economists. This was a frequent concern as Europeans imposed capitalist economic systems on their colonies. In India, as elsewhere, it
was viewed by administrators as a failure of the colonial regime. More
recently it has been seen as a symptom of the incomplete penetration of
capitalism in India, perhaps as an aspect of its colonial status, and therefore as an explanation for its underdevelopment. But for both employers
and workers these informal aspects of the system were less atavisims
of a pre-colonial or pre-capitalist era than significant aspects of the
process of negotiation and adaptation that marked rural and industrial
change in colonial India.

The strength and utility of these adaptations were apparent in the
twentieth century as labor militancy increased. Many members of the
new industrial workforce retained strong links to their rural agricultural backgrounds and even while remaining integrated into their rural
village, industrial workers found industrial work in the city to be a necessary part of their family economy in their home village. The continued rural connections of these workers, as well as the kinship ties that
linked them, depressed wages and alleviated the need on the part of
the companies to provide housing and other services needed by the
growing labor forces. But they also affected labor discipline, making
it difficult for employers to enforce labor contracts in spite of a series
of laws passed by the colonial government between the 1850s and the
1920s that facilitated the recruitment and control of laborers for plantations and industry. These rural connections provided the basis for labor
organization and resistance to management policies especially between
the World Wars, when there were strikes in many of these industries.
Far from being a detriment to the formation of a militant working class,
links to the countryside were important supports for an increasingly
restive labor force. In general strikes that occurred in Bombay in 1928
and 1929, the onset of the strike was marked by an exodus of workers
from Bombay to the countryside, helped by the timing of the strikes
during harvests and rural festivals. The historian Richard Newman
estimates that about 60,000 workers sat out the 1928 strike in their village, and government reports show that about 50,000 workers spent the
1929 strike in their village.[28]

---

[28] Richard Newman, *Workers and Unions in Bombay, 1918–1929: A Study of Organisation
in the Cotton Mills* (Canberra: Australian National University, 1981), 157, 203.

The British experience in colonial India was therefore marked by a series of efforts by the colonial state to gain control of and manage legal, sexual, fiscal, and labor relations between colonizer and colonized, colonizer and colonizer, and colonized and colonized. In each of these relationships, it proved difficult for the colonial state to project its power and authority to the extent that it desired, as colonial subjects – and even Europeans – found ways of evading, manipulating, or ignoring the dictates of the colonial state. The clear identities and boundaries that existed in the minds of British administrators could not be maintained in the fields, factories, and streets of India. In this respect, colonial India served as an unintended model for nineteenth- and twentieth-century European colonialism elsewhere.

The French in Indochina

France retained five *comptoirs* in India, at Pondichéry, Karikal, Yanaon, Chandernagor, and Mahé, even as the British Raj was being consolidated. The few French settlers there were primarily merchants who sought to participate in the trade with India, but they found themselves increasingly marginalized as British control over the princely states of the subcontinent became more formal. But France searched for and found a colonial empire elsewhere in Asia at this time, especially in Indochina. Other European powers had established trading outlets in Indochina, beginning with the Portuguese in the early sixteenth century. Catholic missionaries from France had been there since the seventeenth century, but faced suspicion and occasional persecution from the rulers of Cambodia, Laos, and Vietnam. French merchants established a trading post in Tonkin in the north in 1684, and another one south of Saigon two years later. A trade agreement was negotiated with the government in Annam in 1748, and in 1787 the French assisted an exiled prince of Annam, Nguyen-Anh, to regain his throne as the Emperor Ghia-Long. By 1802 Ghia-Long was ruling over the eastern part of Southeast Asia, called Vietnam, from Tonkin in the north to Cochinchina in the south. Ship-repair facilities and trading privileges in Tourane Bay were tangible results of this intervention for the French.

After the turn of the nineteenth century, however, French activities in Southeast Asia were disrupted by the domestic and European concerns of the Revolution and empire, the weakening of the French position in India as Britain consolidated its position there, and the rapid growth of Singapore as a British trading post in Southeast Asia. With the restoration of the Bourbon Louis XVIII in 1814–15, however, French interest in Indochina increased. Several French voyages into the Pacific during the Restoration – including privately financed voyages by Bordeaux merchants and official naval voyages – had mixed results. Ghia-Long's death in 1820 led to a turn against relations with Europeans at the Annamite court, and it proved difficult for European emissaries to make any headway in improving conditions for trade or for missionaries attempting to convert Indochinese to either Catholic or Protestant Christianity. In spite of this, French trade with Indochina continued to grow, with over fifty merchant vessels sailing there from Bordeaux alone in the four years after 1826.[29] Missionary activity also increased in spite of opposition from the Annam government.

As the Pacific basin and its adjoining land areas became better known, the French began to fear that their European rivals would gain a trade advantage over them in the region. Enticed by the prospect of China as a market for French goods, and concerned about the British establishment of Hong Kong as an entrepôt for that market, the French searched for another entrance into East Asia, and found it in Indochina. The execution of several French missionaries in Indochina in the 1850s led to an unsuccessful diplomatic mission by Charles de Montigny to Siam (Thailand), Cambodia, and Vietnam that sought protection for missionaries in the future. French naval bombardment of Da Nang in the south of Vietnam also produced no positive results, and, with further urging by the Catholic Church, Emperor Napoleon III supported an expedition in 1858 that captured Saigon. But it was only after the end of the War of Italian Unification (1859–60) in Europe and French peace with China in 1860 that the French expeditionary force moved outside that city. The capture of My Tho on April 13, 1861 opened the Mekong Delta and Cambodia to French control, and the Treaty of Saigon in June 1862 with the Annamese Emperor Tu Duc ceded to France three provinces of Cochinchina in the south and opened three ports to French commerce. A Franco-Siamese treaty in 1863 confirmed a French protectorate over Cambodia, the kingdom west of Annam and Cochinchina. By 1866 France had annexed the western provinces of the south, giving France control of the southern portion of the Indochinese peninsula.

Hopes that the Mekong River could provide an opening for trade with southern China, Laos, and Burma were disappointed by the failure of expeditions in 1866–68, but the Red River in the north seemed a possible substitute. A French military expedition in 1873 moved up the Red River towards Hanoi in support of a French arms merchant, J. Dupuis,

---

[29] John Dunmore, *French Explorers in the Pacific: The Nineteenth Century* (Oxford: Clarendon Press, 1969), 229.

whose activities in the Chinese province of Yunnan were interfered with by Annamite functionaries in Hanoi. After the commanding French officer, Lieutenant Francis Garnier, was killed in an engagement with the forces of the Emperor of Annam, the threat of a larger French military expedition made the emperor agree to a treaty with France in 1874. This gave France possession in principle of Cochinchina, established a French protectorate over Annam, and opened the Red River and the ports of Qui Nham, Haiphong, and Hanoi to European commerce.

With the firm establishment of republican institutions in France by 1877, some republicans began to look to extend French influence in Southeast Asia. Beginning in 1879 Admiral Bernard Jauréguiberry, the minister of marine, urged further expansion, and events in Annam played into his hands. By 1881 the Emperor of Annam had once again come under the influence of the Chinese, who refused to recognize the validity of the 1874 treaty between France and Annam and restricted access by French merchants and missionaries to the Red River. In September 1881, the government in Paris, headed by Jules Ferry, ordered the French governor of Cochinchina to demonstrate French power, but without undertaking activities that might lead to military involvement. An expedition led by the naval Captain Henri Rivière was sent to Tonkin, the northern part of Vietnam. Ignoring his instructions, Rivière carried out a plan pushed by merchants and missionaries at Hanoi and Haiphong, capturing the citadel at Hanoi in April 1882. This was a serious blow to the Annamese emperor, and it opened the way for a possible French conquest of Tonkin. Such a move by the French, however, would probably have led to a war with China. While Ferry backed Rivière's actions after the event, neither he, the Annamese, nor the Chinese were interested in pursuing the conflict, and the three parties agreed to a settlement by which Annam accepted a Chinese zone of influence in the north, in Tonkin, and a French one in the south, in Cochinchina.

But in 1883 a second Ferry ministry resumed the French advance, aiming at the conquest of Tonkin. Once again Rivière led an expedition up the Red River, but in May 1883 he was killed. News of his death fueled the perception in Paris not only that French national honor had been damaged, but also that French national interests were at stake in the Red River delta. France sent an expeditionary force that would reach 35,000 men by early 1885. By that time, France had concluded and ratified treaties with Annam and Cambodia, fought and ended an undeclared war with China, and gone through a political crisis in Paris that ended the ministerial career of Jules Ferry, now derisively called "le Tonkinois" by his political opponents. In 1887 a series of

decrees consolidated the various French possessions in Southeast Asia –
Annam, Tonkin, Cochinchina, Cambodia – into a unified government
based in Saigon. This French government ruled Annam, Tonkin, and
Cambodia indirectly through the indigenous princes, but administered
Cochinchina directly. But the decrees did not end government from
Paris – only a telegram away – and the treaties did not end the fighting:
resistance in the region to French control continued into the twentieth
century.[30]

A treaty in 1893 established a French protectorate over Laos, and
having gained at least nominal control of the entire region of Indochina,
the French began a slow process of transformation of the region to
bring the benefits of French civilization. As we will see in Chapter 6,
each colonial empire systematized its governance in retrospect. But as
these colonial administrations developed, they were often marked by
inconsistencies and contradictions. French policies in Indochina were
a combination of grand projects and piecemeal improvisations. For the
administrators sent by the French Republic, the primary concerns were
the creation of institutions that would guarantee stability and the fiscal
resources needed to operate the colonial state in a region in which, in
fact, French control was very uneven. In the case of Vietnam, this meant
co-optation of the elite who had, under the pre-colonial government,
administered the country. In Laos and Cambodia, the French governed
through the states that existed prior to French control. In each of these
areas, the French created a group of indigenous Indochinese who maintained some semblance of their position and status by working with the
colonial regime.

Ironically, given the anti-clericalism of the Republic and the harshly
anti-clerical policies instituted by the Republic in France itself, the French
administration also cooperated, even if uneasily, with the Catholic missionaries who were in Indochina. Those missionaries themselves usually gave at least nominal allegiance to the Republican regime, and in
return the administration left many colonial activities to the missionaries. Hospitals, schools, and similar activities tended to be run by the
Catholic Church after the French took over. This occurred with only
occasional interference from Paris, which often focused on the inability
of the poorly funded missionary schools to teach Indochinese the most
obvious sign of assimilation, the French language. The mission schools
also continued to spread facility with the romanized Vietnamese language, called *quoc ngu*, based on a dictionary that was developed by

[30] Aix-en-Provence, France, Centre d'Archives d'Outre-Mer, Indo, GGI, 6142–64,
    doss. 19.

the Jesuit missionary Alexandre de Rhodes in the seventeenth century. The French allowed the use of only French and *quoc ngu* as official languages. But constructing a new educational system was beyond the capability of the colonial regime, and the difficulties of creating a secular educational system that would teach universal knowledge of French led some French officials before World War I to argue that it would be more practical to teach French only to an elite, while *quoc ngu* was used to spread French ideas to most of the population.[31] In the end, French colonial rule in Vietnam undercut the high levels of popular literacy and the well-educated mandarin elite that had marked the pre-colonial period, leaving most Vietnamese unable to communicate in either of the languages used by their colonial rulers.

French colonial rule sought as well to increase exports from Indochina.[32] As demand for rice grew during the nineteenth century, the central provinces of Cochinchina and the Mekong Delta in the south became important participants in a trade that connected to Hong Kong, Japan, Singapore, the Netherlands Indies, the British East Indies, and Ceylon. Under the French, this continued to be the most important growth sector of the economy: rice exports multiplied thirty times between 1860 and 1928 and by 1930 Indochina trailed only Burma as an exporter of rice. This increased production for the export market, however, came at the cost of the concentration of landholding in the hands of a small part of the population and declining per capita food consumption. At the same time coffee and tea cultivation spread from the area north of Saigon into Tonkin, especially in the Red River valley, and after the turn of the century rubber plantations became one of the most important sectors of the economy. Introduced from Malaya in 1897, rubber cultivation spread in a broad arc from northwest of Saigon east into the *terres rouges* of eastern Cochinchina. The establishment of the Banque d'Indochine in 1875 facilitated investment in France's Asian colonies, and a mining sector also began to develop by the 1890s. Coal was found in several sites in Tonkin, and zinc and tin mines opened in that province in the 1920s. While the expectation was that the colony would not develop industries that would compete with those in France itself, the inability of the metropole to supply some goods, such as steel and cement, for the Indochinese market stimulated their manufacture in the colony. By the period between the World Wars, the policy of

[31] J. P. Daughton, *An Empire Divided: Religion, Republicanism, and the Making of French Colonialism, 1880–1914* (Oxford University Press, 2006), 111.

[32] Pierre Brocheux and Daniel Hémery, *Indochina: An Ambiguous Colonization, 1858–1954* (Berkeley and Los Angeles: University of California Press, 2009), 116–80.

mise en valeur – making the colonies more productive – dictated concerted efforts by the French administration to develop the economic resources of the colony. Electric power plants were constructed in the 1930s, along with a naval arsenal in Saigon and glassworks and porcelain manufactures.

The French also invested heavily in improvements in infrastructure that would link together the different provinces of the region and connect the developing plantations and industries of the interior to the metropole and the world market. In the last years of the nineteenth century and the first three decades of the twentieth, the French devoted significant investment to transportation facilities. Roads were built and improved in many parts of the colony, and harbors at Haiphong and Saigon became important links between the Indochinese interior and both Asian and Western markets for the commodities drawn from Indochina. Saigon, the port for the rice-producing regions of Cochinchina, became one of the most important rice ports in the world as well as the sixth largest port in the French empire.

Perhaps the most ambitious effort on the part of the French at improving the Indochinese infrastructure was the construction of the *Transindochine* railroad. Railroads were the most obvious signs of modernity in Indochina as they were in nineteenth-century Europe, harnessing energy for economic benefit and imposing "modern" practices such as scheduling and timetables on their users. The railway project was first discussed in the late 1870s, with some construction occurring in the 1880s. But it was not until the turn of the century that a railroad was planned that would link together the different provinces of the colony and foster the commercial and moral progress that would justify French colonial control. For its principal planner, Governor-General Paul Doumer, it had the additional advantages of allowing a "peaceful conquest" of the country, and improving relief from natural disasters and famines.[33] It was to link the Chinese border with Hanoi, Saigon, Bangkok, and Phnom Penh, although Doumer's plan was never completed. Constructed at French expense, either through direct state investment or state bonds, the line cost over 4 billion 1939 francs, and took up half of the total French public and private investment in Indochina between 1885 and 1939.[34]

These and other transformations of the Indochinese economy by the French brought with them changes in the forms of labor in the

---

[33] Paul Doumer, *L'Indo-Chine française (Souvenirs)* (Paris: Vuibert et Nony, 1905), 324–48.
[34] David Del Testa, "Workers, Culture and the Railroads in French Colonial Indochina, 1905–1936," *French Colonial History* 2 (2002), 181–98.

colony. Significant differences existed between plantation and industrial workers because of the geographical patterns in which these enterprises developed. The railway workshops at Trường Thi were located in a well-populated part of the colony and were therefore able to draw on a relatively large local labor pool, and those workers maintained strong relationships with their families and kin groups in the surrounding peasant villages. Plantations, in contrast, were located in a relatively sparsely populated part of the interior and depended on *corvée* (forced) labor to construct access roads. Mines also developed in sparsely populated areas. The absence of a local labor supply forced both plantations and mines to seek their labor supply over long distances and institute labor systems that would both attract labor migration and overcome the disadvantages of casual labor. Workers on plantations were often brought in as contract labor, usually on three-year contracts. These plantation workers proved difficult to retain, and plantation owners enlisted the power of the colonial state to enforce contracts against workers who walked away from their commitments. They thus replicated the problems that casual labor created for nineteenth-century European industrialists and for plantations and industries in other Asian colonies and in Africa. The enforcement of the plantation labor system may have contributed to making plantation workers stronger opponents of the colonial regime than the railroad workers by the period between the World Wars. While there were labor protests by the workers in the workshops at Trường Thi in 1923, 1927, 1929, and 1936, they focused on working conditions, and a wave of protests against the colonial regime itself in 1930–31 did not attract their support. Instead, these protests drew upon miners and rubber-plantation workers in other parts of the country. It was only after 1936, as the colonial administration failed to reform labor codes and material conditions in the workshops and towns deteriorated, that the railway workers turned against the French regime.[35]

If labor was difficult to control, so also were the boundaries between colonizer and colonized. French culture in the late nineteenth and early twentieth centuries was pervaded by fears of racial decay from hybridity and disease. In the colonial context, in which the ability of the French to project authority over not only recently conquered colonial subjects but also French men and women who had left behind metropolitan France was in question, these fears contributed to attempts to organize

[35] Del Testa, "Workers, Culture and the Railroads"; Martin J. Murray, "'White Gold' or 'White Blood'? The Rubber Plantations of Colonial Indochina, 1910–1940," *Journal of Peasant Studies* 19 (1992), 41–67.

the physical spaces, public behavior, and private lives of both colonizers and colonized. The development of rubber plantations and other
large-scale agricultural projects by the French required management of
the landscape, and often changed the long-standing agricultural practices of Indochinese. The forests of Indochina in particular attracted
French attention, both as possible sites of exploitation and through the
imposition of French forestry practices on the pre-colonial practices
of the Indochinese themselves. French urban planning, as it built new
cities in Saigon and Hanoi, attempted to create European living conditions for the colonizers as well as control the spaces in which French
could interact with Indochinese. Yet, as elsewhere, these restrictions
were only partially effective, and French discussions of the colony were
marked by anxiety about the potential for disease and physical and
moral degeneration posed by racial interaction. To some extent this
was a concern about political order, and the French prison system that
was constructed in colonial Indochina aimed at isolating and punish-
ing opponents of the regime. It showed few rehabilitation efforts such
as prisons in Europe were attempting at the same time, however, and
its low levels of funding made it a sign of both colonial power and the
limits of that power. Overcrowding, the French inspector Chastenet de
Géry lamented in 1931, "permits them to plan together at leisure all
inclinations at rebellion, which could easily produce a general uprising." Prisoners were sometimes better informed than cadres outside:
ICP (Indochinese Communist Party) member Nguyen Tao recalled
that on his first night in Nam Dinh, after escaping from Hanoi central
prison in 1933, "we held a meeting with five activists ... We talked
about the world situation and the danger of war, the home situation and
the forthcoming task of the revolution ... [D]eprived of news for a long
time and cut off from the rest of the organization, [our friends] wanted
to know everything and asked us question after question." Ironically,
the French prisons in Indochina became veritable "schools for com-
munism" in which opponents of the regime could organize resistance
and, in the process, gain credentials for leadership of the nationalist
movement.[36]

French understandings of the colonial relationship were also expressed
in attempts to control sexual relationships that seemed to threaten
racial degeneration. The efforts by the colonial state to project its power

---

[36] Mark Cleary, "Managing the Forest in Colonial Indochina *c.* 1900–1940," *Modern
Asian Studies* 39 (2005), 257–83; Gwendolyn Wright, *The Politics of Design in French
Urban Colonialism* (University of Chicago Press, 1991); Peter Zinoman, *The Colonial
Bastille: A History of Imprisonment in Vietnam, 1862–1940* (Berkeley and Los Angeles:
University of California Press, 2001), 210, 214.

involved to a remarkable extent measures to control the bodies of both colonial subjects and colonizers and to limit contact between them. *Encongayement* – the French practice of taking an indigenous lover – played out French fantasies about the sexual compliance of indigenous women and demonstrated male French dominance of Indochinese society. But it also challenged the colonial order. There were official hopes after the turn of the century that the arrival of French women in the colony would somehow impose on French men the bourgeois sexual and familial mores of the metropole. French women who emigrated to Indochina thus found themselves in a setting in which traditional gender roles were even more rigidly enforced than in the metropole, with women no matter what their station expected to reinforce colonial rule by maintaining domestic and social hierarchies.

Often disappointed in practice, these hopes had as their underside the controversies that existed among the French over the growing number of *métis*, the products of sexual relationships between French men and Indochinese women. While *métis* existed in every French colony, they were most frequently encountered in Indochina, and in spite of their relatively small numbers – perhaps 20,000 in an Indochina of 20 million *indigènes* and 25,000–35,000 French in 1906 – they attracted great attention from the colonial administration.[37] One concern was that close relationships between French and *indigène* distracted colonizers' energy from the development of the colony. In some instances these relationships were formalized by civil marriage, and their offspring were recognized by their French fathers and received French citizenship. But the more frequent product of those relationships, what was really meant by the term *métis*, was the illegitimate offspring of an Indochinese woman and a French father who did not acknowledge his paternity. These children represented a challenge to the *grand partage*, the clear line the French drew between colonizers and colonized, on which the colonial enterprise depended.

The legal status of *métis* was also an issue that drew increasing attention from the French regime as time passed and the number of *métis* in Indochina increased. Beginning just before World War I, it became

---

[37] This and the next paragraph are based on Emmanuelle Saada, *Les enfants de la colonie: les métis de l'empire français entre sujétion et citoyenneté* (Paris: Éditions la Découverte, 2007), esp. 29, 53, 68, 79, 132, 230. See also Ann Laura Stoler, *Carnal Knowledge and Imperial Power: Race and the Intimate in Colonial Rule* (Berkeley and Los Angeles: University of California Press, 2002), esp. ch. 4, and "'Mixed-Bloods' and the Cultural Politics of European Identity in Colonial Southeast Asia," in Ian Nederveen Pieterse and Bhikhu Parekh (eds.), *The Decolonization of Imagination: Culture, Knowledge and Power* (London: Zed Books, 1995), 129–48.

increasingly unacceptable among French administrators and others in Indochina to leave *métis* with their Indochinese mothers. The sense that children of "French blood" could in some way be socialized to be European, rather than Indochinese, was encouraged by the increasing medicalization of racial theories among French colonial elites. Colonial notables developed schools and other institutions aimed at "reclassifying" *métis*, making them "français d'âme et de qualité." The growth of this sentiment was slow, but by 1928 it had led to a remarkable decree from the French Republic which referred to individuals "de race française," the first reference to race in a French law since the abolition of slavery in 1848. Eurasian men were recruited by the colonial regime as go-betweens in both the civil administration and the military, where their mastery of two languages made them valuable employees. Women were less practically useful to the colonial administration, but nonetheless of great concern: their rare opportunities for schooling – for example at the elite Couvent des Oiseaux in Dalat – were intended to prepare them for their crucial future maternal role, which was seen by some French men and women as improving the human race by blending better "French blood" with the supposedly inferior blood of Indochinese.

As both colonizer and colonized slipped out of the control of the colonial state, therefore, that state sought to regulate the private, intimate lives of all citizens and subjects, creating an impetus for the projection of the power of the colonial state that far exceeded both the intentions of the original colonial conquest and the capacity of that state. A combination of commitment to the colonial goal of progress and a populationist view that indigenous childbearing practices damaged the growth of the indigenous population led to another manifestation of the colonial state's efforts to regulate the physical bodies of its subjects, the creation of training schools for indigenous midwives who would implement French obstetrical practices and reduce infant mortality. Such practices worked only imperfectly. French-trained midwives found it difficult to supplant the indigenous midwives who held the confidence of Indochinese mothers. Medical science also addressed the European colonizers, whose bodies were viewed as under siege by both the tropical climate of Indochina and by contact with colonial subjects. Attempts to regulate prostitution in Indochina, as in India, drew upon fears of indigenous prostitutes as sources of disease. The association made between the colony and disease also led to the creation of a number of hydrotherapeutic spas in Indochina, at Sapa, Tam Dao, and Mau-Son in the north, Bokor in Cambodia, Tanninh in Laos, and most notably at Dalat in Annam, for colonial officials to recover their health. Personnel policies for colonial officials also provided for leaves in the metropole and spas there such as Vichy, which became a colonial haven by the late nineteenth century.[38] But the colony remained a death trap for colonial officials in spite of the efforts of doctors steeped in the truisms of colonial medicine.

The Netherlands East Indies

The Netherlands had been one of the most important colonial powers of the early modern world, but its declining power left it with only vestiges of that empire by the beginning of the nineteenth century. It retained a few small colonies in the western hemisphere in Surinam and Curaçao. Surinam had originally been settled by the British in the 1650s, but was captured by Dutch forces in 1667 and confirmed as a Dutch possession in 1674 by the Treaty of Westminster. Curaçao was claimed by the Dutch West India Company in 1634, and was soon settled with plantations producing corn and peanuts. It also was an important port for ships plying the Caribbean, especially those in the slave trade.

But the most important Dutch holdings were in Southeast Asia. The Dutch East India Company (VOC) had been established in 1602 to exploit the spice trade in the Malay archipelago, and twenty years later the Company was the preeminent European power in the area. The scattered holdings in Southeast Asia that were colonized and exploited in the course of the seventeenth and eighteenth centuries by the VOC made that company one of the most powerful players in Asian trade at the time, dwarfing other European companies. With its base in Batavia (present-day Jakarta) on the island of Java, the VOC extended its trading activities across the Indonesian islands and further east, exporting sugar and spices, as well as Chinese tea, to Europe and developing the administrative, commercial, and military capacity to do so. It did this not only by joining Chinese traders in the existing trade networks that linked the Indonesian archipelago to other parts of Asia, but also by insisting on its monopoly of trade in the region and enforcing that monopoly by force. The Company in this way stimulated the development of middlemen entrepreneurs, Javanese administrators who supplied the Company with cash crops and the Mataram court in the interior of the island with the funds it needed to gain the military support of the

---

[38] Eric Jennings, *Curing the Colonizers: Hydrotherapy, Climatology, and French Colonial Spas* (Durham, NC: Duke University Press, 2006), and *Imperial Heights: Dalat and the Making and Undoing of French Indochina* (Berkeley and Los Angeles: University of California Press, 2011); Thuy Linh Nguyen, "French-Educated Midwives and the Medicalization of Childbirth in Colonial Vietnam," *Journal of Vietnamese Studies* 5, 2 (2010), 133–82.

VOC. The Company's presence in Java therefore stimulated a form of economic development on the island, even if this development was fastened on products that could be sold by the Company in the European market.

The Company's governance of Java was built around a closely interconnected Eurasian elite that used familial ties and patronage to maintain control of the colonial administration. Few European women came to the East Indies during the Company period to accompany the administrators and soldiers who came east from the Netherlands. Children born of sexual relationships between Dutch men and Indonesian women were a frequent occurrence. There is evidence of considerable care by officers of the Company for their illegitimate Eurasian children: boys were sometimes sent to the Netherlands to be educated, and sometimes never returned to Indonesia. Those who did almost never married one of the few women who migrated from the Netherlands and who would be reduced in status by such a marriage. Girls remained in Indonesia, but often married Netherlanders. As Jean Gelman Taylor has shown using genealogies of elite families in Batavia, in the seventeenth and eighteenth centuries the high mortality of Europeans in the colony meant that often these girls were widowed multiple times, and each time they remarried they added to the interconnections between their Indonesian families and the Dutch colonists. These women were usually isolated as a matter of course from the social lives of their husbands and the small European community in Batavia, maintaining Indonesian dress, language, and practices such as betel-chewing. Taylor points, for example, to a late eighteenth-century painting by Johannes Rach showing Governor-General W. A. Alting walking with his wife in front of their Batavia residence. The wife – probably his second wife, the Eurasian Maria Susanna Grebel (the daughter of a freed slave and the widow of another councilor, Huybert Senn van Basel) – wears European-style clothing, but they are accompanied by the signs of Asian status, a slave attendant who carries Maria's betel box. As Taylor points out, studies which have focused on male lineages from father to son in these families miss the important ways in which local women maintained the web of relationships "of patron and protégé as father-in-law, son-in-law, and brothers-in-law" that held the top levels of Batavian society together and provided access to government office.[39]

In the last decades of the eighteenth century the VOC faced increasing competition, notably from the British East India Company, and the

---

[39] Jean Gelman Taylor, *The Social World of Batavia: European and Eurasian in Dutch Asia* (Madison: University of Wisconsin Press, 1983), esp. 62–64, 71.

weakening position of the Netherlands in the European conflicts of the time exposed the VOC to incursions from other powers. In the Fourth Anglo-Dutch War (1780–84), the VOC suffered losses to its East Indies fleet at the hands of the British navy, the seizure of all of its possessions in South Asia, and the surrender or destruction of many of its outposts on Sumatra. The situation worsened in the following decade, and in 1796 the Company was taken over by the Batavian Republic established after the invasion of the Low Countries by France. The charter of the VOC expired on December 31, 1800, and after a British interregnum from 1811 to 1816 its remaining holdings in Asia were taken over by the new United Kingdom of the Netherlands established at the Congress of Vienna at the end of the Napoleonic Wars in Europe.

The Dutch East Indies in the first few decades of the nineteenth century were far from the prosperous empire that had led the VOC to declare annual dividends averaging 18 percent during the seventeenth and eighteenth centuries. But their possession made the Netherlands a significant factor in Southeast Asian colonialism, and they were also an important aspect of the projection of Dutch trade and culture halfway around the globe. Dutch authority was extended over eastern Java and Sumatra in the course of the nineteenth century, and Batavia grew to become a major urban center, the administrative and trading hub of Southeast Asia, rivaling the British colony of Singapore. But this took time to develop. At the beginning of the nineteenth century, the Indies were an economic millstone for the fledgling Netherlands monarchy. Loosely organized village communities were often scarcely touched by the colonial administration, and the most important crop, rice, was for local consumption rather than export.

The VOC had worked within this system, contracting with local rulers to deliver, for a set price, produce for export. The local ruler organized the production of the crop, supervised its harvest, and delivered it to the Company, which then paid the local ruler and exported it for its own profit. But Dutch administrators influenced by the liberal economic theories of the late eighteenth century attempted to make the Indies a profitable colony by administrative reforms aimed at reducing the authority of the indigenous aristocracy, who were seen as useless intermediaries whose corruption and exploitation of the peasantry prevented the development of market-oriented crops on Java. Beginning with Marshal Herman Willem Daendels (governor-general 1808–11), the colonial administration sought to increase its power at the level of the local village, a goal that Stamford Raffles, governor during the British interregnum, also pursued. Raffles introduced a land-rent system that directly taxed the peasantry by the colonial state. By converting the indigenous aristocracy into a salaried bureaucracy in the service of that state, this system hoped to create economic incentives for the peasantry to increase production, especially of cash crops such as coffee, sugar, and indigo that could bring profits on the international market. When the Dutch returned in 1816, they continued Raffles' system.

This assumed a substantial projection of Dutch power into the East Indies, and it proved difficult to displace the local rulers and force greater market participation by the peasantry. Chinese traders also undercut the system: they used their financial resources to help peasants pay the land rent and thereby gained control of village production. The results were therefore less than hoped for by the Dutch administration. Population grew, as did agricultural production, but much of that increase came in rice for local consumption, not in the cash crops that the Dutch hoped would turn the Indies into a profit-making venture.

In 1830, in an effort to increase agricultural production and make the colony more profitable for the Netherlands, Governor-General Johannes van den Bosch instituted a new agricultural system in Java, what came to be called the Cultivation System. For van den Bosch, the incentive system that had been in place for several decades was destined for failure because it only encouraged peasants to grow rice. Instead, he proposed a system of forced production based on the land-rent system introduced in the early nineteenth century. Primarily a set of local arrangements between Dutch administrators and local rulers to orient production towards the European export market, the Cultivation System was introduced for the cultivation of indigo, sugar, and coffee, and made the Indies administration a fundamental participant in the exploitation of the land. Peasants were required to produce crops for export to Europe in place of paying their land rent. If they produced more than the value of the land rent, they were paid cash, but this was not a frequent occurrence. In instances in which there was not adequate labor to maintain production, the government intervened to force peasants to work at the different production tasks. The crops were consigned to the Netherlands Trading Company for shipment (usually on Dutch ships) to Amsterdam and Rotterdam for auction, and the proceeds of the auction went to the Dutch treasury. Officials, both European and Javanese, were paid incentives to increase production in their districts.

The Cultivation System was put in place rapidly beginning in 1830, and by 1840 agriculture in Java had settled into a harsh pattern organized around the production of sugar, indigo, and coffee for the European market. Some land held by Indonesians remained outside the System: there were principalities in which indigenous rulers contracted with private entrepreneurs to establish plantations that in effect competed with the state control of production implied by the Cultivation System. But for many peasant communities, the System forced them to plant *sawah*, irrigated land often used for rice cultivation, in the cash crops required by the Dutch administrators. Coffee production was by far the most profitable of the principal crops produced, in fact usually making up for losses incurred in indigo and sugar cultivation.

The Cultivation System had obvious economic benefits for the Dutch state and for businesses in the Netherlands. Between 1860 and 1866, the Cultivation System produced one third of Dutch state revenues. Amsterdam and Rotterdam became staple markets for colonial produce, enhancing their international role. The use of Dutch ships to bring cargoes from Batavia to the Netherlands made this a period of great prosperity for the Dutch shipping industry. In practice, however, both the Cultivation System and private plantations undercut colonialist assumptions that economic exploitation for the European market would have no effect on Javanese society. The construction of roads in the interior of Java improved communication with coastal settlements. The increased market activity of the System led the peasants themselves to engage more in trade. Sugar factories and other enterprises slowly created a wage labor market, although this was inhibited by the ambivalent attitude of the Dutch administration and the unattractiveness of factory work. Cash payments for produce helped to monetize the Javanese economy. The penetration of the Javanese market by European manufactured goods, especially machine-produced cloths, undercut the long-standing handicraft textile industry in the villages, and drew the peasantry into trading networks that extended from the village to Europe.

The System also placed a steadier and heavier burden of labor on the Javanese peasantry, making it more difficult for them to produce their own crops and handicraft goods. They responded at times by migration to escape heavy labor demands, by clandestine acts of arson or sabotage, by group refusals to carry out orders that were considered unfair, and by occasional acts of violence against individual officials. A recent evaluation of the effect of the Cultivation System on the Javanese peasantry, by Robert Elson, rejects the blanket condemnation that has marked earlier scholarship. But he does conclude that, while the material prosperity of many peasants probably improved, the System's thrust was to conserve the traditional structure of Javanese rural life "in such a way as to inhibit further development for the mass of Java's population."[40]

---

[40] R. E. Elson, *Village Java under the Cultivation System 1830–1870* (Sydney: Allen & Unwin, 1994), 321.

The Cultivation System came under criticism after the middle of the nineteenth century not, however, because of opposition by the Javanese peasantry or the changes it caused in Javanese society and the difficulties this created for the Dutch administration. Events in the 1840s had cast some doubt on the effectiveness of the System itself. Failures of the rice crop and famines in some Residencies in 1844 and 1845 and a typhoid epidemic in the latter half of the 1840s suggested that the ability of peasants to withstand the crises of rural life was being undermined. As early as 1846, in response to these crises, local administrators were instructed to pay more attention to local food production, and planting indigo, a crop that did significant damage to the rural agricultural system, decreased. But a second wave of famines in 1849–50 suggested that these changes had not adequately addressed the problems, and policy-makers who came to power in the Netherlands in 1848 sought to implement liberal economic policies in line with the growing European commitment to free trade and free labor. A new regulation in 1854 continued the System, but aimed at easing the burden of forced labor on the peasantry. It increased control over indigenous officials to prevent the worst abuses of their authority, especially by limiting landholding by local officials, and opening the way for non-government entrepreneurs to enter into direct contracts with peasants. The resurgence of conservatives in the Netherlands in the late 1850s slowed these reforms, but increasingly the need for some private agricultural enterprise was recognized by the Dutch government. The final demise of the Cultivation System came in 1870, when a new Agrarian Law promoted the cultivation of some areas of Java on long-term leases, and a Sugar Act began to dismantle the state-organized sugar industry. After 1870 both the government and Javanese continued to own the land, but the government ceased to act as a planter and land was cultivated on leaseholds granted to private entrepreneurs.

There was, however, no change in the ultimate goal of making the East Indies the financial foundation of the Dutch state. Liberals hoped that a more market-oriented approach would stimulate development and greater prosperity in the Indies, and continue the substantial remittances that had been going from the Indies to the Netherlands since 1830. But events intruded. While more land came under cultivation and production and exports grew, a lengthy downturn in the world economy in the 1880s forced many entrepreneurs into bankruptcy, and after 1885 the economy was increasingly dominated by agricultural banks and corporate management. The profits to the Dutch government also failed to materialize, and the Indies proved to be a losing proposition for the Dutch state for many years. There was substantial growth in the population of Java in the same period, and increases in production may not have been adequate to maintain, much less improve, the living conditions of the Javanese peasantry.

Continuing questions about the economic development of the Indies in the period of liberal economic policies after 1870 led, after the turn of the twentieth century, to a change to what was called the Ethical System, proposed in the late 1890s by commentators (notably C. T. van Deventer) and proclaimed by Queen Wilhelmina in a speech from the throne in 1901. This proposed a moral mission for the Netherlands in its colonies, and the fulfillment of the "debt of honor" that colonialism entailed. In its most radical form – such as van Deventer's – it aimed at repaying the debt that the Netherlands owed to the Indies as a result of its exploitation during the nineteenth century and especially the period of the Cultivation System. The goal of the Dutch administration under this policy was to improve the condition of the indigenous population through education, industrial development, and agricultural improvements. In spite of its goals, however, the Ethical System was predicated on the firm belief that Dutch domination over the Indies was beneficial for the colonies, able to preserve indigenous culture even as it fostered greater integration of the Indies into the world market and transformed that culture with the benefits of "civilization." Indonesian development therefore remained oriented towards the needs of the Dutch economy rather than of the indigenous population of the archipelago. Greater capital investment in the Indies increased the demand for capital goods manufactured in the Netherlands, and thereby the involvement of Dutch industry in the economic development of the colony. Other trading partners acquired significance as well: the closing of the Dutch market to Indonesian goods during World War I increased trade ties with other Asian countries and the United States. But increased participation in the world market exposed the Indonesian economy to the fluctuations of that market, and it was hard hit by severe drops in prices for commodities like rubber and sugar during the depression of the 1930s. The government became more interventionist as a result, and by the last decades of the colonial era it had abandoned its non-interventionist liberal principles and adopted policies that involved more state intervention.

There were certainly local variants on Java, and between Java and Sumatra, which was developed later. But the plantation system created in the second half of the nineteenth century in East Sumatra provides an example of the interactions between the penetration of capitalist export agriculture, the colonial state, and the labor force needed for production of goods for the export market.[41] As in India and Indochina, and, as we will see, many parts of Africa, Sumatra's plantations also show the attempts by colonial powers and Western businesses to create a labor system that conformed to their assumptions about the contrast between free and unfree labor, while at the same time using the power of the colonial state to meet the needs of the plantation economy without necessarily organizing a fully free labor market.

Growing tea, palm oil, tobacco, and rubber, these plantations attracted capital from investors in Great Britain, the United States, France, Belgium, and the Netherlands. But as the plantations developed in the late nineteenth century, it proved impossible to convince the local population to work on them. The labor force for these plantations was therefore initially predominantly Chinese, many of whom came to Eastern Sumatra under indenture contracts that bound them to their employers for a set period of time. The colonial state and its legal system worked to enforce these contracts and to ensure the compliance of the labor force with the conditions established by the agribusinesses that employed it. At the turn of the century, most of these laborers were male; those women who were on the plantations were prostitutes or were subject to sexual exploitation by managers, foremen, and male laborers.

By the 1910s, labor policy began to change on the Eastern Sumatra plantations. Penal sanctions and indenture contracts were phased out, and plantations began to adopt what they termed a "free labor" (*vrija arbeiders*) system. In this system, migration from over-populated regions of central Java was used to create a resident labor reserve in Sumatra. Supply thus normally exceeded demand on the plantations, keeping wages low. Labor settlements that included use of small plots of land by workers shifted some of the costs of maintaining the workers onto them and also were a way to keep workers in Sumatra even during slack periods on the plantations.

With the depression of the 1930s, plantations were able to trim their labor forces and the labor reserve in ways that clearly targeted the family organization of workers. The plantations laid off unmarried men, and the colonial state forced those men to return to their home villages in Java. Married women were also laid off, creating a domestic economy for plantation worker families that reinforced the dependence of the workforce. When the economy improved in 1934, labor

---

[41] Ann Laura Stoler, *Capitalism and Confrontation in Sumatra's Plantation Belt, 1870–1979*, 2nd edn. (Ann Arbor: University of Michigan Press, 1995).

recruiters sought to bring in married couples rather than single men or women. Labor control was therefore closely tied to workers' family and sexual behavior, and the companies and government authorities worked closely together to regulate these issues as they created a labor system that was not slave or indentured, but also was not free. Nor was this a transitional form of labor that might have been a product of the "incomplete" capitalist penetration of Sumatra, or a step on the way to a fully free labor market. Rather, it was an integral part of the plantation system on the island.

Resistance to this labor system took the forms of violence against colonial and plantation authorities as well as union and labor organizing. Overseers and other officials were frequent targets of attacks by workers from the beginning of the twentieth century. On the plantations on Sumatra, the period between the World Wars saw frequent labor actions such as collective refusals to work. These occurred especially on older tobacco estates, and their participants were frequently Chinese rather than Javanese. But they showed little sign of outside influence, especially the "communist agitators" who struck such fear into the government and the plantation authorities. Rather, labor unrest seems to have been focused on local grievances rather than capitalist or colonial domination.

The attempts by the Dutch authorities to regulate workers on the plantations of Java and Sumatra by managing their family and sexual behavior were matched by concerns about the Dutch and other Europeans who came to the Indies to work for the administration, the plantations, or simply to seek their fortunes in Southeast Asia. These demonstrated not only that the boundary between colonized and colonizer tended to lose definition in practice, but also that the colonizers themselves cannot be seen as a single homogeneous actor in the colonization process. The British interregnum at the beginning of the nineteenth century undercut the administrative system based on intermarriage between the Dutch administrative elite and the Indies-born population of European descent. The return to Dutch rule in 1816 did not see a return to this system, as recruitment to civil-service posts became based more on academic qualifications and markers of European origin than on the family connections that had been important during the first two centuries of VOC and Dutch rule. Some of these changes focused on the long-standing customs of Eurasian women: the slave attendant and betel box in the painting of W. A. Alting and his wife disappeared, and European forms of sociability ended customary gender separation, bringing men and women at elite social occasions into the same room to participate in activities such as dancing. Others targeted the sons of

East Indian families. A European education became important to con-
fer facility with the Dutch language. Regulations issued in 1825 aimed
at professionalizing the civil service created the *Radicaal*, a credential
that certified the holder for appointment to civil-service positions.
Introduced by Jean-Chrétien Baud, governor-general in 1833–36 and
minister of colonies from 1839 to 1848, these regulations often favored
European-born candidates over Indies-born, since it was necessary to
attend school in the Netherlands to gain the proper credentials.

This indirect favoritism of Europeans at the expense of those born
in the Indies was most obvious at the middle of the century. In 1842,
a colonial training school was opened in the Netherlands at Delft, and
parents of Indies-born children who aspired to the higher levels of the
civil service were required to send those children to Delft for a significant part of their childhood. In the long run, there are suggestions that
the number of Delft graduates was so small, and the practice of sending
children to the Netherlands for secondary schooling so ingrained in the
families of European descent in the Indies, that its impact was more
psychological than anything else. In May 1848, as news reached Java
of the revolutions that began in February in Paris and spread across
Europe, and of plans by the King of the Netherlands for constitutional
reform, there was rioting in Batavia and demands for the end of the
Radicaal and improvement of educational opportunities in Java itself.
In the years after 1848, under Governor-General Jan Jacob Rochussen,
who had witnessed the May events and seems to have been concerned
about the revolutionary potential of lower-class Indo-Europeans, the
Radicaal was granted to many Europeans born in the Indies (*inlandse
kinderen*), enabling them to aspire to the higher levels of the civil service.
Secondary schools opened in the 1860s and 1870s in Batavia, Surabaya,
and Semarang, and opportunities for Indies-born and educated men
in the civil service improved. Delft continued to provide higher civil
servants, but it did not enjoy anything approaching a monopoly in that
area, and the certificate system ended.[42] Nonetheless, these requirements betrayed a lack of confidence in those *inlandse kinderen*. A part
of this was based on concerns that they would not be able to command
respect from the Javanese they were supposed to govern. But the policy
also betrayed anxieties about the ways in which physical aspects of chil-
drearing could affect national identity and the loyalties of Europeans
born in the Indies: the Dutch minister of colonies worried in 1848 that

---

[42] Ulbe Bosma and Remco Raben, *Being "Dutch" in the Indies: A History of Creolisation
and Empire, 1500–1920*, trans. Wendie Shaffer (Athens, OH: Ohio University Press,
2008), esp. 184–214.

"this upbringing [in the Indies] will have the result that these children who are frequently suckled with the breastmilk of Javanese wet nurses along with their native children, at a more advanced age, will lack any sense of unity with Europeans."[43]

While the fears of the Indies-born that their children would be blocked from administrative posts may have been exaggerated, the nineteenth century certainly saw a decline in the direct political influence of the old colonial elite on the government of the colony, and there is some evidence that the older colonial families instead devoted themselves to landownership and the development of plantation agriculture (Illustration 5). The fate of the van Riemsdijk family may have been shared by many of their friends. Jeremias van Riemsdijk, an immigrant from Utrecht, had become governor-general in 1775, and his son, W. V. H. van Riemsdijk, held numerous offices, including becoming councilor extraordinary in 1793. His position was strengthened by his marriage in 1763 to Catharina Margaretha Craan, herself a Eurasian descended from a Dutch minister. But the sons of W. V. H. and Catharina van Riemsdijk would not continue the family tradition of political office. Those sons were pushed by their father towards management of the family's estates and sugar plantations.[44]

The marriage patterns and career paths of the van Riemsdijk and other families in the Netherlands East Indies, as well as other families in India, French Indochina, and virtually everywhere else in Asia, underscore the inherent instability of the European colonies even as the colonial powers thought of them as conquered and firmly acquired. Throughout the nineteenth and early twentieth centuries, European colonial powers restructured their ties to the Pacific and Asia from earlier trading and missionary ventures into more formal colonial empires. These empires were intended to enhance the global power and economic welfare of the colonial powers, but as had been the case with earlier empires in the Atlantic they were efforts at projecting European power into a vast region of the world in which there already were existing states. Europeans' technology and military power gave them an advantage in many instances, and allowed the formation of new empires that appeared, from the vantage point of London, Paris, and Amsterdam, to be firmly in European control. But it proved difficult for those colonial powers to control the actions and lives of not only their new colonial subjects, but also many of the Europeans who

---

[43] Quoted in Stoler, *Race and the Education of Desire*, 162.
[44] Taylor, *Social World*, 120.

Illustration 5 Planter family in Java, Indonesia, around 1865. The mother (far right) appears Indonesian, while an Indonesian nursemaid holds the youngest child.

"went out" to Asia as a part of the colonial project. In the late nineteenth century, those empires led Europeans to Africa, where the same issues would reappear.

FURTHER READING

Aldrich, Robert. *The French Presence in the South Pacific, 1842–1940*. Honolulu: University of Hawai'i Press, 1990.

Bayly, C. A. *Imperial Meridian: The British Empire and the World, 1780–1830*. London: Longman, 1989.

    The New Cambridge History of India: Indian Society and the Making of the British Empire. Cambridge University Press, 1987.

    Rulers, Townsmen, and Bazaars: North Indian Society in the Age of British Expansion, 1770–1870. Cambridge University Press, 1983.

Bayly, Susan. *The New Cambridge History of India: Caste, Society and Politics in India from the Eighteenth Century to the Modern Age*. Cambridge University Press, 1999.

Belich, James. *Making Peoples: A History of the New Zealanders From Polynesian Settlement to the End of the Nineteenth Century*. Honolulu: University of Hawai'i Press, 1996.

Benton, Lauren. *Law and Colonial Cultures: Legal Regimes in World History 1400–1900*. New York: Cambridge University Press, 2002.

Blainey, Geoffrey. *The Rush That Never Ended: A History of Australian Mining*, 5th edn. University of Melbourne Press, 2003.

Bolton, Geoffrey. *Spoils and Spoilers: Australians Make Their Environment 1788–1980*. Sydney: George Allen & Unwin, 1981.

Boomgaard, Peter. *Children of the Colonial State: Population Growth and Development in Java, 1795–1880*. Amsterdam: Free University Press, 1989.

Bosma, Ulbe, and Remco Raben. *Being "Dutch" in the Indies: A History of Creolisation and Empire, 1500–1920*, trans. Wendie Shaffer. Athens, OH: Ohio University Press, 2008.

Bowen, H. V. *The Business of Empire: The East India Company and Imperial Britain, 1756–1833*. Cambridge University Press, 2006.

Elites, Enterprise and the Making of the British Overseas Empire, 1688–1775. London: Macmillan, 1996.

Revenue and Reform: The Indian Problem in British Politics 1757–1773. Cambridge University Press, 1991.

Brocheux, Pierre, and Daniel Hémery. *Indochina: An Ambiguous Colonization, 1858–1954*, trans. Ly-Lan Dill-Klein, Eric Jennings, Nora A. Taylor, and Noémi Tousignant. Berkeley and Los Angeles: University of California Press, 2009.

Chakrabarty, Dipesh. *Rethinking Working-Class History: Bengal 1890–1940*. Princeton University Press, 1989.

Chandavarkar, Rajnarayan. *Imperial Power and Popular Politics: Class, Resistance and the State in India, c. 1850–1950*. Cambridge University Press, 1998.

The Origins of Industrial Capitalism in India. Cambridge University Press, 1994.

Charlesworth, Neil. *British Rule and the Indian Economy 1800–1914*. London: Macmillan, 1982.

Cohn, Bernard. *Colonialism and its Forms of Knowledge: The British in India*. Princeton University Press, 1996.

Cooper, Nicola. *France in Indochina: Colonial Encounters*. New York: Berg, 2001.

Daughton, J. P. *An Empire Divided: Religion, Republicanism, and the Making of French Colonialism, 1880–1914*. Oxford University Press, 2006.

Del Testa, David. "Workers, Culture and the Railroads in French Colonial Indochina, 1905–1936." *French Colonial History* 2 (2002), 181–98.

Dirks, Nicholas. *Castes of Mind: Colonialism and the Making of Modern India*. Princeton University Press, 2001.

Dunmore, John. *French Explorers in the Pacific*, vol. I, *The Eighteenth Century*; vol. II, *The Nineteenth Century*. Oxford: Clarendon Press, 1965, 1969.

Elson, R. E. *Village Java under the Cultivation System 1830–1870*. Sydney: Allen & Unwin, 1994.

Fasseur, C. *The Politics of Colonial Exploitation*. Ithaca, NY: Cornell University Press, 1992.

Fisher, Michael H., ed. *The Politics of the British Annexation of India, 1757–1857*. Oxford University Press, 1993.

Frost, Alan. *The Global Reach of Empire: Britain's Maritime Expansion in the Indian and Pacific Oceans, 1764–1815*. Melbourne: Miegunah Press, 2003.

Frykenberg, Robert. *Guntur District 1788–1848: A History of Local Influence and Central Authority in South India*. Oxford: Clarendon Press, 1965.

Frykenberg, Robert, ed. *Land Control and Social Structure in Indian History*. Madison: University of Wisconsin Press, 1969.

Ghosh, Durba. *Sex and the Family in Colonial India: The Making of Empire*. Cambridge University Press, 2006.

Gordon, Stewart. *The New Cambridge History of India: The Marathas 1600–1818*. Cambridge University Press, 1993.

Gouda, Frances. *Dutch Culture Overseas: Colonial Practice in the Netherlands Indies, 1900–1942*. Amsterdam University Press, 1995.

Guha, Ranajit. *Dominance without Hegemony: History and Power in Colonial India*. Cambridge, MA: Harvard University Press, 1997.

Jennings, Eric T. *Curing the Colonizers: Hydrotherapy, Climatology, and French Colonial Spas*. Durham, NC: Duke University Press, 2006.

   Imperial Heights: Dalat and the Making and Undoing of French Indochina. Berkeley and Los Angeles: University of California Press, 2011.

Knapman, Claudia. *White Women in Fiji, 1835–1930: The Ruin of Empire?* London: Allen & Unwin, 1986.

Kolsky, Elizabeth. *Colonial Justice in British India*. Cambridge University Press, 2010.

Lawson, Philip. *The East India Company: A History*. London and New York: Longman, 1993.

Levine, Philippa. *Prostitution, Race and Politics: Policing Venereal Disease in the British Empire*. New York and London: Routledge, 2003.

Ludden, David. *The New Cambridge History of India: An Agrarian History of South Asia*. Cambridge University Press, 1999.

Mani, Lata. *Contentious Traditions: The Debate on Sati in Colonial India*. Berkeley and Los Angeles: University of California Press, 1998.

Marshall, P. J. "British Expansion in India in the Eighteenth Century: A Historical Revision." *History* 60 (1975), 28–43.

   East Indian Fortunes: The British in Bengal in the Eighteenth Century. Oxford University Press, 1976.

Metcalf, Thomas. *The Aftermath of Revolt: India, 1857–1870*. Princeton University Press, 1964.

Murray, Martin J. "'White Gold' or 'White Blood'? The Rubber Plantations of Colonial Indochina, 1910–1940." *Journal of Peasant Studies* 19 (1992), 41–67.

Nagtegaal, Luc. *Riding the Dutch Tiger: The Dutch East Indies Company and the Northeast Coast of Java, 1680–1743*, trans. Beverley Jackson. Leiden: KITLV Press, 1996.

Newman, Richard. *Workers and Unions in Bombay, 1918–1929: A Study of Organisation in the Cotton Mills.* Canberra: Australian National University, 1981.

Patel, Sujata. *The Making of Industrial Relations: The Ahmedabad Textile Industry, 1918–1939.* New Delhi: Oxford University Press, 1987.

Prakash, Gyan. *Another Reason: Science and the Imagination of Modern India.* Princeton University Press, 1999.

　Bonded Histories: Genealogies of Labor Servitude in Colonial India. Cambridge University Press, 1990.

Price, Pamela G. *Kingship and Political Practice in Colonial India.* Cambridge University Press, 1996.

Saada, Emmanuelle. *Les enfants de la colonie: les métis de l'empire français entre sujétion et citoyenneté.* Paris: Éditions La Découverte, 2007.

Sinha, Mrinalini. *Colonial Masculinity: The "Manly Englishman" and the "Effeminate Bengali" in the Late 19th Century.* Manchester University Press, 1995.

Stokes, Eric. *The English Utilitarians and India.* Oxford: Clarendon Press, 1959.

　The Peasant and the Raj: Studies in Agrarian Society and Peasant Rebellion in Colonial India. Cambridge University Press, 1978.

Stoler, Ann Laura. *Capitalism and Confrontation in Sumatra's Plantation Belt, 1870–1979,* 2nd edn. Ann Arbor: University of Michigan Press, 1995.

　"'Mixed-Bloods' and the Cultural Politics of European Identity in Colonial Southeast Asia." In Ian Nederveen Pieterse and Bhikhu Parekh, eds., *The Decolonization of Imagination: Culture, Knowledge and Power.* London: Zed Books, 1995, 128–48.

Taylor, Jean Gelman. *The Social World of Batavia: European and Eurasian in Dutch Asia.* Madison: University of Wisconsin Press, 1983.

Tomlinson, B. R. *The New Cambridge History of India: The Economy of Modern India, 1860–1970.* Cambridge University Press, 1993.

Van Niel, R. "The Effect of Export Cultivation in Nineteenth-Century Java." *Modern Asian Studies* 15 (1981): 25–58.

Wright, Gwendolyn. *The Politics of Design in French Urban Colonialism.* University of Chicago Press, 1991.

Yang, Anand A. *Bazaar India: Markets, Society, and the Colonial State in Bihar.* Berkeley and Los Angeles: University of California Press, 1998.

　The Limited Raj: Agrarian Relations in Colonial India, Saran District, 1793–1920. Berkeley and Los Angeles: University of California Press, 1989.

Zinoman, Peter. *The Colonial Bastille: A History of Imprisonment in Vietnam, 1862–1940.* Berkeley and Los Angeles: University of California Press, 2001.

5   The Middle East and Africa

In the course of the nineteenth century, European outposts on the Mediterranean, Atlantic, and Indian Ocean coasts of Africa were pushed inland. Accounts of this extension of European control point to multiple factors in this process: crises of European capitalism, a desire for employment for European elites, a "gentlemanly capitalism" that resulted from the common interests of the British landed elite and the financial and service sector of southeast England, technological improvements, or a "social imperialism" that would focus European workers less on the injustices of European society and more on the power of European nations.[1] While with different emphases, these narratives have in common their focus on events such as the initial European forays into Sub-Saharan Africa in the 1870s, the "loaded pause" of the early 1880s, the Berlin Africa Conference of 1884–85, and the "scramble" that divided up the continent by the turn of the century. The Berlin Conference in particular is often seen as the prelude to "Scramble" and "Partition" by setting out the rules for the expansion of European control in West and Central Africa – notification of the other European powers and effective occupation – and consolidating Belgian control of the Congo Free State. Recent research has undercut this preeminent role for the Conference, and in the middle of the twentieth century, the emphasis on the "Partition" itself was critiqued by two historians of the British empire, John Gallagher and Ronald

[1] V. I. Lenin, *Imperialism: The Highest Stage of Capitalism* (Petrograd, 1917), and J. A. Hobson, *Imperialism: A Study* (London, 1902); R. Robinson and J. Gallagher, with A. Denny, *Africa and the Victorians: The Official Mind of Imperialism* (New York: St. Martin's Press, 1961); P. J. Cain and A. G. Hopkins, *British Imperialism*, 2 vols. (London: Longman, 1993); Daniel R. Headrick, *The Tools of Empire: Technology and European Imperialism in the Nineteenth Century* (New York: Oxford University Press, 1981), and *The Tentacles of Progress: Technology Transfer in the Age of Imperialism, 1850–1940* (New York: Oxford University Press, 1986); Bernard Semmel, *Imperialism and Social Reform: English Social Thought, 1895–1914* (Cambridge, MA: Harvard University Press, 1960); Hans-Ulrich Wehler, "Bismarck's Imperialism, 1862–1890," *Past & Present* 48 (1970), 119–55.

Robinson. They noted a period of "informal empire," in the first half of the nineteenth century, that gave way to formal empire only when necessary to maintain British influence and control in a particular part of Africa. Seeing a basic continuity between the middle and the end of the nineteenth century, Robinson and Gallagher argued that this policy was in fact one of "extending control informally if possible and formally if necessary." They also emphasized the importance of strategic considerations – especially concerns about India – in the "official mind" of British imperialism, and insisted that imperial expansion had been influenced not only by European actors but also by Africans.[2]

The factors motivating the European powers in Africa will certainly appear in this chapter, as we see the expansion of European control in the different regions of Africa and in the Middle East. But sixty years after Robinson and Gallagher's critique of the Partition narrative, we now understand better the need to consider not only European events and European agency in the changes that took place in Africa in the nineteenth century, but also the complexity that existed in Africa prior to and during the arrival of Europeans, the different levels of integration of Africans into the global economic system that was increasingly dominated by European capitalism, and the differing abilities of Africans, African states, and African communities to resist, accommodate, and collaborate with the intruders. This history must begin not with the first footprint of Europeans on Africa, but by recognizing that, while before the middle third of the nineteenth century most European contact with Africa was limited to the coastlines, where European traders had been engaging in commerce for centuries, the continent was crossed by numerous trading routes from its coasts to the interior. Most of these existed without much reference to the Europeans on the coasts. As European contact increased through trade, missionary activity, and the attempts by naval squadrons to end the transatlantic slave trade, the Europeans who came to Africa often found strong states such as the Asante and Tukolor states in West Africa as well as commercialized economies and societies. European entry therefore only added another, albeit a very powerful, participant in African political and economic relations.

That entry took many different forms. Merchants came to trade, first in slaves and then in agricultural products. Naval squadrons attempted

[2] Stig Förster, Wolfgang J. Mommsen, and Ronald Robinson (eds.), *Bismarck, Europe, and Africa: The Berlin Africa Conference 1884–1885 and the Onset of Partition* (Oxford University Press, 1988); John Gallagher and Ronald Robinson, "The Imperialism of Free Trade," *Economic History Review*, 2nd series, 6, 1 (1953), 1–15, esp. 13.

to cut off the transatlantic slave trade in West Africa beginning in the early nineteenth century, and later in the century the British navy patrolled the coast of East Africa to end the indigenous trade between the coast and the island of Zanzibar. In both instances, the naval presence meant European contact with Africans. Missionaries also came spreading Christianity, often preceding the military expeditions and civilian administrations who made the colonial empires. Dutch missionaries came to South Africa in the 1770s, British soon followed them, and after the middle of the nineteenth century famous missionaries such as David Livingstone and less well-known ones sent by the London Missionary Society and other groups brought Protestant Christianity to the continent. The Catholic Society of Missionaries of Africa, called the White Fathers, was founded in Algiers in 1868 by Cardinal Charles Lavigerie, and over the next fifty years it brought Catholicism to virtually every part of the French Sahara, the interior of West Africa and the Sudan, German East Africa, the Belgian Congo, Northern Rhodesia, and Nyasaland. The European colonies established in Africa, whether before or after 1870, represented not only an increase in the European presence in the interior of the continent, but also a restructuring of that presence.

In North Africa, numerous short-distance trade routes crossed the Sahara desert, the semi-arid Sahel to its south, and the tropical savanna of the Sudan even further south. Running from north to south, trade routes crossed the desert from Cyrenaica to Wadai, west of Lake Chad in the Sahel, in and north of the upper Niger River valley, and from Morocco to Senegambia and the Niger. There were also routes in the Nile basin and in the Horn of Africa that brought trade from the Mediterranean and Red Sea coasts into the interior. East–west routes crossed the Sahara, the Sahel, and the Sudan, and in the center of West Africa Timbuktu was the focal point for routes connecting the desert, Senegambia, and the Niger valley. Depending on the region, these routes brought salt, grains, dates, livestock, and slaves. Increasingly in the course of the nineteenth century, European goods such as cotton and woolen cloths and guns were traded for ostrich feathers, tanned and dyed goatskins, and ivory.

West Africa south of the Sahara was not a single economic unit prior to the extension of European control, and trading patterns tended to focus either in the central Sudan and lower Guinea region in the east or the western Sudan/upper Guinea region in the west. Nonetheless, both the east and west of West Africa had strong indigenous economies that made the Europeans who came in from the coast not the agents of incorporation into the European economic system, but instead another set of foreigners who sought to participate in existing economic relations.

The difficulties Europeans had in getting inland from the coast – a development that occurred only around mid-century – were the result of the ability of the indigenous regimes, bolstered by their economic prosperity since the mid eighteenth century, to resist that encroachment. Indigenous traders often proved able to adapt to changes in European demand when, most notably, the slave trade withered and then ended. This was an event of huge proportions for the indigenous traders. However, in many parts of West Africa it led to a shift from the sale of slaves to Europeans to a "legitimate trade" in groundnuts and palm and other oils that Europeans and others were willing to purchase. Rather than being sold into the transatlantic market, slaves remained in West Africa working as laborers on large and small agricultural holdings and as caravan porters and crews on riverboats. Slavery therefore continued to exist within West Africa in spite of the end of the transatlantic trade – indeed, in some places the construction of railroads and peanut agriculture that came with European imperialism utilized slave and other forms of coerced labor – and West African economic networks continued to be linked to European markets. When European dominance did occur, it was not necessarily the result of the ability of Europeans to trade more effectively than others within those existing trade networks, but often of the willingness of Europeans to use force to make their way.[3]

In contrast, Africa south of the equator was marked by an environment that made it difficult to support large populations and effective political units. The region did not produce an agricultural surplus that could be traded, as was the case in West Africa and North Africa. Because of this, it was profoundly affected by the intrusion of the Arab Indian Ocean trading network from its base on Zanzibar Island, the Portuguese colonization of Mozambique and Angola, and Afrikaner and British settlements in the south. By the 1870s, those coastal settlements found nothing resembling the resistance of the hinterlands of West Africa. It was therefore much easier to penetrate into the interior, and European trade stimulated the development of internal trading networks. These trade networks utilized the rivers of the region, and exchanged European goods for cassava and other crops cultivated by the inlanders who lived away from the rivers. The western coast of this region, in contrast, was a major participant in the slave trade until the mid nineteenth century, when slaves were replaced as exports by ivory, palm oil, kola, hardwoods, and wild rubber. In the east, ivory

[3] Martin Klein, *Slavery and Colonial Rule in French West Africa* (Cambridge University Press, 1998).

dominated trade with Europeans. As the ivory frontier moved west, leaving behind it areas such as present-day Tanzania that were denuded of elephants, Africans provided provisions and porters for caravans heading further into the interior. The Portuguese in Mozambique and Angola further south had always left the initiative to African chiefdoms that were able to control trade and production. But by the nineteenth century even this colonial presence was receding, as the slave trade ended and a serious recession ensued. An attempt at growing cotton during the American Civil War (1861–65) quickly collapsed, and ivory, coffee, sugar, and rubber instead became the staple export products of the region's economy. Internal production of foodstuffs and trade continued in these regions, but the violence of the slave and ivory trades was difficult for the African states in the region to control.

Islam in Africa

The Christian missionaries who came to Africa in the nineteenth century often encountered a strong indigenous religion, Islam, which had spread slowly across significant parts of the continent in the years after AD 700. It would be a mistake to view this as a single, monolithic religion. There were divisions within the clerical and scholarly ranks of Muslims between Sunnis and Sufis, and everywhere in Africa Islam interacted with the religious beliefs that marked the indigenous societies into which it spread. In some parts of Africa, the Islamic law of the shari'a was adopted more rigorously than in others, and over time there were fundamentalist revivals that sought to enforce more rigid adherence to the tenets of the religion.

With those caveats in mind, however, we can trace a rough history of the spread of Islam in Africa. It entered the continent through two "doorways." One route was through Egypt, first conquered by Muslims in the seventh century and where Sunni orthodoxy eventually was established. In 1276, a large force of Mamluks – members of an elite military caste – conquered Makuria, and by 1315 a puppet Muslim king had been imposed by the Egyptians. In the ensuing years the Sudanese kingdoms south of Egypt became committed to Islam, increasingly adopting Mediterranean institutions and engaging in trade, especially in slaves, with Egypt. In the early nineteenth century, invasions by Egyptians consolidated Egyptian control there, and Muslim warlords from the north imposed slave regimes serving the Turkish and Egyptian markets. By the middle of the nineteenth century, merchants from Khartoum – some but not all of whom were Muslims – had moved into the southern Sudan as well as west into Uganda and Congo (Map 4).

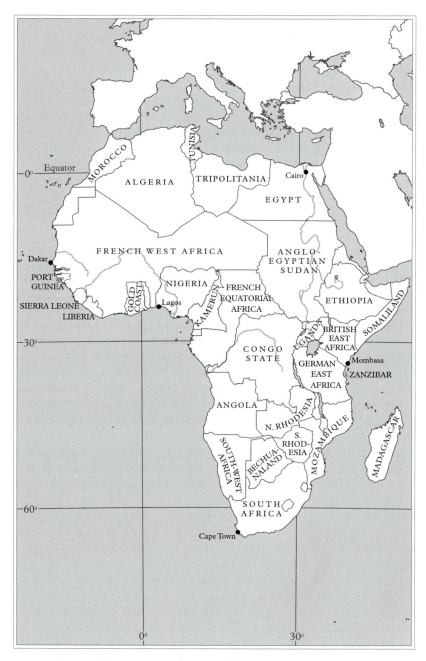

Map 4 The partition of Africa, 1905.

Islam also spread from Egypt west across North Africa. From there it moved south along the trade routes that Berber merchants followed into the Sahara, going from Tripoli towards Fezzan and Kanem Bornu, and from the Sus in Southern Morocco towards Mauritania and Senegal. By the tenth century Muslim traders were established in Awdaghust and Tadmekka, close to the border between the desert and the Sahel, and from there they developed trade links with the Sudanese kingdoms of Ghana and Gao. Over the next several centuries, the border between the Sahara and the Bilad al-Sudan (the Land of the Black People) became increasingly hazy, and the Sahara trade reached as far south as Walata and Timbuktu. From Timbuktu on the Niger River, Islam followed the river systems of West Africa south. The Muslim merchants who moved along these rivers did not themselves proselytize, but religious teachers joined the trade caravans, propagating the Islamic faith among the different tribes between Timbuktu and the coast.

Much of this early spread of Islam was limited to elites and took place in towns and cities. In the seventeenth and eighteenth centuries, however, it spread from urban centers into the countryside and gained converts among the peasants who lived there. This shift was connected to a turn to vernacular preaching and the translation of religious texts into vernacular languages. At the beginning of the nineteenth century, a series of jihads by Islamic reformers turned Islam into a pervasive way of life and religious belief in major parts of West Africa, from the western Sudan to the area inland of the French settlements on the coast of Senegal. One of these began in 1804 and established a new Fulani empire in Hausaland, in the western Sudan. Subsequent jihads in the Masina region around Timbuktu in the 1810s and further west in Futa Toro in the middle of the nineteenth century also had significant effects on pre-colonial West Africa. Reforming elites were installed in power in many parts of the region, and their newfound power allowed the spread of Islamic literacy and educational institutions. Islamic intellectual centers created large permanent walled cities in place of the small nomadic settlements that had previously been typical of the region. Islamic social and political institutions in these regions created solidarity as well, and greatly strengthened the Sufi orders that had not only religious but also political, social, and educational significance as the region faced the incursions from French Senegal that began at mid-century.

This Islamic militancy and the jihads that expressed it not only spread Islam into the countryside but, by establishing political regimes that supported popular Islamic practice, were instrumental in making much of West Africa self-consciously Islamic. These regimes created the basis for the West Africa that Europeans would encounter when they attempted to move inland from the coast of West Africa in the eighteenth and nineteenth centuries. Ironically, the accommodations made by some Muslim leaders with the colonizing powers, the imposition of colonial rule on indigenous conflicts that made it safer for Muslim proselytizers to enter previously unsafe regions of West Africa, and the improvements in transportation and communication brought by colonization meant that Islam spread even more widely after colonization than before. But, especially after the jihad of 'Umar Tal in the middle of the nineteenth century, Islam provided a basis for resistance to European intrusion in West Africa.

Islam also came to Africa by water, opening a second doorway in East Africa. The Indian Ocean connected eastern Africa with a broad and diverse Muslim world spread along its shores, and by the tenth century Arab merchants from the heartland of Islam, in Oman and Hadhramaut, were moving south along the east coast of the African continent. They continued past Somaliland and Ethiopia to the Swahili coast and Zanzibar, where through acculturation and intermarriage they became a significant part of the Swahili world. As elsewhere in Africa, trade provided the basis for the spread of Islam, and by the sixteenth century, a form of Islam had become the majority religion along the coast.

The growing importance of Islam in East Africa made it a rallying point for resistance to the spread of Portuguese rule and Christian missions in the region. The Portuguese were expelled from the coast north of Mozambique in 1728, and in the aftermath of that military victory Islamic influences on Swahili culture grew. The rise of the Omani Sultan of Zanzibar after 1820 provided a home for Muslim scholars and clerics and a consequent rise in the standard of religious education and scholarship. Both on Zanzibar and on the east coast, the nineteenth century also saw Islam become a more popular religion, with missionary teachers making it an advocate for the poor Muslim and non-Muslim peasants of the region. But it was only in the 1830s and 1840s, when trade caravans led by Arabs, Swahili, and sometimes Indians moved inland towards the Great Lakes region in search of ivory and slaves, that Islam began to spread in the interior.

The Portuguese presence on the coast of Mozambique since the late fifteenth century hindered the spread of Islam in that part of East Africa, and it was only in the middle of the nineteenth century that, influenced by the sultanate on Zanzibar and Muslim traders from the north, it began to make its presence felt in the interior of Mozambique. Further south still, the small Muslim communities of southern Africa seem to have come into being largely as a result of migration, whether of political deportees from the East Indies in the late seventeenth and early eighteenth centuries, slaves from Zanzibar and East Africa, indentured servants from South Asia, or, after the outlawing of the Atlantic slave trade in 1807, the cargoes of illegal slaveships captured by the British navy.

The Maghreb and the Ottoman territories

The nineteenth-century expansion of European power in Africa began in the north, where the declining authority of the Ottoman empire provided opportunities for European states. France was the first, invading Algeria in 1830 over a commercial dispute between French merchants and the Dey of Algiers, who ruled in the name of the Ottoman emperor. During the 1830s it proved difficult for the French to move inland from the coastal plain, but in the 1840s France consolidated its control. General Thomas Bugeaud, a former Napoleonic sergeant, led a campaign that aimed at destroying the ability of the tribes to resist French authority. By the end of the decade, he had extended French control south to the Atlas Mountains in a campaign that, recent scholars have emphasized, was marked by extraordinary violence that would presage the nature of French colonial rule.[4] In 1848, events in France served to increase French presence. The Revolution of February 1848 in Paris, which established the Second Republic, was quickly followed in June by a revolt of Parisian artisans and workers. In the aftermath of this revolt, many radicals were sent to Algeria. Three years later, on December 2, 1851, the president of the Republic, Louis-Napoleon Bonaparte, launched a coup d'état against the Republic, soon establishing a Second Empire with himself as Emperor Napoleon III. The republicans arrested in December 1851 became more exiles to Algeria. The French population, therefore, was increased by these infusions of radical republicans. Because of the circumstances that brought many of them to Algeria, a significant part of this settler population, especially in the city of Algiers, was pro-republican and adamantly opposed to the regime of Napoleon III.

The French military regime in Algeria was dominated by military officers whose positions in the ministry of war's directorate of Arab affairs gave them direct influence in the formulation and execution of

---

[4] Benjamin Claude Brower, *A Desert Named Peace: The Violence of France's Empire in the Algerian Sahara, 1844–1902* (New York: Columbia University Press, 2009); Jennifer E. Sessions, *France and the Conquest of Algeria* (Ithaca, NY: Cornell University Press, 2011).

policies in the colony between 1830 and 1870. Many of these officers had been influenced at the École Polytéchnique by the ideas of the utopian socialist Henri de Saint-Simon and his followers Père Enfantin and the Arab specialist Thomas "Isma'il" Urbain. In contrast to the goal of assimilation of Algerians to the French nation espoused by French republicans at mid-century, these officers believed that French and Arab civilizations were at different points in their historical development, and that those different civilizations must continue their evolution within the framework of their own institutions and cultures. These Arabist officers aimed at protecting indigenous cultures and institutions, and favored policies that would maintain and support an "Arab kingdom" in Algeria.

When, in September 1870, the Second Empire of Napoleon III was defeated by the German states in the Franco-Prussian War and another, Third, Republic established, many of the French in Algeria supported this new regime. But the triumph of the Republic, and its support for the aspirations of the French settlers in Algeria, was a defeat for the indigenous peoples of Algeria, whose communal lands had been protected by the military Arab Bureaus against the demands of the settlers. The force of the French army was needed to maintain French rule over the indigenous peoples of Algeria, but the settlers supported the Republic as it restored order in France and Algeria and consolidated a civil government. Thereafter, any hopes of assimilation that had marked earlier republican policies towards the colony gave way to a revival of the earlier policies of association, now marked not so much by the preservation of indigenous Arab culture but by a self-fulfilling disbelief in the ability of Algerian Arabs to become fully French.

Elsewhere in North Africa French financial interests forced attention by the government to the ongoing interest of the British, and the developing interest of Italy, in the provinces of the Ottoman empire. Concerns about the debt of the Tunisian government, the desire of French merchants, banks, and companies for commercial access, along with a professed intention to protect the security of Algeria, led to armed intervention in April 1881. A treaty presented as an ultimatum to the Bey of Tunis gave France control over Tunisian policy, the right to occupy Tunisian territory, the authority to represent Tunisia abroad, and the power to reorganize the finances of the Tunisian state. While the bey remained sovereign in principle, a French resident-general made decisions, using a system of French administrators who doubled the existing Tunisian system: French ministers were placed next to Tunisian ministers, and in the provinces, French "civil controllers" were set up parallel to the Tunisian *caïds*. At the same time France increased its influence in Morocco as French merchants competed with those from other European countries for business in what was still a province of the Ottoman empire. The French role in Morocco was contested by the other European powers, and French claims to primacy there became a bargaining chip in European diplomacy. In the *entente cordiale* between France and Great Britain in 1904 the British government recognized French preeminence in Morocco in exchange for French acceptance of British dominance in Egypt. This was finally confirmed by the European powers, and recognized in a protectorate treaty between France and the Sultan of Morocco, only in 1912. At the same time, Italy captured Tripolitania.

Most of the Middle East territories of the declining Ottoman empire remained at least nominally governed by the Ottoman emperor prior to World War I, but both France and Great Britain had long-standing interests in this area, while the Russian empire began pushing into Afghanistan and Iran in the early nineteenth century. An overriding concern for the British was the security of the Suez Canal, opened in 1869 and an important link to India, and in the decades before World War I it sought to ensure this through a series of treaty arrangements that, while not formally creating colonies, nonetheless allowed the British to exercise significant power in the region. Britain also protected its contact by land between Iraq and India, fending off Russian attempts to extend informal control into Afghanistan and Iran rather than by acquiring formal colonies.

The collapse of the Ottoman empire in the aftermath of World War I brought closer attention by European powers to what was now called the Middle East. The Sykes–Picot agreement of May 1916 established French and British claims to significant portions of Mesopotamia, which Russia agreed to on condition of a promise of territory in eastern Anatolia. The Bolshevik Revolution in 1917 upset this quid pro quo, and the region became even more unsettled with the Balfour Declaration of November 1917, which promised the establishment in Palestine of a Jewish homeland. The Palestinian issue was not settled by the end of the war, but in the peace settlement, France received Syria and Lebanon as mandates from the League of Nations. Britain held similar mandates for Palestine and Mesopotamia.

The Nile valley

The nineteenth century saw exploration of the interior of the continent by Europeans, and the eventual formalization of political control by European powers that embarked on a new competition for overseas territories in the last third of the nineteenth century. Sporadically at first, European powers sought to protect the trading interests of their citizens by establishing formal links with indigenous societies. One initial focus of this was the Nile River basin. Its two tributary streams, the Blue Nile from the east and the White Nile, which originated in the Great Lakes region of the continent, came together in the Sudan and flowed north to Alexandria on the Mediterranean Sea. Cairo, 100 miles from the delta, was the focal point for trade up the Nile, to Damascus and the Red Sea to the east, and to the Fezzan in the west. In the eighteenth century this area was dominated by a military elite, among them the sultan's household troops, the Janissaries, and by a number of grandees, many from the families of Mamluks, the elite slave soldiers used by the Ottomans. These different groups contended for power, with their struggle presided over by a weak representative of the Ottoman emperor in Constantinople.

The first European to venture beyond Cairo was James Bruce, a Scotsman, who in 1769 traveled up the Nile to the Red Sea and then into the interior. By mid February 1770 he had reached Gondar, the principal city of Ethiopia, overlooking Lake Tana, the source of the Blue Nile. Bruce's works proved valuable twenty years later for a French army which invaded Egypt in 1798 under the command of Napoleon Bonaparte. Landing at Alexandria, Napoleon easily defeated the Mamluk army in July 1798. While the British navy trapped the French army in Egypt, a Turkish invasion in July 1799 to regain control of Egypt led to a devastating defeat for the Turks at the battle of Abukir on July 25, 1799. A French expedition south to capture the remaining Mamluks eventually reached Aswan, providing for the first time European documentation of the ancient civilizations upriver. An Orientalist scholar, Vivant Denon, accompanied the French military expedition, viewing and sketching temples. Denon's publication of his findings, and other archaeological discoveries, such as the Rosetta Stone, provided key insights for European scholars into Classical Arabic language and culture. Napoleon also brought with him to Egypt a team of about 160 scientists and scholars, who, over the next three decades, produced the *Description de l'Égypte*, an attempt to create a compendium of French knowledge of Egypt.

Napoleon had come to Egypt not so much to build an empire but to put pressure on France's European enemies. The most persistent of these enemies, the British, forced the surrender of the French in July 1801, but themselves left soon after. With no European presence, a revolt in 1805 led to the appointment of Muhammad 'Ali as viceroy. During his long rule, in which he remained the nominal vassal of the sultan in Constantinople, Muhammad 'Ali consolidated his power by weakening the authority of the Muslim legal scholars who made up the ulama, ending the ability of the Mamluks to control the viceroy, and confiscating land to increase his financial resources. He also expanded his territorial power up the Nile River. Attempts to expand into Greece, in 1822–24, and Ottoman Syria, in 1831–40, ran into the interests of European powers and were less successful. The wars nonetheless consolidated his control within Egypt itself. Most noteworthy in this was the concession by the sultan, Abdulmecid, that made Muhammad 'Ali and his family the hereditary rulers of Egypt.

The one permanent conquest of Muhammad 'Ali, the Sudan, continued to be an object of interest for the government in Alexandria under his successors. After 1854 European traders entered the region around the upper White Nile, stimulating a complex trading system that was focused on ivory but which also brought European goods into the interior and stimulated the slave trade in the southern Sudan and further west. This trading system was soon dominated by Egyptians, Sudanese, and Levantines, who used trading stations as outposts to extend their influence.

The search for geographical knowledge, especially the source of the Nile, motivated subsequent European visitors, and by the 1860s explorers had shown that Lakes Victoria and Albert were the sources of the White Nile. The exploration of the sources of the Nile overlapped with an increasingly contentious situation in Egypt. Under Muhammad 'Ali a slow process of Westernization had begun through the establishment of a small number of schools that taught Western subjects as well as the beginnings of immigration by Westerners into the country. A limited number of Egyptians traveled to France and England for educational opportunities at this time as well. Under the Khedive Isma'il, who came to power in 1863, this Westernization increased, not only with a continued influx of foreigners and the growth of Western educational institutions, but also with the increased control of Egyptian finances by Westerners. Isma'il had inherited from his predecessor, the Viceroy Muhammad Sa'id, concessions granted in 1854 and 1856 to the French engineer Ferdinand de Lesseps and the Suez Canal Company for a canal between the Mediterranean and Red seas. Work on the canal began in 1859, but when Isma'il came to power in 1863 he rapidly incurred a major debt by purchasing shares in the canal company and buying out an agreement to supply labor for the project.

The Suez Canal made Egypt an object of great interest to the European powers, especially Great Britain and France. Its opening in 1869 provided a faster route from Britain to India, and raised the stakes for British diplomacy in the eastern Mediterranean. Isma'il's indebtedness to European lenders continued to grow, and in 1876 Britain and France established a system of dual control over Isma'il's government and Europeans forced the creation of a Caisse de la Dette Publique to supervise Egyptian finances and protect the interests of European investors. This increased Western control of Isma'il's government, and by 1879 significant opposition to this control had developed in the Egyptian elite. This opposition came into the open in April 1879 with the formation of the National Party by discontented army officers, religious leaders, politicians, and intellectuals, and Isma'il was deposed by that opposition later that year. But riots in Alexandria in June 1882 convinced William Gladstone, the British prime minister, that British subjects and interests were in danger, and a British military force – the French declined to join the expedition because of the cost, effectively turning over preeminence in Egypt to the British – intervened in Egypt. What was intended to be a short occupation to guarantee stability and British financial interests would last past the turn of the century, officially ending only in 1915 when Britain declared a short-lived protectorate over the country. During the occupation, the British representative – especially the first, Evelyn Baring (Lord Cromer) – governed as a de facto imperial proconsul. The finances of the Egyptian state slowly stabilized, and in fact Egypt experienced prosperity in the early 1900s, with improved tax collection and a rising world market for cotton. By 1910 that crop accounted for 93 percent of Egyptian exports.[5] Nationalist opposition forced Britain to end its protectorate over Egypt in 1922, although it retained a strong presence and a huge military facility in the Suez Canal zone that not only protected communication with South Asia through the Canal but also figured prominently in British strategic and military planning in the region.

The British occupation of Egypt opened the way for British penetration of the Nile from the north and British control of not only Egypt but also the region to its south. The first challenge was the need for an Egyptian response to the Mahdist movement that dominated the Sudan in the 1880s and 1890s. This movement began in the 1870s as a fundamentalist attempt to purify an Islam that was viewed as corrupt, and its leader, Muhammad Ahmad, gained popular support in the last years of Isma'il's reign. While Muhammad Ahmad drew on the long-standing belief in the Sudan in a divinely inspired Mahdi who

---

[5] G. N. Sanderson, "The Nile Basin and the Eastern Horn, 1870–1908," in Roland Oliver and Sanderson (eds.), *The Cambridge History of Africa*, vol. VI, *From c. 1870 to c. 1905* (Cambridge University Press, 1985), 629.

would restore justice and equality, Isma'il's use of Christians such as the British army officer Charles Gordon as administrators and governors exacerbated the conflict between Egypt on the one hand and the Mahdi and his followers on the other. Attempts by the Egyptians, with British help, to control or arrest the Mahdi in 1881 and 1882 failed, and by the summer of 1882 he had assembled an army that he led north towards El Obeid. His capture of the city in May 1883 opened the way to Egyptian holdings in the northern Sudan.

By 1883 the British were in effective control of the Egyptian government, and a British force commanded by Sir Alexander Hicks moved south to attempt to stem the success of the Mahdi and his army. This army (and Hicks) were massacred at Shakyan, south of El Obeid, on November 5, 1883, creating an uproar not only in Alexandria but in England. The Mahdi's siege of the Egyptian post at Khartoum, at the confluence of the White and Blue Nile, further complicated matters. In 1884, with the British garrison at Khartoum in danger, Charles Gordon, a former governor-general of the Sudan, was sent to escort the garrison out safely, but himself refused to leave. The British Prime Minister, William Gladstone, reluctantly sent a relief expedition in late 1884. With this expedition almost at Khartoum, the city fell on January 26, 1885 to the Mahdist army, with Gordon dying as the city was captured. The relief expedition arrived on January 28, but then withdrew upriver to Egypt, abandoning the Sudan to the Mahdi and his successor, the Khalifa 'Abdullah ibn Muhammed, who established their government across the Nile in Omdurman.

The fall of Khartoum and the almost immediate withdrawal of the British relief army from the Sudan began more than a decade in which Europeans showed little interest in the upper Nile region. The Sudan remained under the control of the Mahdist state in Omdurman. While Belgian colonization of the south bank of the Congo River placed pressure on the Mahdist state in 1891–92 and 1897, attempts to extend Belgian authority eastwards were not successful. Nonetheless, European diplomatic and economic concerns soon revived interest in the region. In 1898 the British sought to establish Egyptian control of the upper Nile before any other European powers could do so. A British army, commanded by Lord Kitchener, moved up the Nile from Egypt, and on September 2, 1898, at the battle of Omdurman, defeated the Khalifa and reasserted Alexandria's control over the Sudan.

Kitchener's victory over the Mahdi was in the name of the Egyptian government, but in its aftermath the British quickly extinguished any Egyptian rights over the Sudan and asserted their own rights by conquest. This effectively made the Sudan a British possession, although in practice British control was limited to the northern part of the region. But the British intent was not just to regain control of the Sudan from Mahdist forces, but also to prevent other European powers from controlling the Nile, and in pursuit of this objective Kitchener continued south. He soon encountered a French expedition led by Captain Jean-Baptiste Marchand that had set out from the French colony of Senegal in 1896. This encounter of two European armed forces at Fashoda raised the specter of a European war sparked by a chance colonial encounter. The crisis ended in November 1898 with the French conceding the Nile valley to the British and Egyptians, while the French received a free hand west of the river.

East Africa

The interior of East Africa was marked in the late eighteenth and early nineteenth centuries by a number of localized tribal communities, principalities, and kingdoms overseen by a weak and ineffective Ethiopian state. At the turn of the nineteenth century, that state was centered on Gondar, but its inability to assert its authority over a number of other princes led to a period of civil war known as the *zemana mesafent*, the "era of the princes" that lasted until mid-century. Beginning in the early 1840s, however, a provincial governor, Lij Kassa Haulu, won a series of victories over his principal competitors, and in 1855 he was crowned the king of kings, taking the name Tewodros, and ending the *zemana mesafent*.

Tewodros drew, even in his throne name, on the messianic legend of a king of kings who would rule the world in peace, prosperity, and righteousness. He himself envisioned an Ethiopia with an effective state that would lead Ethiopians towards prosperity and international respect, even from the European powers. But he faced almost constant rebellions and mutinies throughout his reign, and by 1865 his empire was a shadow of what it had been at its peak in 1861, reduced in size and with only a small army. He no longer commanded the resources necessary to maintain his power, and he was pressed on all sides by resurgent competition. The end came in 1868, when he imprisoned several British subjects and a British military expedition invaded. Tewodros' last bastion at Magdala was captured, and he shot himself just before he was reached by British soldiers.

The British invasion against Tewodros established a temporary European presence, but having defeated him, the British forces departed and European presence in that part of the continent again became negligible. But Tewodros' successors faced internal challenges to their power, notably from a resurgent Shoa in the south. By the 1880s there was also a growing threat from both Egypt and the Mahdist state to the west, and Europeans became more interested in the coast as more shipping traveled through the Suez Canal, the Red Sea, and the Gulf of Aden. In 1889, the death of the Ethiopian king Yohannes opened the way for the Shoan ruler, Menelik, to succeed Yohannes as king of kings. Menelik was forced to cede territory to Italy in the north, effectively shifting the geographic center of Ethiopia further south around its new capital of Adis Ababa. But he ended the internal contention that had plagued his predecessors, and when Italy attempted to assert a protectorate over Ethiopia in 1896, Menelik was able to mobilize forces from almost every part of his country. His crushing victory over the Italian army at Adowa dramatically improved his standing with the other European powers, and he effectively limited French and British influence in his territories. At the same time, he reached a workable relationship with the Mahdist regime in Omdurman, reducing that threat to his regime. After 1900, Menelik headed a regime that stood out not only for its successful resistance to the partitioning European powers, but also for its adoption of European technologies such as the telephone and telegraph to create an effective administrative system that lasted, with little change, for two generations after Menelik.

Further south, in Somalia, the outcome of the last decades of the nineteenth century was less favorable for the African residents. In 1875 Egypt occupied the northern coast, and Britain accepted this occupation as a way of preventing the intrusion of another European power. The collapse of Egyptian power in the Sudan after the fall of Khartoum in 1885, however, opened up a vacuum in the region that other European powers moved to fill. French, Italian, and British protectorates were established in 1889, but making these effective was difficult. An Islamic rebellion led by Muhammad 'Abdallah Hasan began in 1899, successfully preventing the establishment of European control of the interior and leading to withdrawal in 1910 by the European powers to the coastal cities that were, for them, the most important aspect of the region. The interior, left to the different Somali tribes, disintegrated into civil wars that brought Muhammad 'Abdallah Hasan back from exile to establish a stronghold at Taleh that enabled him to dominate northern and central Somalia. The British were able to remove him only in 1920.

Prior to 1800 there was little penetration into the interior of East Africa by Europeans or by traders from the Indian Ocean basin, even though there were some Muslim Swahili settlements on the coast. But a growing population and new states such as the Nyamwezi, Usaguzi, and

Imaliza kingdoms in the interior provided the impetus for the development of regional trading networks in the region between the coast and the lake region and further west. In the late eighteenth century, the Nyamwezi began long-distance trade in the area around the lakes. By 1800 they had reached as far west as Katanga. Nyamwezi adventurers moving east eventually found their way to the Swahili settlements on the eastern coast, and in the early nineteenth century they began to collect ivory in the interior and ship it by caravan to the coast. Other groups soon followed them into the ivory trade. By 1840 Swahili traders were themselves traveling into the interior to trade for ivory. In that year, the Omani ruler Sa'id bin Sultan moved his capital to Zanzibar, which soon became the principal commercial entrepôt in the region, with the hinterland connected to the island through a dense network of trading routes extending from the coastal Swahili towns into the interior areas around the Great Lakes and west of Lakes Victoria and Tanganyika. Slaves captured west of Lake Tanganyika were transported along these routes to the coastal towns where they were sold either to the island of Zanzibar or to Arabia. Ivory made the same journey. In other parts of the interior, such as Rwanda and the area east of Lake Tanganyika, the amount of foreign trade was lower, with cattle the most important product and pastoralism prevalent. Decentralized politically, this large region was held together by its commercial ties to the Swahili towns on the coast.

The extension of Egyptian and British influence in the Nile basin in the 1870s was easily resisted by local rulers south of Lake Kyoga. These moves, however, did have the effect of spurring the local rulers west of Lake Victoria to increase their military capability. The Sultan of Zanzibar also strengthened his state apparatus, a move that concerned the Swahili traders in the coastal towns who had benefitted in the past from the relatively lax control exercised by the sultan. There were certainly some successes for Europeans in the 1870s: the Egyptian occupation of ports on the upper coast in 1875 was accepted by the local elites there, who saw the benefit of British protection for their activities. The continued prosperity of the Swahili trading system and the increased ability of indigenous leaders in the interior of East Africa to resist European power meant that, while the trading system provided the basis for European penetration into the interior, conquest and partition remained in the future. In the meantime, however, British colonial subjects were emigrating from India to the coastal regions of East Africa, attracted by economic opportunities there.

In the 1870s and 1880s the Swahili system itself benefitted from the influx of money from European exploration and missionary activity. A series of middlemen, providing transport, charging tolls, and exchanging goods from the interior for those from the coast, extended as far as the area west of Lake Tanganyika. Protestant and Catholic missionary agencies as well as the International African Association (IAA) established by King Leopold of Belgium began to establish permanent stations in the interior in the 1870s. Two Anglican Church Missionary Society missionaries reached Buganda north of Lake Victoria in that decade, and the White Fathers followed beginning in 1878. The White Fathers placed mission stations alongside the IAA posts as it expanded east from the Congo basin. While the IAA withdrew as Leopold's interests focused on the Congo River basin, the missionaries remained, and by the twentieth century, Lake Tanganyika was described as "a strip of water completely surrounded by White Fathers."[6] While these had humanitarian goals, they also provided the opportunity for Europeans to compete more effectively in the ivory trade and other staple commodities of the Swahili system. Yet this is not, in the 1880s, a story of European triumph and African collapse. Most notable was the attempt by a coalition of indigenous rulers and merchants – the Sultan of Zanzibar, the merchant Tippu Tip, and others – to adapt the Swahili system to the new conditions through the HM Company, an organization that sought to mobilize indigenous political leadership and capital to keep Swahili and Zanzibar control of the ivory trade. Established in 1883–84, the Company was able to work effectively with European merchants and authorities, including the Congo Independent State that was moving in from the west, to both reach this goal and expand colonial control and European business interests.

The HM Company reflected the economic and political power of the Sultan of Zanzibar, and much of this came from the clove plantations on the island. Clove trees were first planted on Zanzibar in 1819, and with the encouragement of the sultan, who himself invested substantially in clove plantations, their cultivation spread across the island.[7] By the 1830s the Zanzibar crop was beginning to make a significant dent in the international trade in cloves, and in the following decade cultivation spread to the plantations of a large part of the Omani community on Zanzibar and to Pemba. The clove plantations increased the demand for slaves on the two islands, and by the middle of the nineteenth century

---

[6] Caroline Oliver, *Western Women in Colonial Africa* (Westport, CT: Greenwood Press, 1982), xiv, 146.

[7] Frederick Cooper, *Plantation Slavery on the East Coast of Africa* (New Haven, CT: Yale University Press, 1977), and *From Slaves to Squatters: Plantation Labor and Agriculture in Zanzibar and Coastal Kenya, 1890–1925* (New Haven, CT: Yale University Press, 1980).

they were dependent on importing slaves from the African mainland. The slave trade brought pressure from the British government to end it, as well as British naval vessels that enforced the European ban on the slave trade. At the same time agriculture on the fertile coastal plains of East Africa became specialized in the production of grain, especially millet, sold not only to the increasing population of the islands but also to the less fertile areas of the Horn of Africa and Arabia. In the course of the nineteenth century agriculture in East Africa had been transformed from family farms with a few slaves to plantations worked by large numbers of slaves. These plantations also produced coconuts and sesame, crops from which oil could be extracted for sale to European traders on Zanzibar.

But a combination of increased European competition, a series of ecological crises that damaged local economies throughout the interior, and the disruptions created by military activities soon led to the collapse of the Swahili commercial system and to European conquest and rule. Locusts, rinderpest, smallpox, sleeping sickness, and drought added to military and political disarray to facilitate the partition of the region among European powers. In the 1880s British, French, and Italian claims to portions of Somaliland were established and acknowledged by the other European powers. An Anglo-German treaty in 1886 recognized British control of Kenya, south of Ethiopia, which guaranteed access to Uganda and the Great Lakes region further inland. At the same time the German explorer Carl Peters was concluding treaties with indigenous rulers in the region. While the German chancellor, Otto von Bismarck, had little interest in colonial expansion, he eventually accepted from Peters territories between Tanga on the coast and Lake Tanganyika. These provided the basis for a German protectorate, recognized as German East Africa in a German–British treaty in 1890. From the west, the Congo Independent State (CIS), the successor to King Leopold's International Association of the Congo and International Congo Association, pressed its claims to the area west of Lake Tanganyika against attempts by both Swahili merchants and European missionaries to maintain their influence there, but the delineation of boundaries by the European powers overcame these efforts and the common border between the CIS and German East Africa was established. The British also extended their control inland into territories allocated to them at the Berlin Conference in 1885. Initially, the Imperial British East Africa Company undertook this project, especially the construction of a railroad from the port of Mombasa to Lake Tanganyika, but in 1895 the British government took over rule of what became British East Africa.

After the conquest and partition of this region was completed, increased European coastal traffic combined with the completion of railways into the interior and steamer service on Lake Victoria to allow more sustained economic development than had been possible in earlier decades. This development built on the Swahili system, but found new products to carry along the older trade routes. Rubber became a major product of German East Africa, British East Africa, and Uganda after 1900, spurring the development of rubber plantations in those areas. The Lake Victoria basin, opened up by a railroad from the coast around the turn of the century and knitted together by daily steamers on the lake, became an exporter of cotton and groundnuts that, because of cheap labor and the low transportation costs on the railway, were competitive in the world market. Steps towards political stabilization were taken through alliances between colonial administrations and local indigenous leaders who, after the collapse of the Swahili system and the profits it had brought to them, were looking for ways to rebuild their wealth and prestige.

As these events were occurring, the plantations of East Africa came under pressure as a result of British insistence that the Sultan of Zanzibar end the slave trade in his territories. In 1873 the British forced the sultan to agree to a treaty outlawing all shipments of slaves by sea and closing the public slave markets on Zanzibar. In 1876 another treaty outlawed slave caravans on land, and slowly these measures disrupted the supply of slaves to the plantations on the coastal plains and on the islands. As that supply weakened so also did the profitability of the plantation system. Slavery was eventually abolished by the British on Zanzibar in 1897, and in Kenya in 1907.

The labor and landholding regimes that would replace slavery were less than clear to the British colonial administrators. Attempting to preserve the plantation system inherited from the pre-colonial era, the British aimed at a steady labor supply under the control of plantation owners, made up of workers who would learn the values of hard work and obedience to supervision. But it became necessary for the state to intervene in the labor market to make laborers behave in the ways expected by the British and needed by the plantation owners. On Zanzibar freed slaves remained on small plots of land they had cultivated prior to emancipation, and some were able to migrate to the town, where they could work as casual laborers in the port. These alternatives allowed freed slaves to determine for themselves whether they would work on the clove plantations. In the end, while the British continued to hold out a free labor system as their goal, they drew back from it in practice. Lost harvests led to the introduction of forced labor on the island in 1904–5, as the colonial state used its power to support the plantations and their need for labor.

In contrast, the British colonial state did not make such an intervention in the grain-producing coastal plantation areas of Kenya. Once the British had consolidated their control, they began implementing a model of economic development that emphasized British immigration and settlement on the highlands through which passed the railroad link between Mombasa on the coast, Nairobi in Uganda, and Port Florence on Lake Victoria. Between 1903 and 1915 large amounts of land were expropriated from the Kamba, Kikuyu, and Maasai tribes in the highlands, and British settlers were granted the best of this land. The Africans who had been there were moved into reserves and a free market in both labor and land was created. In principle, both British settlers and the Arab and Swahili plantation owners in the coastal areas enjoyed the same protection in these capitalist markets. When slavery was abolished in 1907, the land titles of coastal plantation owners were registered and enforced by the British. But no provision was made to allocate land to freed slaves, and so they became squatters on plantation land. This created a paradoxical situation: the plantation owners who controlled the land could profit from it only if they could get the freed slaves to work on it for the profit of the landowner, not as squatters. Yet if the power of the state was used to evict squatters, they would return as plantation workers only if they had no alternative sources of wage labor. The colonial state therefore left squatters in possession of land, but without legal titles. Those with legal titles, the plantation owners, could not profitably cultivate the land. Instead, the state was concerned with providing an adequate labor supply for the settler farms in the highlands. What had been a productive coastal agricultural region before the British took control became locked in paralysis: neither squatters nor landowners had any incentive to improve the land or increase production by experimenting with new crops or investing capital.

West Africa

In West Africa a significant impetus for the extension of colonial control was the campaign against the slave trade and slavery that began in the 1770s, and settlements by the British in Sierra Leone (1787), the Americans in Monrovia (1821), and the French in Libreville (1848) were established for freed slaves. With Great Britain's abolition of the transatlantic slave trade in 1807, its navy assumed the principal responsibility for preventing slavers from leaving the coast of West Africa for the New World. This increased naval presence in the waters around

West Africa both provided support for European merchants who traded along the coast and increased European contact, as the ships occasionally put in to the bays and inlets of the coast for provisions and repairs. The efforts to end the slave trade proved ineffective until the demand for slaves in the New World ended after mid-century, but especially after 1840 the British and French used anti-slave-trade activity as a way of increasing their own influence in Senegambia and the south coast of West Africa.

Beginning in 1854, French troops moved east from Saint-Louis, at the mouth of the Senegal River, and the island of Gorée, further south near the mouth of the Gambia, into the interior of the western Sudan. These efforts ran into the Futa Toro and Tukolor states that resulted from jihads in the first half of the nineteenth century, but made some progress until French focus on developments in Europe and North Africa led to a French withdrawal back towards the coast after 1870. Largely as a result of initiatives taken by military officers, the French advance resumed in the 1880s into the interior of the western Sudan, to the Niger River, and by 1894 to Timbuktu on the Niger Bend, forming the basis for what in 1895 became French West Africa.

Around 1870, a coastal strip from Saint-Louis in Senegal to the mouth of the Niger River was relatively integrated into world trading markets as groundnuts and palm oil replaced the slave trade. In the hinterland behind this coastal strip, however, from the upper Senegal River to Lake Chad, the long-standing indigenous trans-Saharan commerce continued to dominate. For several decades after 1870, in fact, European commercial penetration seems to have been weak and intermittent in this hinterland region. After the convulsions of mid-century, therefore, the interior of West Africa was relatively stable until 1885 or 1890. The gathering European pressure on this region of the continent was felt primarily in Senegambia, the Upper Niger, and the Asante and Yoruba territories near the mouth of the Niger River. It was, rather, internal contests for power, the challenge of expanding Islam, especially in its Mahdist form, and frontier conflicts with non-Muslims that were most disruptive in the two decades after 1870 in this region. But as the French tried to manage these conflicts, they extended their own power. In 1886 they moved against one of the contestants, al-Hajj Muhammad al-Amin (Mamadu Lamine). In May 1887 Ahmad bin 'Umar Tal, ruler of what was left of the Tukolor empire, concluded a treaty with France that established a French protectorate in the region.

The decline of the Tukolor empire had left in its wake successor states that were able to resist French expansion in the 1870s and 1880s. One of the most important of these was the Wassoulou empire, led by

Samory Touré. Samory began to consolidate his power in the Guinea highlands in the 1860s, and his influence spread through the Sudan over the next several decades. But in the 1890s the balance between African political regimes and European power took a decisive shift in favor of the Europeans as French administrators and army officers moved to preempt other European powers and expand French control into the interior. The French occupied territories of the Tukolor and the Dahomey, and by the end of the decade the French had established a series of posts along the Niger River. In 1896 the French defeated the last ruler of the kingdom of Futa Jalon at the battle of Pore-Daka, and two years later they captured Samory Touré. French expeditions from Algeria, the west, and the southeast converged in the region between the French Sudan and Lake Chad in 1899 and 1900. The final defeat, and death, of the warlord Rabah at the battle of Kousseri in April 1900 concluded the French conquest of most of West Africa. The Germans and the British extended their control over territories in West Africa at the same time. These moves were motivated by a desire to increase the profitability of the European presence in West Africa by forcing greater cooperation from Africans, and also by fears on the part of each of these European powers that their European rivals would steal a march on them in the competition for African resources. The indigenous regimes in the hinterland that had been, in 1870, relatively free of European influence now experienced a series of crises of authority that invited greater European intervention and control.

The effect of this European intervention was to stimulate both collaboration and resistance. David Robinson has shown the accommodations reached between the French colonial authorities and Muslim marabouts in Senegal and Mauritania that allowed the French to portray themselves as a "Muslim power" and rule with the collaboration of religious leaders who were not a part of the formal administrative structure of colonial rule.[8] Christian mission stations became significant points of contact between Europeans and Africans, and missionaries themselves at times became agents of imperial power. Conversion, by the same token, brought Africans into imperial networks. The exigencies of ruling a large area with few Europeans and minimal budgets meant that the colonial administrations that began to develop in the 1890s depended on the cooperation of indigenous leaders in some areas. These were not necessarily the long-standing political leaders

---

[8] David Robinson, *Paths of Accommodation: Muslim Societies and French Colonial Authorities in Senegal and Mauritania, 1880–1920* (Athens, OH: Ohio University Press, 2000).

and social elites of West Africa: the European powers did not hesitate to put new leaders in place if they proved more complaisant in opening trade, providing labor, and supporting missionary efforts. The slow origins of what would become indirect rule grew out of these practical considerations rather than an ideological choice. Elsewhere, such as in the western Sudan, where the rise of large indigenous states before the arrival of the French had destroyed the authority of local indigenous rulers, the French were forced to adopt direct administration until the early twentieth century. The French also adopted legal systems that allowed Africans to continue to adjudicate their disputes without the intervention of the French administration. These decisions avoided large concessions held by European companies, allowed the retention of significant indigenous access to natural resources, and, at least initially, maintained a relatively light administrative touch on much of West Africa.

Central Africa

Since its discoveries in the fifteenth and sixteenth centuries, Portugal had been the principal European colonial power on both coasts of Central Africa. In its colony on the west coast, Angola, the large African state systems in the interior, the Kongo, Kasanje, Lunda, and Ovimbundu kingdoms, were all threatened by emerging groups of traders or by competing lineages in the course of the nineteenth century. In spite of these internal conflicts, the ruling groups in these indigenous kingdoms were able to push back efforts in the middle third of the nineteenth century to extend Portuguese influence inland. But as their internal problems continued into the late nineteenth century, these indigenous rulers of Central Africa found it difficult to resist the European incursions that were beginning to come from the south.

On the east coast, in northern Mozambique, the spread of Islam, the absence of a single centralized indigenous state on which Portugal could focus military operations, and the trade in firearms that made the many small centers of indigenous power heavily armed and able to compete with the small forces the Portuguese could muster provided the basis for resistance. In the south, while the dominance of the Sangane state of Gungunyana provided a target for Portuguese efforts at conquest, it posed a formidable military obstacle. The weakness of the Portuguese economy in the middle of the century, and the lack of economic promise of either Angola or Mozambique, also worked against extension of Portuguese control into the interior. Portugal's African colonies were seen more as potential sources of capital to develop the metropole than as sites for economic development, but the prospects for fulfilling even this goal seemed poor. In the 1870s, therefore, there was a general withdrawal back to the coast on the part of the Portuguese and an emphasis on increasing customs revenues.

The agreements reached in 1885 at the Berlin Conference, however, insisted on effective occupation of territory by the colonial power, and raised the possibility of a takeover by other European powers of these lightly held Portuguese colonies. This gave the colonial party in Lisbon more influence and, ultimately, led to a change in government policy to one aimed at controlling the interior of Angola and Mozambique. A treaty in 1891 finally resolved the borders of Angola and Mozambique, but confirmed British control of the area north of the Zambezi. The extension of Portuguese control into the interior after 1891 was slow, hindered by economic crises in Portugal and the absence of adequate resources on the ground in Africa. It was only on the eve of World War I that the interior areas of both colonies could be considered militarily occupied, and these occupations were punctuated by occasional revolts. Economic development proved slow as well. Hopes for gold mining in the Cassinga area in southern Angola were disappointed, as the deposits there were not suitable for large-scale mining. After the consolidation of Portuguese control and the abolition of slavery (formally abolished in the 1870s, but only effectively ended in 1911), efforts were made to force the peasants into the labor market by taxation and forced labor policies. Ivory and rubber booms provided some impetus for wage labor, but they proved short-lived. Southern Angola especially, with poor agriculture and few industrial enterprises, became a labor reserve for plantations, fisheries, and public works within Angola. By the 1920s, temporary migrants were going as casual laborers not only to South West Africa, but also to the diamond fields in northeast Angola, copper mines in Northern Rhodesia, and gold and diamond mines in Southern Rhodesia and South Africa.

If Portugal struggled to maintain its long-standing presence in Africa, other European powers did not face the same limitations. An expedition led by Pierre Savorgnan de Brazza, a French naval officer, sought a route into the interior of the continent up the Ogooué River between 1875 and 1878. After 1879, as they had in Indochina and West Africa, French cabinet ministers favorable to colonial expansion provided the impetus for expansion in this part of Africa. On a second expedition, from 1879 to 1882, de Brazza concluded treaties with the indigenous tribes in the Congo River valley, notably with the king, Makoko, that established a French protectorate over Makoko's dominions and those of his vassals. Returning to France in 1882, de Brazza found support for ratification of his treaties from commercial interests who wished to develop railroads and other ventures in the Congo, as well as from cabinet ministers such as Charles de Freycinet and Admiral Bernard Jauréguiberry, and they were quickly ratified. A third expedition by de Brazza in March 1883 was the occasion for further treaties that extended French influence in the region.[9] By the time of the 1885 Berlin Conference, de Brazza had made France the principal European power north of the Congo River and laid the groundwork for what would become French Equatorial Africa.

South of the Congo River, European influence and control took a different form. The erstwhile *New York Herald Tribune* reporter H. M. Stanley, who first came to Africa in 1871 in search of the Scottish medical missionary David Livingstone, led another expedition between 1874 and 1877, on which he circumnavigated Lake Victoria in spite of "experience of African troubles, native arrogance, and unbridled temper." He then continued west to the Congo basin and to the Atlantic, thus connecting the two great areas of exploration that had dominated European interest for a century. Once back in Europe, he persuaded the King of the Belgians, Leopold II, to create a private company, the International Congo Association (ICA), to exploit the resources of the Congo River basin. With Leopold borrowing money from the Belgian state to finance the venture, Stanley concluded treaties for the Association with over 500 tribal chiefs south of the Congo River in the early 1880s – the result, he thought, of "seeds of good-will [sown] at every place we had touched" – establishing the domination over them of the Association.[10]

Prior to the activities of the Congo Association, indigenous trade networks connected the east and west coasts of Equatorial Africa. There was heavy traffic up the Congo River between its mouth on the west coast and Stanley Pool, another system that extended further up the river to Basoko and the multiple branches of the Congo, and a third linking Luanda and Benguela as far as Katanga. From there, these routes that began on the west coast could link up with the Swahili-speaking traders we have already seen in East Africa who penetrated as far as Katanga and Kisangani (Stanleyville) on the upper Congo. These networks,

---

[9] These events have been advanced as the spark that set off the so-called Scramble for Africa. See Jean Stengers, "The Partition of Africa: l'impérialisme colonial de la fin du XIXe siècle: mythe ou réalité," *Journal of African History* 3, 3 (1962), 469–91; and C. W. Newbury and A. S. Kanya-Forstner, "French Policy and the Origins of the Scramble for Africa," *Journal of African History* 10, 2 (1969), 253–76.

[10] Dorothy Stanley (ed.), *The Autobiography of Sir Henry Morton Stanley* (Boston and New York: Houghton Mifflin Co., 1909), 299, 344.

finally, linked to traders from the Nile who were based in Khartoum. European traders and European goods moved along these networks prior to Stanley's arrival in 1879, along with agricultural and artisanal goods produced by the peoples of the Congo region. The ICA, however, changed this, destroying not only the indigenous participation in trade up the river, but also the agricultural and artisanal economy that contributed to it. After the Berlin Conference in 1885 the ICA became the Congo Independent State (CIS), still completely owned by Leopold and his investors until his death in 1906, when it passed to the Belgian state. The Congo Independent State existed to exploit the region, and this meant ivory and, as the elephant herds were destroyed, rubber and copper mines. In contrast to West Africa, the CIS exploited the Congo through concessions to European companies that would bring the capital needed to develop the transportation of the basin, especially a railroad from the mouth of the Congo to Stanley Pool, and steamers above that point. The heavy labor demands, both for infrastructure and for rubber plantations and mines, were often met by forced labor. Until reforms after 1906, the Congo was a byword for the use of force and, at times, extraordinary violence against Africans by Europeans. Such methods of colonial exploitation led to occasional revolts (and heavy repression) as well as a revival of traditional religions that provided a haven against the forcible imposition of European civilization.

At the same time the French and the British were reaching agreements on the disposition of territories further east. An Anglo-French agreement in 1890 accorded to France a protectorate over Madagascar, while confirming British protection over Zanzibar. While endorsed by Germany later the same year in exchange for French and British recognition of German East Africa, this convention did not include the Madagascan queen, and French attempts to assert control led to an uprising, French annexation and abolition of the monarchy in 1896, and pacification of the island by French troops under the first governor-general, Joseph Gallieni.

South Africa

A significant part of Great Britain's participation in the colonial expansion of the last few decades of the nineteenth century built on its existing control over the southern part of Africa that dated from the first half of the century. Britain gained control of the Dutch colonies on the Cape of Good Hope in the course of the European wars of the 1790s, seizing the colony in 1795 and having possession confirmed at the Congress of Vienna in 1814. As elsewhere, missionary efforts helped colonial expansion. The Dutch sent missionaries to South Africa as early as the 1730s. The Evangelical revival in Great Britain in the 1790s encouraged the foundation of numerous missionary societies, notably the Baptist Missionary Society, founded in 1792, and the London Missionary Society (LMS), established three years later. The first LMS missionaries arrived in South Africa soon after, setting up mission stations among the Khoisan on the fringes of the colony. Later in the century, the LMS would send two of the best-known missionaries to Africa, Robert Moffat, who arrived in 1817, and David Livingstone, who came in 1841.[11]

In the early part of the century, the British struggled on two fronts to extend their influence inland from the Cape. On the one hand, they dealt with ongoing opposition from the Dutch (Boer) descendants of the original European settlers on the Cape, who demonstrated, more often than not, a distinct inclination to resist British government. The second part of the British struggle in the nineteenth century was to assert their control over the different African tribes that inhabited the areas brought under nominal British control. Expansion further north ran into resistance from large African political systems. The most striking example of this was in the northeast, where in the early nineteenth century the leader Shaka created a Zulu state. Shaka's military exploits and consolidation of power made the Zulu kingdom a powerful indigenous force that Europeans had to confront. By the time of his death in 1828 he had not only consolidated a powerful state but also impoverished much of the area in Natal to the west to support his military forces.

In spite of such powerful indigenous forces, the first half of the nineteenth century saw significant attempts to expand South Africa as Dutch and then British settlers moved northwards from the Cape. These settlers established an agricultural system built around cattle-ranching, displacing indigenous cultivators and using the African population as a labor force. As the population of Cape Colony grew, the settlers, and this labor system, pushed north, moving into the Zuurveld just below the Fish River by 1820. The high cost of land there led many whites to move across the river. Resistance by the Xhosa on the eastern side, towards the coast and the Zulu kingdom, closed off expansion in that direction, but in spite of official disapproval the migration continued

---

[11] Elizabeth Elbourne, *Blood Ground: Colonialism, Missions, and the Contest for Christianity in the Cape Colony and Britain, 1799–1853* (Montreal and Kingston: McGill-Queen's University Press, 2002); Tim Jeal, "David Livingstone: A Brief Biographical Account," in John M. MacKenzie (ed.), *David Livingstone and the Victorian Encounter with Africa* (London: National Portrait Gallery, 1996), 11–78.

north. By 1824 the frontier had been extended to the Orange River, and by the end of the decade it had reached the Harts River.

The pressure from whites for land, efforts by the government to protect African laborers from the extremes of the labor system, and the apparent unwillingness of the government of Cape Colony to open up new areas for settlement led in 1836 to the migration of Dutch-speaking farmers out of Cape Colony into the expanses of land beyond its frontiers. These territories had been temporarily cleared of their populations in the previous decade by the wars of Shaka and other African leaders. The Boer Trekkers poured into Natal and Transvaal, in effect trying to escape from Cape Colony and British rule. In part a protest against British policies, in part a continuation of the northward movement of the expanding white population of South Africa, the Great Trek encountered but overcame indigenous resistance in both Transvaal and Natal. Fearing an independent Boer regime that might threaten the security of Cape Colony, the British annexed Natal to the Cape in 1845. In response, many Boers left for the high veld across the Vaal River, and in 1852 the British gave up any claims to control settlers north of the Vaal, effectively making the Transvaal a South African Republic controlled by the Boers. In 1854 Britain also abandoned the area north of the Orange River, which became the Boer-dominated Orange Free State. But especially in 1849–52 settlers from Britain arrived in large numbers, seeking escape from the economic hardships of the "Hungry Forties" in Europe and attracted by the prospect of land. Many of these settlers came to Natal, and in 1852 it became a separate British colony.

By the mid nineteenth century, therefore, only a few small independent African kingdoms – the Zulu, Swazi, and Tswana kingdoms and the chiefdoms in the Transkei – remained in an area dominated by the four principal European colonies, the British Cape Colony and Natal and the Afrikaner Orange Free State and South African Republic (SAR). Most Africans were primarily subsistence farmers and cattle-ranchers, as were some Europeans, especially the Afrikaner farmers of the South African Republic and Orange Free State. But in the middle of the nineteenth century the ivory frontier extending from Zanzibar and Kenya reached the northern Transvaal, creating market pressures for ivory and with it the sale of European goods such as guns. At the same time, market-oriented agriculture by European settlers in the Cape Colony, built on raising merino sheep for their wool in place of cattle-ranching, was increasing in importance and spreading into the Orange Free State. This began to stimulate a market for African labor. The increased dependence of the South African economy on wool made it vulnerable to changes in European production techniques, as occurred in the 1850s and 1860s, and to disruptions in international trade.

But this dependence on wool changed in the last third of the nineteenth century. The discovery of diamonds in Kimberley in 1867 created the first major industrial center in southern Africa, attracting to it not only prospectors who flocked to the region as word of the discovery spread but also European capital to exploit the diamond deposits. Limitations placed on the number of claims that individual miners could hold initially created an ephemeral "diggers' democracy" that even included a number (about 120 in 1875) of Africans. But a period of consolidation quickly followed. Deeper mines became increasingly dangerous, and the labor demands of those mines favored larger claim holders with the resources to mobilize the labor of African migrants into the region. The size of claims slowly increased, and after the repression of a rebellion of small diggers in 1875, the way was open for larger concessions held by joint-stock companies linked to British capital. Further weeding out was stimulated by changes in mining technology and the collapse of the stock market in 1886, and by 1887 two concessionaires, Barney Barnato in Kimberley and Cecil Rhodes on the De Beers mine, controlled both production and distribution.

In 1886, at the same time as the Kimberley diamond fields were being consolidated by large companies, gold was discovered further north in the Witwatersrand. A process similar to that in the diamond fields in the Transvaal, but on an even larger scale, followed, as the commercialization of the economy made available the capital and technology needed to exploit the diamond and gold discoveries. The gold fields lay within the boundaries of the South African Republic, however, and presented a challenge to its Calvinist and fundamentalist Afrikaner residents. Led most prominently by Paul Kruger, a descendant of early eighteenth-century emigrants to South Africa who had been a part of the Great Trek as a teenager, Afrikaners resisted the extension of British influence and authority into the South African Republic. But the gold discoveries undercut the SAR in the long run as the Cape Colony sought to gain control of the interior. In the course of the 1890s this was marked by British annexation of the territories north of the Cape Colony that became British Bechuanaland and the Bechuanaland Protectorate, as well as by increasing tension between the Cape Colony, now led by the mining magnate Cecil Rhodes, and the SAR. Rhodes, a firm believer that the Anglo-Saxon race was destined for greatness, was particularly interested in expanding British rule and his own mining enterprises into the territories that became Southern and Northern Rhodesia. These tensions culminated at the end of the century in the

Boer War, and the eventual consolidation of the south into the Union of South Africa.

The exploitation of colonial Africa

By the outbreak of World War I, European powers had for the most part divided up Sub-Saharan Africa and established colonial administrations. The African empires consisted of Portuguese Angola and Mozambique, the Belgian Congo, two east–west belts, German and French, and a British north–south belt, projected to link the Cape to Cairo. Imperial possessions had become an important characteristic of virtually all European Great Powers as well as several lesser powers. The war in 1914 itself disrupted colonial rule, and there were some military engagements in East Africa between British and German settlers. Recruitment of colonial subjects into the armies of the belligerents changed the perspectives of Africans towards their colonial masters. In the colonies themselves, World War I presented colonial subjects with the spectacle of colonial rulers fighting one another. The French and the British quickly captured the German colony of Togo in West Africa in 1914. Kamerun took longer, with German forces there surrendering in February 1916. In German Southwest Africa, the South African Defence Force, many of whose members had fought against the British during the Boer War, forced the Germans to surrender in July 1915. In German East Africa, volunteers from Kenya and then South African forces under General Jan Smuts spent several years chasing a force of German and colonial troops from German East Africa. The German force, led by General Paul von Lettow-Vorbeck, eventually surrendered on November 23, 1918, twelve days after the Armistice. In the Volta-Bani region of West Africa, the French faced not German troops, but a revolt of the indigenous tribes in 1915 that required the mobilization of the largest colonial army in French history and a campaign that by mid 1916 had led to complete destruction of rebel villages and slaughter that matched the Western Front. Only in 1917 were the French able to capture the rebel leaders and finally crush the rebellion.[12]

But with peace in 1918, colonial rule in Africa resumed, with the principal territorial change the transfer of German colonies to the control of the victorious allies. The peace settlement also brought more attention to the colonies and the extent to which the European powers

---

[12] John Morrow, *The Great War: An Imperial History* (New York: Routledge, 2004), 145.

were fulfilling the promised "civilizing mission" that justified colonial rule. For this reason, and in hope of increasing the economic returns from the colonies, colonial administrations undertook reforms that sought to improve the living conditions of Africans in the aftermath of the war. There is some evidence of improved food and clothing in tropical Africa. There were also improvements in education, with some Africans gaining literacy skills. For African men, this was a preparation for positions in the increasingly industrial economy of the continent. A handful of men even acquired university degrees in Europe. There were also efforts to improve educational opportunities for African women, but this was often seen not in terms of work and upward mobility, but as a complement to their domestic roles.[13]

But it would be an extremely optimistic reading of the early twentieth-century colonial regimes in Africa to focus solely on improvements. European contact itself, through the slave trade and other forms of commerce, had helped create many of the conditions that committed colonizers sought to remedy after they gained control, and the Partition was hardly a peaceful event. Rather, it left in its wake disruptions of normal economic activity, social and political upheaval, deaths from combat and "pacification," and famine and disease. While the transatlantic slave trade ended in the nineteenth century, slavery remained in many parts of Africa, and often Europeans' efforts to end it were half-hearted. The railroads and plantations developed by Europeans in many instances increased indigenous slavery. Not surprisingly, African opposition to the colonial regimes continued to be apparent for much of the colonial period in the form of acts of individual violence and rebellion. The French governor in Mauritania, Xavier Coppolani, was assassinated in 1905, and the Arab population of that colony remained difficult for the French to control at least until 1934. The Abe tribe in eastern Ivory Coast attacked railway stations and cut track in January 1910 in opposition to the harsh labor policies of the French governor, Gabriel Angoulvant. The repression of this revolt was even harsher, with government troops burning villages and executing rebels. There were major revolts by the Bariba and Somba in Dahomey during World War I, and in the French Congo and Ubangi-Shari at the end of the 1920s. In 1931, a revolt by the Pende challenged Belgian rule in the Congo. Only slowly, by the end of the period between the World Wars, did the colonial powers assert their authority in West and Central Africa. Many

---

[13] Ruth Compton Brouwer, "Margaret Wrong's Literacy Work and the 'Remaking of Woman' in Africa, 1929–1948," *Journal of Imperial and Commonwealth History* 23 (1995), 427–52.

Africans, and many parts of Africans' lives, remained outside the control of the colonial powers.

The wars and pacification of the African colonies had a profound influence on European culture in the late nineteenth and early twentieth centuries, as stories of the exploration of Africa and the military exploits that asserted European rule became the stuff of popular novels, plays, and other forms of entertainment. As in the Americas and Asia, the expansion of European colonial empires also was crucial in defining the multiple identities of Europeans that revolved around nation, gender, race, and class. The confrontation between Marchand and Kitchener at Fashoda may have brought Europe to the brink of war, but those military leaders and others like them reflected heroic masculine virtues, and what was at stake was not a dusty outpost in a part of Africa no one had heard of before, but the power and authority of Great Britain, France, and their citizens. The colonial administrators who followed the conquering armies were similarly engaged in the masculine work of building empire. Imperial stories – along with a significant amount of scientific theorizing about racial difference – made Frenchmen, Britons, and other Europeans conscious of their national and racial difference from not only other Europeans but also Africans and Asians. The colonies therefore contributed to the nationalist revival that swept Europe to war in 1914. But by providing each European nation with the common purpose and achievement of imperial conquest and rule, they also helped guarantee that all Europeans, from aristocrats and bourgeois to workers and peasants, would rally to the colors in August of 1914.

European women did not have a significant presence in many Sub-Saharan African colonies, especially those south of the Sahara, until just before World War I. As in India and other Asian colonies, the African colonies were largely a "man's world" marked by frontier conditions during the Partition and for several decades thereafter. When women did begin coming to the colonies to accompany their husbands in the colonial service, they brought subtle and not-so-subtle changes in the culture of the colonizers.[14] The assumption of colonial authorities and commentators often was that European women would police the boundary between colonizer and colonized that was crucial to colonialism, and especially discourage interracial unions. Whatever their

---

[14] Helen Callaway, *Gender, Culture, and Empire: European Women in Colonial Nigeria* (Urbana and Chicago: University of Illinois Press, 1987); Nupur Chaudhuri and Margaret Strobel (eds.), *Western Women and Imperialism: Complicity and Resistance* (Bloomington: Indiana University Press, 1992); Owen White, *Children of the French Empire: Miscegenation and Colonial Society in French West Africa 1895–1960* (Oxford: Clarendon Press, 1999).

pre-colonial accomplishments, these women found themselves forced into a position of domesticity that was already seriously under challenge in the metropole. Lady Lugard, who came to Nigeria in 1902 (she was the second, by only a few months, British wife to come to the colony), had been an accomplished journalist prior to her marriage to the British governor-general, Lord Lugard. But in the colony she had to give up those activities and provide for her husband household management, hospitality and entertaining, and strictly regulated participation in imperial pageantry. Many of the white women who came to the colonies did come, as did Lady Lugard, as wives, and their role was similar to hers albeit at a lower level of the white hierarchy. Africa was viewed as a dangerous climate for Europeans, and wives were assumed to provide an important contribution to the effectiveness of the colonial service by maintaining the health and well-being of their husbands. They themselves were viewed as physically threatened by the colonial environment, however, and were sent home at any sign of ill health or pregnancy. It was the same for their children, and it was only after World War II that the children of colonial administrators remained in the colony. For wives, therefore, their support for their husband's work in the colonies came at the cost of long-term separation from their children.

After World War I, white women became more common in African colonies, and many of these were not wives but rather women who worked as nurses, educators, and eventually, at least in British colonies, as subordinates in the colonial administrations. While these women came more frequently into contact with Africans in the course of their duties, there was a tendency for all Europeans in the colony to seek to maintain a strong boundary between themselves and their colonial subjects. In larger European settlements this took the form of a distinct physical and cultural enclave within which Europeans lived, worked, and socialized. The increased emphasis on domesticity that came with larger numbers of white women contributed to this, but the isolation of colonial administrations went beyond the maintenance of a middle-class family life in the colonies. There was considerable anxiety concerning the possibilities of sexual violence, racial pollution, disease, and miscegenation in the colonies. In Southern Rhodesia, there was a fear beginning around the turn of the century of a "Black Peril" of sexual violation of white women by black men. This was voiced most vehemently by white men in the colony, who supported and passed multiple laws aimed at regulating sexual conduct by white women and black men. Jock McCulloch has argued that the "Black Peril" panics also reflected the failure of the colonial state (the British South Africa

Company) not only to protect Europeans, but also to support male and white authority and to manage the supply of black labor effectively. There was, however, less formal concern about the regulation of sexual behavior by white men, even though there were informal attempts to control behavior that was viewed as symptomatic of degeneration and the loss of European civilization. The presence of mulattos and *métis* was a reminder of the fragility of racial boundaries and the possibilities of what was often considered to be racial pollution. As in French Indochina, orphanages for *métis* were established in parts of French West Africa, and their graduates often found employment in lower levels of the colonial administration: boys worked as schoolteachers, health auxiliaries, and clerks, while girls became midwives, nurses, schoolteachers, and seamstresses. Their racial "intermediacy" in the eyes of the French seemed to predestine them for these positions that involved contact with both French and indigenous peoples. But they could also be viewed as dangerous *déclassés*.[15]

The colonization of Africa obviously also had profound effects on the Africans who became subjects of the European empires. The implantation of colonial governments and the continuation of industrial development during the period between the World Wars brought about major disruptions in the lives of African men and women. European rule forced Africans into commercial agriculture both on plantations and, when they had land, on their own farms, and created huge labor markets in Central and West Africa. At the same time, the specific social, cultural, economic, and political aspects of the colonial regimes reconfigured pre-colonial practices, such as those involving patriarchal familial and kin relations. In some respects, these pre-colonial practices were undercut by the changes in labor demand and opportunity that colonial development brought. In other ways, however, colonial administrations, themselves influenced by European assumptions about the appropriateness of different forms of relationships within families and communities, found themselves attempting to shore up what they understood as pre-colonial practices. Multiple sets of assumptions about masculine and feminine identity cut across racial and class differences in colonial society, as the uneven penetration of capitalism and the limited ability of the colonial state to project power into local spaces took the existing diversity of African society and culture and remolded it.

---

[15] Jock McCulloch, *Black Peril, White Virtue: Sexual Crime in Southern Rhodesia, 1902–1935* (Bloomington: Indiana University Press, 2000); Dane Kennedy, *Islands of White: Settler Society and Culture in Kenya and Southern Rhodesia, 1890–1939* (Durham, NC: Duke University Press, 1987); White, *Children of the French Empire*, 68–69, 123.

The imposition and consolidation of colonial rule in the first half of the twentieth century was therefore a period in which many long-standing economic, political, and social practices, including working conditions and subsistence as well as intimate details of people's lives, came under duress. The inability of both village elites and colonial administrations to control previously subordinated groups, such as young people and women, contributed to a sense of moral upheaval that pervaded both colonial administrations – themselves influenced by perceptions of degeneration in European society and fears of contagion from colonial subjects – as well as those who had controlled village society. In this context, such features of the colonial regimes as indirect rule through carefully selected chiefs facilitated the colonization of not only public power relations but also the domestic sphere, as the chiefs were themselves supported as they sought to redefine the roles and sexuality of women and younger men by making rules concerning marriage and divorce.[16]

As in other colonial settings, the ways in which the colonial regimes attempted to mobilize and manage the labor of their colonial subjects in Africa proved to have widespread implications even outside the workplace. Attempts, even if half-hearted and unsuccessful, to abolish indigenous slavery in the colonies altered labor systems, as did European reinterpretations of indigenous customs concerning property-holding and individual rights.[17] These changes occurred not only in the urban and industrial centers that developed in the late nineteenth and early twentieth centuries, but also in the rural areas that remained agricultural under the colonial regimes. The needs of the colonial states and the transformations brought about by the increased power of the state, the transfer of land from indigenous communities to white settlers, and the monetization of the economy had profound effects on the lives of Africans.

But while the colonial powers in general introduced features of a capitalist economy such as private property and free labor markets, local conditions often forced adaptation of these models. A handful of local studies make these transformations apparent. In the pastoral rural economy in Tanganyika the pre-colonial political and economic systems had

---

[16] Robert Morrell, "Of Boys and Men: Masculinity and Gender in South African Studies," *Journal of African History* 24 (1998), 605–30; Jean Allman, "Rounding up Spinsters: Gender Chaos and Unmarried Women in Colonial Asante," *Journal of African History* 37 (1996), 195–214.

[17] On the persistence of indigenous slavery, see Suzanne Miers and Martin A. Klein (eds.), *Slavery and Colonial Rule in Africa* (London: Frank Cass, 1999), and Suzanne Miers and Richard Roberts (eds.), *The End of Slavery in Africa* (Madison: University of Wisconsin Press, 1988).

been based on complementary and interconnected relations between men and women. This had some patriarchal components, but under the British colonial state these were reinforced and reshaped. Property became more individually defined, a development that increased male control of this vital resource. Men were incorporated into the colonial state and male authority expanded as female domestic and male public spheres were rigidly separated. Far from a simple survival of patriarchalism from pre-colonial into colonial regimes, therefore, the colonial regime reinforced and expanded patriarchal authority even as the pastoral economy remained in place. A similar pattern was apparent in Southern Rhodesia, where, as men were increasingly drawn into a migrant labor force, older forms of patriarchal control were replaced by the combined efforts of male elites and the colonial regime to keep women in the countryside, where they could provide cheap agricultural labor. The colonial regime assisted chiefs, headmen, and other elders in multiple ways to assert their authority, but the most obvious was by requiring women in towns and on European farms to produce marriage registration certificates, which became a kind of "pass document" for African women.[18]

In Swaziland, colonial administrators were concerned that the growth of urban areas such as Johannesburg drew rural labor away from white settlers.[19] These administrators tended to defer to customary law, and village chiefs seeking to maintain their authority emphasized the importance of maintaining patriarchal control over women so that they would remain in the household to provide labor for indigenous farms and to reproduce the family. The efforts to limit female migration, however, proved difficult to implement and were avoided by many women attracted to urban areas not only by the wages available there but also by the opportunity to escape from patriarchal control in their villages. Complaints by both colonial administrators and village chiefs about a decline in discipline often reflected their inability to limit female migration.

Elsewhere, in East Africa, the loss of land by indigenous men, which made it impossible for them to fulfill cultural expectations as adult men

---

[18] Dorothy L. Hodgson, "Pastoralism, Patriarchy, and History: Changing Gender Relations among Maasai in Tanganyika, 1890–1940," *Journal of African History* 40 (1999), 41–65; Sean Hanretta, "Women, Marginality, and the Zulu State: Women's Institutions and Power in the Early Nineteenth Century," *Journal of African History* 39 (1998), 389–415; Elizabeth Schmidt, *Peasants, Traders, and Wives: Shona Women in the History of Zimbabwe, 1870–1939* (Portsmouth, NH: Heinemann, 1992).

[19] Hamilton Sipho Simelane, "The State, Chiefs, and the Control of Female Migration in Colonial Swaziland, c. 1930s–1950s," *Journal of African History* 45 (2004), 103–24.

who could support their families, contributed to a religious revival in the 1920s and 1930s that disrupted the churches attended by indigenous converts to Protestant Christianity. Issues concerning economic change were argued about in terms of their effects on marriage and family relations, and mainstream ministers sought to enforce discipline through fines for sexual indiscretions and by maintaining registers of bridewealth. But revivalists were less literate than oral, interrupting services to confess sinfulness and condemn the greed of large landholders. In particular, the revival provided the opportunity for women to articulate, in the religious terms of salvation and eternal condemnation, their anxieties about the disruptions of traditional gender relations and their concerns about male domination of the missionary churches in East Africa.[20]

The labor needs of the industrial enterprises and cities that accompanied colonial exploitation of the continent also had profound effects. Migration became prevalent in many parts of Africa. In some instances this was stimulated by the pull of employment in the urban areas, but migrants were also pushed by the difficulties in many parts of the continent of surviving on farms. In areas in which plantation agriculture developed, such as on the Transkei sugar plantations in South Africa, African migrant labor replaced indentured labor from other parts of the British empire just before World War I. Colonial regimes contributed as well to rural–urban migration, with policies intended to make Africans consumers of European goods that could be taxed to support the colonial administrations. Plantation, industrial, and urban labor often took the form of casual seasonal labor that avoided permanent settlement. This usually took male family members away from rural communities throughout Africa, altering household responsibilities in those communities as well as family and gender relations. In Lesotho between the World Wars, for example, primarily male labor migration allowed some women in rural Basotho villages to escape from the restrictive patriarchal gender relations that existed prior to colonization, becoming more responsible for the management of the household economy. But the uncertainty of the earnings of migrants, their prolonged absence, and the hardships caused by the economic downturn of the early 1930s and a famine at the same time increased the numbers of women who survived by the makeshifts of prostitution and brewing beer. These practices further undercut social relations in the villages: women who were

[20] Derek Peterson, "Wordy Women: Gender Trouble and the Oral Politics of the East African Revival in Northern Gikuyuland," *Journal of African History* 42 (2001), 469–89.

perceived as "disorderly" challenged the authority of village chiefs, leading to attempts by the colonial administration to regulate both brewing and prostitution.[21] These efforts had mixed success, demonstrating not only the intentions of the colonial states to intervene in intimate aspects of Africans' lives, but also their inability to do so.

These changes were driven by policies aimed at extracting resources and revenues from each colony for the benefit of its colonial master. At the time of the Partition, the European powers had at least implicitly agreed that the African market would remain open, with no protection against goods produced by other European powers or tariff barriers within Africa itself. But as colonial administrations grew in size and expense, and the colonies in Africa and elsewhere became more crucial for the economic prosperity of the metropoles, the colonial powers erected barriers against imports both in Europe and in the colonies. Trade between the developed countries in the northern hemisphere continued to dominate the economies of those countries, but colonies became increasingly important trade partners. France's African colonies had accounted for about 10 percent of its foreign trade in 1920; by 1935, this had doubled. For Britain, Sub-Saharan Africa had accounted for 5.3 percent of its foreign trade in 1930, and 7 percent in 1938. African colonies also became important sources of raw materials such as copper and tin.[22]

The colonial administrations often became what have been called "gatekeeper states," controlling access to the colonial economy by outsiders but also managing access to the global economy by producers, black and white, within the colony.[23] While they were not always completely successful at monopolizing trade between the colony and the global economy, colonial administrations nonetheless sought to collect excise taxes that provided an important part of the administration's budget. By protecting the colonial markets for metropolitan producers of finished goods and by taxing imports and exports, they made colonial

---

[21] Tshidosa Maloka, "Khomo Lia Oela: Canteens, Brothels, and Labour Migrancy in Colonial Lesotho, 1900–1940," *Journal of African History* 38 (1997), 101–22; Luise White, *The Comforts of Home: Prostitution in Colonial Nairobi* (University of Chicago Press, 1990).

[22] Data from Andrew Roberts, "The Imperial Mind," in Roberts (ed.), *The Cambridge History of Africa*, vol. VII, *From c. 1905 to c. 1940* (Cambridge University Press, 1986), 62.

[23] Frederick Cooper, *Africa since 1940: The Past of the Present* (Cambridge University Press, 2002). For an instance in which indigenous producers retained control of colonial production (of rubber in French Guinée), see Emily Lynn Osborn, "'Rubber Fever,' Commerce and French Colonial Rule in Upper Guinée, 1890–1913," *Journal of African History* 45 (2004), 445–65.

subjects subsidize the well-being and standard of living of metropolitan producers.

But colonial governments were concerned with more than collecting taxes. The maintenance of public order was a primary concern for the European administrators of the continent, and while it took different forms, this brought the power of the colonial states to bear on their African subjects. In the French colonies, this was formalized in the *indigénat*, a series of regulations first established in Algeria in 1881 and extended to the rest of the French empire in 1887 that gave administrators the power to punish Africans without obtaining the judgment of a court. While corporal punishment was in principle forbidden, justice came swiftly (one of its advantages in the eyes of administrators), and could include *contrainte par corps fixé*, in which an individual would be tied up as punishment or until their debts or taxes were paid by their families.[24] Similar, if less formalized, practices also existed in the Belgian and British colonies. To a remarkable extent, these administrative powers were used to manage indigenous labor and the labor market. These were important issues for the regimes: as plantations, mines, and ports developed, they stimulated labor migration across the continent, from densely populated regions towards less-populated areas that needed labor. By the interwar period, this labor migration was at least formally free. But some vestiges of older forced-labor regimes continued past World War I, notably in the French *prestation* established in 1912, a "work tax" that required up to fifteen work days from France's colonial subjects.

Much of this migration was to work in the mines that developed in Central and South Africa and was therefore male. But some women also wished to take advantage of opportunities in the growing urban areas of the colonies. However, as we have seen, this female migration was limited by the collusion of village men and colonial administrators in some parts of Africa. Labor was also recruited by private agencies on extended contracts, with chiefs required to provide workers to the labor recruiters, to work on major projects such as road and railway construction. Less-developed areas served as labor reserves for regions with more labor demand. In this way, cocoa growers in Gold Coast and plantations on Mount Cameroun drew labor from the interior of West Africa. There was also a marked trend towards increased urbanization elsewhere in many parts of the continent, and Ibadan, Lagos, Dakar,

---

[24] Gregory Mann, "What was the *Indigénat?* The Empire of Law in French West Africa," *Journal of African History* 50 (2009), 342.

Luanda, Lourenço Marques, Nairobi, Salisbury, and Elisabethville had become substantial cities by 1940.

As exports of minerals such as gold, silver, tin, diamonds, and copper grew in the first half of the twentieth century, the colonies that produced these minerals increasingly experienced difficulty finding enough labor to work the mines. The inability of the labor market to provide cheap labor consistently – and the unwillingness of Africans to be that labor – brought the colonial administrations to intervene in the labor market. Perhaps the most innocuous of these interventions was the use of tax policies to encourage labor migration. These policies imposed taxes on Africans to force them out of localized subsistence economies and into the labor market to earn the money to pay the taxes and provide needed wage labor. Europeans also thought that, separated from the land and their home villages, Africans would be forced to purchase consumer goods, creating demand for imports from Europe. But these policies had unintended consequences. Increases in taxation in the 1930s occurred at a time when export prices were lowest, squeezing the resources of colonial subjects. At the same time industrial demand for labor reduced the available supply for domestic agriculture, contributing to famine conditions in areas such as Niger and Gold Coast. The colonial policies did, in the end, stimulate labor migration, but often not in the quantities needed by the developing European side of the economy.

The interaction of industrial development, labor migration, and colonial governance played out differently in different places. In West Africa, large-scale agricultural projects, such as cotton plantations in the Sudan, cocoa farms in the Gold Coast and Ivory Coast, and groundnut farms in Senegambia competed for labor with gold mining in Gold Coast. Casual labor was the usual practice until after the turn of the century, but other employment options for mineworkers – notably in cocoa cultivation – undercut this system. A labor shortage after 1918 led to increased efforts at labor recruitment in the Northern Territories of the colony, above the Volta River. When these efforts did not solve the problem for the mining companies, they enlisted the help of the colonial state. To make mine work more attractive, some policies that benefitted miners, such as health regulations for mine work, were introduced by the British colonial administration. The state also allowed the formation of labor unions. But it also undertook to organize the labor market through forms of coerced labor recruitment, such as imposition of labor quotas on villages, to draft men to work in the mines.

There were similar processes in Central and South Africa, where mining regions separated by colonial boundaries became linked together through labor migration as the different colonial powers exploited the mineral resources of the region. The gradual expansion north of mining from the 1867 discovery at Kimberley until the period between the World Wars in Northern Rhodesia stimulated the creation of a vast labor market that stretched from South Africa north through Southern Rhodesia, into Northern Rhodesia, west into Katanga, and east into Nyasaland and Tanganyika. As white farmers took over the land, African peasants were forced into this labor market, and the wages available in the mines drew African labor into the industrial enterprises of the region. As in West Africa, this was primarily a casual market at first, with adult men leaving their families behind as they temporarily moved to the mining areas. Both because of the harsh conditions in the mines and competition for scarce labor between mining regions, the colonial state undertook measures to increase labor discipline. Laws required Africans to have passes to enter the mining areas and seek work. Failure to show a pass when requested made Africans liable to a fine or hard labor. Other laws made breach of a labor contract a criminal offense, and the Glen Grey Act of 1894 in Cape Colony imposed a tax on men who could not prove they had been employed for three months of the year. These laws were intended to do more than just control labor: they were meant to bring into existence the compliant labor force that the free market had failed to create by forcing Africans off the land and into that labor force. Cecil Rhodes articulated this, as well as the implicit racism that underlay the colonial system, when he introduced the Glen Grey Act, arguing that "every black man cannot have three acres and a cow, or four morgen and commonage rights ... It must be brought home to them that in future nine-tenths of them will have to spend their lives in daily labour, in physical labour, in manual work."[25]

The same issues surfaced further north as the mining industry in Southern Rhodesia began to make its presence felt around the turn of the century. Relatively high wages on the Rand attracted semi-skilled miners from Southern Rhodesia, and the mining companies turned to the colonial administration for help. Draconian labor legislation – a Masters and Servants Ordinance, pass laws, a Native Regulations Ordinance, and the compound system – reduced Southern Rhodesian miners to virtual slave status, what they called *chibaro*, and they became among the most exploited workers in the African mining industry. Attempts at labor organization in the late 1920s, and a strike at Shamva in 1927, were unable to gain significant improvements and were quickly

[25] Quoted in Shula Marks, "Southern and Central Africa, 1886–1908," in Oliver and Sanderson (eds.), *Cambridge History of Africa*, vol. VI, 463.

repressed. In the end, the profitability of the Southern Rhodesian mines was based on a long-term pattern of declining wages and stringent labor discipline.[26]

In other mining areas, the skill demanded by the deposits created different labor regimes. The area that became Northern Rhodesia did not initially show much promise as a source of minerals in the years immediately after the British South Africa Company gained control of it in 1897, and the Company saw it as a labor reserve for more promising mines in Southern Rhodesia. The peoples of Northern Rhodesia also migrated westwards, into the Katanga region of the Belgian Congo, to work in the mines there. Little changed when the British Colonial Office took over administration from the Company in 1924. But as the Copperbelt mines in Northern Rhodesia began to develop after 1926, they found themselves competing in the Central and South African labor market with mines in Southern Rhodesia, Katanga, and South Africa. The Copperbelt companies made some efforts to improve living conditions for miners, but they also received support from the colonial administration through pass laws and increased police powers in the compounds in which the miners lived.

In the twentieth century, industrial and agricultural development, the growth of cities, the tax policies of the administrations, and labor migration combined to replace ivory and slaves with gold, silver, diamonds, copper, food, and tropical staples as the core of the colonial African export economy. Agriculture itself became more commercial, as in the reserves a labor force made up to a significant extent of women worked to produce the food for the male industrial labor force and other urban dwellers. This increased commercialization of the African economy was fraught with contradictions for the colonial powers. Even those administrators who firmly believed in the civilizing mission of the European powers in Africa found themselves caught up in these conflicts. Cecil Rhodes might coldly consign Africans to labor, but even in the view of a liberal colonial administrator such as the Frenchman Robert Delavignette colonial subjects in Africa had to undertake wage labor so that the colony would have the funds from foreign trade to provide the education, health care, and liberty that the empire promised.[27] In Delavignette's view it was not so much for the wealth of Europeans or the colonial power that Africans worked, but for themselves.

---

[26] Charles van Onselen, *Chibaro: African Mine Labour in Southern Rhodesia 1900–1933* (London: Pluto Press, 1976).
[27] Robert Delavignette, *Freedom and Authority in French West Africa*, trans. Daphne Trevor (London: Oxford University Press, 1950).

But increased labor migration had broader implications, contributing to white settlers' anxieties about relations between blacks and whites and the maintenance of racial boundaries. Colonial officials in the 1920s and early 1930s also tended to mistrust the movement of Africans into a nascent industrial working class, and in many places sought to minimize it or force it to be short-stay migration rather than permanent. Behind this mistrust lay a perception of Africans as fundamentally unsuited for the discipline of industrial labor – this was the basis for the resort to the many forms of coerced labor employed in the colonies – and a vagueness about how much coercion was needed in the supposedly free labor market. Initially, most administrators, owners, and in all likelihood Africans preferred temporary, circular migration that allowed Africans to retain their links to their families, home villages, and tribes, while benefitting for part of the year from the opportunities provided by wage earning. Seen as a better way of providing labor and maintaining social peace, this emphasis – indeed, often insistence – on temporary labor created its own set of problems. From the 1930s on, these were to dominate the concerns of almost everyone in the continent. As the temporary labor surplus created by the depression gave way in the mid 1930s to a return to labor shortage, it became apparent that the presence of alternatives to industrial wage labor – whether in agriculture or in the growing cities of Sub-Saharan Africa – was contributing to the shortage of labor.

Towards the end of the 1930s, therefore, the colonial states and managers of industrial enterprises attempted to resolve the contradictions of their labor policies. This often meant a move away from temporary labor migration and the creation of schemes intended to create a distinct African working class that could be disciplined and accommodated to industrial work. "Development" and "stabilization" programs, featuring the provision of housing for workers and their families and improved living conditions, became ways in which colonial officials sought to have African peasants adapt peacefully to the new economic and social structures in which they lived. The hope was that transformed peasants would become the labor force for reinvented empires that would be productive, orderly, and help recoup the fortunes of the badly battered imperial powers.

Many colonial administrators had in mind an image of an apparent solution to colonial labor problems, the social order of Western Europe between the World Wars. In this view, casual labor needed to be replaced by an organized working class that would be distinct from the potentially dangerous transients who moved back and forth between industrial cities and the countryside, or who lived in the shadows of new industrial cities as in the Copperbelt and Mombasa. These policies envisaged a respectable African working class similar to those at home in Britain, Belgium, and France, a differentiated class that was clearly distinct from the unbounded mass of peasants and casual laborers that administrators saw in Africa. These policy changes did not necessarily reflect a significant change in Europeans' views of Africans, but rather were an attempt to mold part of the indigenous population into a disciplined working class that would improve productivity in the colonies. Stabilization also allowed closer surveillance of family and reproductive practices by African families, and in the industrial regions of the Copperbelt this led between the World Wars to efforts at regulating such practices as breastfeeding of newborns, the use of artificial milk, sexual activity, and intervals between births. These efforts extended European concerns about depopulation to their African subjects, and combined the need to replace expensive white labor with cheaper black labor and to encourage population growth both in the mining areas and in the areas where labor recruitment took place. The result was a sense of population and moral crisis that mobilized significant resources to manage the intimate lives of Africans. In Africa as in the Americas and Asia, that these were only partially successful is an indicator of the limits of colonial power and the ability of colonial subjects to negotiate some of the terms of their subjection.[28]

Creating a distinct African working class, however, brought its own problems for the colonial administrations in the last decades of colonialism. With the significant exception of South Africa, where the Nationalist Party victory in 1948 supported a political decision to buttress the coercive labor system, administrators in the 1940s and 1950s hoped that systematic labor practices and trade unions would assimilate African workers into an industrial culture. Paradoxically, those new labor practices, and the African union leaders who could speak with the colonial authorities, needed to have a payoff for African workers themselves. In the end, unions had to produce benefits, and union leaders had to have legitimacy with African workers in order for the new regime of labor relations to work effectively. This gave African labor leaders the opportunity not only to establish their leadership of what became a thread of the nationalist movement for independence by the late 1950s, but also the ability to present colonial authorities and capitalist enter-

---

[28] Nancy Hunt Rose, "'Le bébé en brousse': European Women, African Birth Spacing, and Colonial Intervention in Breast Feeding in the Belgian Congo," in Frederick Cooper and Ann Laura Stoler (eds.), *Tensions of Empire: Colonial Cultures in a Bourgeois World* (Berkeley and Los Angeles: University of California Press, 1997), 287–321.

prince with a devil's choice: work with the union and improve wages and benefits, or deal with a restive working class.[29]

The complex labor situation in Africa in the first half of the twentieth century was, to some extent, a testimony to the power of the colonial state to change African living and working patterns to conform to the needs of European colonial economies and political control. But the many laws and decrees that proved necessary to make the system work elicited significant resistance on the part of the African labor force. In the eyes of colonial administrators, Africans simply did not understand how to be a labor force. But Africans proved able to negotiate some of the terms of their colonial status. They made pass laws, strict contract laws, and compounds necessary because they understood the labor market in which they worked and often tended to leave poor-paying mines with harsh conditions in favor of better pay and working conditions even if this meant crossing the boundaries drawn by Europeans between colonies. The African colonies may have been the most closely administered of all European colonies, but as in the Americas and Asia they showed the limits and contradictions of European power.

FURTHER READING

Abi-Mershed, Osama W. *Apostles of Modernity: Saint-Simonians and the Civilizing Mission in Algeria*. Stanford University Press, 2010.

Adas, Michael. *Machines as the Measure of Men: Science, Technology, and Ideologies of Western Dominance*. Ithaca, NY: Cornell University Press, 1989.

Brower, Benjamin Claude. *A Desert Named Peace: The Violence of France's Empire in the Algerian Sahara, 1844–1902*. New York: Columbia University Press, 2009.

Cain, P. J., and A. G. Hopkins. *British Imperialism*, 2 vols. London: Longman, 1993.

Callaway, Helen. *Gender, Culture, and Empire: European Women in Colonial Nigeria*. Urbana and Chicago: University of Illinois Press, 1987.

Chaudhuri, Nupur, and Margaret Strobel, eds. *Western Women and Imperialism: Complicity and Resistance*. Bloomington: Indiana University Press, 1992.

Clarence-Smith, W. G. *Slaves, Peasants and Capitalists in Southern Angola 1840–1926*. Cambridge University Press, 1979.

Cooper, Frederick. *Decolonization and African Society: The Labor Question in French and British Africa*. Cambridge University Press, 1996.

From Slaves to Squatters: Plantation Labor and Agriculture in Zanzibar and Coastal Kenya, 1890–1925. New Haven, CT: Yale University Press, 1980.

---

[29] Frederick Cooper, *Decolonization and African Society: The Labor Question in French and British Africa* (Cambridge University Press, 1996), and *On the African Waterfront: Urban Disorder and the Transformation of Work in Colonial Mombasa* (New Haven, CT: Yale University Press, 1987), 212–19.

On the African Waterfront: Urban Disorder and the Transformation of Work in Colonial Mombasa. New Haven, CT: Yale University Press, 1987.

Plantation Slavery on the East Coast of Africa. New Haven, CT: Yale University Press, 1977.

Cooper, Frederick, and Ann Laura Stoler, eds. *Tensions of Empire: Colonial Cultures in a Bourgeois World*. Berkeley and Los Angeles: University of California Press, 1997.

Crisp, Jeff. *The Story of an African Working Class: Ghanaian Miners' Struggles, 1870–1980*. London: Zed Books, 1984.

Dummett, Raymond E., ed. *Gentlemanly Capitalism and British Imperialism: The New Debate on Empire*. London: Longman, 1999.

Elbourne, Elizabeth. *Blood Ground: Colonialism, Missions, and the Contest for Christianity in the Cape Colony and Britain, 1799–1853*. Montreal and Kingston: McGill-Queen's University Press, 2002.

Förster, Stig, Wolfgang J. Mommsen, and Ronald Robinson, eds. *Bismarck, Europe, and Africa: The Berlin Africa Conference 1884–1885 and the Onset of Partition*. Oxford University Press, 1988.

Getz, Trevor R. *Slavery and Reform in West Africa: Toward Emancipation in Nineteenth Century Senegal and the Gold Coast*. Athens, OH: Ohio University Press, 2004.

Headrick, Daniel R. *The Tentacles of Progress: Technology Transfer in the Age of Imperialism, 1850–1940*. New York: Oxford University Press, 1986.

The Tools of Empire: Technology and European Imperialism in the Nineteenth Century. New York: Oxford University Press, 1981.

Jeal, Tim. "David Livingstone: A Brief Biographical Account." In John M. MacKenzie, ed., *David Livingstone and the Victorian Encounter with Africa*. London: National Portrait Gallery, 1996, 11–78.

Jeffries, Richard. *Class, Power and Ideology in Ghana: The Railwaymen of Sekondi*. Cambridge University Press, 1978.

Kanya-Forstner, A. S. *The Conquest of the Western Sudan: A Study in French Military Imperialism*. Cambridge University Press, 1969.

Kennedy, Dane. *Islands of White: Settler Society and Culture in Kenya and Southern Rhodesia, 1890–1939*. Durham, NC: Duke University Press, 1987.

Levitzion, Nehemia, and Randall L. Pouwels, eds. *The History of Islam in Africa*. Athens, OH: Ohio University Press, 2000.

Louis, Wm. Roger. *Ends of British Imperialism: The Scramble for Empire, Suez, and Decolonization*. London: I. B. Tauris, 2006.

Lovejoy, Paul E. *Transformations in Slavery: A History of Slavery in Africa*. Cambridge University Press, 1983.

McCulloch, Jock. *Black Peril, White Virtue: Sexual Crime in Southern Rhodesia, 1902–1935*. Bloomington: Indiana University Press, 2000.

Manning, Patrick. *Francophone Sub-Saharan Africa 1880–1985*. Cambridge University Press, 1988.

Slavery, Colonialism and Economic Growth in Dahomey, 1640–1960. Cambridge University Press, 1982.

Miers, Suzanne, and Martin A. Klein, eds. *Slavery and Colonial Rule in Africa*. London: Frank Cass, 1999.

Miers, Suzanne, and Richard Roberts, eds. *The End of Slavery in Africa.* Madison: University of Wisconsin Press, 1983.

Morrow, John. *The Great War: An Imperial History.* New York: Routledge, 2004.

Oliver, Caroline. *Western Women in Colonial Africa.* Westport, CT: Greenwood Press, 1982.

Oliver, Roland, and G. N. Sanderson, eds. *The Cambridge History of Africa,* vol. VI, *From c. 1870 to c. 1905.* Cambridge University Press, 1985.

Parpart, Jane L. *Labor and Capital on the African Copperbelt.* Philadelphia: Temple University Press, 1983.

Price, Richard. *Making Empire: Colonial Encounters and the Creation of Imperial Rule in Nineteenth-Century Africa.* Cambridge University Press, 2008.

Robertson, Claire C., and Martin A. Klein, eds. *Women and Slavery in Africa.* Madison: University of Wisconsin Press, 1983.

Robinson, David. *Paths of Accommodation: Muslim Societies and French Colonial Authorities in Senegal and Mauritania, 1880–1920.* Athens, OH: Ohio University Press, 2000.

Schmidt, Elizabeth. *Peasants, Traders, and Wives: Shona Women in the History of Zimbabwe, 1870–1939.* Portsmouth, NH: Heinemann, 1992.

Sessions, Jennifer E. *By Sword and Plow: France and the Conquest of Algeria.* Ithaca, NY: Cornell University Press, 2011.

Shorter, Aylward. *Cross and Flag in Africa: The "White Fathers" during the Colonial Scramble (1892–1914).* Maryknoll, NY: Orbis Books, 2006.

Tignor, Robert L. *The Colonial Transformation of Kenya: The Kamba, Kikuyu, and Maasai from 1900 to 1939.* Princeton University Press, 1976.

Van Onselen, Charles. *Chibaro: African Mine Labour in Southern Rhodesia 1900–1933.* London: Pluto Press, 1976.

New Babylon, New Nineveh: Studies in the Social and Economic History of the Witwatersrand 1886–1914, 2 vols. London: Longman, 1982.

Wehler, Hans-Ulrich. "Bismarck's Imperialism, 1862–1890." *Past & Present* 48 (1970), 119–55.

White, Luise. *The Comforts of Home: Prostitution in Colonial Nairobi.* University of Chicago Press, 1990.

White, Owen. *Children of the French Empire: Miscegenation and Colonial Society in French West Africa 1895–1960.* Oxford: Clarendon Press, 1999.

6 Imperial Europe in the nineteenth and twentieth centuries

By the late eighteenth century, the European empires had become imperial nation-states, and the framework within which European history in this period unfolded included both colonial powers and colonies, colonizers and colonized peoples. Colonial subjects were pulled into the economic, political, and cultural systems of empire by the force of conquest, colonial government, and the daily presence of colonizers in their midst. These forces attempted, as we have seen, to control multiple aspects of the lives of the Americans, Pacific islanders, Asians, and Africans who came under colonial rule. While never perfect, this control increased as European states improved their ability to exert power both in Europe and in the colonies. Europeans also felt the force of empire, and European versions of themselves and their home countries were shaped by their colonial experiences. It was virtually impossible for any European to live without contact with the empire and its colonial holdings, products, and peoples. Their perceptions of such central aspects of European civilization as property relations, human and civil rights, political democracy, and industrial capitalism were marked by the colonial empires. All Europeans, as isolated as they may have been from their country's colonies, were drawn into the imperial nation-state.[1]

[1] On the extent of popular support for empire as well as the domestic significance of colonialism see Gary Wilder, *The French Imperial Nation-State: Negritude and Colonial Humanism between the Two World Wars* (University of Chicago Press, 2005); Alice L. Conklin, *A Mission to Civilize: The Republican Idea of Empire in France and West Africa, 1895–1930* (Stanford University Press, 1997); Jean-Pierre Rioux (ed.), *La guerre d'Algérie et les Français* (Paris: Fayard, 1990); Charles-Robert Ageron, *La décolonisation française* (Paris: A. Colin, 1991); Kathleen Wilson, *The Island Race: Englishness, Empire and Gender in the Eighteenth Century* (London: Routledge, 2003); Catherine Hall, *Civilising Subjects: Metropole and Colony in the English Imagination 1830–1867* (University of Chicago Press, 2002); David Cannadine, *Ornamentalism: How the British Saw Their Empire* (Oxford University Press, 2001); P. J. Marshall, "Imperial Britain," *Journal of Commonwealth and Imperial History* 32 (1995), 379–94, and "Britain and the World in the Eighteenth Century: Reshaping the Empire," *Transactions of the Royal Historical Society* 6th series, 8 (1998), 1–18; Bernard Porter, *The Absent-Minded*

Governance by these imperial nation-states was marked by para-doxes and contradictions.[2] The creation of colonial empires brought European states and peoples into close contact with non-Europeans and with parts of the world distant from Europe. Yet these states dedicated significant resources to maintaining boundaries between Europeans and the people they found there. European states were able to project their power into corners of the globe previously inaccessible to them. A remarkably small number of Europeans managed to govern large numbers of non-Europeans and huge swatches of territory. Each of these states also met limits to their power, as they were unable to gain their desired control over territory, colonial subjects, and colonists. The colonial state was a work constantly in progress, but its ultimate end was failure, not only because of resistance and eventual decolonization, but also because even on its best days there were things that the colonial state simply could not get people in the colonies to do.

Colonial expansion meant an additional burden on state adminis-trative systems that were, in many instances, struggling to administer even their European territories. To understand this, we need to remind ourselves of the parallel developments in Europe of individual citizens as rights-bearing and self-governing subjects, on the one hand, and the expansion of the power of the sovereign state on the other, and remem-ber that the increased demands on colonial administrations occurred at the same time as the relationship between European states and their subjects in Europe itself was changing. The "Victorian Revolution in Government" that made it possible for Edwin Chadwick to improve public health in Victorian London, and the centralized power that allowed Napoleon III and Baron Georges Haussmann to rebuild Paris in the 1850s and 1860, also provided the institutional structures within which empires were governed. The representative institutions in the imperial powers that provided legitimacy for government in Europe also supported the colonial empires. As the chartered companies of the seventeenth and eighteenth centuries gave way to colonial rule by European states in the course of the nineteenth, schemes of colonial gov-ernance were formulated in the context of European discourses about

---

Imperialists: What the British Really Thought about Empire (Oxford University Press, 2004).

[2] David Scott, "Colonial Governmentality," Social Text 43 (1995), 191–220; John L. Comaroff, "Reflections on the Colonial State, in South Africa and Elsewhere: Fragments, Factions, Facts and Fictions," Social Identities 4 (1998), 321–62; and Kathleen Wilson, "Rethinking the Colonial State: Family, Gender and Governmentality in Eighteenth-Century British Frontiers," American Historical Review 116 (2011), 1294–322.

the use of power, and these increasingly invoked popular sovereignty as the basis for a more powerful national state. But the European models of citizenship elaborated during the Revolution of 1789 in France, the Revolutions of 1848 in Belgium, the Netherlands, Germany, and Italy, or the parliamentary reforms in Great Britain often were thought ill-suited to colonies whose particular circumstances seemed to contradict the assumptions of those theories. There was little sense of urgency about bringing these forms of governance to the colonies and the peoples who had been there when the Europeans arrived. Some Europeans certainly saw empire as the root of evils such as slavery and the abuses by colonists and colonial administrations that became apparent in the late nineteenth and early twentieth centuries. But many Europeans not only saw no contradiction in their rule over the rest of the world, they increasingly thought of the colonial empires – or at least some parts of them – as extensions of the metropole. The "white settler" colonies of the British empire became, towards the end of the nineteenth century, the focus of ideas about a "Greater Britain" that would recoup the failing power of the island, and for the French the contributions of colonial soldiers to the French cause in World War I helped make France and its dependencies – *la France d'Outre-Mer*, in the phrase that became prevalent then – an indissoluble whole, an "extension of France."[3] The empires also, for many Europeans, brought positive benefits to the colonial subjects. These are very complicated and often contradictory reactions to the growth of empire, but they indicate that the history of colonial governance includes not only the mundane efforts of administrators to maintain and advance European power in the colony, but also the ways in which those administrators, political leaders in Europe, commentators, and individual citizens reconciled the contradictions of the colonial enterprise.

Colonial administrations were not necessarily uniform, nor were they as effective as later treatises made them out to be. Dutch, Belgian, and Portuguese colonies were closely administered from Europe, and even Europeans in these colonies had few civil rights. In the British empire, in contrast, many settler colonies received Responsible Government in the middle of the nineteenth century, with a governor advised by an elected council. The Dominion status received by Canada, New Zealand, Australia, and South Africa in the late nineteenth and early twentieth centuries provided them with their own parliaments and

---

[3] Duncan Bell, *The Idea of Greater Britain: Empire and the Future of World Order, 1860–1900* (Princeton University Press, 2007); Raoul Girardet, *L'idée coloniale en France, 1871–1962* (Paris: La Table Ronde, 1972), 119, 125.

responsible ministries. But other colonies remained more closely administered as Crown Colonies. Colonies without significant settler populations increasingly came under what was called indirect rule. Associated with Frederick Lugard, who served as governor of Nigeria between 1912 and 1919, this was a system in which British administrators governed through control of indigenous rulers and made use of the patron–client relationships of indigenous society. In principle indirect rule made use of those rulers as middle-level administrators, but in practice it proved difficult for the British, including Lugard, to allow substantial African or Asian participation in governance.[4] The practice of utilizing existing indigenous kinship and ethnic structures for colonial rule has recently been characterized as an "invention of tradition" because of the ways in which colonial authorities themselves seemed to construct those structures for their own purposes. Yet colonial administrators recognized that the indigenous rulers they selected had to have some legitimacy. Sir Donald Cameron, a British administrator in Nigeria and Tanzania in the early twentieth century, noted that indigenous loyalties to pre-colonial institutions "form one of the most valuable possessions which we have inherited ... [and] make for law and order in the land as nothing else can." Indirect rule, then, seems more a process in which, as Thomas Spear put it, "far from being created by alien rulers ... tradition was reinterpreted, reformed and reconstructed by subjects and rulers alike."[5]

Representation for colonies in the Parliament at Westminster had been proposed as early as 1776 by Adam Smith. But others cited the great distances between Great Britain and its American colonies. In the opinion of Thomas Paine, that distance was proof that British authority over America "was never the design of Heaven." In a 1775 speech in the House of Commons, Edmund Burke declared "I cannot remove the barriers of the creation," and Jeremy Bentham consistently ridiculed the idea. It was only in the last quarter of the nineteenth century, with improvements in transportation and communication, that some Britons seriously considered the possibility of the British empire as a global federation. That indefatigable proponent of a Greater Britain, J. R. Seeley, declared in 1883 that "[s]cience has given the political organism a new circulation, which is steam, and a new nervous system, which

---

[4] Frederick Lugard, *The Dual Mandate in Tropical Africa* (London: Frank Cass, 1965), 193–229; Colin Newbury, *Patrons, Clients, and Empire: Chieftaincy and Over-rule in Asia, Africa, and the Pacific* (Oxford University Press, 2003).

[5] Cameron quoted in Thomas Spear, "Neo-Traditionalism and the Limits of Invention in British Colonial Africa," *Journal of African History* 44 (2003), 8.

is electricity."[6] The idea of colonial representation at Westminster, however, never caught on, and membership in Parliament remained limited to England, Scotland, Wales, and Ireland, with no provision made for colonies or dominions.

In France, in contrast, representation in Paris for some colonies began as soon as metropolitan France developed a representative system of government after 1789. The Caribbean colonies sent representatives to Paris during the Revolution. The Four Communes of Senegal were allowed representation in Paris under the Second Republic beginning in 1848, but this was abolished in 1852 by Napoleon III. Under the Third Republic, however, many French colonies had representatives in the Senate and Chamber of Deputies. But as France's empire expanded in Africa and Indochina in the nineteenth century, many new parts were designated as protectorates, whose residents did not enjoy the same rights and protections as in the older colonies. French administrators in these colonies attacked what they saw as "feudal" vestiges of aristocratic rule and slavery, but they adopted forms of governance that moved away from the older emphasis on the assimilation of colonial subjects into the French nation and the rights promised by the Revolution and the Republic. But while promoting greater equality within African groups by reducing the authority of chiefs, French policies were also premised on the racial inferiority of its colonial subjects. While these new arrangements sometimes featured direct rule by French officers and officials, as Alice Conklin has noted, "French personnel were too scarce to ever have ruled directly." Territory was administered through local elites, although one of the principal architects of this system in French West Africa, Ernest Roume, cautioned that chiefs should not be granted "commands that are too extensive, which they too often ... abuse, and which only add ... unjustified extra burdens to the population's normal ones." The French also gave some protection to aspects of indigenous cultures such as customary law against the imposition of a universalizing French culture. Instead, they hoped to create a "new African humanity ... as much in their own moral image as marked by indelible difference."[7]

Effective administration in French colonies was in the hands of governors – often military officers – who reported to a number of different ministries in Paris and were often advised by a consultative government

---

[6] Paine, Burke, and Seeley quoted in Bell, *The Idea of Greater Britain*, 72, 83.
[7] Alice Conklin, "Colonialism and Human Rights, a Contradiction in Terms? The Case of France and West Africa, 1895–1914," *American Historical Review* 103, 2 (1998), 430; Roume quoted there on 427.

council of upper-level administrators and representatives of the most important economic and commercial interests. Algeria, after it came under civilian rule in 1873, was administered by the ministry of the interior; others were under the ministry of the navy until a separate ministry of colonies was established in 1894. At the turn of the twentieth century, the Sub-Saharan colonies that France had added to its older holdings in Senegal were grouped into two large administrative units, French West Africa (AOF), established in 1895, and French Equatorial Africa (AEF) established in 1910.[8] These policies reached their most elaborate development in the administration of Morocco by General Hubert Lyautey between 1912 and 1925. Lyautey believed not in assimilating Moroccans to French culture, but associating them with France by creating strict divisions between natives and French. These policies would, Lyautey thought, respect Moroccan culture, lead to its renewal from its degenerated condition when the French arrived, and create a prosperous colonial state.[9]

The creation of colonial administrations and permanent settlements made the experience of colonial life part and parcel of the lives of many British, French, Dutch, and other citizens. For some, a stint in the colonies was a way of seeking upward social mobility. Even if the returns were not the same in the nineteenth and twentieth centuries as they had been for the "nabobs," the British officials of the East India Company such as Robert Clive who had profited so much from eighteenth-century India, many middle-class families sent a son to the colonies to make his fortune. The pervasiveness of colonial experience meant that Europeans increasingly had the experience of constructing railways, dams, and other large projects in environments different from those in Europe. European doctors became more familiar with the medical aspects of colonialism. Even as European medicine rejected environment as a cause of disease – especially tropical diseases such as malaria – the tropical empires of the European powers became dotted with hill stations and hydrotherapy resorts aimed at maintaining the health of the Europeans who went to the colonies. Over time, some of these resorts – Simla in northern India and Dalat in French Indochina – became de facto capitals, housing the administration of the

---

[8] AOF included Senegal, Guinée, Côte d'Ivoire, Dahomey, Niger, Benin, Soudan, and Mauritania; Upper Volta was created as a part of AOF after World War I. AEF included Gabon, the French Congo, and Oubangui-Chari-Chad.

[9] Paul Rabinow, *French Modern: Norms and Forms of the Social Environment* (Cambridge, MA: MIT Press, 1989), 151–56; Conklin, *A Mission to Civilize*, 5,6,78,175; M. le Général Lyautey, *Rapport général sur la situation de la protectorat du Maroc au 31 juillet 1914* (Rabat: Résidence Générale de la République Française au Maroc, 1966), xiv.

colony for much of the year, creating a European oasis in the colony, but at the same time displaying the contradictions of colonialism because of the thousands of colonial subjects needed to construct and operate the resorts.[10]

Colonial governance also depended on Christian missionaries. Missionaries often were drawn from the ranks of literate workers, for whom saving souls in Asia or Africa not only fulfilled God's plan but also provided a path out of the mills of industrial Europe. Evangelical and Catholic missionaries in the Pacific islands, Asia, and Africa often preceded civil colonial administrations, and provided a justification for empire. These activities also affected European religions, providing a field for efforts at the propagation of Christianity, making it a world religion. Catholic orders dedicated to spreading the faith in the colonies grew during the nineteenth century, giving a focus to the religious dedication of Europeans who gave financial support or undertook a vocation to the religious life as a priest, nun, or teaching brother.

In some colonies, such as India and Egypt, missionaries came late, initially resisted by administrators who were less than enthusiastic about the missionary project. Attempts to convert native peoples to Christianity were seen as, at best, disrespectful of indigenous civilization, and at worst potentially dangerous to public order. But most missionaries were convinced that they were bringing the benefits of Western culture and religion to the morally and materially impoverished indigenous populations in the colonies. Some also believed they were in some way gaining absolution for the events connected with the European conquest. Conversion was, however, an ambiguous event: in some instances, such as in south India, both Catholic Jesuits from the French settlements and British Protestant missionaries seem to have consistently misunderstood the intricate synthesis that occurred in the eighteenth and nineteenth centuries between indigenous religious beliefs and both Christianity and Islam. Such syntheses also occurred elsewhere in Asia and in Africa. While Catholic missionary liturgy was inflexible and mostly in Latin, there were some accommodations that not only used the vernacular in informal devotions, but also incorporated African personifications, as in Uganda, where Lent was referred to as Basibie ("they fast"). The Catholic White Fathers in Africa often created bands and choirs that performed European liturgical music,

---

[10] Dane Kennedy, *The Magic Mountains: Hill Stations and the British Raj* (Berkeley and Los Angeles: University of California Press, 1996); Eric T. Jennings, *Curing the Colonizers: Hydrotherapy, Climatology, and French Colonial Spas* (Durham, NC: Duke University Press, 2006).

such as Gregorian chant, during Mass. Indigenous music, such as drumming, was not incorporated into services, but drums were used to call Christians to Mass, and dancing was sometimes included in processions and festivities such as the blessing of a church. If for some missionaries such as Monsignor Victor Roelens, vicar-apostolic of the White Fathers in the upper Congo, Africa was a place of "chronic culture shock," for others missionary activity was a process of slow understanding of African culture and practices. There were, however, limits to this process, and for missionaries as for colonial administrators policing the boundaries between indigenous and European culture was an ongoing concern.[11] For colonial subjects, on the other hand, conversion to Christianity brought entry into the political and social networks of the European empires, and such connections could at times be used by Asians and Africans to exert influence over the terms of colonial control.

But missionaries did more than just preach the Gospel. By the late nineteenth century, they could act as go-betweens as European powers extended their control. In Northern Rhodesia in the 1890s, the good offices of François Coillard, a French Huguenot who had worked in Barotseland on behalf of the Paris Missionary Society since 1885, were an important part of the negotiations that led the local ruler, Lewanika, to adhere to a treaty that opened northwestern Rhodesia to the British South African Company. Missionaries elsewhere, such as Maurice Leenhardt in Melanesia, were precursors of twentieth-century ethnographers, learning local customs and languages.[12] A part of their ability to act as intermediaries came from their familiarity with these aspects of indigenous life. They produced translations of Holy Scripture, hymns, and other materials needed to instruct colonial subjects in the tenets of Christianity. But in Africa in particular this process ran into roadblocks. The multiplicity of languages – in Northern Rhodesia, for example, there were approximately thirty different languages spoken by the 1,500,000 Africans living in the region – made the task very difficult, and there was no common agreement on a single language that might be adopted. In South Africa, some missionaries suggested using Swahili as a common language, but others rejected it, either because it seemed contaminated by Islam or because another language was more

[11] Susan Bayly, *Saints, Goddesses and Kings: Muslims and Christians in South Indian Society, 1700–1900* (Cambridge University Press, 1989); Aylward Shorter, *Cross and Flag in Africa: The "White Fathers" during the Colonial Scramble (1892–1914)* (Maryknoll, NY: Orbis Books, 2006).

[12] James Clifford, *Person and Myth: Maurice Leenhardt in the Melanesian World* (Berkeley and Los Angeles: University of California Press, 1982).

common where they worked. Teaching Christian doctrine in English, of course, required teaching English, and some feared this would encourage Africans to seek lives "beyond their station."[13] Schools became important components of the missions, as did the provision of medical assistance even in the amateurish way possible for most missionaries. The schools, health care, and other services provided by the missions collected Africans around them, and the insistence by the missionaries that those who came to the mission stations obey the missionaries meant that they became a form of colonial authority. Before colonial administrations reached isolated parts of Africa, missionaries even acted as unofficial civil magistrates, making judicial rulings and enforcing penalties, including carrying out floggings of miscreant Africans.

The authority of missionaries was, however, undercut by several factors. Competition between different missionary groups was often an unedifying spectacle. The desire of most missionary groups to gain a monopoly over a particular territory for their own brand of Christianity made cooperation difficult, and the interdenominational war for colonial souls took time and energy away from the task of conversion. By the turn of the twentieth century, some missionaries were aware of practices that weakened the impact of their message. They were also aware that the attack on "heathen" customs accelerated the destruction of indigenous society without providing a coherent alternative. The contradiction between the Christian message of justice and brotherhood and the racist practices of many missions was a further detriment, as was the frequent insistence by missionaries that Africans and Asians abstain from practices – brewing or drinking beer for example – that were condoned for white parishioners. But missionaries were at times able to transcend the national divisions that marked others involved in the colonial venture and critique the process of colonization itself. Even the critics among missionaries, however, remained largely unaware into the twentieth century of the extent to which the appeal of Christianity was limited by these practices.

Rights and the colonies

From the English Glorious Revolution to the American Declaration of Independence and the French Declaration of the Rights of Man, the concepts of individual liberty and rights have been a key aspect of modern world history. The conjunction of the elaboration of these

---

[13] Robert I. Rotberg, *Christian Missionaries and the Creation of Northern Rhodesia, 1880–1924* (Princeton University Press, 1965), 47–48.

theories of human rights in many parts of Europe and the spread of colonial rule created some of the most important paradoxes in the colonial project. As the colonial empires expanded, these concepts became a part of the civilizing mission undertaken by the colonial powers, and the empires were the context within which those conceptions of rights were elaborated. The history of those rights must view them, therefore, not as abstractions but as interacting in a concrete, contingent way with the fundamental fact of European rule over others. Whether through the claims of American colonists that they should enjoy the "rights of Englishmen," or those of *métis* and African slaves that they too enjoyed universal human rights, the colonies provided cultural spaces in which Europeans worked out the implications of these claims.

Yet until the very end of formal empire in the mid twentieth century, the extension of these rights to colonial subjects was contentious, challenging Europeans and colonial subjects alike to reconcile the contradictions between universal promises and particularistic policies. This history has often been written in terms of the failure of the colonial powers to fulfill their promises to the peoples they incorporated into their empires, an account that makes Europeans civilized and enjoying universal rights, and colonial subjects uncivilized, inferior, and incapable of meeting the challenge of becoming like Europeans. It is apparent that whether in the abolition of slavery in the western hemisphere or the treatment of indigenous peoples in Africa and Asia, the colonial powers made particular accommodations for what they saw as exceptions to the Enlightenment principles of universal equality in whose name modern colonialism was justified. This coexistence of particularist colonial regimes, often with racial overtones, with assertions of equality in the Rights of Man or even the Rights of Englishmen seems to be a fundamental aspect of colonial modernity.[14]

The Atlantic slave trade and slavery itself were among the most important links between European colonial powers and their colonies from the early sixteenth century, when the first African slaves were unloaded in Hispaniola, until the mid nineteenth century. The links that the slave trade created between Europe, Africa, and the Americas were an important part of the networks of trade that connected the Atlantic system until the nineteenth century, and colonial products such as sugar and coffee that slaves grew and for which the slave trade paid meant that most Western Europeans' lives were in some way connected to the trade. There were many in Britain, France, Portugal, and the Netherlands who depended on the slave trade for employment and a

---

[14] Wilder, *French Imperial Nation-State*, 24–40.

few whose significant fortunes were made in the trade. Many more consumed products from the colonies that were produced by slave labor: coffee, tea, cotton, and above all sugar were important items of consumption in Europe, yet were produced, at affordable prices, by the labor of Africans who had been brought against their will to the New World, or by their descendants.

By the late eighteenth century, however, this system was seen as an abomination by a growing number of Europeans who regarded it as a betrayal of the values of European civilization, and the struggle to abolish the slave trade and slavery itself was a prominent feature of intellectual, religious, and political life in Europe. Indeed, it drew together many of the strands of European thought about political institutions, gender and sexuality, economic organization, and social behavior, and often provided a focal point for debates about reforms within Europe. The European colonies in the Atlantic world, on which much of the debate about slavery in the eighteenth and early nineteenth centuries was focused, experienced that debate at the same time that attempts at reform of colonial administrations and the restructuring of the relationships between metropoles and colonies took place in that period. Debates about slavery and the slave trade became entangled with the aspirations of the leaders of the colonies and, as the wars of independence developed, of all of the participants in those movements. That independence occurred in a climate of growing opposition to slavery profoundly affected the discussions about independence in the colonies of both North and South America, and opened different paths for post-independence development – for example, commercial agriculture utilizing free, rather than slave, labor – than had been the case earlier. The reward of even partial emancipation, linked to military service, for slave participation opened the way to eventual abolition. In Cuba and Brazil, the major exceptions to this pattern, prosperous plantation economies and the absence of institutions through which abolitionists could affect public policy allowed planters to prevent its definitive abolition until late in the nineteenth century.[15] The discussion of abolition of the slave trade and emancipation of slaves also affected, to differing degrees, the politics, economies, and culture of the European powers. Only rarely were calls for abolition heard in Spain or Portugal, imperial centers that struggled to maintain control over their colonies in the New

---

[15] Emiliano Gil-Blanco, "Spanish Policy towards the Abolition of Slavery in the Nineteenth Century," in Marcel Dorigny (ed.), *The Abolitions of Slavery from L. F. Sonthonax to Victor Schoelcher, 1793, 1794, 1848* (New York: Berghahn Books, 2003), 291–95; Christopher Schmidt-Nowara, *Empire and Antislavery: Spain, Cuba and Puerto Rico, 1833–1874* (University of Pittsburgh Press, 1999).

World at the beginning of the nineteenth century. It was in France and especially in Great Britain that abolitionist movements were strongest and had the most wide-ranging impact.

Debates about the slave trade and slavery itself in France were closely connected to the importance of the Caribbean colonies and their sugar plantations to the metropolitan economy, to the expansion of France in the late eighteenth and early nineteenth centuries, and to the Revolutionary experience of the country at that time. There had been sentiment against the slave trade and against slavery itself prior to the outbreak of the Revolution in 1789. Nonetheless, there appears to have been a remarkable cultural amnesia in France about its participation in the slave trade and its possession of slave colonies for much of the eighteenth century, and there were few depictions of the French colonies or abolitionist sentiments in literary texts in the eighteenth century. Certainly the major figures of the French Enlightenment inveighed against the practice around the middle of the eighteenth century: it was condemned by Montesquieu, Rousseau, Diderot, and others, and the *Encyclopédie* article by the chevalier de Jaucourt on the slave trade described slavery as "a trade which violates religion, morals, natural law, and all the rights of man's nature." But neither Montesquieu in the *Spirit of the Laws* nor Jaucourt in the *Encyclopédie* used French Caribbean slavery as an example in their condemnations of the institution, focusing instead on Oriental or ancient slavery.[16] This continued even as the French experience with slavery and its products was becoming more and more firmly rooted in the Caribbean colonies.

Only after 1770 did slavery and the slave trade become topics of more frequent discussion, not only for French novelists and playwrights but also for authors concerned more directly with issues of political economy. Olympe de Gouges, better known as the author of the *Declaration of the Rights of Women and Citizen* of 1791, wrote several plays – *Zamore et Mirza* (1783–84, published in 1788) and her final play, *L'eslavage des noirs* (published in 1792) – that used slavery as a setting. Germaine de Staël (1766–1817), the daughter of Louis XVI's finance minister Jacques Necker, grew up in close contact with Old Regime figures such as Diderot, d'Alembert, and Raynal, and utilized slavery and the slave trade in several of her early writings that were published before the events of the 1790s in the Caribbean colonies. But while slavery

---

[16] Christopher L. Miller, *The French Atlantic Triangle: Literature and Culture of the Slave Trade* (Durham, NC: Duke University Press, 2008); Doris Garraway, *The Libertine Colony: Creolization in the Early French Caribbean* (Durham, NC: Duke University Press, 2005), 5; Madeleine Dobie, *Trading Places: Colonization and Slavery in 18th Century French Culture* (Ithaca, NY: Cornell University Press, 2010), esp. 48.

was condemned on moral grounds by these *philosophes*, it often was accepted for economic and political reasons. The abolition of slavery was subordinated to the creation of a liberal economic system of free trade and open competition in which, they thought, slavery would be either ameliorated or possibly abolished. In *The History of the Two Indies* (first published in 1770, with expanded editions in 1774 and 1780) the abbé Raynal argued that slavery posed a danger to the colonial order because of a possible "Black Spartacus" who might lead a slave rebellion. But he called for reform of slavery, not abolition. The marquis de Condorcet in his *Reflections on Black Slavery* (1781) claimed that slavery was against human nature, but nonetheless insisted on considering it in the context of France's economic interests.

In the last years of the eighteenth century most French commentators on slavery advocated only gradual emancipation of slaves. Discussions of slavery took place not in the context of the human rights that colored debates about metropolitan France in the Revolutionary assemblies, but of the liberal political economy advocated by the Physiocrats, the influential group of *philosophes* who proposed a number of economic reforms towards the end of the Old Regime. Because the Physiocrats viewed agriculture as the source of wealth, they and their followers subordinated the human rights of slaves to the needs of the French and colonial economy. These commentators therefore often condemned slavery but failed to call for its abolition because they feared abolition's negative effects on agricultural production.

The foundation in 1788 of the Société des Amis des Noirs in Paris represented a practical step towards addressing the issue of colonial slavery, and its founders, Jacques-Pierre Brissot and Etienne Clavière, were strongly influenced by their exposure to British abolitionism during their exiles in England during the 1780s. At the opening of the Estates General in May 1789, the royal minister Jacques Necker condemned slavery and complimented British anti-slavery advocates, but failed to make any concrete proposal.[17] Brissot especially remained an outspoken advocate of abolitionism as he became one of the most important leaders of the Girondist faction in the Revolutionary assemblies of the early 1790s. But slavery was rarely discussed in the assemblies and clubs of Revolutionary Paris, and attempts to reform the colonial regime were countered by the Club Massiac, which represented colonial proprietors

[17] Jeremy D. Popkin, "Saint-Domingue, Slavery, and the Origins of the French Revolution," in Thomas E. Kaiser and Dale K. Van Kley (eds.), *From Deficit to Deluge: The Origins of the French Revolution* (Stanford University Press, 2011), 237.

with a vested interest in the maintenance of slavery and the plantation system.

Many of the leading figures in the Société des Amis des Noirs became prominent figures in the Revolutionary assemblies of the 1790s, and the abolition of slavery is sometimes attributed to the power of Enlightenment concerns for human rights among the revolutionaries. In this view, the abhorrence of slavery and the slave trade was part of a more sweeping "invention of human rights" driven by the "bulldozer force of the revolutionary logic of rights" that began in the late eighteenth century and, from relatively limited statements in the American Declaration of Independence of 1776 and the French Declaration of the Rights of Man and Citizen of 1789, led to a "cascading" extension of the idea of equality and human rights into areas that were not part of the intention of the original framers of those documents.[18] But as a matter of practical politics, abolition of the slave trade and emancipation of slaves proved to be difficult policies to implement even in the Revolutionary turmoil of the 1790s in France. While Girondists such as Brissot may have viewed slavery as antithetical to their vision of a Republican France devoted to liberty, many in the Revolutionary assemblies continued to view its immediate abolition as impractical and dangerous to a national economy that depended heavily on the sugar, coffee, and other products of the Antilles. Anti-slavery figures in France appear to have been a relatively small group who, without popular backing, were unable to bring pressure to bear on the assemblies, and when emancipation occurred it seems to have been forced on the revolutionaries in the Convention by events in the Caribbean. Only when faced with news of Sonthonax's decree in Saint-Domingue in August 1793 did the Convention in Paris extend it to other French colonies on February 4, 1794.[19]

But recalculation of French interest after the Haitian Revolution and the accompanying loss of France's most profitable sugar colony undercut the pragmatic argument to maintain slavery.[20] Those events and the requirement imposed on France by the Treaty of Vienna in 1814 that it take steps to end the slave trade ensured that with the restoration of the

[18] Lynn Hunt, *Inventing Human Rights: A History* (New York: W. W. Norton, 2007), esp. 160–67.

[19] Seymour Drescher, *Abolition: A History of Slavery and Antislavery* (New York: Cambridge University Press, 2009), 179; Jeremy Popkin, *You Are All Free: The Haitian Revolution and the Abolition of Slavery* (New York: Cambridge University Press, 2010).

[20] David Patrick Geggus, "Racial Equality, Slavery, and Colonial Secession during the Constituent Assembly," in *Haitian Revolutionary Studies* (Bloomington: Indiana University Press, 2002), 168.

Bourbon line in the person of Louis XVIII in 1814, debates about slavery became more frequent. Many of these continued the Old Regime habit of displacing slavery elsewhere than the French Caribbean. A novella was published by Claire de Duras in 1823, *Ourika*, that spoke in the voice of a Senegalese girl brought to France. A story that Prosper Mérimée published in 1829, *Tamango*, had a captured African warrior and an African woman as characters and a slave revolt on the Atlantic Middle Passage as a setting. The story, based on events from the 1780s, would find resonance in the twentieth century in the work of the Martinican writer Aimé Césaire and in a film produced in the 1950s. But it displaced events in the Caribbean to Africa, as did a novel published in 1828 by Baron Jacques-François Roger, *Kelédor, histoire africaine*.

Popular anti-slavery in France therefore remained a small movement, without the means to influence the government. The principal anti-slavery figure during the restoration was the abbé Grégoire, a veteran of the Société des Amis des Noirs. But he had also been a member of the Convention that condemned Louis XVI to death, and was a political outcast and an embarrassment to anti-slavery forces. The restoration administration of the colonies was staffed in large part by veterans of the merchant and planter interests. They recreated a new version of the Old Regime *exclusif*, reserving the colonial market for French manufacturers and excluding virtually all foreign sugars from the French domestic market. This made sugar the most profitable crop that could be grown in Martinique and Guadeloupe. With a high demand for slaves in those colonies, the sense grew among many Frenchmen that foreign, especially British, pressure to end the slave trade was unfair punishment for France's misdeeds during the Napoleonic era. This weakened the enthusiasm of the French government for policies limiting the slave trade. Efforts in this direction – a royal ordinance in January 1817, a law of April 1818 – were weakly enforced and had little effect.

Only in the 1820s, as opposition grew to the Legitimist government of Louis XVIII (r. 1814–24) and his even more conservative brother Charles X (r. 1824–30), did abolitionism revive to any significant extent. A Société de la Morale Chrétienne brought together many men who were offended by the moral implications of slavery and the slave trade. They aimed at more than just ending slavery and reforming the colonies, however. Their opposition to slavery was part of a broader concern with reforming public morals and promoting religious education and a vision of the bourgeois family as the basis for French society. After the July revolution in 1830 brought the more liberal duc d'Orléans,

Louis-Philippe, to the throne, a critique by liberal economists such as J. C. L. Sismondi and Jean-Baptiste Say of slavery's inefficiencies as a labor system that should be replaced by free labor began to gain traction. A Société Française pour l'Abolition de l'Esclavage was established in the 1830s by the duc de Broglie (Germaine de Staël's son-in-law). Its membership soon included prominent members of the opposition to the July Monarchy. The Loi Mackau, voted in April 1845, remedied some of the worst aspects of the slaves' condition, but continued the institution of slavery itself. The sugar plantations continued to depend on slave labor in the fields, and popular support for abolition remained weak. In a decade when the government resisted any reforms, abolitionists were unable to influence government policy.

It was only with the collapse of the Orleanist regime in February 1848, and the establishment of a provisional government of the new Second Republic (1848–52) that emancipation became a reality in French colonies. The new minister of the navy, François Arago, appointed Victor Schoelcher, one of the most outspoken proponents of abolition before 1848, chief of the colonial bureau of the navy. Schoelcher persuaded Arago and other members of the provisional government that the time was ripe to move quickly towards abolition. A proclamation on March 3 promised a commission on slavery to prepare an emancipation decree, and news of this proclamation and anticipation of emancipation spread quickly in Guadeloupe and Martinique. The slave system there collapsed as local governments abolished slavery to prevent disorders in the islands. Schoelcher was able to gain approval for an emancipation decree from the provisional government on May 2, officially ending slaveholding by French citizens.

The abolition of slavery in France was, on balance, a relatively small part of the political discussion in France during the first half of the nineteenth century, and French abolitionists remained dependent on moments of political crisis in 1794 and 1848 to obtain results. The British experience was different. Certainly in the late eighteenth century the advocates of abolition there faced a daunting task. There were (and still are) debates about the relative productivity of slavery and free labor, and before the American Revolution slavery was considered an acceptable form of labor in the New World colonies even if not in Britain itself. For most Britons, slavery was something that existed in the Americas, not in Britain. It was American colonists who were slaveholders, and British institutions and policies seemed unconnected to the institution. In Great Britain this disjunction was confirmed in the 1772 Somerset ruling, in which the court held that a slave, James Somerset, brought to Britain from Virginia, was free.

But the imperial crisis of the late eighteenth century that reframed the ways in which government was discussed in Britain also reflected on slavery.[21] Eighteenth-century reformers critiqued the government by describing it as a corrupt aristocratic state, subservient to France, effeminate and weak abroad. As politics spread outside a narrow elite to include provincial urban middle classes and the newspapers, pamphlets, theatres, and coffee houses in which they discussed public affairs, the empire became the chosen field in which true British values of virtue, manliness, and liberty could be asserted against aristocratic corruption and betrayal of the national character. The crisis of empire in late eighteenth-century Britain heightened perceptions that the British empire was an empire of liberty, different from previous empires such as the Roman or Ottoman. It also seemed to require that the empire be defended against challenges to that liberty, and slavery was the most obvious of those challenges. Ignoring efforts by a few American colonial legislatures before the American war to end the slave trade, British rhetoric during the war cast the rebellious Americans as slaveholders, and thus challenged the British to be an empire of free labor.[22]

While not based on ideas as universalist as the Rights of Man that French anti-slavery activists invoked, British anti-slavery thought modeled a polity in which policy was based on general rather than particular interests, justified state intervention in the economy, and promised a stimulus to the economy, since free laborers were also consumers. A Great Britain that dominated the seas with its navy, whose international commerce was pushing the world economy towards greater integration, and whose capital, London, was the major international financial center, began to see abolitionism and anti-slavery as policies that, in the long run, would not only fulfill the moral obligations of many British subjects, but would also reinforce the prosperity and power of the country. This combination of political, economic, and moral factors meant that increasingly after the American War, abolitionists – who established the Society for Effecting the Abolition of the Slave Trade in 1787 – found

---

[21] John Brewer, *The Sinews of Power: War, Money and the English State, 1688–1783* (Cambridge University Press, 1989); Linda Colley, *Britons: Forging the Nation, 1707–1837* (New Haven, CT: Yale University Press, 1992); Kathleen Wilson, *The Sense of the People: Politics, Culture and Imperialism in England, 1715–1785* (Cambridge University Press, 1995).

[22] Christopher Leslie Brown, *Moral Capital: Foundations of British Abolitionism* (Chapel Hill: University of North Carolina Press, 2006); Seymour Drescher, *Abolition: A History of Slavery and Antislavery* (New York: Cambridge University Press, 2009); Robin Blackburn, *The Overthrow of Colonial Slavery* (New York: Verso, 1988), 439–40.

allies in their campaign against the trade even while the empire itself was rarely questioned.

They also found a political system that was changing in ways unlike any other European country at the time. Certainly the political system of Great Britain in the 1780s and 1790s was one in which it was difficult to place pressure on Parliament and the government and that allowed the West Indies interests in Commons and in Lords – in many instances absentee planters living in England on the incomes from their plantations – an impact on public policy out of proportion to their numbers. But as demands for parliamentary reform increased in the late eighteenth and early nineteenth centuries, a parallel and often overlapping movement for abolition was pushed forward by middle-class men and women, both in London and the provinces, who were influenced by the Evangelical revival in British Protestantism, Quakerism, the tradition of Rational Dissent and, in the nineteenth century, Utilitarianism.

These activists, led by figures such as William Wilberforce, James Stephen, and Lucy Townsend, were instrumental in making the end of the slave trade palatable to the leaders of the British government. They were joined by an increasingly vocal civil society that adapted to the political arena advertising methods developed to sell products for mass consumption. The Somerset decision itself had seen an outpouring of comment in newspapers and pamphlets, and parliamentary debates and government policy were soon being discussed in newspapers not only in London but also in the provinces. As abolitionism gathered strength in the late 1780s, it also used these media. Images of the horrific conditions on slave ships played an important role in turning public opinion against the trade and towards its abolition. Incidents like the Zong case in 1781, in which slaves sickened by the long voyage from West Africa were deliberately thrown overboard so that owners of the slave ship could collect insurance on them, provided the grist for letter-writing, newspaper, and pamphlet campaigns. The abolitionist movement was an innovator in new forms of expressing public opinion, using petitions, publicity, and local organizing committees to pressure Members of Parliament. Petition campaigns in 1788 and 1792 and in the early 1830s drew together abolitionists from across the country, linking members of an increasingly assertive middle class that would, especially after Waterloo, bring reform to many different areas of British life. It also drew women into the public sphere, and many of those who would provide leadership in the Victorian feminist movement began their political activism in anti-slavery activities.

Abolitionism was, Seymour Drescher has noted, "a reform for good seasons," and when it was possible to mobilize public opinion for reform, abolitionists were able to do so for their specific cause. When the movement for reform felt government repression, as during the 1790s and after the Peterloo Massacre in 1819, anti-slavery agitation also suffered.[23] But once the House of Commons had been reformed in 1832, the abolitionist movement shifted into high gear: in the election called after passage of the Reform Bill, the Anti-Slavery Agency Committee pressed candidates to pledge to vote for emancipation. Hundreds did pledge, and many of them were elected. In the aftermath of the election, abolition came in a compromise between the West Indies interest and the new abolitionist Members of Parliament, allowing a brief "apprenticeship" period before complete emancipation. The popular movement had become so powerful that even the long-standing opponent of abolition William Cobbett – who in 1818, in exile in America, wrote of the benefits of exile: "No Wilberforces. Think of that! No Wilberforces" – pledged his support for the emancipation law during the 1832 election campaign.[24]

The abolition of the slave trade, and the emancipation of slaves in the American colonies of Spain, Great Britain, and France, were complex movements that depended not only on the articulation of conceptions of human rights, but also on the development of European political systems that allowed abolitionists to influence public policy. They also depended on particular contingencies, such as the need by Latin American revolutionaries such as Simón Bolivar and American presidents such as Abraham Lincoln to gain political support for policies not directly related to slavery itself. The failure of post-emancipation labor markets to provide adequate labor meant that slavery was succeeded by another form of bonded labor, indentures that brought Asians, Africans, and Pacific islanders to the Caribbean sugar plantations as well as to enterprises elsewhere in the colonial empires. Slavery itself remained an issue as European empires spread to other parts of the world: in Africa and Asia, colonial administrators often found ways of avoiding the end of indigenous slavery in the interests of developing the colonies as economic resources for the metropole. In many instances, the expansion of European empires increased indigenous slavery. The hopes of Wilberforce, Schoelcher, and other abolitionists for an end to slavery ultimately proved chimerical: at the beginning of the twenty-first century, while it is almost universally condemned and is in retreat, slavery remains a presence in the world.[25]

[23] Drescher, *Abolition*, 231.
[24] Brown, *Moral Capital*, 378.
[25] Drescher, *Abolition*, 455; David Northrup, *Indentured Labor in the Age of Imperialism, 1834–1922* (Cambridge University Press, 1995).

Colonialism in elite and popular culture

The interconnections between discourses about liberty, empire, and nation had powerful effects on the organization of European politics. As we have followed the spread of European colonialism from the Atlantic to Asia and Africa, we have seen how the differences between Europeans and their colonial subjects in the nineteenth century became more and more territorial, cultural, and racial. At the same time, imperial nation-states, especially Great Britain and France, became more rationalized, authoritarian, and disciplinary not only in defense of the birthrights of Englishmen and the Rights of Man, but also to institute European rule and preserve order in the colonies. The cultural aspects of these imperial regimes, both in Europe and in the colonies, justified European rule, emphasized the differences between Europeans and non-Europeans, and policed the boundaries between the culture and society of the colonists and that of their subjects.

One aspect of this was Orientalism, "a style of thought" that distinguished between "the Orient" and "the West." By describing the Orient in authoritative terms, Orientalists – often academics – produced an Orient over which the West ruled.[26] Studies of Persian language, such as those pioneered by the Englishman Sir William Jones (1746–94), opened up a civilization that was viewed as at least the equal of the ancient Greek and Roman civilizations that were the subject of European inquiry. Other philological scholars, such as Jones' fellow Englishman Edward William Lane (1801–76) and the Frenchmen Silvestre de Sacy (1758–1838) and Ernest Renan (1823–1892), also contributed to the development of an approach to the Orient that drew its authority from its claim to scientific rigor. Geographical and other learned societies encouraged a broader approach that drew on the methods and insights of a number of developing academic disciplines. These inquiries also, however, served the interests of the growing colonial presence in South Asia and the Middle East, providing practical language skills and information on Persian and Hindu civilizations that were used by colonial administrators. An imperial proconsul such as Warren Hastings dedicated himself to the study of South Asian civilization even as he pursued policies that increased British control of that civilization.

These divisions between Europe and the Orient were diffused through many different parts of European culture. The academic study of the Orient became institutionalized as part of the training of prospective colonial administrators in institutions like the École Publique

[26] Edward Said, *Orientalism* (New York: Random House, 1978), 2.

des Langues Orientales, established in Paris in 1795, the French École Coloniale, founded in 1889, and the School of Oriental (and African) Studies founded in London in 1916. Orientalism also infused the works of travelers to North Africa, the Middle East, and South Asia. Accounts by the vicomte de Chateaubriand (1812), Alphonse de Lamartine (1835), Gérard de Nerval (1851), and Maxime du Camp (1852) made it a staple of nineteenth-century literature. Epic poems by Lord Byron, such as *The Corsair* and *Childe Harold's Pilgrimage*, and novels by Gustave Flaubert (*Salammbô*) and others were inspired by real or imaginary trips to the Orient. Orientalism was also a popular genre of academic painting, beginning in the late eighteenth and early nineteenth centuries. *The Battle of Aboukir* (1806) by A.-J. Gros was a collection of brightly colored flags and costumes, threatened beauty, nudes, and violence. Many painters – some well known, such as Eugène Delacroix (1798–1863) or Jean-Léon Gérôme (1824–1904), others less known, such as Edward Lear (1812–88) or Prosper Marilhat (1811–47) – chose Orientalist subjects. In many cases this was the result of an Orientalist tour taken early in their lives that inspired them for the rest of their careers. For others, their inspiration was less direct contact or travel than a version of the Orient gained from reading works such as Edward Lane's *Manners and Customs of Modern Egyptians* (1836). Jean-Auguste-Dominique Ingres, for example, painted several well-known Orientalist works, including *La grande odalisque* (1814), *Odalisque à l'esclave* (1839), and *Le bain turc* (1862), even though he never traveled to the Orient.

Orientalist paintings were popular with the art-buying public from the 1820s until late in the nineteenth century. Local artists trained by the British East India Company, the "company painters," provided versions of the South Asian empire that adorned the halls of Company headquarters in London.[27] Wealthy bourgeois and princes decorated their apartments with Orientalist paintings, and governments purchased them for the museums that became more widespread in the course of the century. The French government in particular purchased numerous Orientalist paintings from the annual Salon, and displayed them in Parisian and provincial museums. But these images also had popular resonance. Sketches in the *Journal de Voyages* and other popular illustrated magazines circulated images of the Orient and hung on the walls of the rooms of less wealthy travelers of the imagination. Prints of harems and dancing girls decorated bachelor apartments and military

---

[27] Mildred Archer, *Company Paintings: Indian Paintings of the British Period* (London: Victoria and Albert Museum, 1992), 11–18.

barracks. Shareholders in the Suez Canal reminded themselves of their investment by hanging paintings of the desert on their walls.

At the end of the nineteenth century photography undercut the market for Orientalist paintings but made possible the diffusion of these images to a much broader audience. In particular, postcards with Orientalist themes gained popularity after the turn of the century. These postcards made it possible not just for the cultural elite who had taken a tour of the Orient or could purchase paintings, but also for the "tourist, the soldier, the colonist" to participate in the circulation of Orientalist images.[28] They focused on the harem, a symbol of the Orient that expressed colonial power over the bodies of colonized women and eroticized those bodies for the pleasure of the colonizers. Figures of women in harems, some drawing on the traditional form of the odalisque, provided a kind of "soft porn" that circulated through the postal systems of France and other countries. That it was all a fiction – photographers were not allowed inside harems, and the pictures were taken of models posing in studios, often in Paris – allowed these images to write European fantasies onto the colonial subject even while using a format – the photograph – that seemed to present reality transparently.

Imperial architecture and design also showed the interactions between metropole and colonial civilization. As the European presence in the colonies increased from the eighteenth century through the twentieth, colonizers made their presence known through the construction of buildings and even whole cities. While some of these structures, such as those the British built in Egypt, adapted Orientalist decorations, they were often in European styles, becoming symbols of colonial power. The alteration of the physical environment of the colonies by colonial governments was based on the conviction that the moral principles of European civilization could be made manifest through material settings. Forts and Government Houses erected in colonial cities were also clear assertions of imperial power. The contrast between the indigenous styles of Mughal princes in India, for example, and the combination of Greek revival and Palladian styles found in the Town Halls, Residency Buildings, and Government Houses erected in Calcutta, Bombay, Hyderabad, Madras, and Lucknow made British authority in India evident (Illustration 6). The Sydney and Melbourne Government Houses erected in Australia in the middle of the nineteenth century made similar points.

---

[28] Malek Alloula, *The Colonial Harem* (Minneapolis: University of Minnesota Press, 1986), 4.

Illustration 6 Government House, Bombay, 1810.

In India the challenge to British power in the Revolt of 1857, and the reassertion of that power after the transition to Crown rule, were represented by increased adoption by the British of Indian forms to legitimize their rule. In architecture this led to an Indo-Saracenic style that featured the arches and domes that marked Mughal palaces. Architects like R. F. Chisolm (the Revenue Board Building in Madras, completed 1871) and Major C. Mant (Mayo College, Ajmer, completed 1885) used a mixed style that placed the British as successors to the Mughals. The contradictions of imperial power, however, were difficult to resolve in stone. When the capital of British India was moved from Calcutta to Delhi at the beginning of the twentieth century, there were some attempts to reconcile Indo-Saracenic and classical Western forms. But there was also an overwhelming desire to "embody the idea of law and order which has been produced out of chaos by the British Administration," as Herbert Baker, one of the architects involved in designing New Delhi, put it. Even more forceful was Edwin Lutyens, whose Viceroy's Residence, a massive dome-and-colonnade structure sited on Raisina Hill overlooking the new government quarter below, adopted some Indic forms. But while its massive form can be read as an attempt by Edwardian Britain to reassert its slipping control over India, it also demonstrated the inability of Lutyens to create in his architectural design a successful relationship between the British and the peoples – both Hindu and Muslim – of South Asia.[29]

French colonial buildings in Indochina and Madagascar avoided adoption of any indigenous design influences for much of the nineteenth century, perhaps an expression of the French desire to assimilate colonial peoples into the French nation.[30] The Palace of the Governor General in Antananarivo in Madagascar, built in 1889–92, the Saigon Hôtel de Ville in Indochina (1902–8), and the Governor-General's Palace in Saigon, built in 1873, employed the baroque style to express the absolute power of the French. The Medical School at Antananarivo (1897) expressed the power of Western science in its neo-classical façade. When the capital of Indochina was moved to Hanoi in 1900, the governor-general, Paul Doumer, built a new *beaux-arts*-style governor-general's palace in that city and surrounded it with monumental gardens that imposed the French presence on the landscape of the city. Other municipal buildings, such as the Saigon Theater opened in 1895, not only expressed French power in its form, but also were the site for the performance of French culture, with classics performed by visiting theater troupes and plays written by colonial officials filling out the bill. Train stations built around the turn of the century were modeled on those of the metropole, themselves expressions of the control of nature by Western science and technology.

In the early twentieth century French architects began to accommodate indigenous influences in design, but as the French became more settled in their rule, they undertook major construction projects in which the colonies became a terrain on which metropolitan ideas could be expressed. Inspired by theorists such as the Swiss Le Corbusier and supported by colonial proconsuls such as Joseph Gallieni and Hubert Lyautey, the "urbanists" Tony Garnier, Henri Prost, Ernest Hébrard, Georges Cassaigne, and André Jully planned "modern" cities that they hoped would improve public health and the movement of traffic. Their goal was to create an environment that would combine historical and natural elements into what Paul Rabinow has called "one of the most complete examples of modernity," a planned city that would regulate modern society. These urbanists created plans for European cities, such as Garnier's *cité industrielle* and Prost's plan for the Belgian city of Anvers, but administrative and legal obstacles often prevented them

---

[29] Baker quoted in Thomas R. Metcalf, *An Imperial Vision: Indian Architecture and Britain's Raj* (Berkeley and Los Angeles: University of California Press, 1989), 226.

[30] Gwendolyn Wright, *The Politics of Design in French Urban Colonialism* (University of Chicago Press, 1991).

from fully implementing their theories in Europe itself. The colonies, however, could provide the opportunity for them to do so, not so much because Indochina, Madagascar, Algeria, and Morocco were blank slates but because supportive colonial administrations could overcome obstacles to reconstructing urban spaces. Projects in Hanoi, Saigon, Haiphong, Casablanca, and Algiers did incorporate existing historical cities in their plans, but their linear design and emphasis on distinct urban functions separated peoples: housing for Europeans was often set apart from the older parts of the cities – preserved in the name of respect for indigenous culture – inhabited by the colonial subjects, and industrial zones were distinct from the administrative areas and those for housing and recreation for European elites. While these projects, such as the Grand'Place (now the Place des Nations Unies) in Casablanca and the Administrative Quarter in Rabat incorporated Moroccan ornamentation, in their grandeur and spatial form they clearly demonstrated the difference between subordinate colonial subjects and the dominant French. Most fully expressed in Morocco, where Lyautey as governor-general was able to claim by decree the powers that urban administrations in France lacked, their implementation showed the fact of colonial power and the ability of that power to impose its desires on the indigenous landscape and peoples. After World War II, as colonial administrations sought to maintain colonial rule by improving standards of living for colonial subjects, urbanism continued to be an important instrument in French hands.[31]

While urbanists hoped that colonial experiments would lead to broader application of their theories in Europe, colonial influences on urban design and architectural style in Europe itself were limited. They can be seen in Orientalist designs, *chinoiserie* and *japonnerie*, the "Hindoo style" of the early nineteenth century, and the Egyptian revival architecture and Indo-Saracenic style later in the century.[32] But sweeping transformations of the cityscape required extraordinary authoritarianism, reminiscent of the rebuilding of Paris and other major French cities under the Second Empire (1851–70), and this was not an example many Republican politicians wished to emulate after 1870. Architects might wish to incorporate colonial experiments in their projects, but they

---

[31] Rabinow, *French Modern*, 12, 277–319; Zeynep Çelik, *Urban Forms and Colonial Confrontations: Algiers under French Rule* (Berkeley and Los Angeles: University of California Press, 1997); Janet L. Abu-Lughod, *Rabat: Urban Apartheid in Morocco* (Princeton University Press, 1980).

[32] Mark Crinson, *Empire Building: Orientalism and Victorian Architecture* (London: Routledge, 1996); Raymond Head, *The Indian Style* (University of Chicago Press, 1986).

needed clients who would build their designs. Such buildings were rare in France, and reflect some colonial connection. The École Coloniale in Paris, designed in 1898 by Maurice Yvon, employed Orientalist mosaics on its façade. The Institut Franco-Musulman, designed in 1926 by Maurice Mantout, Maurice Trenchant de Lunel, Robert Funez, and Charles Heubèz, drew inspiration from a mosque in Fez, and features a courtyard inspired by the Alhambra and decorative effects executed by North African craftsmen.

In Britain, the nabobs who returned in the late eighteenth century after making their fortunes in India were not anxious to demonstrate their difference from the rest of the British elite: the point was to gain acceptance in the landed gentry that ruled England. Nonetheless, several of them remembered their service in the homes they built after their return.[33] The house at Daylesford in Gloucestershire built in 1788 by Warren Hastings featured a Mughal-inspired dome. Around the turn of the nineteenth century, another nabob, Sir Charles Cockerell, employed Hastings' architect, his own brother, Samuel Pepys Cockerell, to design a country house at Sezincote, Gloucestershire, that featured numerous Indian aspects, including a large dome. Sezincote influenced the Royal Pavilion built by the Prince of Wales at Brighton between 1787 and 1822. The final architect employed by the prince, John Nash, gave it a distinctive Indian style when he took over management of the project in 1817. The finished building featured Mughal onion domes, turrets, tent roofs, and Orientalist styles in the interior décor and furnishings.[34]

More often, small decorative details were the only signs of colonial influences on buildings constructed in Europe. However, India gave to Great Britain and much of the rest of the world a particular house style, the bungalow, which while detached from its Bengal origins, became pervasive from the British seacoast to Southern California and almost everywhere in between.[35] Initially inspired by the huts of Bengali peasants, by the late eighteenth century what were called bungalows had become the working and residential space of British officers and commissioners in India. After the turn of the nineteenth century, the style was adapted to provide annexes or temporary housing outside Calcutta for the British, and in the second half of the nineteenth century, bungalows – low one-story, spacious houses with broad verandas – were built to provide housing for the British who came to India to run the colony.

---

[33] Patrick Conner, *Oriental Architecture in the West* (London: Thames and Hudson, 1979).
[34] John Dinkel, *The Royal Pavilion Brighton* (New York: Vendome Press, 1983).
[35] Anthony King, *The Bungalow: The Production of a Global Culture*, 2nd edn. (New York: Oxford University Press, 1995).

A feature of hill stations such as Simla, bungalows became associated with what was viewed after the 1857 Revolt as a healthier and safer rural environment. By the early twentieth century, it was the usual style of European-occupied houses in the interior of India. The design found its way to Britain before the turn of the nineteenth century – Sezincote featured a bungalow near the main house – and the term came to refer not to a specific style of building but the use to which it was put. As late Victorians discovered the seashore and its supposed health and recreational benefits, several bungalows were constructed in 1869–70 at Westgate on the Kent seashore. Many more followed, and by the 1890s bungalows were a cheap answer to concerns about rural housing and the development of suburbs outside the large cities of Great Britain. In the early twentieth century, it acquired overtones of both bohemianism and the moral value of the countryside, where a "simpler life" could be found. Fraught not only with material implications in its organization of space but also with its cultural meanings, the bungalow remains a lasting vestige of Britain's imperial role in India.

The relative absence of buildings in Europe with colonial influences was more than made up for by colonialist fiction. Expressing imperialist ideas of European superiority and hegemony and demonstrating European control over its colonial possessions, this became a staple of European literature during the nineteenth century. It provided its readers with ways of thinking about colonization, and described the colonies to those who never left Europe. Figurative language and fictional plots and characters placed Europeans at the center of an empire, while the colonies and their peoples were outside European civilization. Characters began new lives in the colonies, overcoming the limits placed on them by metropolitan society or by the disasters of their own lives. But while the colonies offered great freedom for Europeans, breaking taboos about sexual behavior, class, and race often had disastrous consequences.

The colonial empires elicited strong reactions from Europeans as they grew in the course of the eighteenth and nineteenth centuries. In the late eighteenth century, the British politician Edmund Burke viewed India with both astonishment and also terror, "ungraspable" in its sublimity. His friend the Orientalist William Jones, in contrast, was awed by the grandeur of the classical Sanskrit texts that he found in India.[36] At the height of imperial expansion at the end of the nineteenth

---

[36] Michael J. Franklin, "Accessing India: Orientalism, anti-'Indianism' and the Rhetoric of Jones and Burke," in Tim Fulford and Peter J. Kitson (eds.), *Romanticism and Colonialism: Writing and Empire, 1780–1830* (Cambridge University Press, 1998), 48–66.

century, colonialist fiction expressed the self-confidence of European societies that were imposing their will on huge expanses of the world. Gilbert and Sullivan operettas, boys' tales by G. A. Henty, and the novels of the French naval officer Pierre Loti conveyed this confidence and the moral superiority of European culture. But after the turn of the century, as the contradictions of the empires became more apparent, fiction such as Joseph Conrad's *Heart of Darkness* and E. M. Forster's *A Passage to India* used colonial settings not to praise European civilization, but to point out its banality at home and failings abroad. While Henty and Loti may have convinced many Englishmen and Frenchmen to go out to the colonies, by the twentieth century Conrad and Forster were demonstrating the dangers and ambiguities of a colonial career. From images of masculine triumph and national glory, the colonies had become a symbol for anxiety about the validity of the colonial project and the decadence of European civilization.

Travel literature was a development closely related to fiction and one that drew heavily on the colonies for subject matter. These accounts communicated the experience of travel to readers in Europe who themselves never left their native countries. The earliest travel accounts were similar to the scientific reports of explorers or accounts by missionaries of their struggles to convert colonial subjects to Christianity. But in the course of the nineteenth century, travel accounts acquired a distinctive form that separated them from other descriptions of the colonies, such as fiction, the tour guides that began appearing in the mid nineteenth century, and the ethnographic accounts of anthropologists. Travelers were able to write about faraway places from both inside and outside European culture.

Travelers' voices were usually male, but by the late nineteenth century female voices were also being heard. At a time when separate gendered spheres were carefully marked in European culture, and when female fiction was considered scandalous, women travel writers such as Mary Kingsley and Isabella Bird were able to write in ways that subverted the gender conventions of European culture. These accounts were part of a larger role for the empire in the feminist movement, especially in Great Britain. By linking their own cause with the mission of what they saw as the most powerful force for reform in human history, the British empire, feminists such as Josephine Butler placed themselves, considered a subordinated part of the superior British race, in the position of protectors of colonial – and especially Indian – women. Because of the moral superiority of British women and their role as mothers of the British race, the emancipation of British women, and especially the vote, would, in their views, not only fulfill the destiny of the British nation but also improve the condition of Indian women that was evident in such practices as sati, the harem, and prostitution, even though those Indian women themselves were rarely, if ever, granted the ability to represent themselves. French feminists such as Hubertine Auclert made similar arguments about Algerian women.[37]

Images and impressions of colonial possessions were also available in museums and in the international and other exhibitions that became frequent events in Europe in the late nineteenth and early twentieth centuries. As a form of spectacle or performance, the representations to Europeans of the colonies made them a part of everyday life that might be as commonplace as the Luxor Obelisk that graced the center of the Place de la Concorde in Paris after 1836, a symbol of the growing French presence in Egypt. In other instances, museums displayed artifacts brought back from colonial Africa and Asia. These exhibits joined the colonies and metropole through communication of a form of scientific truth – an exhibit assembled by scientists, and displayed in a museum that claimed to communicate the truth – and a popular imagination inspired by exhibits such as the Benin bronzes brought back by a British military expedition in 1897 and displayed in Liverpool's Mayer Museum, the Pitt Rivers Museum in Oxford, and the Horniman Free Museum and the British Museum in London.

With less scientific pretense, other exhibitions provided Europeans with descriptions of the colonies. The Barnum and Bailey Great Show in London in 1897 included a performance entitled "The Mahdi: or For the Victoria Cross. A Realistic Reproduction of Life in the Soudan." Performers from Africa took prominent parts in these exhibitions, with Zulus, Asante, and others imported from Africa to sit in recreations of their homelands as European viewers walked past. Such importations were not, however, without their dangers: in 1899 the star performer in a "Savage South Africa" exhibition in London became engaged to an Englishwoman, Miss Kitty Jewell. Arousing outrage over the dangers to British womanhood of exposure to the male African performers, this event generated a heated debate in which not only the place of colonial

---

[37] Antoinette Burton, *Burdens of History: British Feminists, Indian Women, and Imperial Culture, 1865–1915* (Chapel Hill: University of North Carolina Press, 1994), and *At the Heart of the Empire: Indians and the Colonial Encounter in Late-Victorian Britain* (Berkeley and Los Angeles: University of California Press, 1998); Julia Clancy-Smith and Frances Gouda (eds.), *Domesticating the Empire: Race, Gender, and Family Life in French and Dutch Colonialism* (Charlottesville: University Press of Virginia, 1998); Hubertine Auclert, *Les femmes arabes en Algérie* (Paris: Société d'Éditions Litteraires, 1900).

subjects in the British nation was discussed, but also the nature of that nation itself.

The exoticism, and eroticism, that marked European cultural representations of colonial subjects found popular expression, especially in France, in the phenomenal popularity from the mid 1920s until after World War II of Josephine Baker. Born in 1906, Baker was an African American who had grown up in East St. Louis, and had experienced American racism in race riots there in 1917. At the age of 15 she headed to New York, and appeared in the Harlem reviews *Shuffle Along* (1921) and *The Chocolate Dandies* (1924). When that show closed in New York, it moved to Paris, opening on the Champs Elysées as *La revue nègre*, with Baker as a featured dancer. The show had a major impact on Parisian night life: as one historian has commented, "Audiences of the Revue Nègre were looking at scenes that purported to represent American Negro life, but they were seeing in their minds' eyes the jungles of Africa and the palm-fringed beaches of the Pacific."[38]

As African Americans made their mark in French entertainment and popular culture between the wars, through the work of jazz musicians and writers who found French racism less oppressive than that in the United States, Baker became not just one of the most popular American performers in Paris, but an international star. Baker's career was remarkable on several counts. But her representation of a version of colonial subject to the French – who never seemed to care that she was from the United States, not Africa – is perhaps most revelatory of the ways in which Europeans interacted with their colonial connections in the first half of the twentieth century. Baker drew on long-standing French images of African women as "sexualized savages" that had been present in French culture through the work of Balzac, Baudelaire, Loti, and others, and the fascination with primitivism that was a fundamental part of the Cubism of Fernand Léger and the poster art of Paul Colin, who designed the original poster for *La revue nègre* in 1925. Seeing in an African American woman a representation of the subjects in their African and Pacific colonies, Frenchmen wrote on Baker's image the exotic and erotic fantasies that had been a part of the imperial experience since its beginnings. Transported to a Parisian music hall, Baker carried on the tradition of the Tahitian women who had so fascinated European explorers such as Joseph Banks in the eighteenth century.

The colonies were presented in an even more spectacular fashion in public exhibitions. The Netherlands held a colonial exhibition

---

[38] Phyllis Rose, *Jazz Cleopatra: Josephine Baker in her Time* (New York: Doubleday, 1989), 22.

in Amsterdam in 1883 that featured a recreated East Indian village, including inhabitants from Java, along with other ethnographic exhibits. It attracted 1.5 million visitors and brought home to the Dutch the reality of their colonial empire. At the Stanley and African Exhibition held in 1890 in the Victoria Gallery on Regent Street in London, exhibits were contributed by a wide range of groups with interests in Africa: the colonial service, the British armed forces, the Royal Geographical Society and the Anthropological Society, the British Museum and the Horniman Museum, and the Anti-Slavery Society. Treating visitors as explorers, the exhibition led them through displays of African material culture, charts, and maps that reflected the supposedly scientific purposes of the exhibition. It even showed two boys from Swaziland, Gootoo and Inyokwana, in the slavery section.

The Crystal Palace Exhibition in 1851 in London began the custom of temporary exhibitions that showcased the national and industrial accomplishments of Europe, and many of these featured the colonies. By the time of the Paris Universal Exposition of 1889, colonial powers were using these exhibitions not only to display the possibilities for trade with their colonies, but also to provide Europeans with lessons on the power of Western technology and culture and to create pride in the accomplishments of the metropole. Both France and the Netherlands recreated indigenous villages on the Esplanade des Invalides for this Exposition. Dancers from the East Indies and North Africa were also featured in exhibits that were among the most popular in the Exposition and attracted attention from Émile Zola, Edmond de Goncourt, and other writers. The popularity of the expositions suggests that these lessons resonated well with the thousands of Europeans who visited them.

There were French Colonial Exhibitions in Marseilles in 1906 and 1922, and the British held their own Colonial Exhibition at Wembley in 1924–25. But in many respects this exhibition of the colonial world to European audiences reached its spectacular pinnacle at the 1931 Parisian International Colonial Exposition. Organized in the Bois de Vincennes in eastern Paris under the direction of Hubert Lyautey, now a marshal of France and commissaire-général of the Exposition, it was further proof – after Indochina, Madagascar, and Morocco – of Lyautey's belief in the ability of architecture and physical space to shape human behavior and of his policy of association between French and indigenous culture. The pavilions for European nations were designed in art deco style, while – in what may have been one of the most important imports of colonial architecture into France, even if most of the buildings were torn down in 1932 – the colonial pavilions reflected "native" styles.[39] Beginning at the main entrance at the porte de Picpus, the exposition was publicized as a "Tour du Monde en Un Jour" (A Tour of the World in One Day). Visitors first visited a Section Métropolitaine that displayed goods produced in France for export to the colonies. Next, a Musée des Colonies, the only permanent building on the site, displayed France's history as a colonial power. After viewing a Cité des Informations on investment, emigration, and business relations with the colonies, the visitor proceeded past the Madagascar pavilion down the avenue des Colonies, with its displays on Oceania, the French Caribbean, Somalia, Tahiti, the French Establishments in India, Indochina, French West and Equatorial Africa, and the North African possessions of Morocco, Algeria, and Tunisia. Dominating these exhibits was a recreation of Angkor Wat in Cambodia. The French colonial pavilions were supplemented by those dedicated to the Belgian Congo, the Dutch East Indies, and the nascent Italian empire. At the northern edge of the grounds, alongside Danish and Portuguese displays, the United States pavilion, a reconstruction of George Washington's home, Mount Vernon, celebrated the eighteenth-century struggle against colonialism by the United States but also American control over the Philippines, Hawai'i, Alaska, the Panama Canal zone, and its other Caribbean and Pacific holdings. The Dutch pavilion, in the form of a Balinese temple, featured fifty Balinese dancers whose popularity rivaled that of Josephine Baker's performances in Paris nightclubs. The Exposition may have contributed to the significance of a "colonial modern" style in art, in which colonial influences made their way into the works of European artists.[40]

The Exposition did not go without contestation of its positive portrayal of European colonies. A campaign to keep Parisians from visiting the Exposition began in 1930 and continued through 1931. Socialists drew attention to the human costs of colonial conquest and the harsh repression by colonial governments, and the French Communist Party not only pointed out the prevalence of coerced labor in the empire, but also drew attention to labor disputes in Indochina, Algeria, Morocco, Tunisia, and in the League of Nations mandated territories of Lebanon and Syria. At the end of October 1931 a Counter-Exhibition – officially titled *La vérité sur les colonies* (The Truth about the Colonies) – opened in Paris, supported by a variety of political and cultural opponents of

[39] Patricia A. Morton, *Hybrid Modernities: Architecture and Representation at the 1931 Colonial Exposition, Paris* (Cambridge, MA: MIT Press, 2000).
[40] Herman Lebovics, *True France: The Wars over Cultural Identity* (Ithaca, NY: Cornell University Press, 1992).

the Third Republic. Surrealists such as Louis Aragon, André Breton, Paul Éluard, Tristan Tzara, and Georges Sadoul displayed art from different colonies. Other parts of the exhibition drew attention to the anti-colonial nationalist movements around the globe. Another room was dedicated to the Soviet Union, contrasting the repressive colonial policies of the European imperial powers with the nationality policy of the Soviet Union.[41]

Race and hybridity

One of the striking aspects of Europe between the mid nineteenth and mid twentieth centuries is the profound cultural and racial pessimism that came over Europeans at the same time as they were apparently triumphing over, almost literally, the rest of the world. This pessimism grew out of anxieties about the many changes – industrialization, urbanization, political democracy, the decreased influence of older elites – that were occurring in European society and political life. While social changes often produce cultural anxieties, the particular aspect of this in nineteenth- and twentieth-century Europe was that it was often expressed in scientific and medical language, as those articulating these theories drew on the rising prestige of the natural sciences to make their arguments. For many French men and women, the defeat in the Franco-Prussian War in 1870–71 seemed to indicate not only the need for military reforms if France was to compete successfully with the newly unified Germany, but also a decadence of the French nation that did not bode well for attempts by *la grande nation* to recapture its former glories. Public figures and military officers such as comte (Albert) de Mun and Hubert Lyautey shared this opinion with many others.[42] By the late nineteenth century, many in France saw rampant violent crime, vagrancy, prostitution, and alcoholism around them and took them as indicators of national degeneration. This sense acquired a medical hue in the first decade of the twentieth century, as doctors and psychiatrists used their professional training to articulate a "hygienic" theory of degeneration, first applied to criminals and then to the nation itself. Similar theories of decline, extending medical and biological analyses of deviance to the nation, were prevalent elsewhere as well. In Germany the liberal Max Nordau attacked modernism and its

---

[41] Catherine Hodeir and Michel Pierre, *L'exposition colonial, 1931* (Brussels: Éditions Complexe, 1991), 111–34; Panivong Norindr, *Phantasmatic Indochina: French Colonial Ideology in Architecture, Film, and Literature* (Durham, NC: Duke University Press, 1996), 52–71.
[42] Rabinow, *French Modern*, 118, 289.

accompanying insanity, alcoholism, and crime in medical terms, claiming to describe a "sickness of the age." In Austria, psychiatrists listed sexual "deviancies" as signs of moral decay that undercut national vitality. The British undertook a national debate in the decade before World War I on the deterioration, degeneracy, and decadence of the British nation. In France, novelists such as Émile Zola portrayed hereditary degeneration in best-selling novels. The medicalization of discussions of degeneration in the decade before World War I also contributed to the rapid growth of the science of eugenics, which aimed at using medical expertise to improve the racial "stock" of the British, French, or German nations.[43]

The racial concerns that colored discussions of degeneration and eugenics inevitably reflected on colonial society. The colonies were seen by some as a laboratory in which a healthy modern society could be created, giving them a cultural significance beyond the possible strategic and economic benefits they might bring. But the colonial empires also contributed to the elaboration of racial differences in European culture. In the eighteenth century, race was a concept that was rarely used and usually meant lineage except when needed in pro-slavery arguments. Some scholars have argued that it became a weapon in the political and cultural attack on aristocratic power in the late eighteenth century.[44] This conception of race changed, however, in the course of the nineteenth century. West Indian planters who described their slaves as "Quashee" – "lazy, mendacious, incapable of working without the whip, mentally inferior, and sexually depraved" – were matched by abolitionists who saw them as "meek victim(s) of white oppression, grateful to his or her saviours, ready to be transformed."[45] Later, by mid-century, after the great experiment of emancipation had been tried, there was a turn towards racial distinctions as a way of explaining the inability of freed slaves to reach the levels of "civilization" intended by their emancipators. Thomas Carlyle was not alone in blatantly claiming that blacks could never be the equal of whites.

In the nineteenth century perceptions of racial difference increasingly drew on theories and a vocabulary taken from the physical sciences, especially biology. Missionaries created their own versions of the

---

[43] Robert A. Nye, *Crime, Madness, and Politics in Modern France: The Medical Concept of National Decline* (Princeton University Press, 1984), 329, 330–38; Daniel Pick, *Faces of Degeneration: A European Disorder, c. 1848–c. 1918* (Cambridge University Press, 1989), 21.

[44] Ann Laura Stoler, *Race and the Education of Desire: Foucault's "History of Sexuality" and the Colonial Order of Things* (Durham, NC: Duke University Press, 1995).

[45] Hall, *Civilising Subjects*, 321.

slaves, freedmen, Asians, and Africans among whom they worked and tried to convert to some version of Christianity, placing them in a hierarchy in which Europeans dominated. "Race" came to mean that there were a fixed number of human types, but biological differences were taken to signal both physical and cultural differences. Biological essentialism replaced earlier cultural versions of racial distinction. Thus, not only the existence of races but also the implications of hybridity dominated European discussions of the colonies. By the middle of the century, the idea of race had become so powerful that its claims to be an essential determinant of human behavior had become an important part of both scientific theory and popular discussion. As late as 1942, the French eugenicist René Martial, a member of the faculty of the School of Medicine in Paris, argued that "instability [was] the dominant characteristic of *métis*."[46]

The more frequent contact between Europeans and non-Europeans as a result of imperial expansion certainly contributed to the importance of racial thinking among both elites and the general population. The British in India made distinctions between the different peoples and castes of South Asia, especially after the middle of the nineteenth century. The Gurkhas and Sikhs who remained loyal to the British in 1857 increasingly were viewed as "martial races" from which the Indian army could recruit its best soldiers. The Paharis of Simla, the Lepchas of Darjeeling, and the Todas of Ootacamund, located where the British were developing hill stations, were unrelentingly portrayed as noble savages. Other tribes were consigned to the status of "criminal tribes," assumed to be threats to public order and the subjects of legislation that remained in effect until independence in 1947. Similarly, the French in Algeria carefully distinguished between the Arab population that was hopelessly separated from French civilization and the Kabyles who, if they would only give up their Muslim religion and convert to Christianity, could easily be envisioned as assimilable into the French nation.

These racial theories of the late nineteenth century drew particular power from their ability to mobilize scientific discourses in their support, and formed the basis for a hierarchy of races and the dominance of one race over another. Foremost among these discourses was the focus in nineteenth-century biology on evolution. Evolutionary theory was concerned with the heredity of physical characteristics, but there was no

---

[46] Quoted in Ann Laura Stoler, *Carnal Knowledge and Imperial Power: Race and the Intimate in Colonial Rule* (Berkeley and Los Angeles: University of California Press, 2002), 109.

agreement among scientists about exactly how evolution worked in the physical world. One theory, Lamarckism, was based on the work of the French biologist Jean-Baptiste Lamarck (1744–1829), who claimed that changes in the environment could produce new characteristics in races that then became hereditary. Charles Darwin's (1809–82) work, which argued for the hereditary transmission of physical characteristics but was less concerned with environmental or social influences than that of Lamarck, was among the most influential, especially in Great Britain. An extension of Darwin's theories of evolution, Social Darwinism, emphasized the importance of competition between races through natural selection, and was able to draw on the scientific ideas of Darwin to legitimate its own views about racial difference and hierarchy.

While to some extent those who discussed racial difference were interested in distinguishing between what they viewed as different races, they were also concerned with racial mixing, or hybridity. The Frenchman Paul Broca (1824–80) held that racial hybridity had possible degenerative or suicidal consequences. By the last third of the nineteenth century, these racial views gained resonance in a number of different places. They contributed to debates in Britain about the relationship between the Irish and the English, while the rising power of a unified Germany after 1871 posed the question of the relationship between Germans and other Europeans. Eugenicists who were concerned about the policies to be taken towards the industrial working classes used this language, often referring to workers as similar to "alien tribes." But these racial theories also helped shape the increased contact between Europeans on the one hand and Sub-Saharan Africans and Asians on the other, providing theories with the imprimatur of science that helped Europeans interpret the peoples and societies that they found in the colonies. The combination of the language of science with views about racial difference proved to be a powerful and long-lasting consequence of European contact with non-Europeans.

The scientific debates about race overlapped with similar debates about gender, as biological theories about the essential differences between men and women became increasingly prevalent and found their cultural expression in expectations about masculinity and femininity. The search for male identity that Catherine Hall has found in the biography of Edward Eyre, the British governor on Jamaica at the time of the Morant Bay rebellion, was writ large as concepts of citizenship were elaborated – and empowered – in the second half of the nineteenth century through increasingly representative political institutions. It is a truism, of course, that this participation was gendered, as the "manly citizen" received the vote and the middle-class woman did not. But what needs to be underscored is the use of similar biological models of superiority and inferiority to inform judgments about both women and colonial subjects: if middle-class women were biologically incapable of political participation – a conclusion reached by many male commentators in the nineteenth and twentieth centuries – that provided a model by which colonial subjects could also be seen to be incapable because they acted as if they were the "effeminate babu." The subordination of women in Europe reinforced the subordination of colonial subjects in the empires as those colonial subjects were feminized.

But these hierarchies always seemed in danger. Europeans had been concerned about the threats to European civilization posed by the slave colonies of the New World and the sexual dangers inherent in the low proportion of white women in the Caribbean islands and the availability of slave and mulatto women. Eighteenth-century French discourses about the sugar colonies dismissed them as places of libertinage where moral indiscretion was the norm.[47] This view emphasized the threat to social order posed by free mulatto women and black slave women. Metropolitan writers accorded those women not only a natural predisposition to erotic excess, but also the ability to utilize this in order to control white males. Reinforced in the nineteenth century by biological theories of hybridity and the supposed dangers of miscegenation, these ideas gave a particular impetus to the efforts by colonial administrations to manage sexual relations between Europeans and colonial subjects, and to concerns about the growing numbers of mixed-race children being born in the colonies. In the twentieth century, these concerns were reflected in discussions about eligibility for citizenship rights and other privileges in the racialized colonies of Asia and Africa.

By the beginning of the twentieth century, these multiple interactions between the colonial powers and the colonies had made the imperial framework a "naturalized" assumption for French, British, Dutch, Portuguese, and Belgian men and women. Properly governed by imperial nation-states, the colonies would benefit from European rule and form an important resource for the maintenance of European civilization, supplementing the metropole in the competition between nations that marked early twentieth-century Europe. The raw materials and markets they provided for metropolitan economies became powerful evidence in support of the "New Imperialism" of the pre-World War I era. Politicians such as Joseph Chamberlain and Jules Ferry were convinced of the need for colonies if their countries were to hold their position in the world, and they argued for investments that would enhance this

---

[47] Garraway, *Libertine Colony*, 194–239, 29.

ability. With little hesitation, European leaders committed Asians and Africans to World War I, assuming that the colonies would be willing reservoirs of manpower for the Western Front. Europeans also viewed their national identities in terms of the colonies. Scientifically explained contrasts with colonial subjects positioned Europeans in racial hierarchies that justified colonial rule and exploitation. Masculine and feminine qualities were drawn from colonial experience and examples. For many Europeans, the colonies also provided a space for the imagination, sparked by literature, art, exhibitions, and academic disciplines like Orientalism and anthropology to envision a better, perhaps happier world in place of a Europe that, increasingly in the twentieth century, seemed decadent and in decline. What few imagined was that the colonial empires would end.

FURTHER READING

Abu-Lughod, Janet L. *Rabat: Urban Apartheid in Morocco*. Princeton University Press, 1980.

Ageron, Charles-Robert. *La décolonisation française*. Paris: A. Colin, 1991.

Ajayi, J. F. Ade. *Christian Missions in Nigeria 1841–1891: The Making of a New Elite*. Evanston, IL: Northwestern University Press, 1965.

Alloula, Malek. *The Colonial Harem*. Minneapolis: University of Minnesota Press, 1986.

Anstey, Roger. *The Atlantic Slave Trade and British Abolition, 1760–1810*. London: Macmillan, 1975.

Arnold, David. *Colonizing the Body: State Medicine and Epidemic Disease in Nineteenth-Century India*. Berkeley and Los Angeles: University of California Press, 1993.

Bayly, Susan. *Saints, Goddesses and Kings: Muslims and Christians in South Indian Society, 1700–1900*. Cambridge University Press, 1989.

Blackburn, Robin. *The Overthrow of Colonial Slavery 1776–1848*. New York: Verso, 1988.

Bloembergen, Marieke. *Colonial Spectacles: The Netherlands and the Dutch East Indies at the World Exhibitions, 1880–1931*, trans. Beverley Jackson. National University of Singapore Press, 2006.

Brah, Avtar, and Annie E. Coombes, eds. *Hybridity and its Discontents: Politics, Science, Culture*. London and New York: Routledge, 2000.

Brewer, John. *The Sinews of Power: War, Money and the English State, 1688–1783*. Cambridge University Press, 1989.

Burton, Antoinette. *At the Heart of the Empire: Indians and the Colonial Encounter in Late-Victorian Britain*. Berkeley and Los Angeles: University of California Press, 1998.

Burdens of History: British Feminists, Indian Women, and Imperial Culture, 1865–1915. Chapel Hill: University of North Carolina Press, 1994.

Cannadine, David. *Ornamentalism: How the British Saw Their Empire*. Oxford University Press, 2001.

Çelik, Zeynep. *Urban Forms and Colonial Confrontations: Algiers under French Rule*. Berkeley and Los Angeles: University of California Press, 1997.

Chafer, Tony, and Amanda Sackur, eds. *Promoting the Colonial Idea: Propaganda and Visions of Empire in France*. New York: Palgrave, 2002.

Clancy-Smith, Julia, and Frances Gouda, eds. *Domesticating the Empire: Race, Gender, and Family Life in French and Dutch Colonialism*. Charlottesville: University Press of Virginia, 1998.

Clark, Linda L. *Social Darwinism in France*. Birmingham, AL: University of Alabama Press, 1984.

Clifford, James. *Person and Myth: Maurice Leenhardt in the Melanesian World*. Berkeley and Los Angeles: University of California Press, 1982.

Colley, Linda. *Britons: Forging the Nation, 1707–1837*. New Haven, CT: Yale University Press, 1992.

Comaroff, Jean, and John Comaroff. *Of Revelation and Revolution: Christianity, Colonialism, and Consciousness in South Africa*. University of Chicago Press, 1991.

Comaroff, John L. "Reflections on the Colonial State, in South Africa and Elsewhere: Fragments, Factions, Facts and Fictions." *Social Identities* 4 (1998), 321–62.

Conklin, Alice. *A Mission to Civilize: The Republican Idea of Empire in France and West Africa, 1895–1930*. Stanford University Press, 1997.

Conner, Patrick. *Oriental Architecture in the West*. London: Thames and Hudson, 1979.

Coombes, Annie E. *Reinventing Africa: Museums, Material Culture and Popular Imagination in Late Victorian and Edwardian England*. New Haven, CT and London: Yale University Press, 1994.

Crinson, Mark. *Empire Building: Orientalism and Victorian Architecture*. London: Routledge, 1996.

Curtin, Philip D. *Death by Migration: Europe's Encounter with the Tropical World in the Nineteenth Century*. Cambridge University Press, 1989.

Dinkel, John. *The Royal Pavilion Brighton*. New York: Vendome Press, 1983.

Dobie, Madeleine. *Foreign Bodies: Gender, Language and Culture in French Orientalism*. Stanford University Press, 2001.

Trading Places. Ithaca, NY: Cornell University Press, 2010.

Foucault, Michel. "Governmentality." In Graham Burchell, Colin Gordon, and Peter Miller, eds., *The Foucault Effect: Studies in Governmentality*. University of Chicago Press, 1991, 87–104.

Garraway, Doris. *The Libertine Colony: Creolization in the Early French Caribbean*. Durham, NC: Duke University Press, 2005.

Gouda, Frances. *Dutch Culture Overseas: Colonial Practice in the Netherlands Indies, 1900–1942*. Amsterdam University Press, 1995.

Hale, Dana S. *Races on Display: French Representations of Colonized Peoples, 1886–1940*. Bloomington: Indiana University Press, 2008.

Hall, Catherine. *Civilising Subjects: Metropole and Colony in the English Imagination 1830–1867*. University of Chicago Press, 2002.

Head, Raymond. *The Indian Style*. University of Chicago Press, 1986.

Hodeir, Catherine, and Michel Pierre. *L'exposition colonial, 1931*. Brussels: Éditions Complexe, 1991.

Hunt, Lynn. *Inventing Human Rights: A History*. New York: W. W. Norton, 2007.

Jennings, Eric T. *Curing the Colonizers: Hydrotherapy, Climatology, and French Colonial Spas*. Durham, NC and London: Duke University Press, 2006.

Jennings, Lawrence C. *French Anti-Slavery: The Movement for the Abolition of Slavery in France, 1802–1848*. Cambridge University Press, 2000.

Jullian, Philippe. *The Orientalists: European Painters of Eastern Scenes*. Oxford: Phaidon, 1977.

Kennedy, Dane. *The Magic Mountains: Hill Stations and the British Raj*. Berkeley and Los Angeles: University of California Press, 1996.

King, Anthony. *The Bungalow: The Production of a Global Culture*, 2nd edn. New York: Oxford University Press, 1995.

Lebovics, Herman. *True France: The Wars over Cultural Identity, 1900–1945*. Ithaca, NY: Cornell University Press, 1992.

Metcalf, Thomas R. *Imperial Connections: India in the Indian Ocean Arena, 1860–1920*. Berkeley and Los Angeles: University of California Press, 2007.

An Imperial Vision: Indian Architecture and Britain's Raj. Berkeley and Los Angeles: The University of California Press, 1989.

The New Cambridge History of India: Ideologies of the Raj. Cambridge University Press, 1994.

Midgley, Clare. *Women against Slavery: The British Campaigns, 1780–1870*. London and New York: Routledge, 1992.

Miller, Christopher L. *The French Atlantic Triangle: Literature and Culture of the Slave Trade*. Durham, NC: Duke University Press, 2008.

Newbury, Colin. *Patrons, Clients, and Empire: Chieftaincy and Over-rule in Asia, Africa, and the Pacific*. Oxford University Press, 2003.

Norindr, Panivong. *Phantasmatic Indochina: French Colonial Ideology in Architecture, Film, and Literature*. Durham, NC: Duke University Press, 1996.

Northrup, David. *Indentured Labor in the Age of Imperialism, 1834–1922*. Cambridge University Press, 1995.

Nye, Robert A. *Crime, Madness, and Politics in Modern France: The Medical Concept of National Decline*. Princeton University Press, 1984.

Oldfield, J. R. *Popular Politics and British Anti-Slavery: The Mobilisation of Public Opinion Against the Slave Trade, 1787–1807*. Manchester University Press, 1995.

Peer, Shanny. *France on Display: Peasants, Provincials, and Folklore in the 1937 Paris World's Fair*. Albany: State University of New York Press, 1998.

Pick, Daniel. *Faces of Degeneration: A European Disorder, c. 1848–c. 1918*. Cambridge University Press, 1989.

Pitts, Jennifer. *A Turn to Empire: The Rise of Imperial Liberalism in Britain and France*. Princeton University Press, 2005.

Rabinow, Paul. *French Modern: Norms and Forms of the Social Environment*. Cambridge, MA: MIT Press, 1989.

Rose, Phyllis. *Jazz Cleopatra: Josephine Baker in her Time.* New York: Doubleday, 1989.

Rotberg, Robert I. *Christian Missionaries and the Creation of Northern Rhodesia 1880–1924.* Princeton University Press, 1965.

Scott, David. "Colonial Governmentality." *Social Text* 43 (1995), 191–220.

Sharpe, Jenny. *Allegories of Empire: The Figure of Woman in the Colonial Text.* Minneapolis: University of Minnesota Press, 1993.

Stevens, MaryAnne, ed. *The Orientalists: Delacroix to Matisse: European Painters in North Africa and the Near East.* London: Royal Academy of Arts, 1984.

Stoler, Ann Laura. *Carnal Knowledge and Imperial Power: Race and the Intimate in Colonial Rule.* Berkeley and Los Angeles: University of California Press, 2002.

Thornton, Lynne. *The Orientalists.* Paris: ACR Édition Internationale, 1983.

Turley, David. *The Culture of English Antislavery, 1780–1860.* London and New York: Routledge, 1991.

Wilson, Kathleen. *The Island Race: Englishness, Empire and Gender in the Eighteenth Century.* London and New York: Routledge, 2003.

"Rethinking the Colonial State: Family, Gender and Governmentality in Eighteenth-Century British Frontiers." *American Historical Review* 116 (2011), 1294–322.

The Sense of the People: Politics, Culture and Imperialism in England, 1715–1785. Cambridge University Press, 1995.

Wright, Gwendolyn. *The Politics of Design in French Urban Colonialism.* University of Chicago Press, 1991.

The end of empire in the middle of the twentieth century is in many recountings an uncomplicated finale to the story of European colonial expansion and rule.[1] In this view, indigenous elites demanded autonomy and eventually independence for the colonies in which they lived. In the British empire, this accelerated attempts to move colonies along a path to membership in the Commonwealth of Nations, while at the same time transforming the Commonwealth away from political federation towards an economic trading zone. In the French empire, the longtime practices that considered the empire to be a constituent part of the Republic led first to an unsuccessful war in Indochina and then an even more disastrous one in Algeria. These major imperial defeats were paralleled by Belgian withdrawal from the Congo, the Dutch departure from Indonesia and, in the 1970s, the end of the last European empire, the African possessions of Portugal. No matter what the vision of empire that had existed in the imperial powers in 1945, therefore, those empires were quickly liquidated.

These colonial conflicts make up one of the most remarkable events of twentieth-century history, and they often seem to have been inevitable. There had, of course, been doubts about the value of the colonies on the part of some Europeans almost from the beginnings of the empires, with the controversies over the Atlantic empires in the late eighteenth century and the decades preceding the Partition of Africa particularly marked by these concerns among the intellectual and political elites of the colonial powers. In the twentieth century these arose again. The contradictions of colonial rule that had caused unease in the writings

---

[1] See, for example: Derek W. Urwin, *A Political History of Western Europe since 1945*, 5th edn. (London: Longman, 1997), 112–21; J. Robert Wegs and Robert Ladrech, *Europe since 1945: A Concise History*, 4th edn. (New York: St. Martin's Press, 1996), 101–20; Michael Crowder (ed.), *The Cambridge History of Africa,* vol. VIII, *From c. 1940 to c. 1975* (Cambridge University Press, 1984); Jean Plauchais, *L'empire embrasé, 1946–1962* (Paris: Éditions Denoël, 1990); Raymond F. Betts, *France and Decolonisation 1900–1960* (New York: St. Martin's Press, 1991).

of E. M. Forster and Joseph Conrad became more apparent leading up to World War II. The collapse of colonial rule in the first years of World War II seemed to many observers to confirm the critiques of the "degeneracy" of the West that had been prevalent for more than a generation. Visitors to the colonies during the 1930s and after World War II, such as the British novelists W. Somerset Maugham and Anthony Burgess and the French poet Jean Cocteau, were struck by the apparent moral degeneracy of European colonial society, and the phrase "whisky-swilling planters" seemed accurate to many. The defeats of the British, French, and Dutch by the Japanese in the early years of World War II, punctuated by the fall of Singapore to the Japanese in 1942, were for many an obvious outcome of that degeneracy. The abandonment of their colonial subjects to the Japanese by the British at Singapore seemed to confirm their unfitness for imperial rule. For some the feminization of colonial society seemed a reversal of the natural gender order and subversive of male rule. A heightened sense of white prestige and purity and "maintaining form" seemed to run through colonial society, even as Eurasians and Euro-Africans made obvious the inability of colonial society to maintain racial boundaries. Harold Macmillan, who as British prime minister would liquidate much of the British empire, saw anti-colonial nationalism in demographic terms, fearing that the rising tide of non-Europeans would swamp Western civilization. Others found the inevitability of colonial crisis in grand theories of history. For the anti-colonial French Marxists who published their views in *Les Temps Modernes* in the 1950s, the independence of France's most important colony, Algeria, was the outcome of the human struggle for liberation. The French liberal Raymond Aron viewed Algerian independence as part of a similar, if non-Marxist, wave of history.[2]

In retrospect, the meaning of the events at mid twentieth century is less clear.[3] There were many ceremonies transferring power from colonizer to colonized. But in some cases, this was more a shift to

[2] W. Somerset Maugham, *The Gentleman in the Parlour: A Record of a Journey from Rangoon to Haiphong* (Garden City, NY: Doubleday, Doran & Co., 1930); Anthony Burgess, *The Long Day Wanes: A Malayan Trilogy* (New York: Penguin, 1981); Jean Cocteau, *Tour du monde en 80 jours* (Paris: Gallimard, 1983); Wm. Roger Louis, "The Dissolution of the British Empire in the Era of Vietnam," in *Ends of British Imperialism: The Scramble for Empire, Suez and Decolonization* (London: I. B. Tauris, 2006), 561; Christopher Bayly and Tim Harper, *Forgotten Armies: The Fall of British Asia, 1941–1945* (Cambridge, MA: Belknap Press, 2005), 59–69; Todd Shepard, *The Invention of Decolonization: The Algerian War and the Remaking of France* (Ithaca, NY: Cornell University Press, 2006), 63–69, 83–100.
[3] Early recognition of this can be found in J. D. Hargreaves, *Decolonization in Africa* (London: Longman, 1988).

"informal empire" than absolute independence. Post-colonial leaders such as Ghana's Kwame Nkrumah argued that a "Neo-colonialism" continued to hold his country in Europe's grip, determining defense and social policies.[4] In settler colonies such as Kenya and Southern Rhodesia, white minorities resisted black majority rule that would call into question the validity of the colonial settlements. The willingness of former colonial powers to intervene politically and militarily in newly independent colonies cast doubt on the extent to which the new nations of the 1970s were free agents. By the end of the twentieth century the interdependence of the economies of different parts of the world suggested that, whatever decolonization meant, it did not mean freedom from many of the political, economic, and social forces that had marked the colonial era. Placed in the context of the shift in form of Europe's ties to the Americas, Oceania, Asia, and Africa, the complex outcomes of "decolonization" suggest that it was not the end of the arc of European colonialism but rather, as in the late eighteenth century and again in the second half of the nineteenth, yet another reconfiguration of the relationship between Europe and the rest of the world.

Certainly a number of factors coalesced in the mid twentieth century to force rethinking of this relationship. As had been the case since the seventeenth and eighteenth centuries, diplomatic considerations weighed heavily in the decisions of the colonial powers. But they also faced concerted opposition from colonial subjects, and the economic, political, and military costs of maintaining the empires often became intolerable. In the decades leading up to World War I, the colonies had been not only a crucial part of the game of Great-Power diplomacy, but real counters as those Powers contemplated another war in Europe. Lord Curzon was hardly alone when he noted in 1901 that "As long we rule India we are the greatest power in the world. If we lose it we shall drop straight away to a third rate power."[5] During the Great War, the British used Indian troops on the Western Front, replacing them in colonial garrison duty by Territorials from Great Britain itself. The French, for their part, increasingly included troops from the colonies in their military planning, anticipating the problems of keeping the Mediterranean open to bring North African troops to France for a European war. The French government also listened attentively to the plans of Colonel Charles Mangin, who argued in *La force noire*, published in 1910, that Sub-Saharan Africa was a viable source of soldiers and that the *tireurs*

---

[4] Kwame Nkrumah, *Neo-Colonialism: The Last Stage of Imperialism* (London: Heinemann Educational Books, 1965).

[5] Quoted in John Morrow, *The Great War: An Imperial History* (London: Routledge, 2004), 9.

sénégalais, soldiers recruited in France's African colonies since 1857, should be expanded. Those colonies, Mangin thought, could provide 500,000 soldiers for the metropole.[6] The French began expanding the *tireurs* in 1912, and, alone among combatants, used significant numbers of African troops on the Western Front.

The colonial contributions to the British and French efforts in the Great War encouraged some colonial subjects, in India and West Africa, to hope for concessions of colonial autonomy and citizenship rights. Such was not, however, to be the case, and, if anything, Great Britain and France, convinced that the colonies had been key in winning victory, exerted more control over their colonies after peace came in 1918. But World War II also damaged the imperial powers militarily and economically, limiting their ability to maintain their power around the globe. Britain, Belgium, the Netherlands, Portugal, and France were dwarfed internationally after 1945 by two powers, the United States and the Soviet Union, and increasingly had to accommodate their colonial policies to the views of those powers. While strategic interests certainly came into play, the Soviet Union was also avowedly anti-colonial for ideological and strategic reasons. While direct Soviet intervention in Europe's colonies was rare, the self-appointed task of the Soviet Union was "to make the world safe for revolution." It viewed colonies as integral supports for the capitalist economic system, and also saw nationalist movements in the colonies as instruments through which the revolutionary goal of the Soviet Union to overthrow the capitalist system could be achieved. The United States also professed to be anti-colonial, but its policies tended to back its Western European allies, especially Great Britain and France, as they struggled to reassert colonial control after 1945. By the 1950s, as the Cold War with the Soviet Union became the focus of American foreign policy, the United States supported its allies' colonial efforts but urged them to make some accommodation with nationalist groups in the colonies and to avoid debacles such as the French war in Indochina. Thus, while the United States was willing to let the French try to repress the rebellion in Algeria, it had to be done quickly or not at all: US Deputy Under Secretary of State Robert Murphy told a French diplomat in 1956 that "we agree to let you try. If you truly believe that you can solve the problem by force, do it but do it quickly ... But if you cannot reestablish calm quickly, then make all the necessary concessions."[7] The existence after 1946

---

[6] Charles Mangin, *La force noire* (Paris: Hachette, 1910).
[7] Odd Arne Westad, *The Global Cold War: Third World Interventions and the Making of Our Times* (Cambridge University Press, 2005), 72; Matthew Connolly, *A Diplomatic*

of an international forum, the United Nations, in which movements for independence could air their grievances against the colonial powers further undercut the colonial regimes.

As with the earlier reformulations of colonial relationships, decolonization was not a process that the colonial powers themselves completely determined. In each colony, we have seen, opposition to colonial rule developed almost as soon as that rule had itself been established. This has sometimes been described in relatively homogeneous terms, as conflicts between "colonial authorities" and "colonial subjects." But there certainly were Europeans who were outspoken in support of both reforms and the end of the empires, often making themselves the objects of harsh repression by their governments. Within the colonies themselves, there were disagreements among colonial subjects about whether the future should bring reform, autonomy, or independence. Recent scholarship has increasingly emphasized that these disagreements often brought about political alliances between indigenous nationalists of various stripes and the colonial regimes. These developments meant that the only possible outcome was not necessarily the complete independence of the colonies, and the imperial powers certainly did not see that as the expected or even likely outcome when they began restructuring their relationships with their colonies at mid-century. But the outcome of that restructuring was often not the peaceful transition to European-style democracy and economic prosperity envisaged in the rhetoric of empire, but economic, social, and political disruption and, in some cases, chaos.

Great Britain

Relative pessimism about the future of the empire had been a significant strain in British political thought in the 1860s and 1870s, but by the 1880s a number of Britons were both more optimistic about its future and willing to rethink how it should be organized so that it could avoid the seemingly inevitable "decline and fall" of empires. While India was becoming more prominent as an exotic outpost of British power in Asia, with Victoria crowned Empress of India in 1876, others were focusing on what they called the "settler colonies," in South Africa, Canada, New Zealand, and Australia. These came to be called Dominions in the late nineteenth and early twentieth centuries, although this designation brought them no new powers beyond Responsible Government. At

Revolution: Algeria's Fight for Independence and the Origins of the Post-Cold War Era (Oxford University Press, 2002), 101.

the same time a "Greater Britain" movement gained some prominence, drawing support from across the political spectrum and with some of its proponents organizing the Imperial Federation League in 1884 to promote a closer and more equal relationship between Great Britain and those colonies and the possibility of representation in Westminster for the settler colonies. In the mind of one of its most prominent advocates, J. R. Seeley, it held out the prospect of a global nation-state, although others, such as Goldwin Smith, Regius Professor of Modern History at Oxford, ridiculed the idea. The connections between the Dominions were a common Anglo-Saxon race (and so the United States was sometimes included as another member of the federation) as well as nationality and values, thus excluding India and justifying imperial rule over the subcontinent. Based on speculation about the willingness of the Dominions to be tied more closely to London – the socialist critic William Clark noted in 1885 that "It is such an honour, they [federalists] think to be connected with England, that they assume that the interest of the Colonies must lie in such a union" – and the practicalities of a global political organization, Greater Britain as a global nation-state foundered around the turn of the twentieth century, with the Boer War providing perhaps the deadliest shot at the idea.[8]

Edwardians who dreamed about the future of the empire thought more in terms of a multinational commonwealth. This was envisioned as a free association of former colonies with Britain, in which the Crown continued to act as constitutional head of state. Periodic Colonial Conferences beginning in 1887, and called Imperial Conferences after 1911, brought together the leaders of these colonies. While these conferences were the occasion for efforts by some British leaders, notably Joseph Chamberlain and Alfred Milner, to press for greater imperial unity and tariff policies based on Imperial Preference, they also allowed the Dominions to demonstrate greater independence from Westminster in their policies. By the Balfour Declaration of 1926 Great Britain and the Dominions agreed that they were equal in status, and their free association in the "British Commonwealth of Nations" was formalized by the Statute of Westminster in 1931.

The Commonwealth provided a model – albeit an ambiguous one – for what might happen in the future to other British colonies. The assumption was that non-white colonies in Africa and Asia, and the former plantation colonies in the West Indies, with white minorities dwarfed by the descendants of the slaves freed in the nineteenth

---

[8] Clark quoted in Duncan Bell, *The Idea of Greater Britain: Empire and the Future of World Order, 1860–1900* (Princeton University Press, 2007), 61.

century, would eventually follow. Yet those involved in colonial affairs before World War II could hardly imagine the dramatically changed circumstances brought on by that war. There was often sporadic fighting in almost all of the colonies. But even colonies that were relatively untouched by fighting nonetheless found themselves providing previously untold quantities of materials and manpower for the war effort. The crescent of colonies in Southeast Asia from Burma through Malaya and the Straits Settlements were more directly affected. Japanese conquest in the early years of the war turned the region into a cauldron of refugees, death, and material destruction that lasted well after 1945. The Japanese occupation would open up possibilities for the colonial subjects of the region, disrupting the structures of colonial government that had been in existence for generations and weakening the power of the British imperial state. The occupation pushed aside pre-war nationalists as well as colonial governments, and gave Burmese and Malays military training and experience. In 1945, they would be a different kind of nationalist leadership, more youthful, assertive, and militaristic than the pre-war elites who had cooperated with the British.

Even though Dominion status seemed far away for most British colonies in 1945, the intention of British policy-makers at the end of the War was that the old imperial relationship between Britain and its colonies should be reshaped from one of domination into one between relatively equal partners in order to accommodate indigenous demands for reform and to increase the economic contribution of the colonies to the imperial power. By securing the cooperation of moderate indigenous leaders, they hoped, the rising tide of nationalism in the colonies could be used to shape nations that cooperated with British interests. In the event, however, these hopes proved illusory: in colony after colony, from India to South Africa, Britain was forced to make the best of a bad situation, ceding control to new leaders who were themselves the products of the educational institutions – often missionary schools – created by the British in the colonies beginning before World War I, and with government experience gained in systems of indirect rule. While in some instances these new nations remained within the umbrella of the Commonwealth, that structure itself lost much of its internal rigor, becoming only a loose confederation of independent nations with widely varying ties to Westminster. If the hope was that the empire would be reshaped in such a way that it would continue to sustain Britain's role as a Great Power in the post-war world, that proved impossible to realize. Instead, British policy moved from an initial phase of disengagement under the immediate post-war Labour government (1945–51), through the attempts by the Tory governments of Winston Churchill and Anthony Eden to maintain British imperial power, to the era of liquidation under Harold Macmillan after 1957. The end result was the effective end of the formal British empire: between 1945 and 1965, the colonial population was reduced from 700 million to 5 million, of whom 3 million were in Hong Kong.[9]

India and Pakistan

For Britain, the most traumatic instance of decolonization occurred in India, long considered the jewel of the British empire and one that had dominated British global strategy. By the twentieth century, Indian society included a growing number of South Asians who had acquired the Western-style education that had been available on a limited basis since the early nineteenth century. These Indians held a number of administrative and judicial appointments, and sought to expand the opportunities for such positions. Even in the early twentieth century there was pressure on the British government to grant some kind of autonomy to its Indian colony. The two principal organizations demanding this change in status dated from the late nineteenth and early twentieth centuries. The first was the Indian National Congress, a Hindu organization founded in 1885. At the beginning of the twentieth century this gave birth to the Congress political party committed to Hindu participation in Indian affairs. The second movement, the All-India Muslim League, was founded in 1906 and represented many of the Muslims of South Asia. Its principal strengths were in the northeast and northwest of the subcontinent.

Indian support for the British cause during World War I went largely unrewarded by any significant change in the colonial government, and the immediate post-war era was marked by protest campaigns demanding further reforms. In what became a catalyst turning many future nationalists against the British, one of these demonstrations, in the Punjab city of Amritsar on April 13, 1919, led to British and Indian troops firing on a crowd, killing 379 and wounding more. Newer nationalist leaders, notably the London-trained lawyer Mohandas Gandhi and Cambridge-educated Jawaharlal Nehru, also came to the fore after the war. A civil disobedience campaign in 1922 led to Gandhi's arrest and imprisonment, and in 1930 he led a campaign against the government salt monopoly in the form of a 200-mile march to the sea

---

[9] William Roger Louis, "The Dissolution of the British Empire," in Judith M. Brown and William Roger Louis (eds.), *The Twentieth Century*, vol. IV of *The Oxford History of the British Empire* (Oxford University Press, 1999), 330.

Illustration 7 Civil disobedience campaign against the salt laws in India, 1930.

(Illustration 7). A reform act passed in 1935 made some concessions to Responsible Government at the level of the provinces and princely states, but when World War II broke out in 1939, its provisions for the central government had not yet come into effect. Elections at the provincial level, however, had already shown the strong support enjoyed especially by the Congress among many Indians.

During World War II the British viceroy brought India into the war on the British side by decree, without consulting the leaders of either the Congress or the Muslim League. With the Japanese rolling across French Indochina, Thailand, Burma, Malaya, and Singapore in 1941 and 1942, and threatening the eastern parts of Bengal, the British refused to consider any reforms until the end of the war. The British declaration of war for India against the Axis Powers led to the resignation of the Congress ministries in the provinces and a demand for immediate independence. On August 8, 1942 the All-India Congress Committee passed a "Quit India" resolution demanding an end to British rule. The British response was the arrest of the principal Congress leaders, and a loud attack on the Congress in Parliament by pro-colonialists like Prime Minister Winston Churchill, who condemned the resolution as meant "to hamper the defence of India against the Japanese invader who stands on the frontiers of Assam."[10]

[10] Quoted in Bayly and Harper, *Forgotten Armies*, 250.

After the war, the Labour government elected in 1945 adopted a policy that favored Indian independence. While this policy was brought on by the weak British economy and the difficulties Prime Minister Clement Attlee experienced working out an agreement with Indian nationalist leaders, it was also the result of fears that the Indian army, the only force capable of preserving public order, would dissolve and the subcontinent descend into disorder and violence. With this background, Attlee announced – to derisive cries of "scuttle" from Tories – in the House of Commons on February 20, 1947 that India would be turned over to Indian control by June 1948. He also appointed as viceroy to India Lord Louis Mountbatten, a member of the royal family with a record of cooperation with nationalist groups in Burma. The major difficulty was working out some reconciliation of Hindu and Muslim interests, and this proved impossible. The final resolution came when on August 14/15, 1947 the subcontinent was partitioned between a largely Hindu India and a primarily Muslim Pakistan, which included the territories in the northeast (present-day Bangladesh) and northwest (present-day Pakistan). Both newly independent countries became members of the British Commonwealth.

British Southeast Asia

While Tories such as Churchill had clung to the empire, the partition of India drove home the realization that the British did not possess the resources to reassert imperial control over many parts of the pre-war empire and began a process in which the British government tried to restructure colonial relationships and influence through the Commonwealth. But while in early 1948 Ceylon gained independence and joined the Commonwealth as Sri Lanka, other parts of Southeast Asia proved less easily handled, emphasizing for us the multiple actors involved in the process and the limits to European control. Indeed, for Burma, Malaya, and Singapore the end of the war in late 1945 only opened the door on another era of armed conflict. While the Japanese surrendered, a large number of Japanese soldiers remained in the peninsula, and their final repatriation was not completed for years. Chinese and Indian minorities made up substantial parts of the population, and their ultimate disposition and relationship to their home countries – India in the process of gaining independence, China in a civil war between the Kuomintang and the Chinese communists – remained to be resolved. The status of British investment and holdings, and the future configuration of the British role in the region, was also open to question. The region was further destabilized by the struggles of the

Dutch to reassert their control in Indonesia. In each of these colonies, the outcome was determined by different local factors. In all of them, however, the British found themselves reacting to events rather than controlling them.

Burma had received the most autonomy prior to the war, under a 1936 agreement that gave it limited autonomy and created a colonial government in which a Burmese cabinet worked with the British governor. These cabinets were headed before the war by two relatively cooperative members of the Burmese elite, Ba Maw and U Saw. With the collapse of Burma in 1941 to the Japanese invasion, the British and Burmese governments went into exile in Simla in India, where they waited out the war. When they returned in October 1944, the British policy, espoused by the governor, Reginald Dorman-Smith, envisioned slow progress towards a Dominion of Burma under the British Crown and governed by Dorman-Smith's candidate, U Saw. But nationalist groups led by a veteran of the wartime Burma National Army created under the Japanese occupation, Aung San, as well as the Burmese Communist Party, opposed this policy. A White Paper issued by Churchill's government in May 1945 in fact made Dorman-Smith appear moderate, postponing independence indefinitely. With the advent of Attlee's Labour government and the appointment of Admiral Louis Mountbatten as commander of the Southeast Asian Command, however, British policy became more favorable both to Burmese independence and to Aung San as the potential leader of an independent Burma. A deteriorating situation in Burma itself in late 1946, highlighted by the threat of an armed insurrection that Aung San was only barely able to prevent, led to Attlee's disavowal of the White Paper on December 20, 1946, and a rapid move on the part of the British to reach agreement on independence. On January 2, 1947, Aung San and Tin Tut, a member of the Burmese civil service, went to London to negotiate with the British. An agreement reached later that month planned on independence in early 1948, without any commitment on the part of the Burmese to remain within the Commonwealth.

The smooth progress hoped for in January 1947 was disrupted in July, however, when Aung San was assassinated along with other leaders of the nascent Burmese government. Rumors flew about British involvement in the assassination, although no proof was found of that and in September 1947 U Saw, the pre-war prime minister, was convicted of organizing it. Thakin Nu, a Buddhist socialist who favored land reform and some nationalization, but was viewed by the British as a moderate, was persuaded to take over as prime minister at least until independence. In an atmosphere of hope and economic, political, and social unrest, Nu welcomed independence on January 4, 1948.

Malaya had suffered as much as Burma during the Japanese occupation, and when the British returned in 1945 they sought to tighten imperial ties in hopes of continuing the economic returns they had enjoyed since the beginnings of the colony. A federal constitution was worked out with the princes of the peninsula, essentially following the old model of indirect rule. But the inability of the colonial government to deal with the dislocations of the post-war period had by 1948 frustrated the British and created the threat of an insurrection by the Malayan Communist Party (MCP). The MCP decided by May 1948 to await a British provocation, but assassinations of rubber planters by local MCP members, acting on their own initiative, pushed the British towards the declaration of an Emergency in June, 1948. While it was a retreat from liberal democracy and guarantees of individual civil rights, the Emergency made it possible to round up the unprepared MCP leadership. It also accelerated the timetable for the transfer of power, and led the British to strengthen their Malay allies by conceding them some powers. As time went on, this became "a slow but steady hemorrhaging of power" from the British to the Malays. The first federal elections were held in 1955, and independence as a member of the Commonwealth came in 1957. The Emergency remained in effect until 1960, however, along with significant British military and police assistance, ending not only the MCP's hopes for a communist regime but also British hopes for a liberal democracy.[11]

Singapore had much the same experience. It had been excluded from the Malayan Federation created after the war, but was brought into the Federation of Malaysia in 1963, only to depart again in 1965 over concerns that its large Chinese population would destabilize the ethnic balance that the British and their Malay allies were trying to maintain on the peninsula. A moderate constitution offered by the British in 1955, with strong repressive powers that the British thought were needed to maintain security, found little favor among Singapore liberals who hoped for a full liberal democracy. But the British soon found an ally in Lee Kuan Yew, a Cambridge-educated lawyer from an old Singapore family who accepted those compromises and established an authoritarian regime on the island. In Singapore as in Malaya, therefore, the decisions made by the British and their allies during the transfers of power certainly eliminated the possibility of a communist regime

[11] Christopher Bayly and Tim Harper, *Forgotten Wars: Freedom and Revolution in Southeast Asia* (Cambridge, MA: Belknap Press, 2007), esp. 498.

similar to those that were established in post-war China and Vietnam. But the legacy of these decisions was also to eliminate other possibilities, most notably the liberal parliamentary democracy that the British had claimed as the ultimate goal of colonial rule.

The Middle East

More problematic for the British was the situation in the Middle East, where in 1945 Britain had few formal colonies but was the principal European power and exerted economic, political, and military influence throughout the region. British policy hoped to transform the relationship between Britain and governments in the Middle East away from the previous system of British dominance through alliances, mandates, or formal concessions into an informal role that would be more equal but that would preserve British power, its predominant place in the Middle East, and its access to the oil resources of the region, especially in Iran. This restructuring policy, characterized by the British as "non-intervention" and "partnership," had only modest success. It was perhaps most successful in the pro-British kingdom of Transjordan, where a treaty revision in 1948 (of a treaty only concluded in 1946) confirmed the kingdom as Britain's most dependable Middle Eastern ally.

But elsewhere, the British policy seeking a new partnership with Arab nationalists turned into a steady retreat. The British mandate in Mesopotamia ended in 1932 with the establishment of the nominally independent state of Iraq. Under King Faisal, the Hashemite monarch that the British installed, and his successors, British influence remained – marked by treaties and military intervention – until the 1950s. In 1948, after a series of attacks on British personnel, Britain declared its mandate in Palestine at an end. Jewish settlers there declared an independent Israeli state, and in the first of a series of wars quickly defeated their Arab neighbors. The formal changes in the relationship between Great Britain and the Middle Eastern states, however, masked a continuity of domination in the region. Britain took steps to marginalize other European powers, and used alliance treaties, concessions, and a strong military presence to continue an informal British empire in the Middle East.

In the oil-exporting states of Iran, Iraq, and Saudi Arabia, nationalists demanded pricing changes and the American company Aramco's acceptance in December 1940 of a fifty–fifty split of profits in Saudi Arabia created similar demands elsewhere in the region. The Anglo-Iranian Oil Company, which not only produced the largest share of Iranian oil but also controlled the world's largest refinery at Abadan, resisted the new arrangement. The nationalization in May 1951 of Iran's oil industry by the prime minister of Iran, Mohammed Musaddiq, led some in the British cabinet to call for intervention. At the time, Britain was forced to accept Musaddiq's actions and a similar arrangement in Iraq. However, in August 1953, the United States organized a coup that overthrew Musaddiq and placed the more amenable shah on the throne of Iran, restoring Western control of Iran's oil supplies.

British power in the Middle East had begun to crack with the oil crisis, and what remained of British power in the Middle East ended with the Suez crisis in 1956, which took place under a Conservative government headed by Churchill's former foreign minister, Anthony Eden. The 1948 war, and the seizure of power in Egypt by military officers in 1952, had already greatly diminished the British role there, and lingering issues troubled relations between the two countries. British and American concerns about Egypt's move under Gamal Abdel Nasser towards the Soviet Union heightened tension. When the United States withdrew promised financial support to Nasser's government for a dam at Aswan that would provide irrigation for cotton-growing in the Nile valley, Britain and the World Bank followed suit. In response, Nasser nationalized the Suez Canal. With the lessons of Munich and the Persian crisis of 1951 in mind, Eden quickly moved to intervene. Israel, with the covert diplomatic support of France and Britain, launched an attack on Egypt towards the canal, and Britain and France landed a military expedition, nominally to protect the Canal. But the United States – now a primary determinant of British and French policies – opposed the intervention in the United Nations, and an action that fifty years earlier would have been accepted with barely a murmur ended with an ignominious withdrawal by the British and the French.

Africa and the Caribbean

The failure of the Suez intervention was not only a diplomatic defeat for Great Britain. Even if it was not the crucial event in British decolonization that some historians have claimed, it nonetheless demonstrated how isolated British imperialism had become in the post-war era, and seriously damaged the political influence of Tory imperialists who had opposed Indian independence in 1947 and hampered Anthony Eden's efforts at negotiation over the Suez Canal in the early 1950s. When Harold Macmillan replaced Eden as prime minister in 1957, he rapidly moved towards granting greater autonomy and ultimately political independence to virtually all of Britain's remaining colonies. The impact of these changes in policy was most noticeable in Africa; if Labour had been instrumental in Asian decolonization, the Tory government began the process in Africa. After the election of 1959, Macmillan enjoyed his own majority in the House of Commons, giving him freedom of action from Tory imperialists. He confirmed his policy in a speech given to the South African Parliament on February 3, 1960, in which he declared that "The wind of change is blowing through this continent, and, whether we like it or not, this growth of national consciousness is a political fact. We must all accept it as a fact, and our national policies must take account of it."[12]

The pressures for some reformulation of the relationship between Great Britain and its colonies grew across Sub-Saharan Africa as attempts to end casual labor and create a British-type working class that would contribute to economic development in fact created an increasingly expensive labor system. The British administration and the businesses operating in the mining areas of Central and Southern Africa and on the Mombasa docks were faced with trade unions that worked effectively for their members in increasing benefits and wages. Even between the wars, attempts by the British administration to control these unions had generated disputes with Africans. There were also broader disagreements over the imposition of European cultural values on Africans, often through the mission schools that had been the most important part of the colonial educational system established for Africans. In 1929 in Kenya, a dispute over attempts to end female circumcision proved to be a flashpoint for growing African nationalism, and there were similar disagreements elsewhere. By the late 1950s, the costs of maintaining stability and fostering development were more than the struggling British economy could bear. After becoming prime minister in 1957, Macmillan asked for "something like a profit and loss account for each of our Colonial possessions." Robert L. Tignor has pointed out that, at least in the cases of Egypt, Nigeria, and Kenya, no such calculation was carried out, and decolonization proved to be more expensive than any planner could suspect.[13] But Macmillan's question reflected a shift in British attitudes towards empire that set the scene for its rapid end. In British West Africa, an area with few white settlers, the process, at least from the British point of view, was relatively simple. The Gold Coast became independent as Ghana in 1957, an action

---

[12] Harold Macmillan, *Pointing the Way 1959–1961* (London: Macmillan, 1972), 473–82.
[13] Frederick Cooper, *Decolonization and African Society: The Labor Question in French and British Africa* (Cambridge University Press, 1996), esp. parts III and IV, 395; Robert L. Tignor, *Capitalism and Nationalism at the End of Empire* (Princeton University Press, 1998), 394.

that is sometimes seen as a British experiment with African rule. It was joined by Nigeria in 1960, Sierra Leone in 1961, and Gambia in 1965. In East Africa, Uganda became independent in 1963. Tanganyika did so in 1964, then joined with Zanzibar to form Tanzania in 1965.

The British colony of Kenya experienced the struggle for independence in a way that both underscores the complexity of popular indigenous movements for greater autonomy and the profound consequences of the decisions made by both colonizers and colonized.[14] The colonial regime alienated land from Africans and distributed it to a large number of British settlers. This was especially the case in the Central Highlands that had been occupied by the Kikuyu tribe prior to British colonization. The British built a regime of indirect rule, with colonial authority dependent on the ability of chiefs who worked with the regime to maintain their legitimacy within Kikuyu society. The hope of an eventual roll-back of the land alienation and its redistribution among the Kikuyu provided the basis for this legitimacy. But others in Kikuyuland who had benefitted from the colonial transformation of the economy resented the chiefs' dominance of positions of influence and the patronage that flowed from the colonial state. This was the basis for pre-World War II indigenous organizations, notably the Kikuyu Central Association (KCA), founded in 1924, which gained strength by opposing colonial policies that interfered in the lives of Kikuyu, notably the ban on clitoridectomy instituted in 1929. The apparent failure of attempts to roll back the original land alienations from Kikuyu also undercut the authority of the chiefs.

The goal of the KCA before World War II was not so much the end of British rule as an end to the disenfranchisement and dispossession that had, to that point, been the experience of colonialism. But the British banned the KCA after 1945, and refused to make an accommodation with moderate Kikuyu leaders. Policies intended to increase exports made the colonial state more intrusive, allowing the reformed heir of the KCA, the Kenya African Union (KAU), to strengthen its position as champion of the peasants who were forced to implement land reforms.

The declining authority of the chiefs, the growing discontent of peasants, the failure of legal protest to remedy the increasing poverty and hopelessness of many Kikuyu, and the exactions of the colonial state came to a head in 1952 with the beginning of the Mau Mau revolt in the Central Highlands. The British viewed Mau Mau, a traditional

---

[14] Daniel Branch, *Defeating Mau Mau, Creating Kenya: Counterinsurgency, Civil War, and Decolonization* (Cambridge University Press, 2009).

Kikuyu oathing ceremony, as a combination of traditional mysticism and communist insurgency. But especially in the beginning it seems to have reflected more the conflicts within Kikuyu society between elite factions, as chiefs who continued to cooperate with the British and their patrons fought with the KAU and its supporters. The oathing involved in Mau Mau served as a form of political mobilization for the KAU, with many who took the oath forced to do so, and those who refused to take the oath dealt with violently. A vicious civil war between Kikuyu ensued, in which alliances were fluid and many Kikuyu, Daniel Branch has noted, were both Mau Mau and loyalist in the course of the revolt.[15] The British perception of Mau Mau as a nationalist revolt against colonial rule led the colonial state to undertake efforts to repress the revolt: declaration of an Emergency in 1952 was marked by the detention of suspected Mau Mau leaders and was followed by military action against their followers (Illustration 8). By 1954 Mau Mau was in decline, and by 1956 the loyalist Home Guard had reasserted colonial control over the region. Those suspected Mau Mau who had been detained were released in growing numbers in the late 1950s, and with the end of the Emergency in 1960 and negotiations for independence progressing, they awaited the culmination of that process for what they assumed would be their control of the post-colonial state and implementation of the land reforms they had been demanding.

But the decline of Mau Mau brought to the foreground the Kikuyu loyalists who had cooperated with the British, and as the British turned over more authority in the early 1960s it was those loyalists, rather than the radical nationalists who had led Mau Mau, who moved into positions of authority. Those loyalists appeared to be targeted for retribution as Kenya approached independence in late 1963. But the need to maintain a consensus at the national level dampened efforts to pursue radical policies of land redistribution or retribution. The post-colonial state led by Jomo Kenyatta, a moderate Kikuyu who nevertheless had been detained by the British as a suspected leader of Mau Mau on the first night of the Emergency in 1952, instead maintained private property – which had been guaranteed in the independence agreements concluded with the British – and followed policies aimed at economic development through private enterprise.

The situation was more complex in Central Africa, where there were not only white settlers but also significant natural resources at stake. A Central African Federation of Northern Rhodesia, Southern Rhodesia, and Nyasaland was established in 1953. But it broke apart

---

[15] Branch, *Defeating Mau Mau*, 20.

Illustration 8 Examination of papers of possible Mau Mau by an officer of the Kenya Regiment, Kenya, January 31, 1953.

over the insistence by the Macmillan government on an electoral system that would give equality to black African and white British votes. In 1964, Nyasaland became independent under majority black rule as Malawi. Similarly, Northern Rhodesia gained independence in 1964 as Zambia under majority black rule in spite of settler opposition. But in

Southern Rhodesia, the leaders of the white minority issued a Unilateral Declaration of Independence on November 10, 1965, sparking a long guerrilla war. This finally ended in 1980, after international sanctions and military action, with the establishment of a formally independent Zimbabwe with majority black rule under Robert Mugabe, the Marxist leader of the Zimbabwe African Nationalist Union.

Conflict between majority blacks and minority whites similarly complicated matters in South Africa. It gained Commonwealth status in 1910, but the electoral victory of the Nationalist Party in 1948 led to the revival of the political influence of the Afrikaner population and the implementation of a system of legal apartheid. This system formalized racial distinctions between a white "race group" and multiple others, and limited the rights of the majority black population while protecting the privileges of the white population by law. The system often faced resistance from Africans and required the use of force and violence to be maintained. In 1960 South African police opened fire on an anti-apartheid demonstration in the township of Sharpeville in the Transvaal, killing sixty-nine people (Illustration 9). In 1961, under Prime Minister Hendrik Verwoerd, the union act with Great Britain was unilaterally discarded by South Africa and it became a Republic. The Republic aimed at maintaining the apartheid policy and separate development for blacks and whites. Black resistance continued, however, notably in 1976, when a massive demonstration in Soweto against the introduction of Afrikaans as the language of instruction in schools led to the deaths of more than 700 people. A policy creating Bantustans, or homelands, for native tribes was implemented, but came under harsh international criticism. When in 1976 the government under Balthazzar Joannes Vorster began to give "independence" to the homelands, other countries refused to recognize them and the Zulus in fact refused independence on these terms. A new constitution, in 1983, restored some rights to Indians and some of mixed-race parentage, but reshaped the government away from the British parliamentary style and towards a strong presidency. Only in 1994 was the constitution revised to allow majority rule, with Nelson Mandela, a leader of the African National Congress that opposed apartheid and who had been imprisoned by the South African government between 1962 and 1990, becoming the first black president of South Africa.

Elsewhere, Great Britain continued to liquidate its empire in the course of the 1970s and 1980s, in a process that seemed in most cases to demonstrate the inability of the British government to keep up with the aspirations of its colonial subjects. This was especially apparent in the Caribbean, where beginning with a conference at Montego Bay in

Illustration 9 Crowd gathers in Sharpeville, South Africa, March 21, 1960, a few hours before police opened fire on them, killing sixty and wounding hundreds.

1947 attempts were made to create a federation that would include all of the islands in the British West Indies. The two mainland territories, British Guiana and Honduras, declined to join this and, while the federation did come into existence in 1958, it collapsed in 1961 in the face of the desire of the larger islands of Jamaica and Trinidad to escape the limits on their actions that seemed to come from the smaller islands. Barbados became independent in 1966, and in 1967 Antigua, Dominica, Grenada, St. Kitts, Nevis, Anguilla and St. Lucia (and eventually St. Vincent) became "associated states" linked to Britain. In the late 1970s and early 1980s, however, all but Anguilla chose complete independence from Great Britain.

France

For many British colonies, the outcome of "decolonization" was not a complete severing of the relationship with Westminster, but a restructuring of that relationship through the rapidly evolving notion of the British Commonwealth. The French as well sought ways after 1945 to maintain a "Greater France." The constitutions adopted in 1946 and

1958 for the French Republic both included provisions that allowed greater autonomy for colonies within the Republic's framework. These structures – called the French Union in 1946 and the French Community in 1958 – never functioned effectively, however, and while France was able to maintain cultural, economic, and diplomatic links with most of its colonies, "decolonization" was a wrenching and conflicted process for the French and for many of their colonial subjects.

For much of the nineteenth century, as French colonial holdings spread in Asia and Africa, a barely articulated assumption held that the new peoples of the French empire would, in time, join French citizens of the metropole in enjoyment of the universal rights articulated during the Revolution of 1789 and embodied in the Republic. The consolidation of the empire in the twentieth century was assisted by a broad republican consensus in support of the empire that included virtually all political parties across the political spectrum, and that by the 1930s even included, in tepid form, the French Communist Party. The support offered to France by the colonies during World War I only strengthened this consensus. There was as well a general agreement on the "civilizing mission" of France in the colonies, a belief that squared well with the messianic view that many republicans took of the French Republic. Ironically, Jacques Marseille has shown, this belief in the grandeur of France's imperial mission reached is fullest expression and celebration after 1930, by which time those most directly concerned with the economic aspects of the empire had reached the conclusion that it was no longer a positive factor in French economic performance.[16] In the twentieth century French colonial policy was a contradictory combination of universal *fraternité* with a sense of significant differences between European French and their colonial subjects. Even as the empire strained French economic and social resources, created diplomatic tensions with its allies, and generated increased opposition in the colonies, virtually all French men and women, whether politicians or ordinary citizens, believed firmly that the empire was beneficial for both the metropole and the colonies, and for that reason must be maintained.

The republican consensus, and its idealistic goals, flew in the face of the reality of conditions in the colonies between the wars, however, as forced labor, the *indigénat*, and very limited educational opportunities – not to mention restrictions on political activity by colonial subjects – made the experiences of the colonial subjects of the Republic very

---

[16] Jacques Marseille, *Empire colonial et capitalisme français: histoire d'un divorce* (Paris: Albin Michel, 1984).

different from that of its citizens. Accession to that citizenship for colonial subjects was possible, but it required proving "Frenchness" through education, facility with the French language, and, often, abjuring indigenous religions. These were standards of assimilation that few colonial subjects were able or willing to meet. Critiques of these aspects of the empire were most likely to come from the political left in France, but when those politicians came to power in 1936 in the Popular Front, a coalition of the Radical, Socialist, and Communist parties, they were able to do little to change the situation. The Popular Front proposed some reforms, especially in the African colonies. Attempts were made to extend to the colonies social welfare reforms that workers in France itself received as a result of the sit-in strikes that heralded the election of the Front in May 1936. Greater civil liberties were instituted for colonial subjects, they received a limited right to organize labor unions, and some of the harshest aspects of the *indigénat* were mitigated. But these policies ran into local opposition from French settlers – most vehemently in Algeria, where the unsuccessful Blum–Violette proposal of 1936 would have expanded the civil liberties of Algerian Muslims – and often from French colonial administrators as well. There were some members of the Popular Front cabinet who wished to reform the colonial relationship, notably the minister for colonies, Marius Moutet. But while the Socialists such as Moutet who came to the fore in 1936 tried to extend to the colonies a humanism inspired by Jacobinism and the values of the French Republic, they nevertheless remained supporters of the colonial empire and still relied on the ultimate authority of the colonial power over its colonial subjects. The Front therefore exposed the limits of colonial reform. For many *évolués*, colonial subjects who had received some French education and who for the most part filled lower-level civil-service and educational positions, the Popular Front proved a major disappointment in their hopes for greater autonomy within the empire. For that reason, the late 1930s was one of disillusionment with the prospect of any reforms occurring within the colonial empire, and a shift towards hopes for eventual independence.[17]

The Syrian and Lebanon mandates gave the French a first taste of the difficulties of maintaining imperial control. The collapse of the Ottoman empire at the end of World War I had changed the context within which these territories existed, and French administrative policies pitted different minority groups in the region against one another. The French not only faced elite nationalists who wished to gain control

---

[17] Tony Chafer and Amanda Sackur (eds.), *French Colonial Empire and the Popular Front: Hope and Disillusion* (New York: St. Martin's Press, 1999).

of the state from the French while maintaining the patronage networks that allowed them to control, and claim to speak for, most of the population of the territories. But, as Elizabeth Thompson has shown, both the French and the indigenous elites also faced more radical claims for social, political, and legal reform from an Islamic populist movement, labor unions, and women.[18] While these groups challenged the political dominance of the elites, they also put into play the paternalist foundations of that dominance, making the appropriateness of different gender roles an important aspect of the relations between the French and the Syrians and also of relations between different groups in the Arab population. In this context, French policies only made matters worse. An administrative reorganization in 1924 alienated the Arab population in Syria, and a revolt in the Druze region in southern Syria in 1925 spread to Damascus and Hama. The French response was to bombard some parts of Damascus in October 1925 and again in April 1926. In January 1936 a general strike in Damascus that spread to other parts of the country underscored the strength of the opposition to the French regime in Syria, and when the Popular Front government came to power in France later that spring it quickly moved to negotiate treaties for both Syrian and Lebanese independence. But while these treaties were to take effect in 1939, opposition in France and the outbreak of World War II prevented their implementation. The Lebanon mandate was unilaterally abolished by the Lebanese in 1943, a move that was grudgingly accepted by the French. The Syrian mandate lasted until the final withdrawal of French troops in 1946, in spite of numerous attempts by Syrian groups to gain independence.

World War II underscored the difficulties France faced elsewhere in its empire. The Third Republic collapsed in 1940 after the German invasion of France, and two different successors, the collaborationist Vichy regime of Philippe Pétain and the Free French movement led by Charles de Gaulle, claimed to be the legitimate French government. This competition extended to the colonies as well. While some, such as AEF, quickly rallied to the Free French, pro-Vichy administrators elsewhere, as in AOF and Indochina, remained loyal to Pétain well into the war. Vichy instituted policies that intensified the exploitation of colonial subjects, through increased forced-labor demands and harsher *indigénat* practices, and instituted more stringent racial policies. The

---

[18] Philip S. Khoury, *Syria and the French Mandate: The Politics of Arab Nationalism, 1920–1945* (Princeton University Press, 1987); Elizabeth Thompson, *Colonial Citizens: Republican Rights, Paternal Privilege, and Gender in French Syria and Lebanon* (New York: Columbia University Press, 2000).

replacement in the course of the war of Vichyite administrators by Free French – in fact, often incomplete, as de Gaulle continued some Vichy administrators in office, and they continued hounding pro-Free French colonial subjects – did little to improve conditions. At war's end, for many French colonial subjects, especially the *évolués*, discontent with the practices of the colonial regime had turned into anti-colonialism.

Indochina

The French conquest of Indochina did not eliminate older political structures in Cambodia, Laos, and Vietnam that were built on village communities, ethno-cultural identities, and the continued existence of princely courts in Cambodia and Laos and the royal state in Vietnam. But the French created plantations in many parts of the country that changed crops and made production more oriented towards rice and rubber for the world market while reducing the ability of peasants to grow their food. It also stimulated the growth of the cities of Saigon, Haiphong, and Hué, and other islands of industrial development. Ironically, the imposition of Western values of progress on French colonies – teaching French and the romanized version of Vietnamese, *quoc ngu*, and construction of modern transportation and urban systems – facilitated communication throughout the colony and created public spaces in which the European idea of nationalism could be turned against the colonial authorities. Especially after 1867, some members of the Indochinese elite cooperated with the French colonial regime. But there were some who did not, and from the late nineteenth century there was an inchoate anti-colonial movement in the colony. This was reflected in literary works that argued for a return to the pre-colonial royal states and rebellions such as the Can Vuong movement, the revolt in Binh-Thuan in Cochinchina in 1885, as well as instances of banditry and piracy in Tonkin around the turn of the century.[19]

In the early twentieth century, however, a nationalist movement began to develop that argued for more modern goals. Some of these nationalists, best represented by Phan Boi Chau, hoped that Vietnam could be turned into a modern, Western-style nation-state that would throw off French colonial rule. Others, such as Phan Chu Trinh, thought the same goal could be accomplished by cooperating with the French and forcing them to live up to their promises of developing the colony. A

---

[19] David G. Marr, *Vietnamese Anticolonialism, 1885–1925* (Berkeley and Los Angeles: University of California Press, 1995); Aix-en-Provence, France, Centre d'Archives d'Outre-Mer, Indo GGI, 12334–36.

mutiny by Vietnamese infantrymen in February 1930 at Yen Bay north of Hanoi was quickly followed by other attacks on French administrators and headquarters in the region coordinated by the anti-colonial Vietnamese Nationalist Party (Viet Nam Quoc Dan Dang, VNQDD), and the French reacted with arrests of activists in the VNQDD and aerial and infantry attacks on villages suspected of supporting the rebels. At the same time as the mutiny, a major strike of rubber plantation workers occurred north of Saigon, a prelude to similar strikes in 1932 and 1936–37. In April and May, 1930, a series of strikes and demonstrations broke out in Annam and, in spite of harsh repressive action by the French army, the two provinces of Nghê-An and Ha Tinh required major military operations that lasted until October for the French to regain control of them. Unrest there continued into the following year. In the aftermath of these revolts, many leaders of the nascent nationalist movement, including both the VNQDD and the recently established Indochinese Communist Party (ICP), were either imprisoned or forced into exile. This left the nationalist movement in disarray for much of the 1930s, until the Popular Front government that came to power in France in 1936 released many of those imprisoned in 1930–31 and allowed Vietnamese political parties, including the ICP, to participate openly in local politics. These parties joined in a widespread protest movement that included rubber plantation strikes in Cochinchina, strikes in 1936 and 1937 against the arsenal in Saigon, May Day demonstrations in that city in 1937, peasant demonstrations in Cholon province, and railway strikes in Cochinchina and Annam. In this context, attempts by the Vichy government during World War II to export to the colonies its theories of "National Revolution" only stimulated nationalist opposition to French rule in many French colonies, including Indochina. While the Communist Party in Indochina had always had a nationalist agenda, its resistance to French rule became increasingly infused with nationalist rhetoric while the rhetoric of class struggle that had been prominent between the wars faded.[20]

During World War II, Indochina was occupied by the Japanese, but the occupiers governed the country through the pro-Vichy French administration. In March 1945, as it became apparent that the Japanese were losing the war, they ended the pretense of French rule and established a puppet government under the Emperor Bao Dai. This destroyed the French administrative structure at the local level. As the Japanese withdrew after their surrender in August 1945, the Allies, especially the

[20] Eric T. Jennings, *Vichy in the Tropics: Pétain's National Revolution in Madagascar, Guadeloupe, and Indochina 1940–1944* (Stanford University Press, 2001).

French, attempted to reassert control over Indochina. In the eastern part, Vietnam, however, they faced competition from the Vietminh, a broad coalition of nationalist groups opposed to French rule that was dominated by the ICP. The Vietminh was headed by Ho Chi Minh, a leader who in the 1920s and 1930s had been attracted to Lenin's linking of imperialism to a crisis of capitalism and to his strategies of broad-based coalitions against colonialism. Lenin's successor in the Soviet Union, Josef Stalin, had only limited interest in Southeast Asia and mistrusted Ho, and so the Vietminh received only nominal support from the Soviet Union for its plans for an independent Vietnam. While the French and their American allies tried to regain control of Indochina, Ho declared Vietnamese independence on September 2, 1945.

The newly established Democratic Republic of Viet Nam (DRV) faced numerous difficulties in the aftermath of September 2. The French wished to move military forces to Vietnam as quickly as possible in order to regain control of the country and re-establish the colonial regime. At the same time, several hundred thousand Chinese troops were in northern Vietnam to disarm the Japanese, and a smaller British force was in the south for the same task. But in 1945 the British forced the Vietminh out of Saigon, released the French who had been imprisoned by the Japanese, and rearmed Japanese forces so they could assist in the reassertion of European authority in Vietnam. While some Americans in Vietnam were sympathetic to Ho and the nationalist movement, as tension escalated between the United States and the USSR in 1946 American policy-makers in Washington became convinced that Ho and the Vietminh were not nationalists but agents of the Soviet Union. With the tacit approval of the United States, the French began to reassert their rule in Vietnam. In the south, the British forces helped in this task. In the north, where neither the French nor the DRV wished the Chinese to remain, they reached an agreement in March 1946 that recognized Vietnamese autonomy within a "French Union," a new version of the French empire. But important issues were left unsettled, especially the fate of Cochinchina, and it proved impossible for Ho to resolve those issues in a Paris political atmosphere that, by the summer of 1946, had degenerated into political squabbling and cabinet crises. But the March agreement facilitated the return of French military forces into the country, and they moved to reassert French control against the DRV. The shelling of Haiphong by the French on November 20, 1946 was the first conflict in a long war of independence. The Vietnamese war was one of the first examples of what came to be called a People's War, a guerrilla struggle that the French army, accustomed to conventional warfare, found impossible to win. The climax of the war came in 1954, when the French established a base at Dien Bien Phu in the northwest of the country. Beginning on March 13, 1954 it came under siege by the Vietminh, a battle that culminated on May 7, when the Vietminh forces overran the base. A new government in Paris, headed by Pierre Mendès-France, came to power in June committed to ending the war at an international conference that had convened in Geneva. An agreement was reached on July 21, 1954 that envisaged Vietnamese independence and reunification by 1956 and effectively ended the French presence in Indochina. Laos and Cambodia also reached agreements with France in 1953 that provided for their independence.

Tunisia, Morocco, Algeria

While the French had always faced resistance to its rule in its North African colonies in Tunisia, Morocco, and Algeria, World War I marked an important shift in the basis of opposition to French rule. The disconnected tribal resistance in the countryside that had been dealt with more or less effectively by the French military began to be joined by urban resistance that sprang from an Islamic revival, the *salafiyya* movement, that urged Maghrebin Muslims to return to doctrinal purity. French rule in Tunisia and Morocco faced some challenges between the World Wars, notably the Rif War of 1925–26 in Morocco and the challenges posed by the Destours (Constitution) movement in Tunisia. This movement, established in 1920, drew on Salafī teachings and sought a return to Tunisia's pre-colonial 1859 constitution. There were also strike waves in the North African colonies in the years just before World War II. With French attention focused on Indochina and then Algeria after 1945, nationalist movements in both Tunisia and Morocco were able to gain influence. In Morocco the Istiqlal Party issued a call for independence in 1944, and an Arab Maghreb Liberation Committee launched military attacks on the French in October 1955. In 1956 the French acknowledged Moroccan independence under the restored King Mohammed V. In Tunisia, the Neo-Destours party, founded in 1933–34, was organized by younger nationalists, but they made little headway until the early 1950s. A campaign of bombings and attacks on French facilities then forced the French to agree to independence in 1956.

Algeria was more problematic for the French. The loss of Indochina was controversial in France, but its importance paled when compared with the movement for Algerian independence that soon appeared on the horizon. In contrast to Indochina, Algeria had a stronger settler presence, with about 11 percent of the population in 1950 made up of *pieds noirs*, the descendants of the French settlers who had been coming to Algeria – either of their own free will or as political exiles – since the middle of the nineteenth century. Algeria was also more assimilated into the French administration, governed not through the ministry of the colonies, but through the ministry of the interior.

Algerian discontent with the colony's relationship with the government of the Republic in Paris had roots going back more than a generation. One of these, which had support in the countryside, was primarily cultural, reflecting the views of reformist Islamic theologians who above all wished to preserve Islamic purity. Its principal organization, the Association des Ouléma d'Algérie, was established in 1931, and initially supported political reforms, including universal suffrage, that would integrate Muslims into the French nation. The disappointment of these plans in the late 1930s led the ulama to move towards supporting independence from France. Another organization, which attracted Algerian intellectuals in the 1930s, was the Jeune Algérien movement, best represented by Ferhat Abbas, a pharmacist who admired the principles of the French Revolution of 1789 and hoped that France would provide Algerians with equal rights, including the right to remain Muslims even as they were assimilated by France. Another organization, Étoile Nord-Africaine (ENA), was established in 1926 in the North African immigrant community in Paris and was headed by Messali Hadj, a recent immigrant from Algeria. Supported by the French Communist Party, ENA's goal was the independence of Tunisia, Morocco, and Algeria. It was dissolved by the French government in 1929 as a subversive organization, and when it was reconstituted in 1933 it had shed its connection to the Parti communiste français (PCF). In January, 1937, after the disappointment of the failure of the Popular Front to carry out meaningful colonial reforms, the ENA was again dissolved by the French government and the Parti du Peuple Algérien (PPA) was established in March under Messali Hadj's leadership.

In 1943, Ferhat Abbas, Messali Hadj, and other Algerians issued a manifesto that demanded an Algerian constitution and the summoning of a Constituent Assembly for the country, to be elected by all inhabitants of Algeria. While this manifesto initially considered the possibility of a continued relationship with France, by 1945, under the influence of the PPA, its supporters had moved to demanding complete independence. Nonetheless, as the Fourth Republic regained control of Algeria at the end of the war – a process marked by the harsh repression of popular demonstrations in Sétif and the rural Constantinois on May 8, 1945 – the nationalist movement remained split, with Messali Hadj, Ferhat Abbas, and others competing for its leadership. After Messali's Mouvement pour le Triomphe des Libertés Démocratiques split in 1953 between Messalists and centrists, the Revolutionary Committee of Unity and Action (CRUA) was formed in March 1954 to work towards the unity of the factions of the nationalist movement. Later that year CRUA became the Front de la Libération Nationale (FLN), and on November 1, 1954 the FLN launched attacks on French installations throughout the country. By 1956 – two years into the war – nearly all the nationalist organizations in Algeria, with the principal exception of Messali and his followers, had joined the FLN and it reorganized itself into a provisional government headed by Ferhat Abbas.

The French response to the November 1 attacks was a nearly unanimous commitment to maintain Algeria as a part of France, a policy summed up in the slogan of "Algérie Française." The government of the Fourth Republic, still headed by Pierre Mendès-France, began a military effort to end the rebellion. This war would last over seven years and lead not only to Algerian independence but to the collapse of the Fourth Republic. FLN strength grew slowly at first, but gained international support in debates in the United Nations. This support – even if tepid – from Tunisia, China, and the Soviet Union not only placed pressure on France to reach an accommodation with the rebels but also increasingly forced France to deal with the FLN rather than any other "*interlocuteurs valables*" who might accept a resolution short of independence. The Algerian war proved difficult for the French to win, with the French army, still reeling from defeats in France in 1940 and Indochina in 1954, struggling to defeat an enemy organized not in European style but in small cells that struck quickly and then disappeared. French attempts to maintain control and provide protection for its supporters against the FLN often failed, exposing those supporters to FLN retribution. By 1956 the French army was forced to use conscripts from metropolitan France to fight the war. In late 1956, the war came to Algiers itself, as a terrorist campaign by the FLN against the European sectors of the city brought a response in the form of the torture, arrest, and killing of much of the leadership of the FLN by French troops. While a military defeat for the FLN, it hardened attitudes in France and among Algerians. The city of Algiers became clearly divided between the Algerian quarter, the Casbah, and the *pied noir* quarter, Bab-el-Oued. The *pieds noirs*, the officer corps of the army, and many French men and women reached the conclusion that the Algerians were little better than murderers who could not be negotiated with, while the heavy-handed French response, including the use of torture, to the FLN terrorist campaign recruited many Algerians to the cause of Algerian independence.

The war in the countryside dragged on after the battle of Algiers, and the inability of the Fourth Republic to resolve the Algerian situation led to an army revolt on May 13, 1958 that gained support from the *pieds noirs* in Algiers. A Committee of Public Safety was established there under General Jacques Massu. With invasion of the metropole by the French army seemingly imminent, a government crisis ensued in Paris. The president of the Republic, René Coty, insisted that the Assembly allow the recall to power of Charles de Gaulle, the wartime leader of the Free French. On May 13, 1958 de Gaulle was given emergency powers to govern and write a new constitution, thus ending the Fourth Republic and leading to the Fifth, with a much stronger president and a substantially weakened assembly.

De Gaulle never appears to have contemplated the possibility of restoring French rule in Algeria as it had existed before 1954, and he viewed Algeria as a relatively minor part of his overall project of rejuvenating his country and having it "marry its century." In early June 1958 he visited Algeria, giving speeches in a number of cities in the colony (Illustration 10). Ambiguously declaring in Algiers that "I have understood you" to his audience of *pieds noirs*, he began the process of withdrawal, making concessions that recognized the possibility of independence, and then accepted the FLN as the representative of Algeria. By early 1960 this policy created discontent among the army command. Public disagreement by Massu and his recall by de Gaulle sparked the Affair of the Barricades, a demonstration in Algiers by *pieds noirs* and army groups in which the Algerian police were fired upon, perhaps by paratroops, as they attempted to break up a crowd in the central *place* of the city. In January 1961 discontented army officers established the Secret Army Organization, and in April 1961 a Generals' Revolt against the government threatened an invasion of Paris itself by the French army. De Gaulle moved quickly to squelch the revolt and imprison its leaders, and on March 18, 1962, the Evian Accords ended both the Algerian War and French control of its closest-held colony.

Sub-Saharan Africa

The process of decolonization was more straightforward and less violent in France's other African colonies, although as elsewhere it began as a reform process, not as a movement towards independence. During World War II, there were attempts on the part of both the Free French and indigenous leaders from AOF and AEF to restructure

Illustration 10 Charles de Gaulle speaking in Constantine, Algeria,
June 5, 1958, during a three-day visit to Algeria soon after becoming
the head of the French government.

the colonial relationship. A circular by Félix Eboué, the Free French
governor-general of AOF and a close advisor of General Charles de
Gaulle, had focused on easing the harshness of the *indigénat* and on
improving the position of the *évolués* in the French colonies. The most
important of these attempts came in January 1944, when a conference of
the governors of the Sub-Saharan colonies was convened by the Gaullist
French Committee for National Liberation (CFLN) in Brazzaville in
French Equatorial Africa. Conferences of colonial governors had been
held before, in 1917, 1934–35, and 1936, and so the conference cannot
be dismissed as a hasty response to the international situation. The
Programme Général prepared in advance by the commissariat for colonies of de Gaulle's Free French movement outlined numerous options
for reforming the empire: its transformation into a federation of associated territories and peoples, economic reforms that would provide for
economic planning, investment in the colonies and opening them up to
more trade, the abolition of the *indigénat* and forced labor, educational
progress, more representation in the government of the colonies, and

opening the prospect of acquisition of French citizenship to *indigènes* "based on intellectual and moral level or services rendered to the French cause." But recent scholarship has shown the contradictory aspects of the conference. Some colonial governors, such as the governor of Togo, rejected any reforms. The governor of Guinée was so hostile to the proposed reforms that he was asked not to attend the conference. Other governors, however, were concerned about the decentralizing tenor of the proposed reforms because they conflicted with their strong commitment to a unitary, "Jacobin" French Republic: as one governor put it, "No French federation: [instead,] the French Republic." Brazzaville certainly marked a shift in French policy towards the Sub-Saharan colonies. But it did not consider a path to independence, only reform, and many colonial governors not only pressed for limits on the reforms at the conference itself but also lagged in implementing its recommendations. Its long-term effects on colonial governance were therefore less than the initial promise. These differences between the governors and the proposals of the CFLN were significant but, as the historian Charles-Robert Ageron has warned, should not be overestimated. As Ageron concludes, it "announced the end of the colonial Old Regime and the good news of the transfiguration of the Empire."[21]

Critics of Brazzaville noted that it also made clear that most French intended to maintain colonial control over Sub-Saharan Africa after liberation. But several factors made it also apparent that the pre-war system could not be re-imposed. The United States in particular was asserting its anti-colonialism. President Franklin Roosevelt made clear, in a radio address on February 23, 1942, that the principles of the Atlantic Charter of self-determination agreed on with Winston Churchill in August 1941 applied to the entire globe, and that the United States had not entered the war in order to restore Europe's colonial empires. The United States was also formulating plans to transform the empires into a form of international trusteeship that would lead to either independence or international control. As Africans rallied to the Free French cause against the Vichy regime and Nazi Germany, their claims for improved conditions therefore gained leverage.

These pressures led the Free French to make some efforts at restructuring the relationship with the colonies in ways that would maintain French control in spite of the demands from the colonies for greater autonomy and accession to the civil liberties enjoyed by French citizens.

---

[21] Charles-Robert Ageron, "Aperçus historiques sur la Conférence de Brazzaville," in Institut Charles de Gaulle/Institut d'Histoire du Temps Présent, *Brazzaville, janvier–février 1944: aux sources de la décolonisation* (Paris: Plon, 1988), 353–57, 369.

New laws granted Africans the right to participate in a number of kinds of political activity that had, up to this point, been limited to French citizens in the metropole. The constitution of the Fourth Republic that was approved by popular referendum in October 1946 created a system which, in some ways, reinforced the assimilationist approach to French colonies, insisting that the Republic was indivisible. It included the colonies as "overseas territories" within that Republic, and continued control by the French government over the internal affairs of the colonies. The civil service that administered them was likewise controlled by Paris. Citizenship (although not necessarily the franchise) was extended to all Africans by the first Loi Lamine Guèye in May 1946, which included the provision that Africans could remain under customary law. Coerced labor and the *indigénat* were also abolished and a revised criminal code extended the jurisdiction of courts, and the exercise of legal rights, to Africans. Each of the federations had an elected Grand Conseil, and each of the colonies also sent deputies and senators to Paris as members of the two chambers of the French National Assembly. They also sent representatives to a new Assembly of the French Union and to an Economic Council of the French Union. While voting was initially limited based on status, and the system of representation was based on electoral colleges that privileged Frenchmen, by 1956 the system had been extended to virtually universal adult suffrage and a single electoral college. While in most cases ineffectual as a means of representing France's colonial subjects, these assemblies and the increased frequency of elections after 1944 meant that political activity became more prevalent in AOF and AEF.

Other reforms of the Fourth Republic also were intended to improve the conditions of France's African citizens. But while the post-war reforms were envisaged as a way of maintaining the colonial relationship between Paris and Africa in a restructured form, each reform created a larger public sphere within which demands for greater autonomy could be articulated. Trade unions were legalized in 1946. The second Loi Lamine Guèye, passed in June 1950, equalized working conditions and pay between French and African civil servants. A Labor Code was passed in 1952 setting minimum wages and limits on working hours, and providing for paid holidays, collective bargaining, and the validity of collective agreements.

These reforms certainly encouraged some African leaders to believe that their future might lie with a reformed French empire. But they also often empowered one indigenous faction over others, and for that reason did not end opposition to French rule. The French were in fact faced with a very factionalized African political landscape that made widespread acceptance of any reforms difficult to achieve. The political parties that developed in the colonies were often narrowly focused, reflecting the ethnic and local basis of political power for the new African leaders and privileging not the large federations (AOF and AEF) but the smaller territories within them. The most significant effort at creating a broad coalition came in West Africa, where the Rassemblement Démocratique Africain, or RDA, was formed at a congress of primarily communist-leaning African leaders at Bamako in October, 1946. Its manifesto remained within the bounds of the French Union, calling for reforms that would provide equal political, social, individual and cultural liberties, democratically elected local assemblies, and free choice about the nature of the union between France and Africa. Linking African political parties from most French colonies in West Africa, the RDA was the most important political organization in the region between 1946 and 1950, and continued to play an important role to the end of the colonial era. Student groups and youth groups also developed in the course of the 1950s. As their frustration grew at the slow pace of French progress towards fulfilling the promises held out in the 1946 constitution, these groups challenged the older political leadership of the nationalist parties. By the middle of the 1950s, a wide-ranging nationalist movement existed, made up of the political parties, trade unions that catered to évolués and wage laborers, and student and youth groups. That movement, however, was badly divided on its strategies and ultimate goals.

These pressures from within the federations, as well as the attention demanded of the French by the Algerian War, led to the Loi-Cadre of 1956. Its political reforms not only created universal suffrage, but also enhanced the authority and competence of the territorial assemblies, allowing them to elect African executives called Conseils du Gouvernment. The African leaders of these Conseils became, in effect, prime ministers, strengthening the role of African political parties in each territory. The heavy costs of empire also influenced the system established by the Loi-Cadre. The goal of linking compensation to Africans with that paid to French civil servants and to workers in the metropole created a favored class of workers in the colonies whose wage and benefit costs the French government could no longer support. French officials saw this as a situation in which the colonies had acquired the state apparatus and social standards of European countries without also developing the capacity to pay for them. The Loi-Cadre of 1956 separated the territorial civil service in the federations from the civil service in the metropole and gave responsibility for funding territorial services to the territorial assemblies. It therefore shifted the financial burden from the colonial administration to those assemblies, and forced the African politicians who sat in them to make the difficult decisions about how to pay for government services.

At the same time, the government in Paris was being weakened by the Algerian crisis, which in 1958 led to the collapse of the Fourth Republic and the creation of a new Republic that more pragmatically recognized the expense and growing autonomy of the colonies. Further, the creation of the European Economic Community in 1958 created an alternative engine of metropolitan prosperity in which it was difficult to fit the colonial empire. While the new 1958 constitution established a French Community that would include both the metropole and the colonies, it gave the colonies the option of voting in a referendum (on September 28, 1958) on whether to join the Community or choose immediate independence. Membership in the Community would mean a position of autonomous Republic within the Community and continued French aid, while independence meant an end to all French assistance. Of the territories in AEF and AOF, only one, Guinée, voted no and immediately received independence.[22] The new constitution did not in fact recognize the federations, and in 1959 they were officially eliminated.

With African leaders already discussing independence, the referendum in 1958 was too little, too late, and the Community it established did not provide the institutional means of maintaining the colonial relationship between France and its members. The government in Paris soon decided that independence was the easiest way out of the intractable situation in Sub-Saharan Africa. By the end of 1960 members of the Community all had acquired at least the form of political sovereignty. That sovereignty, however, came as a part of a continued relationship with France. This was the form desired by many political leaders of the territories who had built their political careers on their relationships with Paris, and who had supported a "yes" vote in the 1958 referendum. That their principal support came from within their particular colony, rather than at the level of the federation, set them apart from other members of the nationalist coalition, drawn from the trade unions and student and youth groups. These nationalists often held a vision of complete independence, but in the larger framework of West or Equatorial Africa.

With Madagascar gaining independence as the Malagasy Republic in 1960, France ended its African empire even as it fought to maintain control of Algeria. The French insistence on assimilation of its colonies

---

[22] Twelve territories voted; Togo and Cameroun, which France held as UN Trust Territories, did not vote.

into a Greater France served to complicate the experience of decolonization for that country, as in both Indochina and Algeria it fought long, bloody, and ultimately unsuccessful wars to hold on against indigenous uprisings. Elsewhere, what was called decolonization often involved continued cultural, economic, and military cooperation between France and its former colonies. The loss of empire proved traumatic for the French post-war generation, whose conception of France and belief in the universal validity of French culture – the assumptions that justified the empire itself – were called into question by the rejection of French rule by its colonies and the reduction of France to the metropole and a handful of territories in the Caribbean and Pacific.

The Netherlands and Belgium

The colonial holdings of the Netherlands and Belgium presented stark contrasts between the relatively small metropolitan powers (10.1 and 8.6 million population respectively in 1950) and the size of Dutch Indonesia (82.9 million in 1950) and the Belgian Congo (14.5 million in 1950). While both of these countries attempted to maintain their colonial holdings after World War II, they both faced not only indigenous discontent but also the limitations imposed on their colonial policies by the demands on government resources for reconstruction and development at home. Both, then, eventually saw their empires dissolve in the course of events that rapidly overtook belated attempts to reform the colonial relationship.

The Dutch had replaced the "culture system" of the nineteenth century with a form of indirect rule in the twentieth. Under this administrative system, the indigenous village structure was maintained, and the local village leader was co-opted into the system of Dutch rule. While one effect of this paternalistic system was to increase the authority of the village leader, it also made him an agent of the colonial power and rendered these leaders ineffective as agents of democratization as pressures for greater indigenous rule began to increase after 1945. The situation was further aggravated by the plantation system that dominated Indonesian agriculture, producing commodities for export but failing to improve living conditions. Even in the prosperity of the 1920s, the standard of living of the rapidly increasing population (from 37.7 million in 1905 to 67.5 million in 1930) failed to rise. The depression after 1930 proved catastrophic. Indonesia was firmly embedded in the world economy, yet suffered more than it profited from its effects.

While the Dutch did not make the same efforts towards cultural assimilation as did the French – there was little insistence on the use of the Dutch language, little missionary activity, great leeway allowed for the practice of Islam, and little effort to provide educational institutions for most Indonesians – those Indonesians who did receive a Western-type education found few opportunities to utilize that education, with Indonesians making up only 221 of the 3,039 senior officials in the colony in 1940.[23] While there appears to have been little consideration in the Netherlands of the prospects for assimilation or association between the metropole and its Indonesian colony, there was strong sentiment in the Netherlands that Indonesia should remain a part of the Netherlands even if that required the kind of repressive policies that marked earlier eras of Dutch rule. The representative institutions the Dutch created in Indonesia after World War I provided a forum for nationalist leaders to criticize the colonial administration, but effectively limited their power to affect policies or to assume responsibility for governing. Even as other colonies obtained greater autonomy or, as in the case of the US Philippines, a deadline for independence, a relatively moderate resolution passed by nationalist leaders calling for a conference to develop a ten-year plan for greater autonomy within the framework of the Dutch constitution was rejected by the government in favor of greater administrative decentralization. Intellectual ferment was most obviously expressed by *pemuda*, young men who rejected the older generation's bureaucratic ways and who began to foment an Indonesian Revolution. An Islamic revival during the period between the World Wars, and the presence of the first Communist Party in Asia, the Partai Komunis Indonesia (PKI), founded in 1920 and the survivor of vicious Dutch repression in the late 1920s, raised the threat of an Islamic social revolution.

The Japanese invasion in 1942 came, therefore, as a welcome event for some Indonesians, with a number of nationalists willing to collaborate with the occupying forces. As in other parts of Southeast Asia, the Japanese occupation of Indonesia during World War II not only disrupted colonial rule for the duration of the war, but created opportunities for changes in the colonial relationship. The occupation was more exploitative than elsewhere, and many members of the indigenous elites were compromised by their cooperation with the Japanese. By 1942 the

---

[23] Rudolf von Albertini, *Decolonization: The Administration and Future of the Colonies, 1949–1960*, trans. Francisca Garvie (New York and London: Africana Publishing Company, 1971), 489–90.

pressures of American anti-colonialism had forced the Dutch to promise a kind of Commonwealth, a partnership in which local autonomy would be paired with Dutch direction of foreign policy and defense, tariff and currency policies. This became the basis of post-war Dutch policy, but the chances of its success were seriously compromised by the Japanese removal of the Dutch colonial administration, dissemination of anti-Dutch propaganda, release of imprisoned nationalist leaders, and formation of a constitutional commission in October 1944. Even as Japan was moving towards capitulation in the summer of 1945, an independent Republic of Indonesia was proclaimed on August 17, 1945 by the nationalist leaders Sukarno and Muhammad Hatta, presenting the restored Dutch administration with a fait accompli that preempted its plans for a Commonwealth. To the disappointment of Malay leaders in exile, who hoped for a greater Indonesia, or *Indonesia raya*, that would include the Malay peninsula, Sukarno's brief statement made no mention of Malaya.

Indonesia was transferred by the Western allies to Lord Louis Mountbatten's Southeast Asian Command in August 1945, after the Japanese surrender, and it was the British, not the Dutch, who sent the troops to carry out the reconquest. Mountbatten utilized the 65,000 Japanese troops on Java to maintain public order, and local British commanders also turned to the Japanese for help. The intervention culminated with disastrous events in September 1945 in Surabaya, the largest naval base in Southeast Asia after Singapore, when a British force was set upon by an overwhelming force of civilians and Indonesian soldiers loyal to the Republic. A month later, a fragile ceasefire was negotiated, but it took another month before the British forces in Surabaya were relieved.

The Dutch government initially ignored the Republic, considering it a Japanese creation and its leaders collaborators and traitors. But by November 1946, in an agreement brokered by the British, it was forced to accept many of the Republic's claims. In turn, the Republic gave up its claim to represent the outer provinces. In the following years Dutch attempts to retain predominance by playing off Java, Sumatra, and other parts of the archipelago against one another failed. After two "police actions" involving military intervention the United States and United Nations forced an agreement, signed on November 2, 1949, by which all of the Dutch territories in Indonesia, with the exception of West New Guinea, were to be transferred to a new organization called the United States of Indonesia.[24] This would be part of a Dutch-Indonesian Union,

---

[24] The United States of Indonesia consisted of the Republic of Indonesia and fifteen other autonomous states.

in which both partners were sovereign but also recognized the Queen of the Netherlands as sovereign. By 1954, this Union had become unworkable, and it was terminated by Indonesia.

By the period between the World Wars Belgium hoped to be able to continue indefinitely as an imperial power in the Congo. Indigenous agriculture concentrated on cotton for export and food production, while the rubber plantations and mining industry that developed in Katanga and Kivu provinces were participants in the developing world economy of the early twentieth century. These industries drew indigenous labor into those provinces, not only draining the populations of non-industrial areas but creating concentrations of population in the industrial areas. But the copper and diamond resources of the region attracted foreign investment, and the mining companies and the Belgian administration tried, in paternalistic fashion, to deal with the social issues created by economic developments. While there were successes in comparison with other European colonies in Africa, these efforts nonetheless could not prevent severe social dislocation in the indigenous population.

The Belgian administration tended to leave education to the Catholic missions in the Congo, and while this created a widespread educational system, its purpose – backed by the administration – was to create a broadly literate population that could be an efficient workforce rather than a highly educated indigenous elite capable of moving into the higher levels of the colonial administration. Universities were established in the Congo only in the mid 1950s, and few Congolese traveled to Europe to obtain university degrees. The colony was marked by a strong color bar, not only in access to elite positions but also in everyday life, with segregated residential areas, transportation, and sociability. A system of indirect local rule that used tribal chiefs as the agents of the colonial administration was hampered until mid-century by the multiplicity of tribal units and by the failure of the Belgian administration to prepare those chiefs for administrative service. Only in 1957 did the Belgians attempt to incorporate European-trained Congolese into local administrations, a decade after similar developments in French and British colonies. A 1952 law allowed some *évolués* the possibility of legal equality with Belgians, but it required an application that would be evaluated in terms of the level of "civilization" of the applicant, and the number of such assimilated Africans remained low. Since even Belgians in the Congo did not have voting rights, legal assimilation did not open political participation to Africans.

As nationalist movements developed in other parts of Africa after 1945, the Belgian administration remained content to continue its paternalist policies in the Congo. Even proponents of colonial reform tended to advocate lengthy delays – thirty years or longer – before significant autonomy would be granted. Congolese manifestos in 1956 calling for effective parliamentary institutions were ignored by the administration. Events soon proved the weakness of this policy. The economic boom ended in 1957, and with it the ability of the growing economy to meet the rising expectations of the African population. Unemployment increased in Leopoldville, Stanleyville, and Elisabethville, and the difficulties new immigrants had in finding employment increased tensions within those urban areas themselves. Nationalist sentiment was fostered by attendance by Congolese at a world exhibition in Brussels in 1958, and that December Patrice Lumumba, one of the founders and the president of the Mouvement National Congolais (MNC), attended a pan-African congress in Ghana (Illustration 11). Rioting in Leopoldville in January 1959 increased the pressure on the government in Brussels. A declaration by the king, on January 13, 1959, that Belgian policy would aim at independence for the Congo finally broke the stalemate, although the statement was little more than a vague promise of eventual independence. Colonialist circles in Belgium noted the absence of an indigenous elite that could take over running the colony and the need therefore for a lengthy transitional period. But leaders of the growing nationalist movement in the Congo called for independence in 1960 or 1961. It became apparent to the Belgian government that the failure to address potential Congolese autonomy had created a situation in which, at best, only the protection of Belgian economic interests and an orderly withdrawal might be obtained.

Attempts in 1959 to create indigenous parliamentary institutions and a brief transitional period failed. A round-table meeting of representatives of the Belgian government and Congolese selected by that government finally agreed in early 1960 on a date of June 30, 1960 for independence. While Patrice Lumumba, head of the MNC, and the first prime minister of the independent Republic of the Congo, claimed that "Independence does not mean a break with Belgium, nor the expulsion of Belgians from the Congo," and undertook to guarantee the property of European enterprises,[25] the newly installed Congolese government immediately faced conflicts about the extent to which Belgian officials would continue to have authority after independence. The Congolese troops of the Force Publique mutinied against its European officers within days after independence. The replacement of those officers by

---

[25] Jean Van Lierde (ed.), *Lumumba Speaks: The Speeches and Writings of Patrice Lumumba, 1958–1961*, trans. Helen R. Lane (Boston: Little, Brown and Company, 1972), 152.

Illustration 11 Congolese premier Patrice Lumumba and Ghanaian president Kwame Nkrumah meeting in Accra, Ghana, August 8, 1960.

Congolese, and the accompanying mass flight of European administrative cadres, speeded up the decolonization process and Africanized the political system of the independent Congo. But the months after independence saw efforts supported by the mining industry to isolate the wealthiest parts of the Congo and establish a secessionist regime in the province of Katanga, led by Moise Tshombe and his Conakat party. With public disorders and troops from Belgium, United Nations-authorized troops from Ghana, and the Force Publique squaring off against one another, the years after independence witnessed a violent civil war in the Congo that only ended, along with Tshombe's secession, in 1963.

Portugal

With the end of the Algerian War, and the independence of Sub-Saharan Africa, the Belgian Congo, and Dutch Indonesia, formal European overseas colonies had virtually disappeared. Only the Portuguese colonies in Africa, a few vestiges such as the Falkland Islands, and islands in the Caribbean and the Pacific and Indian oceans remained. In the early 1970s, that Portuguese empire itself disappeared, a victim of not only the post-war impetus for colonial independence that affected the British, French, Belgian, and Dutch empires, but also the inability of the Portuguese government to mount an effective defense of its colonial control of Angola, Guiné (Bissau), and Mozambique. The fascist governments of Dr. Antonia de Oliveira Salazar, from 1932 to 1968, and Dr. Marcello Caetano after 1968 refused to countenance any decolonization, instead progressively incorporating the African colonies into a tighter relationship with European Portugal that left no room for decentralization or the devolution of political authority. Reforms, such as the abolition in 1961 of the status of *assimilado* and conferral of the status of Portuguese citizens on all inhabitants of Angola, Mozambique, and Guiné (Bissau), did little to change the material or legal situation of colonial subjects given the underdeveloped economy and the absence of political and civil rights in Portugal itself.

Overt opposition to the restrictions – if not the fact – of Portuguese rule began to become apparent in the 1950s, with a series of disturbances in the colonies that were harshly repressed. In 1953 about 1,000 people were killed in labor disturbances on the islands of São Tomé and Príncipe. In 1960 police fired on cotton laborers in northern Mozambique, killing about 500, and the following January a number of cotton workers in Angola were killed by troops. About fifty dockworkers in Guiné (Bissau) were killed when their strike was broken up by the increasingly active International and State Defense Police, an organization that had carried out the repression of political activity in Portugal since the inception of the dictatorship in the 1930s.

As important in the long run was the development of anti-colonial organizations in the Portuguese colonies. This was assisted by contacts made by students from the colonies during university studies in Portugal itself. The personal relationships formed during their studies would, over the next decade, create an illusion and at times the reality of a coordinated anti-colonial movement. At the same time, however, organizations calling for the end of Portuguese rule were formed in each of the colonies consisting of more or less effective alliances between a European-educated elite and local groups in the colonies. These sometimes found strength in particular ethnic groups or regions, such as the Bakongo ethnic group in Angola. They also drew some inspiration from the Portuguese Communist Party and other reformist groups in Portugal.

When colonial uprisings began in the early 1960s in all three colonies (1961 in Angola; 1961 in Guiné (Bissau); 1964 in Mozambique), Salazar sent Portuguese troops to reassert control. As the experience of the French in Indochina and Algeria and the British in Kenya had already shown, colonial guerilla wars far from Europe and in which the rebels enjoyed the tacit support of much of the population were difficult to win. With most European colonial powers already losing their empires the international situation proved to be more favorable to the rebels than to the attempts by the Portuguese government to suppress them. US anti-colonialism in the 1960s was muted because of the desire of the United States to maintain its military bases in the Azores, and this gave way to more direct support for the Portuguese effort once the Nixon administration came into office in 1969. But the growing number of colonies, especially in Sub-Saharan Africa, that had gained independence in the 1960s, and their increasing weight in the General Assembly of the United Nations, lent support to the rebellions in each of the Portuguese colonies as the wars dragged on through the 1960s and into the 1970s.

In 1973 discontented officers in the Portuguese army formed the Armed Forces Movement (AFM), which initially sought more effective prosecution of the colonial wars and an end to the favoritism given recent recruits to the officer corps. The moral leader of the AFM was General Antonio de Spinola, who served in Angola and as military governor of Guiné (Bissau). An AFM uprising in Lisbon and in provincial barracks on April 25, 1974 brought an end to the Caetano dictatorship with remarkable speed. The AFM formed a Junta for National Salvation (JNS) to govern, and a Republic was proclaimed on May 14. By the end of September the AFM had entered both the JNS and the provisional government of the Republic, acting as a watchdog to ensure continuation of the revolution. A constitutional law promulgated on July 26, 1974 recognized the right to self-determination by the African territories, including independence. Lisbon recognized the independence of Guiné (Bissau) on September 17, 1974, a year after rebels had unilaterally declared independence. The islands of Cabo Verde (July 5) and São Tomé and Príncipe (July 12) followed the next year. The transition had already occurred, in late June, in Mozambique, although it was only a prelude to a civil war that lasted through the 1980s and into the 1990s.

A lengthy process of negotiation had set November 11, 1975 as the date for independence in Angola. But the situation on the ground was complicated by the division of the revolutionary movement into three competing groups and intervention, in the course of the late summer and fall of 1975, by outside military forces. South African and Zairean troops were backed by the United States and other Western powers, while Cuban troops intervened in support of the Marxist-inspired and Soviet-backed Movimento Popular de Libertação de Angola. By February 1976, the internal dispute over control of the newly independent Angola seemed to have been resolved through the defeat by Cuban forces of both the South African and Zairean invasions. Yet Angolan independence was only an early step in what would become a decades-long civil war stoked by the interests of South Africa and Zaire in the region, the willingness of the United States and the Soviet Union to play out their Cold War conflicts in Africa, and the factional disputes within Angola itself. Only in 2002 did the civil war in Angola finally come to an end.

Russia

If the twentieth century saw a decline in the power of the Western European colonial powers, the Russian empire followed a different path. World War I presented the Russian empire with a major governmental crisis, and its lack of success on the battlefield and the inability of the tsarist government to manage the war effort led to its overthrow in 1917 by liberals whose goal was not only to win the war but also to consolidate liberal political institutions. They in turn faced mutinies by Russian soldiers and sailors by autumn 1917. Power then passed into the hands of the most radical actors in Russian politics, the Bolshevik faction of the Russian socialist movement. Rapidly ending the war and consolidating their power in a civil war that lasted until 1922, the Bolsheviks re-established the dominance of Russia over most of the territories previously controlled by the tsars.

The resulting Soviet Union remained a diplomatic pariah for much of the period between the World Wars, and the German invasion of the Soviet Union in 1941 proved to be one of the biggest challenges faced by the Soviet state. But when peace came in 1945 the Soviet army was further west than Russian forces had been since 1815. Over the next several years, new outposts were incorporated into the Soviet empire, as the Eastern European countries from Poland through Czechoslovakia, East Germany, Hungary, Bulgaria, and Romania came under Soviet control as nominally independent but actual satellite "People's Democracies." In 1955, these countries joined with the Soviet Union as members of the Soviet-led Warsaw Pact alliance against the United States and Western Europe.[26]

As with the other empires discussed in this book, the Soviet Union frequently faced resistance from its subject peoples. In the Asian parts of the empire this often built on religious and ethnic differences from the dominant Russians. Both Orthodox Catholics who wished to practice their religion freely and the growing Muslim population presented significant problems for the Soviet governors and were a rallying point for ethnic and nationalist opposition to Russian rule. But the best-known resistance movements were in the Eastern European countries. Worker riots in East Berlin in 1953 were brutally repressed, and in 1956 reform movements in Poland and Hungary threatened Soviet control of the area. The replacement of hard-line communist leaders with more moderate reformers, who were willing to end the collectivization of agriculture, ended the Polish crisis. But in Hungary in November 1956 and in Czechoslovakia in 1968 military intervention proved necessary to maintain Soviet control. The Cold War competition with the United States strained the economic capability of the Soviet Union, and by the 1980s it was apparent that the rigid economic policies that had marked the Soviet system since the 1920s were not able to support both the demands of the Soviet military for weapons and those of the peoples of the Soviet Union for higher standards of living.

A series of reform movements, beginning in Poland in 1980, spread through the other People's Democracies. By the middle of the decade these had taken root in the Soviet Union itself. Instigated by Mikhail Gorbachev, who became First Secretary of the Communist Party of the Soviet Union (and de facto ruler of the USSR) in 1985, these reforms aimed at decentralizing government and opening the economy to market forces. With remarkable speed in the fall of 1989 the authoritarian communist governments of the Eastern European countries collapsed, replaced by Western-looking governments that challenged their subservience to the Soviet Union. Gorbachev's attempts to ride the wave of reform in the Soviet Union ultimately failed, and the Union itself began to crumble. The Baltic states of Lithuania, Estonia, and Latvia

---

[26] Albania and Yugoslavia were also People's Democracies, but were able to avoid Soviet domination in ways that the other Eastern European countries were not.

began asserting their independence in 1988, and disaffection spread quickly to other republics of the USSR and even to parts of the Russian Soviet republic itself. By 1991 Ukraine, Azerbaijan, Georgia, Moldavia, Uzbekistan, Tajikistan, Kyrgystan, Turkmenistan, and Kazakhstan all had declared independence. Gorbachev's attempts to maintain some semblance of unity among the constituent parts of the Soviet Union ultimately failed, and on December 26, 1991, the Soviet Union ceased to exist. The principal successor state, Russia, remained a power to be reckoned with internationally, but smaller states now made up much of the territory of the tsarist and Soviet empires.

Post-colonial Europe

The preceding accounts of events after 1945 in different parts of the world should make clear that the end of formal European control over much of the rest of the world did not completely sever the links between the imperial powers and their colonies. Indeed, from a wider perspective, formal colonialism was only one of the ways in which relations between Europe and other parts of the world have been structured. Our contemporary world, both in Europe and in its former colonies, continues to be marked by the legacies of colonialism as, in the era since 1970, those links have been reconstructed in economic, demographic, and cultural terms.

Perhaps most obvious are the economic links that tie the former metropoles to former colonies. The consolidation of formal European empires in the late nineteenth century was a part of a process of globalization of the economies of Europe and the rest of the world. At the same time, the volume of international trade expanded as Europe and North America industrialized. Along with the increase in volume came the breakdown of the older barriers that had separated the world into distinct commercial regions. In the twentieth century the economic links between the developed north and the less-developed southern hemisphere were important characteristics of the world economy. London, until after 1945, was the most important financial center in the world as commercial relations became more complex and its banking community emphasized the maintenance of stable exchange systems. The industrialized economies of Europe and the United States exchanged manufactured goods between themselves in this economic structure, but they also depended on the southern hemisphere for raw materials which were acquired at relatively low prices, then processed and resold into southern hemisphere markets as manufactured goods. In the culmination of the informal and then formal empires of the nineteenth century, it became vital for the industrial economies of Europe to maintain close ties with the south, both to ensure a supply of raw materials and also to maintain their markets in those countries. The economic disruptions caused by war and depression between 1914 and 1945 seemed to make these imperial ties more vital for European powers even as they adopted economic policies aimed at favoring metropolitan industries and agriculture over those in their colonies.

The movements for independence that crossed Asia and Africa after 1945, however, undercut the political supports for these economic arrangements, as colony after colony gained independence from its European master. What followed was the construction of a new international economy that was increasingly based on free trade. But new world organizations came into existence to control this world economy. The International Monetary Fund and the International Bank for Reconstruction and Development, created in 1944, and the International Development Association established in 1960 attempted to stabilize exchange rates and provide funds for development. Other agreements tried to open up international trade. The General Agreement on Tariffs and Trade, established in 1947, negotiated rounds of tariff reductions. The Uruguay Round of negotiations in 1995 created, as a successor to the General Agreement on Tariffs and Trade, the World Trade Organization, devoted to maintaining predictability and openness in trade worldwide.

As a result of these developments, the former imperial powers, joined by the United States, maintained significant influence on the economic conditions and policies of what were called less-developed countries, and even after independence many colonies found themselves in economic relationships with their former imperial rulers that severely limited their ability to act independently. The quarter century of economic boom that followed World War II did not eliminate disparities in economic productivity and standards of living between the former imperial powers and the former colonial parts of the world, nor did it significantly alter international trade patterns. The terms of trade remained in favor of industrial economies during much of the boom, so that even as the economies of the less-developed countries grew at unprecedented rates between the 1950s and the 1970s, they did so at a pace slower than that of the industrial economies.

The global movement of capital and goods that characterized the international economy after decolonization was accompanied by a global labor market that brought migrants from the former colonies to Europe. Many of these migrants were citizens of the former European colonial power, or had immigration rights as a consequence of the independence agreements of their native countries. The influx of non-European immigrants has been one of the most important social and political developments in Europe since the 1960s, introducing greater ethnic diversity into European populations and raising questions about not only immigration policies but also long-standing European policies regarding citizenship. During the 1970s, when the long post-war growth of the European economy broke, immigration restrictions were imposed in most European countries. In spite of these restrictions, however, provisions for family reunification – wives and children joining husbands who had migrated to Europe already – meant that significant immigration flows continued to the end of the twentieth century and beyond.

It has, however, been less immigration itself than the status of existing residents of non-European origin or heritage that has created controversies in Europe in recent decades. Many immigrants do not wish to return to their country of origin, and the European-born children of immigrants have no experience of those countries should they move to them. Their knowledge of Turkish or Arabic is often scanty or non-existent, and they would face problems of the equivalence of credentials obtained in Europe with those granted in their parents' home countries. At the same time, however, it has proved difficult for European societies to assimilate or accept these minorities. The 1980s and 1990s witnessed the growth of extreme-right-wing movements in most Western European countries that raised issues about the nature of national identity, often in explicitly racist terms. Their electoral success tempted conservative politicians to take anti-immigrant positions, and this has legitimized the issues and confused positions in European politics. The colonial issue of the post-war decades has therefore seemed to become the immigration issue of the late twentieth century.

The mid-twentieth-century changes in the relationship between the European colonial powers and their colonies also led to significant cultural reflections on the colonial experience and the meaning of the end of formal colonies. The way in which decolonization occurred brought to the fore the paradoxes contained in European ideas and assumptions about national identity and the relationship between European identity – often stated in universal terms, such as the French dedication to the "Rights of Man" – and the particular characteristics of colonial subjects. By forcing the definition of concepts such as national identity and citizenship that had been left vague during the colonial era, decolonization opened avenues to European identity for some groups who had been considered marginal. But it did so at the cost of more firmly excluding colonial others. Todd Shepard has shown how the French experience in the Algerian War on the one hand defined Algerian Jews, whose status as French citizens had been denied by the Vichy regime during World War II, as clearly French. At the same time, however, rigid boundaries were erected between French national identity, on the one hand, and Algerian Muslims, on the other, in spite of the promises made since the conquest in the 1830s that rule by the French Republic would ultimately lead to assimilation of those peoples into the French nation. Decolonization, therefore, effectively separated the experience of French colonial rule from reflection about universal Republican values.[27]

More broadly, the era after colonialism has seen a self-consciousness about the effects of colonialism on the rest of the world, a movement termed "post-colonialism." The hybridization of indigenous and imperial cultures has assumed a major place in this movement. Post-colonial authors, film-makers, and artists have produced a body of work that reflects on the experiences of the peoples who were colonized, and on the effects of colonization and migration on both migrants and on the countries that have sent and received them. Historians have themselves re-examined the colonial past to draw a broader, less triumphalist version of what colonial conquest and rule entailed. All of these works have emphasized in particular the experiences of indigenous peoples, women, and migrants. By being critical of and refusing to accept the assumptions of European colonialism, post-colonial authors, historians, and artists have created a new perspective on the relations between Europe and the rest of the world.

Médard's story

Martinique, the French sugar colony in the Caribbean, has since the end of World War II not only been incorporated into France as a *département*, but also joined to European France by migration, improved communications, more frequent travel, and the investment links and other economic ties built around its desirability as a tourist destination. The elimination of the indigenous Carac population soon after contact in the early seventeenth century means that the current population of Martinique is a mixture of French *colons*, the descendants of slaves from different parts of Africa, and Euro-Caribbeans. In these respects, the history of Martinique over the last 350 years has been similar to that of other European colonies. And as with every place touched by

---

[27] Shepard, *Invention of Decolonization*, 272, 170.

Europe's colonial past, the island's population has stories that are the product of that past.

Many of these stories, and by far the easiest to discover, are about the French missionaries, soldiers, administrators, and slaveholders who came to Martinique and who linked the island to the broad diplomatic, economic, and cultural accounts that have made up much of this narrative of European colonialism. But one of these is the story of Médard Aribot, who was born in 1901 in Sainte-Luce on Martinique, a descendant of the slaves who had been brought to the island when it was one of France's sugar colonies.[28] He grew up mostly in the commune of Diamant on the south coast of the island, living in a cave by the sea, fishing, crabbing, and never setting foot in a schoolhouse. At some point he began carving wooden sculptures of the ships he could see in the ocean and figures of people on the island. One of those sculptures was of Colonel Maurice de Coppens, a planter who owned a sugar distillery just outside Diamant. Coppens was a candidate for the Chamber of Deputies in 1925, when he was killed during what was called the Guerre du Diamant, a riot sparked by electoral corruption by the French elite and the French governor of the colony.

Médard himself was not a participant in the Guerre du Diamant. He first came to official notice, and therefore to us, through a series of petty crimes he committed in the course of the 1920s and early 1930s. In 1933 he was sentenced to the *bagne*, the French prison in French Guyane, under an 1885 law aimed at "purifying" France of recidivists. Médard spent around twenty years in Guyane. Until 1939 he was confined as a *relégué collective* to Saint-Jean, a camp about 17 kilometers up the Maroni River from the administrative center of Saint-Laurent. In spite of a singularly unimpressive disciplinary record – he seems to have continued his habit of petty larceny – he was then transferred to the status of *relégué individuelle*, which allowed him to live by himself in Guyane as long as he reported to the authorities twice a year. He seems to have returned to his native island only in the 1950s, one of the last *relégués* to leave after the *bagne* was ended at the end of World War II. Setting himself up in a seaside shack on Martinique, he began a career as an artist, turning out woodcarvings that earned him only a small income. His past, however, stayed with him in an unusual way. It had been his sculpture of Colonel de Coppens that had been paraded by the socialist workers during the Guerre du Diamant, an event that

---

[28] Médard's story is told by the American anthropologist Richard Price in *The Convict and the Colonel* (Boston: Beacon Press, 1998).

remained alive in popular memory in Martinique. But Médard himself became a participant in the riot in popular memory. By the 1970s, he was a symbol of resistance to the corruption of French colonial rule, with his time in the *bagne* attributed to his having made an image – a "photo" – of Coppens. That symbolic identity, however, over time made many of his neighbors uncomfortable as they tried to accommodate themselves to the continued French presence on the island and the cultural *francisization* that gathered strength in the last decades of the twentieth century. By the 1990s, long after his death, he had acquired a different identity in the memories of those on the island: his carvings were seen as important works of art, and his imprisonment disappeared from view. Médard's story became one that was intertwined with the birth of the *Département de Martinique*, a place supposedly as French as the Côte d'Azur or the Seine.

Médard's story reminds us of the continuity of imperialism and colonialism, and the inability of a narrative from exploration and conquest to high imperialism and then decolonization to contain the many aspects of those parts of the global past. The occasional reformulations over the past three centuries of the relationships between Europe and other parts of the world have affected both the control by Europeans of their colonial subjects and the ability of those subjects to create the history of European colonialism. Each of those reformulations has reconfigured boundaries between Europeans and colonial others, and opened up new possibilities for all participants in the colonial project. Each of them, as well, has closed off possibilities. Often, these closures have been accompanied by an erasure of the memory of their presence, an erasure that the revived study of the history of European colonialism offers us, whose world has been so profoundly shaped by the colonial past, the opportunity to reverse.

FURTHER READING

Bayly, Christopher, and Tim Harper. *Forgotten Armies: The Fall of British Asia, 1941–1945*. Cambridge, MA: Belknap Press, 2005.
  Forgotten Wars: Freedom and Revolution in Southeast Asia. Cambridge, MA: Belknap Press, 2007.
Bell, Duncan. *The Idea of Greater Britain: Empire and the Future of World Order, 1860–1900*. Princeton University Press, 2007.
Branch, Daniel. *Defeating Mau Mau, Creating Kenya: Counterinsurgency, Civil War, and Decolonization*. Cambridge University Press, 2009.
Burgess, Anthony. *The Long Day Wanes: A Malayan Trilogy*. New York: Penguin Books, 1981.
Chafer, Tony. *The End of Empire in French West Africa: France's Successful Decolonization?* New York: Berg, 2002.

Chafer, Tony, and Amanda Sackur, eds. *French Colonial Empire and the Popular Front: Hope and Disillusion*. New York: St. Martin's Press, 1999.

Cocteau, Jean. *Tour du monde en 80 jours*. Paris: Gallimard, 1983.

Connelly, Matthew. *A Diplomatic Revolution: Algeria's Fight for Independence and the Origins of the Post-Cold War Era*. Oxford University Press, 2002.

Gifford, Prosser, and Wm. Roger Louis, eds. *Decolonization and African Independence: The Transfers of Power, 1960–1980*. New Haven, CT: Yale University Press, 1988.

Gifford, Prosser, and Wm. Roger Louis, *The Transfer of Power in Africa: Decolonization 1940–1960*. New Haven, CT: Yale University Press, 1982.

Holland, R. F. *European Decolonization 1918–1981: An Introductory Survey*. New York: St. Martin's Press, 1985.

Horne, Alistair. *A Savage War of Peace: Algeria 1954–1962*. New York Review Books, 2006.

Hyam, Ronald. *Britain's Declining Empire: The Road to Decolonisation 1918–1968*. Cambridge University Press, 2006.

Jennings, Eric T. *Vichy in the Tropics: Pétain's National Revolution in Madagascar, Guadeloupe, and Indochina 1940–1944*. Stanford University Press, 2001.

Lebovics, Herman. *Bringing the Empire Back Home: France in the Global Age*. Durham, NC: Duke University Press, 2004.

Louis, Wm. Roger. *The British Empire in the Middle East 1945–1951: Arab Nationalism, the United States, and Postwar Imperialism*. Oxford: Clarendon Press, 1984.

Ends of British Imperialism: The Scramble for Empire, Suez and Decolonization. London: I. B. Tauris, 2006.

McQueen, Norrie. *The Decolonization of Portuguese Africa: Metropolitan Revolution and the Dissolution of Empire*. New York: Longman, 1997.

Manning, Patrick. *Francophone Sub-Saharan Africa 1880–1985*. Cambridge University Press, 1988.

Marr, David G. *Vietnam 1945: The Quest for Power*. Berkeley and Los Angeles: University of California Press, 1995.

Vietnamese Anticolonialism, 1885–1925. Berkeley and Los Angeles: University of California Press, 1971.

Maugham, W. Somerset. *The Gentleman in the Parlour: A Record of a Journey from Rangoon to Haiphong*. Garden City, NY: Doubleday, Doran & Co., 1930.

Mazower, Mark. *No Enchanted Palace: The End of Empire and the Ideological Origins of the United Nations*. Princeton University Press, 2009.

Morrow, John. *The Great War: An Imperial History*. London: Routledge, 2004.

Munro, J. Forbes. *Colonial Rule and the Kamba: Social Change in the Kenya Highlands 1889–1939*. Oxford: Clarendon Press, 1975.

Price, Richard. *The Convict and the Colonel*. Boston: Beacon Press, 1998.

Shepard, Todd. *The Invention of Decolonization: The Algerian War and the Remaking of France*. Ithaca, NY: Cornell University Press, 2006.

Sorum, Paul Clay. *Intellectuals and Decolonization in France*. Chapel Hill: University of North Carolina Press, 1977.

Stora, Benjamin. *Algeria 1830–2000: A Short History*, trans. Jane Marie Todd. Ithaca, NY: Cornell University Press, 2001.

Thomas, Martin. *The French Empire at War 1940–45*. Manchester University Press, 1998.

The French Empire between the Wars: Imperialism, Politics and Society. Manchester University Press, 2005.

Tignor, Robert L. *Capitalism and Nationalism at the End of Empire*. Princeton University Press, 1998.

The Colonial Transformation of Kenya: The Kamba, Kikuyu, and Maasai from 1900 to 1939. Princeton University Press, 1976.

Index